A BIBLIOGRAPHY
OF THE
DANCE COLLECTION
OF
DORIS NILES & SERGE LESLIE

A BIBLIOGRAPHY

OF THE

Dance Collection

OF

DORIS NILES & SERGE LESLIE

Annotated by SERGE LESLIE

PART IV A–Z
Mainly 20th Century Publications

With a Preface by
SIR SACHEVERELL SITWELL

LONDON
DANCE BOOKS LTD
1981

Princeton Book Co. Publishers
P.O. Box 109, Princeton, NJ 08540

Copyright © 1981
Serge Leslie

ISBN 0 903102 56 0

First published 1981 by
Dance Books Ltd, 9 Cecil Court
London WC2N 4EZ

This edition limited to 525 copies
(25 not for sale)

Photoset by
Rowland Phototypesetting Ltd
Bury St Edmunds, Suffolk
Printed in Great Britain by
Biddles Ltd, Martyr Road,
Guildford, Surrey

To
SIR SACHEVERELL SITWELL

ACKNOWLEDGEMENTS

My warmest thanks to Alexandra Glebow Glenn who kindly read the Russian entries and corrected them; to Nancy and Jill Anne Bowden who gave editorial assistance; and to David Iglesis who read through the French and Italian entries.

INTRODUCTION

THERE MUST BE, there ever must be an inherent sadness when any comprehensive literary project comes to, or appears to approach completion. But knowing its compiler, and having some little working knowledge of the scope of his enterprise, I would think, it is perhaps unlikely that this will be the end of it. The most unexpected item, something long looked for and obviously hopeless to find, will turn up eventually in an unexpected and improbable place. As an instance of the sort I would mention the good luck of a family friend of the past, the pianist Frederick Dawson, once well known in his day in the North of England. He had studied Grieg's piano concerto under Grieg himself, and gave the first performance of the concerto in England. Dawson was a native of Leeds, and a keen researcher into the somewhat sparse musical history of his birthplace. He knew of the existence of a lithograph by a Leeds drawing master of Paganini's one and only concert in Leeds. Dawson set himself to find a copy of this, and after thirty years and nearly in the centenary of its appearance, found this lithograph 'waiting for him', as he said to me, in the dreary window of an old bookshop in Wolverhampton. Such is exactly in the pattern, I would think, of several of Serge Leslie's lucky finds in his field of books on dancing. Not that it is only luck, but as ever the result of diligence and intensive thought and care on the part of the searcher. Quite often too, with the looked for reward in the end.

It is much in character with the compiler of the four volumes of this unique bibliography, that he has expressed the wish that this fourth volume should be less associated with himself than to do honour to his and my old friend Cyril Beaumont, who was indeed unique of his kind and unlikely to occur more than this once in any dance-lover's or balletomane's lifetime. I had known him since I first went to buy books on the Russian Ballet from him in, I think, the Winter term or half of 1913 while I was at school at Eton. A friendship in fact dating from sixty-five years ago, and during what amounts to some three entire generations in time. Later, during my stays or visits, and while I lived in London, hardly a day would pass without my looking in at his shop in Charing Cross Road to talk to him, rather in the spirit of the 'flaneurs' who walk along the quais in Paris looking at the bookstalls. Topics of conversation with Cyril were endless. He was a lively 'raconteur' himself and a gifted mimic, but we would discuss as well Napoleon's campaigns, Japanese woodcuts on which he was an authority, and as well book illustrations of all sorts and kinds, not forgetting Jacques Callot, Stefano della Bella, and every conceivable topic of the sort. Then came the return of Diaghilev's Russian Ballet to London only a few months before the end of the war in 1918, and not more than a year or two after that Diaghilev's great revival of Tchaikowsky's *Sleeping Princess*, the last appearance in history, as he said himself, of the old St. Petersburg. And it was indeed, though it seemed much longer at the time, only some two or three years after the collapse of the old Russia of the Tsars. Aged myself about twenty-two or twenty-three I attended almost every performance of Tchaikowsky's masterpiece at the old Alhambra theatre and Cyril Beaumont was there every night, it seemed. It was in this way, and as a result of this enthralling existence, that one becomes a lifelong lover and aficionado of the Dance.

The list of Cyril Beaumont's writings on ballet given in this volume of Serge Leslie's *Bibliography* is truly astonishing and must run into some hundreds, I would think, of items large and small. It is little wonder that Serge Leslie regards him as mentor and guide in this respect, and reveres him for his factual accuracy and the most reliable of witnesses as to what he saw and heard. Indeed one could say that their friendship apart, as far as the art of the dance is concerned, they are lucky to have been alive at the same time, for the one complemented the other; Cyril Beaumont as living commentator on the present that he lived in and Serge Leslie as a literary collector and anthologizer of the past. Taking all of this in account it is not surprising that Serge Leslie himself and his wife Doris Niles Leslie are both dancers themselves, on the professional side of the curtain and not mere spectators of the dance. This is the explanation of their enthusiasm for the technical minutiae of an art in which both have been participant, and of their respect for the old traditions and strict technique which are so necessary and indeed imperative if it should continue to improve and flourish.

It is a fascination for an amateur like myself to browse through these four volumes and revive memories now almost a lifetime ago. How well I remember when Cyril Beaumont issued his reprint of that old masterpiece by Gregorio Lambranzi, the early eighteenth century Venetian dancing master. Its technical interests apart, its illustrations of the dances are on a par almost with the aforementioned Jacques Callot and Stefano della Bella. They inhabit indeed an entire world of fascination to themselves. I remember giving it to Diaghilev and how excited he was by this publication, and with what enthusiasm he turned the pages; and am still wondering what can have become of the copy of the original edition in the library of Lyhar Strachey. For it had the plates beautifully handcoloured and was conjectured to have belonged probably to Lambranzi himself. What a wonderful theatrical relic to have in one's possession! Having worked a little myself, on the ephemera of the art, on the lithographs of the great dancers Taglioni, Cerrito, Fanny Elssler and so forth; and so descending to a lower order on music-hall covers by Concanen, a minor English master on his own, I can feel the strong emotional pull of the theatre in such things, the nocturnal relics of a long distant and defunct past. Theatrical relics and memories, just because of their ephemeral quality, must be perhaps the most nostalgic of all recallings of the kind. Not least because where the art of the dance is concerned it is dumb and silent, there is no word spoken. It is all played in silence, and the memories of it are of music, movement and expression.

For someone like myself who was so assiduous an attendant on the Ballets Russes there is of course a particular interest in the huge numbers of items connected with it, and this is the place to make a reaffirmation of the extraordinary impact of Léon Bakst's stage settings. He may not have been a great painter, but nothing in the lifetime of the present generation is going to cause the same sensation as his *Schéhérazade*. It was a *coup de théâtre* of epoch making force from the moment the curtain lifted. Nothing to equal it as a stage picture had ever been seen before. But Diaghilev, tireless innovator that he was, produced a still more transcendental tour de force of stage craft in Picasso's setting for *Le Tricorne* less than a decade later. Even old programmes of the Ballets Russes are now treasured possessions because of their lavish illustration of such masterly productions. Bakst's costume drawings for these ballets are almost eerily typical of those first years before the First World War.

But it is of course the earlier items in the collection that are of outstanding interest. And I am wondering because I only had the typescript in my hand for a day or two before going on holiday where I am writing this, whether it records that early volume of the time, I think of Charles II, with the intriguing *A Chacoon for a Green Harlequin*. Chacoons' meaning of course songs or chanson in theatrical slang, and it being quite clearly a book of instruction for young or beginning harlequins. I hope the reader will agree that no book could be more fascinating. It seems to lead straight on to Antoine Watteau's exquisite drawings and paintings of *Le Théâtre Italien*, Watteau being the most 'stage struck' of all great masters.

All this must be by far the most comprehensive of all book collections dedicated to the art of ballet and the dance. And what a pleasure it is to know that its future is assured and that its permanent home is to be in the city where the great dancer and choreographer Noverre spent the most fruitful years of his life. It is not to be dispersed as was so likely to happen, and thrown to the four winds. Serge Leslie has kindly given me a note of what he considers to be the rarest and most interesting of the books he has collected. For their scope lies far beyond my own amateur interest in the theme. They are in many languages; Czech, Hungarian, Greek, Russian obviously, beside the more to be anticipated French, English, Italian and so on. And the scope has sensibly enlarged itself beyond the frontiers of the strict classical tradition to include folk dancing in almost every conceivable country. In this wide province, where the Spanish dance's richness and complexity of forms gives balance or alternative to Russian dance, I have a note of *El Baile Flamenco* by Alfonso Puig, a Catalan name most decidedly. Barcelona 1976. And I cannot write this without its stirring my memory of having seen the great Pastora Imperio dancing at about four in the morning in one of the *casetas* at the Feria in Seville, in 1947, in the euphoria of the war just ended. She was the greatest, it is said, of all Flamenco dancers – her mere preliminary walk round the stage being famous, as, too, her wonderful hands and arms and the electric flash of her green eyes. How typical, too, it is of things Spanish that even now no one knows why it is called Flamenco. Surely not meaning a Flemish origin, while even the bright colours of the Flamingo have been called in not altogether inappropriately. However this explanation too seems unlikely, and it seems as though it will remain forever a mystery. This surely where the magic is concerned is its safe-keeping.

And another of the titles of Spanish books is no less intriguing. This is *"El Trionfo de las Castanuelas"* a volume devoted to castanets; The sub-title *O Mi Viaje a Crotalopolis* can mean nothing else surely than a journey or sojourn in Seville? The mere title of the book revives one of the most exciting and blood stirring memories of a lifetime, in the aforesaid and unforgettable euphoria of arriving in Spain, the war just over and ended. I would lie on my bed dozing and dreaming in the lovely heat of early afternoon, with the scent of orange blossom drifting in through the window, until at about five o'clock the most extraordinary snapping and crackling sound would begin in the distance and seemingly from all directions at once. Coming nearer and nearer, too, and now with the footsteps of a huge crowd approaching. It was the women and children of Seville, perhaps a thousand or more of them, walking to the Feria from all over the town, and crackling their castanets as they came along. If this was not the Spanish dance itself, it was certainly the prelude to it, and the most exciting prelude imaginable. It was indeed one of the musical excitements of a lifetime, and no one who heard it could ever forget it. I have often thought that the only comparable sensation would be to have heard the Gypsy bands playing from all over the fairgrounds of Nijni Novgorod.

What a happy time even with its inevitable disappointments Serge and Doris Niles Leslie must have had in forming this library of books on their beloved subject. For it is certainly a labour, or perhaps one could call it a task or even a bond of love between them. Millionaires, this is the moral, are not the only collectors. Others find no less enjoyment in their devotion to a chosen theme. Its prizes are not in prices reached in salerooms, but in the acquisition of some long sought for volume, or on occasion something unexpected and an entire surprise. And all the time through the years it has been in pursuance of an aim. Not the mere acquiring of anything that came along and caught their eye. The haphazard has only entered into it with the feeling that as with the lithograph of Paganini mentioned earlier in this preface, it was waiting for them of its own volition determined to form part of their collection. Books on such occasions can become almost human in their wish to find a home. In conclusion one could say that the authors and collectors we are discussing are certain to be remembered for these four volumes. They will be indispensable authority on their beloved subject, and more than a little of their pleasure in the task distils itself and is present and discernible in the pages. May there still be a few more treasures for them to find. What a delight it would be to anticipate their wishes and to be able to lay one or two of them in the path before them.

SACHEVERELL SITWELL
August 1978

CYRIL W. BEAUMONT – IN MEMORIAM

DURING THE final seven or eight weeks of Cyril Beaumont's illness I visited him daily. At his bedside were friends, those we both knew and those mutually presented for the first time. One of the latter, a lady, after a short presentation said, "Any friend of Cyril Beaumont is a friend of mine". Thus it was with Cyril: any one a friend of the Dance or Ballet or the literature thereof might be considered his friend. To those who knew him well and those who only knew him through his writings he has left a wonderful legacy of books and articles.

The legacy is larger and fuller than most of us thought or were aware of and until the contents of his flat at 68, Bedford Court Mansions are finally and systematically itemized, with its many, many note books, letters and manuscripts we will not know the true extent.

Of his books, it is relatively easy to find a reasonably complete listing: *Ballet Annual No. 6, 1952* – Forty Years of Writing on the Ballet; *Dance and Dancers Dec. 1961* – Beaumont Anniversary Supplement; and the 1974 edition of *Who's Who*. Salient of course in all three compilations would be *A History of Harlequin*, *A Bibliography of Dancing*, *A Manual of the Theory and Practice of Classical Theatrical Dancing* (Cecchetti), *The Complete Book of Ballets*, *The Romantic Ballet in Lithographs of the Time* (with Sacheverell Sitwell), and *Five Centuries of Ballet Design*. These are unique, not only for their beauty or utility, or both, but because they seem to be the first of their kind to appear in print.

Less well known, I presume, except to collectors, are the twenty-six volumes of *The Beaumont Press 1917–1931*; largely books of poems and letters, limited editions beautifully illustrated and taste-fully bound. Careful descriptions of these works may be found in Beaumont's *The First Score* and B. T. Jackson's *The Beaumont Press* in *The Private Library*, Spring 1975.

Now about articles. I knew there were some very fine ones, having entered several in *Bibliography of the Dance Collection of Doris Niles and Serge Leslie Part III* but until one day several years ago, when Cyril announced he was beginning a 'mining operation' and began passing the results on to me, I did not realize their number or quality. The 'mining operation' was carried on in a store room adjacent to the flat's kitchen where broken water pipes above had flooded this room which was replete with books, paintings, lithographs, magazines and letters. He now began to salvage a few items at a time. First, *Dance Journal* which he edited and published at 75, Charing Cross Road from 1925 on with its excellent articles: Teaching of Dance History, June 1925; Michel Fokine, Feb. 1933; the History of Choreography, in four parts, Vols. III & IV, a very lucid comparison of several systems. Then, early *Dancing Times*: The Life of A Ballet Girl in the Sixties, Dec. 1924; Serge Diaghilev, Nov. 1929; Taglioni Treasures, Sept. 1966. Almost weekly he had another armful for me as I evinced interest in the ever growing collection of articles: *Ballet*, Maria Mercandotti, May 1948; Pushkin and his Influence on Russian Ballet, Dec. 1947, Jan. 1948; and Some Dancers of the Diaghilev Ballet, Sept. 1949.

Perhaps you knew all these – I did not. But did you know these? *Dancing World*: Some New Paintings of the Russian Ballet, June 1922; Marie Taglioni and La Sylphide, Dec. 1923; Pavlova, Lopokova and 'Hassan', Oct. 1923; *Opera & Ballet*: Pavlova, Autumn 1924; and *Dancing Life*: The Sleeping Princess, Dec. 1921. Interspersed with literally hundreds of articles came to life manuscripts and typescripts: a six page typescript of *L'Oiseau de Feu*, possibly 1912, Cyril was not quite sure; but his memory of the contents of articles was amazing and he often quoted from them in our conversations. The last published article that I am aware of was Cartophily – As Applied to Dancers, *Dancing Times*, Feb. 1975, reviewing an album called *Der Kunsterlische Tanz*. There was a similar album, *Die Tanzbuhnen der Welt*, which the Weurtemburgische Landesbibliothek had mailed him at my request. It arrived a few days before the end but we went through the entire book and even though the artists were mainly Austrian or German he knew many of them and his comments were amazing. One of the last books he asked for was *Grimaldi's Memoirs*.

His last book was *Bookseller at the Ballet*. I was aware for some months that it had been completed but not indexed. I offered my services, which were accepted, and we began at once to establish the card index. Some six weeks were spent around the kitchen table where promptly at noon he began to prepare a hot lunch for one o'clock service. He cooked well and carefully, usually a chop, a boiled potato, one slice of bread and butter and usually some form of custard.

Bookseller at the Ballet ended with the passing of Serge Diaghilev and Cyril felt that the greatest part of his life and work had ended with this era. Certainly his friends cannot accept this and I submit these words for their approval. Considering the many fine and outstanding books Cyril Beaumont has published over the years, *Bookseller at the Ballet* must be a landmark. However it is not the complete Beaumont and this will assuredly not be written as he was the only one who could have successfully accomplished this task. So as the history and story of the Diaghilev Ballet Company is sometimes divided into three *époques* with the first period (1909–1914) considered the finest, so might Beaumont's activities as author, critic and bookseller be divided into scores with the years 1910–1929 the most important and evidently he felt this to be true. However, what to say about the next score? Certainly at this period there was no ballet company that replaced the Diaghilev Company, but in the field of publications *The Complete Book of Ballets, The Ballet Called Giselle, The Romantic Ballet in Lithographs* (with Sacheverell Sitwell) and other remarkable books were written and published. Then the period 1950–1959 saw ten years of criticism for *The Sunday Times*, and publications – *The Ballet Called Swan Lake, Ballets of Today, Ballets Past and Present* and others – which merit fast attention. Passing rapidly from 1960 to 1975, during which time the knowledge of Beaumont's works spread to all countries having an interest in the ballet, his active correspondence with artists and choreographers world-wide formed an unrevealed pattern of activity. This, combined with the spread of Cecchetti Schools and Societies, has created a yeast aiding cultures growing in these countries.

The writings of Cyril Beaumont were not meteoric in their flight across the sky but rather a constellation which remains fixed and beautiful for all to study and admire.

SERGE LESLIE – July 19, 1976
67 Redcliffe Gardens, London

A BIBLIOGRAPHY

OF THE

Dance Collection

OF

DORIS NILES & SERGE LESLIE

Note: *in the following descriptions, the size of page is given height first; and where a page number is enclosed within brackets, it indicates that such a page or pages are not numbered. Binding, whether cloth or leather, is full, unless otherwise stated.*

ABRAMOVA (CHURA MARINA, Redaktor). ALEKSI ERMOLAEV. Sbornik Statei. Moskva, Iskusstvo 1974.

F'cap 4to (8·4 × 6·2 ins.). 232 pp. illus. Orig. white cloth.

A collection of articles by various Soviet authors on Ermolaev's (Yermolayev) choreography and roles. See Chujoy, *Dance Encyclopedia* (enlarged and revised ed.), for information in English, also Roslavleva, *Era of the Russian Ballet, Bibliography* Part III.

ADAMI (GIUSEPPE). FANNI BALLERINA DELLA SCALA. Romanzo. Milano-Roma, Rizzoli. 1942.

Cr. 8vo (7·1 × 4·5 ins.). 270 pp. Orig. dec. wrapps.

A novel, the third edition.

ALARCON (PEDRO DE). THE THREE CORNERED HAT. Newly translated by William H. Warden. New York, Vantage Press [1952].

Demy 8vo (8·4 × 5·3 ins.). ix + 50 pp. Orig. red cloth.

The story on which the Massine ballet of the same name is founded. See also *Bibliography, Part I*, Alarcon for another edition. Also Part I Beaumont, *The Three Cornered Hat*; Part II, Picasso, *Le Tricorne*; Part III, *Covent Gardent Ballet Books* No. 3.

ALBERTIERI (LUIGI) & PALMER (STUART). IL MIO MAESTRO CECCHETTI. New York, The Dance Magazine Feb. 1929.

Roy. 4to (12·4 × 9·6 ins.). pp. 16, 17, 60 illus. Orig. dec. wrapps. (Helba Huara)
An illustrated article. See also *Bibliography*, Part I Albertieri, Luigi, *The Art of Terpsichore* and Part IV, Beaumont, Cyril, *Cecchetti*.

ALBERTS (DAVID). PANTOMIME: ELEMENTS AND EXERCISES. Photographs by C. James Gleason. Lawrence, The University Press of Kansas. 1975.
Med. 8vo (9·6 × 6·4 ins.). 69 pp. illus. Orig. white cloth.
To judge from the photographs the author is a true *mime*, not a *grimacier*, who is able to mirror inner thoughts and impulses most impressively; but the *mime* sequences for three players seem rather barren structures for action.

ALEKSANDROV (Y.). TAM GDE ROJDAETSYA TANETS. Moskovskii Rabochii 1977.
Demy 8vo (8·3 × 6·3 ins.). 78 pp. + a large section of plates. Orig. dec. wrapps.
A short history of the Bolshoi School of the Dance followed by many photographs of students and 'Jeunes Soloists' of the Bolshoi Company. The title may be roughly translated *There Where the Dance is Born*.

ALEXANDRE (ARSÈNE). THE DECORATIVE ART OF LÉON BAKST. Notes on the Ballets by Jean Cocteau. Translated from the French by Harry Melvil. New York, Dover Publications. 1972.
Demy 4to (11·7 × 9 ins.). x + 52 pp. + 48 illus. in colour and 29 in black and white. Orig. dec. wrapps.
An excellently produced inexpensive republication of the 1913 edition, the plates only slightly smaller than the original Diaghilev souvenir programmes reproductions.

ALEXANDROVICH (MATVEEV). TEATR OPERI I BALETA IMENI S. M. KIROVA. Leningradskii Gosudarstvennoe Opera Akademicheskii. [1972].
Cr. 4to (10·1 × 8·4 ins.). 112 pp. illus. Orig. dec. boards.
Opera and Ballet at the Kirov Theatre. With well reproduced scenes from standard repertory it contains one photograph of Baryshnikov's *Eve and Adam*. See also Degen, A. and Stupnikov, I., *Mastera Tantsa* for repertory of this theatre from 1917–1973. Also

Bibliography Part III Chistyakova, V. V., *Leningradskii Balet Segodniya.*

ALFORD (VIOLET) & GALLOP (RODNEY). THE TRADITIONAL DANCE. London, Methuen & Co. 1935.
Cr. 8vo (7·2 × 5·6 ins.). xv + 204 pp. incl. Index. Illus. Orig. orange cloth.
A general survey of traditional dances in Europe and the British Isles.

ALGVERE (LINDA) & ABOLIMOV (PETRA). ZOLOTOPRAKHI. Balet v 3-k deistviyakh 7 mi kartinakh. Teatr Operi i Baleta Zstonskoi SSR. Zstoniya. Dekada Zstonskogo Iskusstvo i Literauri v Moskve 1956.
Demy 8vo (8 × 5 ins.). 16 pp. illus. Orig. dec. wrapps.
An illustrated programme with cast, artists and synopsis. *Zolotoprakhi* (Gold Spinners) with music by Zugen Kapp and choreography by Boris Knoblock. Listed in Slonimsky's *Vse o Balete* (p. 365). See also *Bibliography*, Part III, *Frangopulo*, Marietta, 75 *Baletnikh Libretto* and Soviet Ballet, The, 100 *Baletnikh Libretto* (pp. 109–110) where *Kalevipoeg*, another ballet by Zugen Kapp, is to be found.

AMBASSADE DE FRANCE (LONDRES). A LETTER TO CYRIL BEAUMONT. Londres le 21 Février 1951.
Cr. 4to (9·6 × 8·2 ins.). 1 p. Xerox.
A copy of a letter announcing the coming presentation of 'la Croix de Chevalier de la Légion d'Honneur' on 21 April 1950 (date of award), presentation date on 7 March 1951.

[AMBERG (GEORGE)]. THE THEATRE OF EUGENE BERMAN. [New York], The Museum of Modern Art. [1947].
Cr. 4to (10 × 7·4 ins.). 32 pp. illus in black and white with one double fold in colour. Orig. dec. wrapps.
See also A. Delarue and J. Levy, *Bibliography*, Part III.

AMERICAN DANCER (THE). The Managing Director, Ruth Eleanor Howard. Vol. I No. 1. Stage Ballroom Screen. Los Angeles, June 1927.
Demy 4to (11·6 × 8·6 ins.). 40 pp. illus. Orig. dec. wrapps.

Nine volumes of this magazine from June 1927 to December 1936 in original stamped blue folios containing 114 issues. Although Vol. I of Belknap's *Guide to Dance Periodicals* is from 1931–1935, many of the articles published during 1927–1930 are included.

AND (METIN). TURKISH DANCING. A Pictorial History of Turkish Dancing from Folk Dancing to Whirling Dervishes – Belly Dancing to Ballet. Ankara, Dost Yayinlara. 1976.
 Cr. 4to (10·4 × 7.6 ins.). 182 pp. with 194 illus. incl. 101 in colour. Orig. dec. wrapps.
 The quality and profusion of the illustrations draw one to that section, only to find they are not captioned. In the list of illustrations we find Shaman and Shamaness, Mevlevi Dervishes, Çengi (dancing boys and girls), Köcek or Tavsan (dancing boys), Kanto dancer (cafe singer and dancer). Knowledge of these and other terms will help in the appreciation of the unusual illustrations. See also *Bibliography*, Part III, And, Metin.

ANDERSON (JACK). DANCE. New York, Newsweek Books. [1974].
 Cr. 4to (10 × 7·2 ins.). 192 pp. illus. with many in colour. Orig. brown fabrikoid.
 Salient points of the dance and ballet in a smooth-running essay from *Ballet Comique de la Reine* to present day. Fine illustrations, particularly those of the 17th and 18th centuries.

ANONYMOUS. ARTE OU METHODO FACIL DE APRENDER A DANCAR AS CONTRADANCAS FRANCEZAS. Nova edicao Porto Em casa de F. G. da Fonesca, editor. 1862.
 F'cap 8vo (6·7 × 4·1 ins.). 36 pp. illus. with diagrams. Orig. yellow printed wrapps.
 A manual of social dancing with text in Portuguese. The dances originated in France.

ANSELME (JACQUES). DEUX LETTRES DE JACQUES ANSELME À ANTOINE BOURNONVILLE. Paris, Bulletin de la Société des Historiens du Théâtre. 1946.
 Demy 8vo (8·2 × 5·3 ins.). pp. 1–5. Orig. printed wrapps.

An excerpt from *Bulletin* of Avril–Juin 1946 containing two letters by Jacques Anselme with comment by Paul Bournonville.

ANTHONY (GORDON). A CAMERA AT THE BALLET. Pioneer Dancers of the Royal Ballet. London, David & Charles. [1975].
Demy 8vo (9·6 × 6·5 ins.). 96 pp. illus. orig. orange cloth.
Once again Anthony with his unique fairness divides the text and illustrative space equally among participants and closes the book with an Epilogue on Constant Lambert.

ANTHONY (GORDON). MARGOT FONTEYN. Phoenix House, London. [1950].
Med 8vo (9·5 × 5·7 ins.). 132 pp. with a frontis. in colour and 60 other plates. Orig. cloth.
The first of the *Phoenix House* editions with an Introduction by Ninette de Valois. See *Bibliography*, Part III, Anthony, for a later edition.

ANTHONY (GORDON). THE SADLER'S WELLS BALLET. With an Introduction by Eveleigh Leith. London, Geoffrey Bles. [1948].
Med. 8vo (9.7 × 7.2 ins.). xvi + 47 numbered plates. Orig. cloth.
A reprint of the edition first published in 1942.

ANTHONY (JAMES R.). PRINTED EDITIONS OF ANDRÉ CAMPRA'S L'EUROPE GALANTE. New York, G. Schirmer 1970.
Med. 8vo (9·4 × 6·4 ins.). pp. 54–73 illus. Orig. printed wrapps.
An article in *The Musical Quarterly* for Jan. 1970, Vol. LVI No. 1. Reproduction of the musical score.

ARRIGONI (PAOLO) E BERTARELLI (ACHILLE). RITRATTI DI MUSICISTI ED ARTISTI DI TEATRO. Conservati nella Raccolta Delle Stampe e dei Disegni. Catalogo Descrittivo. Milano, Tipografia del Popolo d'Italia MCMXXXIV.
Demy 4to (11·1 × 7·5 ins.). x + (iii) + 454 + (ii) pp. illus. Orig. printed wrapps.

The illustrated catalogue is in two parts: I. Musicisti, Cantanti, Comici e Ballerini; II. Acrobati, Atleti, Cavallerizzi, Domatori Giuocatore di Pallone, Poeti Estemporanei, Prestigatori, Ragazzi-Prodigo. There are also dancers and choreographers in the final listing (Secolo XIX) pp. 379–419. The Catalogue lists 5,636 numbered items. Index.

ARRUGA (LORENZO). PERCHE' CARLA FRACCI.
[Venezia Padova], Blow-Up [di Marsilio Editori 1974].
 Demy 4to (11·6 × 8·2 ins.). 79 pp. illus. Orig. dec. wrapps.
 Primarily a book of photographs in half-tone with text. See also Lidova, *Les Saisons de la Danse* (June 1972); *Dance Magazine Portfolio* (Jan. 1974); and John Gruen, *The Private World of Ballet*, Penguin (pp. 196–201).

ARUNDELL (DENNIS). THE STORY OF SADLER'S WELLS 1683–1964. London, Hamish Hamilton. [1965].
 Demy 8vo (8·3 × 5·3 ins.). xiv + 306 pp. incl. Index. Illus. Orig. blue cloth.
 See Chapter 17: Years of Achievement (p. 199); 18: Opera and Ballet (p. 216); 19: Success Again (p. 230). Consult the Index for listing of dancers' names.

ASCHENGREEN (ERIK). THE BEAUTIFUL DANGER: Facets of the Romantic Ballet. Translated from the Danish by Patricia N. McAndrew. New York, Dance Perspectives Summer 1974.
 Med. 8vo (9 × 6 ins.). 52 pp. illus. Orig. dec. wrapps.
 Issue No. 58 of *Dance Perspectives*. See also *Bibliography*, Part III, *Theatre Research Studies* II.

ASSOCIATION PHILANTHROPIQUE. ASSOCIATION PHILANTHROPIQUE DES ARTISTES DE L'OPÉRA. Fondée le Ier Juillet 1835. Exercice 1892. Paris, Imprimerie Chaix 1893.
 Med. 8vo (9·2 × 6·1 ins.). 15 pp. Orig. printed blue wrapps.
 A list of Artists of the Paris Opera receiving pensions, giving date of birth, amount of pension, etc. Perrot (Jules I believe) receives a grant in 1871 (No. 1,104,196) and on page nine reference is made to 42 days of assistance at 2 francs daily. 1892 is mentioned as the year of his death and there is a Ve. Perrot who received a pension of 176·65 francs and a Ve. Perot one of 106·65.

Could this be one of his wives? The roster contains many names, M. Bretin and Flora Fabbri Bretin, Mme. Fuchs née Taglioni (Louise Taglioni) and many others.

ASSOCIATION PHILANTHROPIQUE. ASSOCIATION PHILANTHROPIQUE DES ARTISTES DE L'OPÉRA. Fondée le Ier Juillet 1835. Exercice 1901. Paris, Imprimerie E. Lefévre 1902.
Med. 8vo (9·2 × 6·1 ins.). 15 pp. Orig. printed wrapps.
A further list of artists receiving pensions. On p. 5 Perrot is listed with grant No. 747,213 and on p. 14 EM Perrot admitted in 1867 under No. 163. See also *Bibliography*, Part III, *Théâtre Impérial de L'Opéra*, Caisse Speciale de Pensions de Retraits.

ATKINSON (MARGARET F.) & HILLMAN (MAY). DANCERS OF THE BALLET. Biographies. New York, Alfred A. Knopf. [1955].
Roy. 8vo (10 × 6·6 ins.). xvii + 174 + (ii) pp. incl. index. Illus. Orig. boards with cloth spine.
A collection of Biographies of leading dancers from the United States, England and France, well illustrated and in alphabetical order.

ATLAS (HELEN V.). NATALIA BESSMERTNOVA. Brooklyn, Dance Horizons 1975.
Med. 8vo (9 × 7 ins.). 23 pp. illus. Orig. dec. wrapps.
A monograph published by *Dance Horizons* called *Dance Horizons Spotlight Series*. Photographs by Mira.

AUSTIN (RICHARD). THE BALLERINA. [London], Vision. [1974].
Demy 8vo (8·3 × 5·2 ins.). 128 pp. incl. Index. Illus. Orig. cloth.
The book includes essays on Pavlova, Spessivtseva, Fonteyn and Makarova.

AUSTIN (RICHARD). BIRTH OF A BALLET. [London], Vision. [1976].
Demy 8vo (8·3 × 5·2 ins.). 151 pp. illus. with photogs. and line drwgs. Orig. red cloth.
The story of a ballet *Black Angels* with choreography by Christopher Bruce. The sketches are by Judy Ling Wong. See also

Bibliography Part I Conyn, *Three Centuries of Ballet* (Chapter XIII p. 103) and Part IV Crisp and Clarke, *Making a Ballet*.

AUSTIN (RICHARD). IMAGES OF THE DANCE. [London], Vision. [1975].

Demy 8vo (8·3 × 5·2 ins.). 183 pp. incl. Index. Illus. Orig. black boards.

In this book, dancers are brought into focus against a background of poetry and music. The image of Natalia Makarova (pp. 158–170) seems clearest to the author. The eight photographs of attitudes and positions seem superfluous in this kind of book.

AVALIANI (NOI) & ZHDANOV (LEONID). Compilers. **BOLSHOI'S YOUNG DANCERS.** Moscow, Progress Publishers. 1975.

Cr. 4to (10·2 × 8 ins.). 320 + (x) pp. illus. Orig. dec. black boards.

Studies of the following 10 dancers each having several authors contributing: Vasiliev, Maximova, Lavrovsky, Bessmertnova, Vladimirov, Sorokina, Akimov, Golikova, Bogatiryov and Ratchenko. Translated into English by Natalie Ward. Printing very clean and photography excellent.

BAJOV (P. P.). KAMENNII SHVETOK. Leningrad 1957.

Med. 8vo (8·4 × 5·7 ins.). 8 pp. Orig. printed wrapps.

The libretto for Prokofiev's *The Stone Flower*, first choreographed by K. Muller for Sverdlosk (1944 according to Swift). This is the Grigorovitch version with A. I. Gribov as *Danila* and I. A. Kolpakova as *Katerina*.

BAJOV (P. P.). KAMENNII SHVETOK. Moskva, Bolshoi Teatr 1958.

Med. 8vo (9·1 × 6·1 ins.). 20 pp. illus. with pen drwgs. Orig. dec. wrapps.

The libretto for Lavrovsky's production at the Bolshoi of Grigorovitch's *Stone Flower* with decorations by Virsaladze. The dancers (not listed) were: Plisetskaya, Vasiliev, Maximova and Levashov.

BAJOV (P. P.). SKAZ O KAMENNOM SHVETKE. Moskva, Sovetskii 1961.

F'cap 8vo (6·4 × 5 ins.). 45 pp. illus. with photogs. and mus. ex. Orig. printed wrapps.

The most complete exposition of libretto, musical fragments and photographs of both Lavrovsky versions of *Stone Flower* for the Bolshoi; the first with Ulanova and Preobrajenskii and the second with Plisetskaya and Vasiliev. See Chujoy & Manchester, *The Dance Encyclopedia* for more details.

BAKER (BLANCHE). DRAMATIC BIBLIOGRAPHY. An Annotated List of Books on the History and Criticism of the Drama and Stage and on the Allied Arts of the Theatre. New York, The H. W. Wilson Co. 1933.
Med. 8vo (9·9 × 6·4 ins.). xvi + 320 pp. incl. index. Orig. blue cloth.
Contents: I. Drama and Theatre. II. Production and Stagecraft. III. Pageantry, Religious Drama, Entertainment. IV. Anthologies, Bibliographies, Directories. Main listing of Dance Material under Part II Sec. 6. The form of this book was closely observed in Paul Magriel's *Bibliography of Dancing* published by Wilson later in 1936, although the annotations in this present work are more complete.

BAKHRUSHIN (Y[URI] A[LEKSEEVICH]). ISTORIYA RUSSKOGO BALETA. Izdanie 2-e Moskva, 'Proveshtsenie' 1973.
Demy 8vo (8·3 × 5·5 ins.). 253 + (i) pp. with 56 pages of composite plates. Orig. dec. brown cloth.
The second edition of *History of Russian Ballet*, which according to Koegler's *Concise Oxford Dictionary of Ballet* is the official text book in use in all Russian ballet schools. See *Bibliography*, Part III, for comment on the original edition.

BAKST (LÉON). BAKST. London, The Fine Art Society Ltd. 1973.
Square (8·1 × 8·1 ins.). 40 pp. n.n. with 136 numbered illus. Orig. dec. wrapps.
A catalogue of an exhibition held at the Fine Art Society Dec. 3, 1973–Jan. 4, 1974. The authenticity of some of the items seems dubious.

BALANCHINE (GEORGE). BALANCHINE: DEMIGOD OF THE DANCE. New York, Newsweek 1964.
Demy 4to (11 × 8·3 ins.). pp. 51–56 illus. Orig. wrapps.

An article in May 4th issue of *Newsweek*. See also *Bibliography*, Part III, Balanchine, George.

BALANCHINE (GEORGE) & MASON (FRANCIS). BALANCHINE'S COMPLETE STORIES OF THE GREAT BALLETS. Revised and Enlarged Edition. New York, Doubleday & Co. 1977.

Med. 8vo (9 × 6 ins.). xxvi + 838 pp. incl. index. With over 75 new photogs. Orig. black cloth spine and boards.

The latest edition of Balanchine's *Complete Stories of the Great Ballets*, with extra material strikingly illustrated with photographs.

BALANCHINE (GEORGE) & MASON (FRANCIS). 101 STORIES OF THE GREAT BALLETS. Garden City, Doubleday & Co. 1975.

Cr. 8vo (7 × 4·1 ins.). xiv + 541 pp. incl. index. Orig. dec. wrapps. Stories of the ballets continuing in the vein of previous books, Balanchine's *Complete Stories of the Great Ballets* and *New Complete Stories of the Great Ballets*.

BALDICK (ROBERT). THE DUEL. A History of Duelling. London, Spring Books 1970.

Med. 8vo (9·5 × 6·5 ins.). 212 pp. with 47 plates, 43 line drwgs. and 8 engr. Orig. red cloth.

W. G. Raffé in his *Dictionary* under *Five Positions* and *Cinq Pas* states these positions employed in Ballet came directly from earlier schools of Fencing in France and Spain. I fear his thesis is on rather shaky ground; however there are several illustrations here that show quite correct ballet positions.

BALLET REVIEW. BALLET REVIEW No. 1, 1947. Edinburgh, The Albyn Press.

Cr. 4to (9·6 × 7·2 ins.). 63 pp. illus. Orig. dec. wrapps.

See *The Soviet Ballet in 1946* by W. G. Raffé (pp. 14–16) and *The Male Dancer* by Rose Tenent (pp. 17, 18).

BALLETS DES CHAMPS-ELYSÉES (LES). Paris, Realités 1946.

Roy. 4to (12·2 × 9·4 ins.). pp. 14–27, 89–91 illus. some in colour. Orig. dec. wrapps.

An article in the Oct. 1946 issue of *Realités*, fully illustrated. See also Beaumont, Cyril, *Les Ballets des Champs-Elysées*.

BALLETS DU GRAND THEATRE DE MOSCOU (LES). LES BALLETS DU BOLCHOI. [Paris, Editions Cercle d'Art 1958].

Cr. 4to (10·4 × 8·2 ins.). 93 pp. with many illus. Orig. dec. wrapps.

Repertory and personnel for the Bolshoi's first appearance in Paris. Brief biographies of Oulanova, Fadëitchev, Plissetskaïa, Lepechinskaïa, Jdanov, Kondratov, Radounski, Lediakh and Strouchkova. (sic.)

BALLETS RUSSES DE SERGE DE DIAGHILEV (LES). LES BALLETS RUSSES DE SERGE DE DIAGHILEV 1909–1929. Ville de Strasbourg 1969.

Demy 8vo (8·4 × 5·5 ins.). 331 pp. + 127 num. illus. and 10 full page plates in colour. Orig. illus. wrapps. (Bakst).

A very important catalogue of an exhibition of Diaghilev material held at *L'Ancienne Douane* 15 May–15 Sept. 1969 in Strasbourg. Contents: A Preface by Serge Lifar, Introduction by Victor Beyer; La Musique dans les Ballets by Jean-Daniel Ludmann. Each piece is preceded by a cast list, argument, followed by the items on display. The catalogue closes with biographies, bibliography and Representations des Ballets Russes. See also *Bibliography*, Part III, Ville de Strasbourg.

BARLANGY (ISTVAN). [MIME TRAINING AND EXERCISES]. Budapest 1964.

Demy 4to (11·4 × 8·3 ins.). 12 pp. typescript + 10 pp. of stick drwgs. on parchment paper. Orig. grey wrapps.

The mss., I believe of *Mime Training and Exercises*, in Hungarian, with excellent and precise drawings. The mss. is signed by Istvan and Juliette, Budapest 1964. See *Bibliography*, Part III, for the publication in English.

BARNES (CLIVE). BALLET IN BRITAIN SINCE THE WAR. London, Thrift Books No. 21. [1953].

Cr. 8vo (7·2 × 4·5 ins.). 92 pp. Orig. green wrapps.

Before arriving at his American eminence Barnes was Ballet Critic of *The Times* and a contributor to *Ballet Annual, Dance and Dancers, About the House* etc.

BARNES (CLIVE). INSIDE AMERICAN BALLET THEATRE. New York, Hawthorn 1977.

Demy 4to (11 × 8·3 ins.). 182 + (ii) pp. illus. Orig. blue buckram.

A very attractive picture book which because of its many topics — New Productions, Heritage, Classic Repertory, The Dancers, The Choreographers, Family Album, Galas — and too few pages (182), can but scan the almost 40 years' life of *American Ballet Theatre*.

BARNES (PATRICIA). MARIS LIEPA. Brooklyn, Dance Horizons 1975.

Med. 8vo (9 × 7 ins.). 23 pp. illus. Orig. dec. wrapps.

A monograph published in the *Dance Horizon Spotlight Series* with photographs by Mira.

BARNEY (DANFORD). WILL WE EVER HAVE AN AMERICAN BALLET? New York, Dance Lovers Magazine, March 1924.

Demy 4to (11·5 × 8·4 ins.). pp. 36, 37, 58 illus. Orig. illus. wrapps. (Fokine).

An interview with Michel Fokine. Among the illustrations are photographs of three groups of students in which Doris Niles appears.

BARON (JOHN H.). LES FÉES DES FORÊTS DE S. GERMAIN BALLET DE COUR 1625. With transcription of the text and music for Act II. Edited with commentary by John H. Baron. New York, Dance Perspectives, Summer 1972.

Cr. 4to (9 × 7·3 ins.). 53 pp. illus. Orig. dec. wrapps.
Issue No. 62 of *Dance Perspectives*.

BARTHOLOMEW (NINO). MIRACLE IN THE GORBALS. As Told by the Beggar. Drawings by Sheila Graham. [London, The Kelgee Publications. 1945].

Demy 8vo (8·2 × 5·4 ins.). 8 pp. illus. with drwgs. Orig. dec. wrapps.

See also *Bibliography* Part I, Haskell, *Miracle in the Gorbals*.

BARYSHNIKOV (MIKHAIL). BARYSHNIKOV AT WORK. Mikhail Baryshnikov Discusses his Roles. New York, Alfred A. Knopf 1976.

Roy. 4to (11·2 × 10 ins.). 252 pp. illus. Orig. black fabric.

An album of fine photographs by Martha Swope, Introduction by

Charles Engell France and most intelligent discussion of his roles by Baryshnikov. This artist is one of the few male dancers of *today* whose work merits detailed examination. See also Péres, Louis, *Mikhail Baryshnikov* and Victor, Thomas, *The Making of a Dance*.

BAZAROVA (N.). KLASSICHESKII TANETS. Metodika Obucheniya v Chetvertom i Pyatom Klassakh. Iskusstvo Leningradskoe Otdelenie 1975.

Cr. 4to (8·4 × 5·4 ins.). 181 + (ii) pp. illus. with line drwgs. Orig. cloth spine and boards.

A Russian manual on the classic dance. See also *Bibliography*, Part III, Messerer, Asaf; Vaganova, Agrippina; and Part IV, Messerer, Asaf; Soviet Ballet, The; and Tarasov, N. for other manuals.

BEATON (CECIL). THE MONTE CARLO BALLET RUSSE. London, Vanity Fair n.d.

Roy. 4to (12 × 8.2 ins.). 3pp. xerox. Illus.

An article containing an interesting paragraph on the author's visits to the Beaumont 'Shrine of Ballet', at 75 Charing Cross Road.

BEAUMONT (CYRIL W.) & BARZEL (ANN). ADOLPH BOLM. London, The Ballet Annual No. 6 1952.

Med. 8vo (9·6 × 7·2 ins.). pp. 54–55. Orig. dec. cloth.

An article in *The Ballet Annual* No. 6. See also *Bibliography*, Part I, John Dougherty, *Perspective on Adolph Bolm*.

BEAUMONT (CYRIL W.). AGNES DE MILLE AND WARREN LEONARD. London, The Dance Journal, Feb. 1933.

Demy 8vo (8·3 × 5·2 ins.). pp. 43–46 illus. Orig. dec. wrapps.

The Dance Journal Vol. V No. 1. A review of the London debut of these artists at the *Arts Theatre*, Nov. 30th 1933.

BEAUMONT (CYRIL W.). ALICIA MARKOVA. London, The Ballet Annual No. 10 1956.

Med. 8vo (9·6 × 7·2 ins.). pp. 52, 53 with one full page illus. Orig. dec. cloth.

An article in *Ballet Annual* No. 10. See also *Bibliography*, Part I, Beaumont, *Alicia Markova*.

BEAUMONT (CYRIL W.). ANNA PAVLOVA. London, The Dance Journal Feb. 1931.
Demy 8vo (8·3 × 5·2 ins.). pp. 304–309 illus. Orig. dec. wrapps.
The Dance Journal Vol. III No. 7. See also Beaumont, Cyril W., *Pavlova* and *Pavlova, Lopokova and Hassan*.

BEAUMONT (CYRIL W.). ANTONY TUDOR: CHOREOGRAPHER. London, Skelton Robinson. [1949].
Demy 8vo (8·1 × 5·1 ins.). pp. 166–180. Orig. cloth.
An article in *British Ballet* edited by Peter Noble, reviewing after a decade Tudor's success of *Jardin aux Lilas*, at the Mercury Theatre where it was produced.

BEAUMONT (CYRIL W.). APPROACH TO BALLET. London, The Critic's Circular. Vol. X No. 41, Summer 1954.
Demy 4to (11 × 8·4 ins.). p. 3. Orig. wrapps.
An article.

BEAUMONT (CYRIL W.). LES ARCHIVES INTERNATIONALES DE LA DANSE. London, The Dance Journal 1933.
Demy 8vo (8·3 × 5·2 ins.). pp. 126–127. Orig. dec. wrapps.
An article in *The Dance Journal* Vol. V No. 3. See also *Bibliography*, Part I, *Archives Internationales de la Danse*.

BEAUMONT (CYRIL W.). THE ART AND PROFESSION OF THE ACADEMIC DANCER II. London. Opera & Ballet, July 1924.
F'cap 4to (8·3 × 5·2 ins.). pp. 22, 24, 16. Orig. dec. wrapps.
An article in Vol. 2 No. 7 of *Opera and Ballet*. There is also a second article, *Century Old Dancers* (Burmese Dancers at Wembley) by Mr. Beaumont and one by Harcourt Algeranoff, *Stage Dancing in Japan* (pp. 11, 12, 26) with one illustration.

BEAUMONT (CYRIL W.). THE ART OF ENRICO CECCHETTI. London, Dancing World, April 1922.
Demy 4to (10·7 × 8·3 ins.). p. 20. Orig. dec. wrapps.
An article marking the Fiftieth Anniversary of Enrico Cecchetti's first appearance on the stage in a principal role.

BEAUMONT (CYRIL W.). THE ART OF MAUD ALLAN.
London, The Dancing World, Aug.–Sept. 1922.
    Cr. 4to (10·7 × 8·3 ins.). with one plate. Orig. dec. wrapps.
    An article. See also *Bibliography*, Part III, Allan, Maud, *My Life and Dancing*.

BEAUMONT (CYRIL W.). THE ART OF NINETTE DE VALOIS. London, Dancing Life No. 3, Jan. 1922.
    Demy 4to (11·2 × 8·6 ins.). pp. 52, 53 incl. one page of photogs. Orig. dec. wrapps.
    An article written at the time of De Valois' appearances with her pupils in London Music Halls. The first monograph in book form about de Valois was by Kate Neatby – *Ninette de Valois and the Vic-Wells Ballet*. This issue has for its cover a photograph of Lydia Kyasht.

BEAUMONT (CYRIL W.). THE ART OF RUTH ST. DENIS. London, The Dancing World, July 1922.
    Cr. 4to (10·7 × 8·3 ins.). Orig. dec. wrapps.
    An article. See also *Bibliography*, Part II, St. Denis.

BEAUMONT (CYRIL W.). ASHTON'S CINDERELLA. London, Ballet, Feb. 1949.
    Demy 8vo (8·3 × 5·2 ins.). pp. 6–26 illus. Orig. dec. wrapps.
    An article in *Ballet* Vol. 7 No. 2. This issue is largely devoted to Cinderella.

BEAUMONT (CYRIL W.). ASHTON'S DON JUAN. London, Ballet Jan. 1949.
    Demy 8vo (8·3 × 5·2 ins.). pp. 13–15 with one illus. Orig. dec. wrapps.
    An article in *Ballet* Vol. 7 No. 1. Review of Ashton's *Don Juan* with music by Richard Strauss. See also Fokine's *Don Juan* with music by Gluck, *Bibliography*, Part I, Beaumont, *Complete Book of Ballets*.

BEAUMONT (CYRIL W.). AUDREY ASHBY. Some Remarks on Training. London, The Dancing World Jan. 1924.
    Demy 4to (11 × 8·4 ins.). p. 23. Orig. dec. wrapps.
    An article about a dance recital given by Audrey Ashby at the Chelsea Palace Theatre Nov. 17, 1924.

BEAUMONT (CYRIL W.). AUGUSTE VESTRIS. London, Ballet Aug. 1947.
Demy 8vo (8·3 × 5·2 ins.). pp. 46–55 illus. Orig. dec. wrapps.
An article in *Ballet* Vol. 4 No. 2. See also Beaumont, *Gaetano and Auguste Vestris in English Caricature.*

BEAUMONT (CYRIL W.). THE AUTOBIOGRAPHY OF A PREMIER DANSEUR. London, The Dance Journal Oct. 1931.
Demy 8vo (8·3 × 5·2 ins.). pp. 455–458. Orig. dec. wrapps.
A review of Anton Dolin's autobiography *Divertissement* in *The Dance Journal* Vol. III Nos. 10 and 11.

BEAUMONT (CYRIL W.). THE AUTOBIOGRAPHY OF A PRIMA BALLERINA. London, The Dance Journal 1930.
Demy 8vo (8·3 × 5·2 ins.). pp. 71–76. Orig. dec. wrapps.
A review of Tamara Karsavina's reminiscences: *Theatre Street* in *The Dance Journal* Vol. III No. 2 April 1930.

BEAUMONT (CYRIL W.). BALANCHINE'S BALLET IMPERIAL. London, Ballet May 1950.
Demy 8vo (8·3 × 5·2 ins.). pp. 13–19 illus. Orig. dec. wrapps.
An article in *Ballet* Vol. 9 No. 5.

BEAUMONT (CYRIL W.). BALET SADLERS WELLS V PRAZE. [Praha]. Britzky Magazin Zari 1947.
Cr. 4to (10 × 7 ins.). pp. 19–23. illus. Orig. dec. wrapps.
An article. Text in Hungarian.

BEAUMONT (CYRIL W.). THE BALLET CLUB – THE CAMARGO SOCIETY. London, The Dance Journal June 1931.
Demy 8vo (8·3 × 5·2 ins.). pp. 420–424. Orig. dec. wrapps.
An article on the second season of *Camargo Society* in their theatre in Ladbroke Road in *The Dance Journal* Vol. III No. 9.

BEAUMONT (CYRIL W.). THE BALLET CLUB. London, The Dance Journal Dec. 1931.
Demy 8vo (8·3 × 5·2 ins.). pp. 576–580 illus. Orig. dec. wrapps.

A review of The Ballet Club's third season with presentations of *Mercury, Cross-gartered, Lady of Shalott* and *Lac des Cygnes* in *The Dance Journal* Vol. III No. 12.

BEAUMONT (CYRIL W.). A BALLET FOLLOWED BY SOME DIVERTISSEMENTS. London, The Dancing World, April 1923.

Cr. 4to (10·7 × 8·3 ins.). p. 24. Orig. dec. wrapps.

An article about performances of Vera Savina (Massine), Loie Fuller's Ballets Fantastiques and performances at the Margaret Morris Theatre.

BEAUMONT (CYRIL W.). THE BALLET GIRL – THEN AND NOW. Part I. 'Then'. London, The Dancing Times July 1922.

Med. 8vo (9·2 × 6·4 ins.). pp. 845–847 illus. Orig. dec. wrapps.

A very sympathetic article about Albert Smith's *The Natural History of the Ballet Girl* which runs in several issues. See *Bibliography*, Parts II & III, Smith, Albert for the original edition and also the reprint. See also Beaumont, *The Life of a Ballet Girl in the 'Sixties'*.

BEAUMONT (CYRIL W.). THE BALLET GIRL – THEN AND NOW. With Drawings by Randolph Schwabe. Part II – 'NOW'. London, The Dancing Times Aug. 1922.

Med. 8vo (9·2 × 6·4 ins.). pp. 925–929 illus. with drwgs. Orig. dec. wrapps.

The second part of an article begun in the July 1922 issue of *The Dancing Times*. However the observations are no longer those of Mr. Smith but rather those of Cyril Beaumont.

BEAUMONT (CYRIL W.). THE BALLET GUILD PRESENT A PERFORMANCE IN HONOUR OF MR. CYRIL W. BEAUMONT. [London]. The Peoples Palace 1944.

Demy 8vo (8·2 × 5·2 ins.). 4 pp. Xerox.

A Xerox of a programme presented March 18, 1944, consisting of: *The Swan Lake, The Nymphenburg Garden, Slavonic Dances, Divertissement*, and *Victorian Bouquet*. Assisting artists have signed the programme.

BEAUMONT (CYRIL W.). THE BALLET OF THE LILAC FAIRY. London, The Dancing World Feb. 1924.

Cr. 4to (10·7 × 8·3 ins.). p. 21. Orig. dec. wrapps.

An article. Also in this issue: Part IV of *A History of Ballet in Russia* also by Cyril Beaumont.

BEAUMONT (CYRIL W.). BALLET RAMBERT. London, Ballet Dec. 1949.
Demy 8vo (8·3 × 5·2 ins.). pp. 17–24 illus. Orig. dec. wrapps.
An article in *Ballet* Vol. 8 No. 6. See also *Bibliography* Part I Haskell, *The Marie Rambert Ballet* and Part III Clarke, *Dancers of Mercury*.

BEAUMONT (CYRIL W.). THE BALLET THEATRE. London, Ballet Sept. 1946.
Demy 8vo (8·3 × 5·2 ins.). pp. 18–24 + illus. Orig. dec. wrapps.
A review of Ballet Theatre's first visit to Covent Garden in July 1946 in *Ballet* Vol. 2 No. 4.

BEAUMONT (CYRIL W.). BALLET'S DEBT TO FAIRY TALE. London, Ballet Jan. 1947.
Demy 8vo (8·3 × 5·2 ins.). pp. 41–44. Orig. dec. wrapps.
An article in *Ballet* Vol. 3 No. 1.

BEAUMONT (CYRIL W.). LES BALLETS DES CHAMPS-ELYSÉES. London, Ballet June 1946.
Demy 8vo (8·3 × 5·2 ins.). pp. 19–24 + illus. Orig. dec. wrapps.
Ballet Vol. 2 No. 1. His first notice of this company.

BEAUMONT (CYRIL W.). LES BALLETS DES CHAMPS-ELYSÉES. London, Ballet July 1946.
Demy 8vo (8·3 × 5·2 ins.). pp. 20–24 + illus. Orig. dec. wrapps.
His second notice of this company in *Ballet* Vol. 2 No. 2.

BEAUMONT (CYRIL W.). LES BALLETS DES CHAMPS-ELYSÉES. Nederlands, Dans Kroniek, [July 1948].
Roy. 4to (12·1 × 9 ins.). pp. 124–129 with illus. Orig. dec. wrapps.
An article, text in Dutch.

BEAUMONT (CYRIL W.). LES BALLETS DES CHAMPS-ELYSÉES. London, Ballet Nov. 1948.
Demy 8vo (8·3 × 5·2 ins.). pp. 7, 8, 13–18 with one drwg. Orig. dec. wrapps.
An article in *Ballet* Vol. 6 No. 2. The return of this company on August 31 to the Prince's Theatre.

BEAUMONT (CYRIL W.). LES BALLETS DES CHAMPS-ELYSÉES. Contemporary French Design. London, The Studio. 1948.
Cr. 4to (9·6 × 7·3 ins.). pp. 12–17 illus. incl. 2 in colour. Orig. dec. yellow wrapps.
An article in the July 1948 issue of *The Studio* with designs by Clavé, Lepri, Maclès, Beaurepaire and others.

BEAUMONT (CYRIL W.). LES BALLETS DES CHAMPS-ELYSÉES. London, Ballet Nov. 1949.
Demy 8vo (8·3 × 5·2 ins.). pp. 15–30 illus. Orig. dec. wrapps.
An article in *Ballet* Vol. 8 No. 5. The company – a favourite of Beaumont's – disbanded in 1950: this was the final visit to London.

BEAUMONT (CYRIL W.). BEHIND THE SCENES AT THE OPERA IN TAGLIONI'S DAY. An Extract from the Memoirs of Dr. Véron. London, The Dancing Times Jan. 1924.
Med. 8vo (9·2 × 6·4 ins.). pp. 403, 405, 406 illus. Orig. dec. wrapps.
An article translated by Cyril Beaumont. See *Bibliography*, Part II, Dr. L. Véron.

BEAUMONT (CYRIL W.). BONNE BOUCHE. London, Ballet June 1952.
Demy 8vo (8·3 × 5·2 ins.). pp. 33–43 illus. Orig. dec. wrapps.
An article in *Ballet* Vol. 12 No. 6. See also *The Sunday Times* April 6, 1952 for a review which appeared two days after its *première*.

BEAUMONT (CYRIL W.). BOOKSELLER AT THE BALLET. Memoirs 1891–1929. London, C. W. Beaumont 1975.

Demy 8vo (8·3 × 5·1 ins.). 426 pp. with 48 illus. Orig. brown cloth.

This volume incorporates the long out of print *Diaghilev Ballet in London*, and in it Beaumont recounts the first 38 years of his life, ascribing his education to much reading, the friendship of Osbert and Sacheverell Sitwell and Diaghilev's *Ballets Russes*, and his first interest in ballet to seeing Pavlova at the insistence of Alice Beha, who later became his wife.

The pages on his childhood in North London reveal a self-contained, imaginative and resourceful boy with an excellent memory, whom those of us who knew him in later years can at once recognise. His activities as a bookseller, ballet historian and critic and publisher of fine books, as well as his work as a dance educator (which included codifying and publishing the major part of the Cecchetti system of ballet training) are recorded so modestly that the reader must pause and consider these achievements before he can appreciate their scope and importance.

BEAUMONT (CYRIL W.). THE BRITISH DANCER.
Some Criticisms and Suggestions. London, Opera Feb. 1924.

F'cap 4to (8·2 × 6·5 ins.). pp. 13, 14, 20. Orig. dec. wrapps.

An article in Vol. 2 No. 2 of this monthly. The issue also contains material on the Diaghilev Company (pp. 8, 32).

BEAUMONT (CYRIL W.). THE BRITISH DANCER.
Some Criticisms and Suggestions. London, The Dance Journal Dec. 1924.

Demy 8vo (8·3 × 5·2 ins.). pp. 12–15. Orig. dec. wrapps.

An article in Vol. I No. 1 of *The Dance Journal*. Reprinted from *Opera*.

BEAUMONT (CYRIL W.). A BURMESE PWÈ AT WEMBLEY. London, Opera & The Ballet June 1924.

F'cap 4to (8·2 × 6·5 ins.). pp. 21, 30. Orig. dec. wrapps.

An article in *Opera & The Ballet* Vol. 2 No. 6. In two parts, see *Century Old Dances* for final instalment. Also *Bibliography*, Part I, Beaumont, for description of a special hand coloured illustrated edition of this article.

BEAUMONT (CYRIL W.). LA CAMARGO. London, The Dance Journal June 1934.

Demy 8vo (8·3 × 5·2 ins.). pp. 112–118. illus. Orig. dec. wrapps.

An article in *The Dance Journal* Vol. VI No. 2. See also *Bibliography*, Part I, Beaumont, *Three French Dancers of the 18th Century* and Part II, Letainturier-Fradin, *La Camargo*; also Montague Nathan, *Melle Camargo*.

BEAUMONT (CYRIL W.). THE CAMARGO SOCIETY. London, The Dance Journal Dec. 1930.

Demy 8vo (8·3 × 5·2 ins.). pp. 282–286. Orig. dec. wrapps.
A review of the initial performance of *The Camargo Society* Oct. 19, 1930 in *The Dance Journal* Vol. III No. 6.

BEAUMONT (CYRIL W.). THE CAMARGO SOCIETY – THE VACANI MATINEE. London, The Dance Journal, Aug. & Oct. 1931.

Demy 8vo (8·3 × 5·2 ins.). pp. 468–469, 523. Orig. dec. wrapps.
Review of The Camargo Society's *The Jackdaw and the Pigeons, Pomona* and *Job*. Also Miss Vacani's Recital with her pupils. *The Dance Journal* Vol. III Nos. 10 and 11.

BEAUMONT (CYRIL W.). THE CAMARGO SOCIETY. London, The Dance Journal Feb. 1932.

Demy 8vo (8·3 × 5·2 ins.). pp. 615, 616. Orig. dec. wrapps.
The Dance Journal Vol. IV No. 1. A review of *Fête Polonaise* and *A Woman's Privilege* amongst other ballets during Camargo's second season at the Savoy Theatre.

BEAUMONT (CYRIL W.). THE CAMARGO SOCIETY. London, The Dance Journal April 1932.

Demy 8vo (8·3 × 5·2 ins.). pp. 650, 651. Orig. dec. wrapps.
The *Dance Journal* Vol. IV No. 2. Further review of Camargo's second season with *The Lord of Burleigh, La Création du Monde, Valse-Fantasie* and *Façade* under scrutiny.

BEAUMONT (CYRIL W.). THE CAMARGO SOCIETY. London, The Dance Journal June 1932.

Demy 8vo (8·3 × 5.2 ins.). pp. 699, 700, 677. Orig. dec. wrapps.
The Dance Journal Vol. IV No. 3. During a four week season at the Savoy Theatre (beginning June 6th), Anton Dolin and Olga Spessivtseva appeared in *Swan Lake*.

BEAUMONT (CYRIL W.). THE CAREER AND TRAGEDY OF VASLAV NIJINSKY. London, The Dance Journal Dec. 1933.
Demy 8vo (8·3 × 5·2 ins.). pp. 281–290. Orig. dec. wrapps.
The Dance Journal Dec. 1933 Vol. V No. 6. An important review of the book *Nijinsky* by Romola Nijinsky.

BEAUMONT (CYRIL W.). CARLOTTA GRISI AND GISELLE. London, The Dance Journal April 1931.
Demy 8vo (8·3 × 5·2 ins.). pp. 344–349 illus. Orig. dec. wrapps.
The Dance Journal Vol. III No. 8.

BEAUMONT (CYRIL W.). CARTOPHILY – APPLIED TO DANCERS. London, The Dancing Times Feb. 1975.
Demy 4to (11·2 × 9 ins.). pp. 250 illus. Orig. dec. wrapps.
A review of the album *Der Kunsterlische Tanz* which is a collection of cigarette cards representing dancers, captioned and neatly pasted down in an album. See *Bibliography*, Part I, *Kunsterlische Tanz, Der*, for the original edition.

BEAUMONT (CYRIL W.). A CATALOGUE OF MOST DESIRABLE BOOKS. London, C. W. Beaumont & Co. 1916.
Med. 8vo (9·1 × 6·3 ins.). 20 pp. Orig. illus. wrapps.
This is catalogue No. 29 which includes Association Items, 1st Editions of Esteemed Authors, Books from Eragny and Vale Presses and a Selection of French Books of Exceptional Interest. Also contains two items related to the dance: Scott, *Dancing in All Ages* and Willy, *Danseuses*.

BEAUMONT (CYRIL W.). CECCHETTI CHOREOGRAPHIC COMPETITION. London, The Dancing Times Jan. 1967.
Demy 4to (11·4 × 9 ins.). p. 215 with 2 illus. Orig. dec. wrapps.
An article in *The Dancing Times* Vol. LVII No. 676.

BEAUMONT (CYRIL W.). THE CECCHETTI METHOD OF TEACHING CLASSICAL BALLET DANCING. [Cecchetti Council of America 1953].

Cr. 8vo (7·5 × 5 ins.). 4 pp. n.n. Orig. printed wrapps.
A pamphlet consisting of excerpts from an article appearing in *Ballet Annual* No. 2. Issued complimentarily by the Cecchetti Council of America.

BEAUMONT (CYRIL W.). CECCHETTI'S LEGACY TO THE DANCE. London, The Ballet Annual No. 2, Adam & Charles Black 1948.

Med. 8vo (9·6 × 7·2 ins.). pp. 59–70 illus. Orig. cream cloth.
An article very well illustrated. See also *Bibliography*, Part I, Beaumont and Cecchetti; Part III, Beaumont, Cecchetti and Celli, and also three more articles in this Part IV: Beaumont, *The Art of Enrico Cecchetti*, *The Cecchetti Method* and *Enrico Cecchetti, The Jubilee of a Great Artist*.

BEAUMONT (CYRIL W.). THE CENTENARY OF ENRICO CECCHETTI. London, The Dancing Times June 1950.

Demy 8vo (8·6 × 5·3 ins.). pp. 542 + illus. Orig. dec. wrapps.
An article in issue No. 477 of *The Dancing Times*. See also Beaumont, Cyril W., *The Art of Enrico Cecchetti*.

BEAUMONT (CYRIL W.). CENTURY OLD DANCES. London, Opera & The Ballet July 1924.

F'cap 4to (8·2 × 6·5 ins.). pp. 20, 21. Orig. dec. wrapps.
An article in *Ballet & The Opera* Vol. 2 No. 7. See *A Burmese Pwè at Wembley* for Part I of this article.

BEAUMONT (CYRIL W.). THE CHARACTERS IN SWAN LAKE. London, Ballet March 1950.

Demy 8vo (8·3 × 5·2 ins.). pp. 20–26 illus. Orig. dec. wrapps.
An Article in *Ballet* Vol. 9 No. 3. See also *Le Lac des Cygnes at Covent Garden, Swan Lake* and *Bibliography*, Part I, Beaumont, *The Ballet Called Swan Lake*.

BEAUMONT (CYRIL W.). CHECKMATE AND MAM'-ZELLE ANGOT. London, Ballet Jan. 1948.

Demy 8vo (8·3 × 5·2 ins.). pp. 7–15 illus. Orig. dec. wrapps.
An article in *Ballet* Vol. 5 No. 1. The Sadler's Wells Ballet at Covent Garden.

BEAUMONT (CYRIL W.). THE CHOREGRAPHE MICHAEL FOKINE. London, The Dancing World Aug.–Sept. 1923.

Demy 4to (11 × 8·4 ins.). pp. 32, 33, 55 with one illus. Orig. dec. wrapps.

An article. Mr. Beaumont's book *Michel Fokine and His Ballets* was not published until 1935. Further material in this number by Beaumont includes: *Critical Notes on Some Recent Dancing* (pp. 35, 36), and *The Truth about the Diaghilev Company* (p. 27).

BEAUMONT (CYRIL W.). CHRISTIAN BERARD 1902–1949. England, The Studio Oct. 1959.

Cr. 4to (9·6 × 7·5 ins.). pp. 75–80 illus. some in colour. Orig. dec. yellow wrapps.

An article in the October 1959 issue of *The Studio*. See also Berard, *Bibliography*, Part IV and Buckle, *Modern Ballet Design*, Part I.

BEAUMONT (CYRIL W.). A CHRISTMAS DREAM FOR BALLETOMANES. London, The Dancing World Christmas 1922.

Demy 4to (11 × 8·4 ins.). pp. 23–30 illus. Orig. dec. wrapps.

An article containing a reproduction of a programme (Grand Gala Performance of the Russian Ballet), Diaghilev Dec. 23 1922. Also the stories of *Le Carnaval*, *Prince Igor*, *La Boutique Fantasque* and *Le Spectre de la Rose*.

BEAUMONT (CYRIL W.). THE CHRISTMAS TREE. A Fantastic Ballet in one Act. Music by Fred Adlington. Choreography by Flora M. Fairbairn and Cyril W. Beaumont. London, March 11, 1926.

Cr. 4to (9·7 × 7·4 ins.). 8 pp. incl. printed wrapps.

The programme for the first performance of *The Christmas Tree* by the Cremorne Company at the New Scala Theatre March II, 1926. See also Payne, Wyndham for notes on the costume designs. Also Beaumont, *The Circus*.

BEAUMONT (CYRIL W.). THE CIRCUS. A Burlesque Ballet in Three Scenes by Cyril W. Beaumont. Choreography by Flora M. Fairbairn and Cyril W. Beaumont. London, Nov. 29 & Dec. 2, 1926.

Cr. 4to (10·2 × 8·2 ins.). 4 pp. incl. Orig. dec. wrapps.
The programme for the second performance of the ballet *The Circus* as performed by The Mayfair Co. of English Dancers (amalgamated with the Cremorne Company) with Phyllis Strickland as First Soloist. The matinee and evening performances were held in The Duke's Rehearsal Theatre. See also Payne, Wyndham.

BEAUMONT (CYRIL W.). THE COMPLETE BOOK OF BALLETS. London, Ballet April 1952.
Demy 8vo (8·3 × 5·2 ins.). p. 20. Orig. dec. wrapps.
Three paragraphs in *Ballet* Vol. 12 No. 4 in which the author points out additions to the latest edition of this work.

BEAUMONT (CYRIL W.). COPPELIA 1946. London, Ballet Dec. 1946.
Demy 8vo (8·3 × 5·2 ins.). pp. 47–52 + illus. Orig. dec. wrapps.
Ballet Vol. 2 No. 7. The issue also contains *Coppelia* 1870 by Ivor Guest.

BEAUMONT (CYRIL W.). COSTUME FOR BALLET. London, Ernst Benn 1928.
Cr. 4to (10·6 × 8·2 ins.). pp. 105–122 illus. with drwgs. by Randolph Schwabe. Orig. dec. cloth.
An article in *Robes of Thespis*, edited by George Sheringham and R. Boyd Morrison for Rupert Mason. See also Beaumont's *The Costume of the Male Ballet Dancer (Dance Journal Supplement* Dec. 1936) and *Ballet Design Past and Present; Design for the Ballet*; and *Five Centuries of Ballet Design*.

BEAUMONT (CYRIL W.). THE COSTUME OF THE MALE BALLET DANCER. London, The Dance Journal Christmas Supplement Dec. 1936.
Demy 4to (11 × 8·6 ins.). pp. 18, 19 illus. Orig. dec. wrapps.
An article, an early one on this subject.

BEAUMONT (CYRIL W.). CRANKO'S PINEAPPLE POLL. London, Ballet June 1951.
Demy 8vo (8·3 × 5·2 ins.). pp. 16–23 illus. Orig. dec. wrapps.
An article in *Ballet* Vol. II No. 5. See also Beaumont's articles in *The Sunday Times* for reviews of Cranko's other earlier ballets.

BEAUMONT (CYRIL W.). CRITICAL NOTES ON SOME RECENT DANCING. London, The Dancing World Aug. & Sept. 1923.
Demy 4to (11 × 8·4 ins.). pp. 35, 36. Orig. dec. wrapps. An article.

BEAUMONT (CYRIL W.). CYRIL BEAUMONT ON BALLET BOOKS. London, The Sunday Times 1955.
A Catalogue and Magazine of *The Sunday Times Book Exhibition*, Royal Festival Hall Nov. 14–28 1955. See also Beaumont, *The Literature of The Ballet*, published in *British Book News* 1949.

BEAUMONT (CYRIL W.). DANCE CRITICISMS APPEARING IN THE SUNDAY TIMES 1950–1959 by Cyril W. Beaumont. London, The Times.
Sup. Royal 4to (14·2 × 10 ins.). 164 pp. illus. Xerox. Bound in folio.

Xerox copies of some 400 articles in Beaumont's press-cutting books. The articles are of various length, some are illustrated and all represent material not reprinted. The first date line is April 9, 1950 and the article is the *Obituary of Vaslav Nijinsky*. The whole represents a wealth of criticism about companies and individuals appearing in London during 1950–1959.

BEAUMONT (CYRIL W.). THE DANCE JOURNAL. Official Organ of the Imperial Society of Dance Teachers (Incorporated with the Cecchetti Society). Editor: Cyril W. Beaumont. London, The Whitefriar Press Ltd.
Demy 8vo (8·3 × 5·2 ins.). Vol. I. comprising 12 Nos. all illus. Bound in full blue buckram, orig. wrapps. bound in.

A privately circulated journal of which the New Series began on December 1924 with Vol. I. No. 1. Below are listed only the articles either initialled or bearing the full name of Cyril Beaumont, the editor. The page numbers given reflect the textual sequence, although in some cases they appear out of numerical order.

No. 1. The British Dancer, Some Criticisms and Suggestions (pp. 12–15). 2. *Le Jugement de Pâris* by J. G. Noverre, translated by C. W. Beaumont (pp. 31, 32). 3. Sur les Pointes (pp. 42, 48). 4. *Giselle ou les Wilis* by Vernoy de Saint Georges, Gautier and Coraly, translated by C. W. Beaumont (pp. 78–80). 5.6.7. *Giselle ou les Wilis* (p. 126). 8.9. On Examinations in the Cecchetti Syllabus (pp. 43, 44, 41). 10. On Teaching of Dance History (pp.

49, 50). 11.12. *The Dancing Master* by P. Rameau translated by C. W. Beaumont (pp. 84–98).

BEAUMONT (CYRIL W. Editor). THE DANCE JOURNAL. VOL. II. London 1928.

Demy 8vo (8·3 × 5·2 ins.). Vol. II comprising 12 Nos. all illus. Full blue buckram, orig. wrapps. bound in.

No. 1. A History of Ballet in Russia (1613–1880) (pp. 8–14). A Discovery (pp. 18–25). The Dancing Master (pp. 29–42). 2. A History of Ballet in Russia (pp. 50–59). The Dancing Master (pp. 65–74). 3. A History of Ballet in Russia (pp. 76–85). The Autobiography of Isadora Duncan (pp. 89–96). *The Dancing Master* (pp. 103–114). 4. 5. A History of Ballet in Russia (pp. 129–138). *The Dancing Master* (pp. 202–210). 6. Enrico Cecchetti (pp. 223–228). *The Dancing Master* (pp. 234–241). A History of Ballet in Russia (pp. 243–250). 7. Enrico Cecchetti (pp. 260–267). A History of Ballet in Russia (pp. 280–286). The Dancing Master (pp. 287–290). 8. La Argentina (pp. 297–299). A History of Ballet in Russia (pp. 303–308). *The Dancing Master* (pp. 321–322, 320). *Marie Taglioni* by André Levinson translated by C. W. Beaumont (pp. 325–328). A History of Ballet in Russia (pp. 344–352). *The Dancing Master* (pp. 356–358). 10. 11. *Marie Taglioni* (pp. 370–375). A History of Ballet in Russia (pp. 451–458). 12. *Marie Taglioni* (pp. 466–474). A History of Ballet in Russia (pp. 485–490, 492). *The Dancing Master* (pp. 493–498).

BEAUMONT (CYRIL W. Editor). THE DANCE JOURNAL. VOL. III. London 1930.

Demy 8vo (8·3 × 5·2 ins.). Vol. III comprising 12 Nos. all illus. Full blue buckram, orig. wrapps bound in.

No. 1. *Marie Taglioni* (pp. 19–24). A History of Ballet in Russia (pp. 43–46). 2. *Marie Taglioni* (pp. 61–67). The Autobiography of a Prima Ballerina (Karsavina) (pp. 71–76). A History of Ballet in Russia (pp. 81–82). 3. *Marie Taglioni* (pp. 97–101). A Dancer on the Horizon (Harold Turner) (pp. 108–109). The History of Choreography or Dance Notation (pp. 114–119). 4 & 5. *Marie Taglioni* (pp. 140–144, 147). A History of Ballet in Russia (pp. 252–256, 242). 6. The Danseuses Viennoises from the French of Théophile Gautier, translated by C. W. Beaumont (pp. 264–267). *Marie Taglioni* (pp. 273–276). The Camargo Society (pp. 282–286). A History of Ballet in Russia (pp. 293–296). 7. Anna Pavlova (pp. 304–309). *Marie Taglioni* (pp. 313–316). Applause and the Dancer (pp. 331-333). Three Dance Performances (pp. 335, 336, 327). 8. Carlotta Grisi and *Giselle* (pp. 344-349). *Marie Taglioni* (pp. 356-361). A History of Ballet in Russia (pp. 374-376). 9. La Argentina (pp. 385-386, 389). Fanny Elssler (pp. 393-397, 415). *Marie Taglioni* (pp. 400-404). The History of Choreography or Dance Notation (pp. 408-412). The Ballet Club – The Camargo Society (pp. 420-424). 10 & 11. *Marie Taglioni* (pp. 440-442). The Autobiography of a Premier Danseur (Anton Dolin) (pp. 455-458). The History of Choreography or Dance Notation (pp. 459-463). The Camargo Society – The Vacani Matinee (pp. 468-469, 523). 12. *Marie Taglioni* (pp. 549-552). The Ballet Club (pp. 576-580). Fanny Elssler (pp. 581-584).

BEAUMONT (CYRIL W. Editor). THE DANCE JOURNAL. VOL. IV. London 1932.

Demy 8vo (8·3 × 5·2 ins.). Vol. IV comprising 6 Nos. all illus. Full blue buckram, orig. wrapps bound in.

No. 1. The History of Choreography or Dance Notation (pp. 608-612). The Camargo Society (pp. 615-616). 2. *Marie Taglioni* (pp. 627-629). Some Notes on the ballet shoes worn by Anna Pavlova (p. 635). Fanny Elssler (pp. 646-649). The Camargo Society (pp. 650-651). 3. The History of Choreography or Dance Notation (pp. 678-685). Mary Wigman (pp. 692-693). Fanny Elssler (pp. 694-698). The Camargo Society (pp. 699-700, 677). 4 & 5. Auguste Vestris (pp. 716-721). *Marie Taglioni* (pp. 725-731). 6. Auguste Vestris (pp. 858-861). *Marie Taglioni* (pp. 883-884).

BEAUMONT (CYRIL W. Editor). THE DANCE JOURNAL. VOL. V. London 1933.

Demy 8vo (8·3 × 5·2 ins.). Vol. V. comprising 6 Nos. all illus. Full blue buckram, orig. wrapps bound in.

No. 1. Michel Fokine (pp. 19-24). Agnes de Mille and Leonard Warren (pp. 43-46). *Marie Taglioni* (pp. 47-48, 27). 2. Michel Fokine (pp. 62-70). Gaetano Vestris Gives a Lesson in Deportment to the Prince de Lamarc (pp. 90-91). 3. Marie Sallé (unsigned) (pp. 108-127). Les Archives Internationales de la Danse (pp. 126-127). Michel Fokine (pp. 132-136). 4 & 5. Michel Fokine (pp. 158-163). Marie Sallé (pp. 168-170). Michel Fokine (pp. 268-267). 6. The Career and Tragedy of Vaslav Nijinsky (pp. 281-290). Michel Fokine (pp. 316-320).

OF DANCING BE 45

BEAUMONT (CYRIL W. Editor). THE DANCE JOURNAL. VOL. VI. London 1934.
Demy 8vo (8·3 × 5·2 ins.). Vol. VI comprising 5 Nos. all illus. Full blue buckram, orig. wrapps bound in.
No. 1. Madeleine Guimard (pp. 30–35, 60). Michel Fokine (pp. 84–88). The Kurt Jooss Ballet (pp. 65, 88). 2. La Camargo (pp. 112–119). Not Although but Because . . . A Dialogue with Michel Fokine (pp. 126–129, 125). The Haunted Ballroom (pp. 136–138). Michel Fokine (pp. 141–143, 147, 150). 3. Leontine Beaugrand (pp. 170–176). Michel Fokine (pp. 191–195, 242, 274). 4. Emma Livry (pp. 320–328). Michel Fokine (pp. 362–368, 313).

BEAUMONT (CYRIL W. Editor). THE DANCE JOURNAL. VOL. VII. London 1935.
Demy 8vo (8·3 × 5·2 ins.). Vol. VII. comprising 4 Nos. all illus. Full blue buckram, orig. wrapps bound in.
No. 1. The National Ballet of Lithuania (pp. 29–31). Michel Fokine (pp. 47–52, 43). 2. Pauline Duvernay (pp. 95–104). Michel Fokine (pp. 128–132, 112). 3. Michel Fokine (pp. 167–172, 193, 233, 258). 4. Michel Fokine (pp. 351–356).

BEAUMONT (CYRIL W. Editor). THE DANCE JOURNAL. VOL. VIII. London 1936.
Demy 8vo (8·3 × 5·2 ins.). Vol. VIII comprising 4 Nos. all illus. Full blue buckram, orig. wrapps bound in.
No. 1. Michel Fokine (pp. 48–56). 2. Michel Fokine (pp. 91–98). 3. Michel Fokine (pp. 231–234, 176). 4. Michel Fokine (pp. 279–282, 261, 240).

BEAUMONT (CYRIL W. Editor). THE DANCE JOURNAL. VOL. IX. London 1937.
Demy 8vo (8·3 × 5·2 ins.). Vol. IX comprising 4 Nos. Full blue buckram, orig. wrapps bound in.
1. Michel Fokine (pp. 41–44, 40). 2. Marius Petipa (pp. 100–105). 3 & 4. Marius Petipa (pp. 302–304).

BEAUMONT (CYRIL W. Editor). THE DANCE JOURNAL. VOL. X. London 1938.
Demy 8vo (8·3 × 5·2 ins.). Vol. X comprising 4 Nos. Full blue buckram, orig. wrapps bound in.
1. Marius Petipa (pp. 40–42, 64). 2. Marius Petipa (pp. 121–124). 3. Marius Petipa (pp. 311–312, 141, 157, 167, 218).

BEAUMOUNT (CYRIL W. Editor). THE DANCE JOURNAL. VOL. XI. London 1939.

Demy 8vo (8·3 × 5·2 ins.). Vol. XI comprising 3 Nos. Full blue buckram, orig. wrapps bound in.
I. Jules Perrot (pp. 41–45, 57 with 1 illus.). 2. Jules Perrot (pp. 113–116, 111). The essay was never completed.

In addition to these articles by Cyril Beaumont, the Journal abounds in dances both classical and folkloric with full descriptions and contains a most interesting Symposium, on, How I arrange my dances by the following: Quentin Tod, Gunter Hess, Anton Dolin, Madge Atkinson, George Balanchine, Lois Hunter, Lois Hutton & Helene Vanel, Leonide Massine, Mary Wigman, Adolph Bolm, Alexandre Sakharoff, Ninette de Valois and Yeichi Nimura.

BEAUMOUNT (CYRIL W.). DANCER ON THE HORIZON. London, The Dance Journal June 1930.

Demy 8vo (8·3 × 5·2 ins.). pp. 109, 108. Orig. dec. wrapps.
Vol. III No. 3. An article about Harold Turner.

BEAUMONT (CYRIL W.). DANCERS IN UNEXPECTED PLACES. London, The Dancing Times Aug. 1968.

Med. 4to (11·1 × 8·5 ins.). pp. 584–588 illus. Orig. dec. wrapps.

An article attempting to determine to what extent dancers have contributed to or inspired industrial design. The illustrations are of dancers on clocks, plaques, candelabrum, pipes, paper dolls, 'Livres des Dames', etc.

BEAUMONT (CYRIL W.). THE DANCER'S LIBRARY. A Bibliography of Modern Books. London, The Dancing Times April 1938.

Med. 8vo (9·2 × 6·4 ins.). Orig. dec. wrapps.

An article complete in the following three issues: April 1928 (pp. 36–38); May 1938 (pp. 151, 152); June 1938 (pp. 296, 299). See also *A Bibliography of Books Relative to The Art of Dancing*, contained in the British Museum. This ran from Oct. 1922 through 1924. Later published in book form in 1929. See also Beaumont, *The Literature of the Ballet*.

BEAUMONT (CYRIL W.). THE DANCING MASTER by P. Rameau. Translated by Cyril W. Beaumont. London, The Dance Journal Dec. 1927.

Demy 8vo (8·3 × 5·2 ins.). pp. 84–98, 29–42, 65–74, 103–114, 202–210, 234–241, 287–290, 279, 321, 322, 320, 356–358, 493–498 illus. Orig. dec. wrapps.
The Dance Journal issues from Vol. I No. 12 and Vol. II Nos. 1, 2, 3, 4, 5, 6, 7, 8, 9, 12. The publication of this work in serial form stopped with Chapter XXXIII, *Of The Balancé*. Published in book form by Beaumont in 1931.

BEAUMONT (CYRIL W.). DANCING SCHOOLS OR ROBOT FACTORIES. London, The Dancing World 1923.

Demy 4to (11 × 8·3 ins.). p. 20. Orig. dec. wrapps.
An article. Also in this issue, Some Remarks on Ballet Training by Judith Espinosa.

BEAUMONT (CYRIL W.). THE DANSEUSES VIENNOISES. By Théophile Gautier. Translated by Cyril W. Beaumont. London, The Dance Journal Dec. 1930.

Demy 8vo (8·3 × 5·2 ins.). pp. 264–267 illus. Orig. dec. wrapps.
An article in *The Dance Journal* Vol. III No. 6.

BEAUMONT (CYRIL W.). DERRA DE MORODA: MARION MORGAN DANCERS. London, The Dancing World Nov. 1923.

Demy 4to (11 × 8·4 ins.). p. 21. Orig. dec. wrapps.
An article. Also in this issue Part V of A History of Ballet in Russia 1741–1756 (pp. 27, 48, 51).

BEAUMONT (CYRIL W.). DESIGNS FOR BALLET. Sydney, The Harbour Press.

Cr. 4to (10·6 × 8·3 ins.). pp. 5, 6. Orig. dec. wrapps.
An article in the catalogue for An Exhibition for Theatre & Ballet.

BEAUMONT (CYRIL W.). DE VALOIS' DON QUIXOTE. London, April 1950.

Demy 8vo (8·3 × 5·2 ins.). pp. 9–18 illus. Orig. dec. wrapps.
An article in *Ballet* Vol. 9 No. 4.

BEAUMONT (CYRIL W.). THE DIAGHILEFF COMPANY. London, Opera Feb. 1924.

F'cap 4to (8·2 × 6·5 ins.). pp. 8, 32. Orig. dec. wrapps.

An article in *Opera* Vol. 2 No. 2. The text concludes with the announcement of De Valois' and Dolin's departure for Monte Carlo to join the company.

BEAUMONT (CYRIL W.). DIAMOND JUBILEE DINNER SPEECH FOR THE IMPERIAL SOCIETY OF TEACHERS OF DANCING. London, Dance Journal Winter 1964.

Demy 8vo (8·3 × 5·4 ins.). pp. 14–18 illus. Xerox.

A Diamond Jubilee Dinner given at Quaglino's, Tuesday Oct. 1964.

BEAUMONT (CYRIL W.). A DISAPPOINTMENT AND A SURPRISE. London, The Dancing World Mar. 1923.

Cr. 4to (10·7 × 8·3 ins.). p. 23. Orig. dec. wrapps.

An article. The Disappointment: Julie Sedowa at the Coliseum; the Surprise: Massine and Lopokova at Covent Garden.

BEAUMONT (CYRIL W.). EMMA LIVRY. London, The Dance Journal Dec. 1934.

Demy 8vo (8·3 × 5·2 ins.). pp. 320–328 illus. Orig. dec. cloth.

The Dance Journal Vol. VI No. 4. See also *Bibliography*, Part I, Beaumont, *Three French Dancers of the 19th Century* and Part II, Quatrelles L'Epine, *Emma Livry*.

BEAUMONT (CYRIL W.). THE EMPEROR AND THE NIGHTINGALE. London, The Studio 1944.

Roy. 8vo (9·6 × 7·3 ins.). pp. 13–17 with 7 illus. incl. 2 in colour. Orig. green wrapps.

An article about Martin Harvey's Costume Designs for *The Emperor and the Nightingale* appearing in the Jan. 1944 issue of *The Studio*.

BEAUMONT (CYRIL W.). ENRICO CECCHETTI. The Jubilee of a Great Artist. London, The Observer Jan. 8, 1922.

A single column on (p. eleven) of this number of *The Sunday Observer*. An article, the first by the author about Cecchetti.

BEAUMONT (CYRIL W.). LES ETOILES DE LA DANSE. London, Ballet Feb. 1948.

Demy 8vo (8·3 × 5·2 ins.). pp. 13–18 with one illus. Orig. dec. wrapps.

An article in *Ballet* Vol. 5 No. 2.

BEAUMONT (CYRIL W.). A FAMILIAR SUBJECT VIEWED AT A NEW ANGLE. London, The Dancing World Oct. 1922.

Demy 4to (11 × 8·4 ins.). p. 22. Orig. dec. wrapps.

Some timely and practical suggestions for an all-English ballet. The issue also contains a longer article by the author: Some Stages in Academic Ballet (pp. 28, 29) with two illustrations.

BEAUMONT (CYRIL W.). FANNY ELSSLER. London, The Dance Journal June 1931.

Demy 8vo (8·3 × 5·2 ins.). pp. 393–397, 415; 581–584, 646–649, 694–698. Illus. Orig. dec. wrapps.

The Dance Journal Vol. III Nos. 9 and 12, Vol. IV Nos. 2 and 3.

BEAUMONT (CYRIL W.). FIFTY YEARS A FOLLOWER OF BALLET. The Fascinating story of Cyril Beaumont. London, Ballet Today June 1957.

Demy 4to (11 × 8·4 ins.). pp. 17–18 with one illus. Orig. dec. wrapps.

An unsigned article in *Ballet Today*.

BEAUMONT (CYRIL W.). FIFTY YEARS OF MALE DANCING. London, The Dancing Times Oct. 1960.

Med. 8vo (9·1 × 6·1 ins.). pp. 28–31 illus. Orig. dec. wrapps.

Fleeting impressions of male dancers from Mikhail Mordkin to Wlodzimierz Tracewski.

BEAUMONT (CYRIL W.). FOKINE'S BALLETS. London, The Dancing Times Oct. 1942.

Demy 8vo (8·5 × 5·3 ins.). pp. + illus. Orig. dec. wrapps.

An article in No. 385 of *The Dancing Times* of Oct. 1942. See also Beaumont, C. W., *The Chorégraphe Michel Fokine, Michel Fokine* and *Michel Fokine and his Ballets*.

BEAUMONT (CYRIL W.). FORTY YEARS WRITING ON THE BALLET. London, The Ballet Annual No. 6. 1952.

Med. 8vo (9·6 × 7·2 ins.). pp. 69–78 illus. Orig. dec. cloth.

An article. See also *Dance and Dancers*, Dec. 1961, The Beaumont Anniversary Supplement.

BEAUMONT (CYRIL W.). FOUR GISELLES. London, Ballet Mar. 1951.

Demy 8vo (8·3 × 5·2 ins.). pp. 10–15 illus. Orig. dec. wrapps.
An article in *Ballet* Vol. II No. 2. The four are Kaye, Alonso, Markova and Chauviré. See also *Bibliography*, Part I, Beaumont, *The Ballet Called Giselle*.

BEAUMONT (CYRIL W.). FOUR OPINIONS ON ASHTON'S SYLVIA: AN ACCOUNT. London, Ballet Oct. 1952.

Demy 8vo (8·3 × 5·2 ins.). pp. 5–10 illus. Orig. dec. wrapps.
An article in *Ballet* Vol. 12 No. 10. The other opinions were by Tony Mayer, Ivor Guest and Richard Buckle.

BEAUMONT (CYRIL W.). FREDERICK ASHTON – English Choreographer. London, Mayfair Publications 1949.

Med. 8vo (9·6 × 7 ins.). pp. 6–12 illus. Orig. blue cloth.
An article in *Souvenirs de Ballet*, edited by Duncan Melvin. See *Bibliography*, Part II, Melvin, Duncan.

BEAUMONT (CYRIL W.). A FRIEND FOR ALL SEASONS. [London]. Bertram Rota. [1975].

Demy 8vo (8·3 × 5·3 ins.). pp. 69–72. Orig. tan cloth.
An article appearing in *Sacheverell Sitwell*, A Symposium edited by Derek Parker. See also *Bibliography*, Parts II and III, Sitwell.

BEAUMONT (CYRIL W.). THE FUNERAL OF VASLAV NIJINSKY. London, The Ballet Annual Fifth Issue 1951.

Med. 8vo (9·6 × 7·2 ins.). pp. 106–108 with one illus. Orig. cream cloth.
An article in *The Ballet Annual* No. 5.

BEAUMONT (CYRIL W.). GAETANO AND AUGUSTE VESTRIS IN ENGLISH CARICATURE. London, Ballet March 1948.

Demy 8vo (8·3 × 5·2 ins.). pp. 19–29 illus. Orig. dec. wrapps.
An article in *Ballet* Vol. 5 No. 3. See also Beaumont, *Auguste Vestris*.

BEAUMONT (CYRIL W.). GAETANO VESTRIS GIVES A LESSON IN DEPORTMENT TO THE PRINCE OF LANMARCK. London, The Dance Journal April 1933.
Demy 8vo (8·3 × 5·2 ins.). pp. 90, 91. Orig. dec. wrapps.
The Dance Journal Vol. V No. 2. Cyril Beaumont translates this episode from the *Souvenirs de la Marquise de Créquy* de 1710 à 1803.

BEAUMONT (CYRIL W.). GARLAND FOR NIJINSKY – ARTIST AND DANCER. London, The Ballet Annual No. 5 1951.
Med. 8vo (9·6 × 7·2 ins.). pp. 47–53 illus. Orig. cream cloth.
An article in *The Ballet Annual* No. 5. The drawings are by Natalie Gontcharova and Michel Larionov.

BEAUMONT (CYRIL W.). GISELLE OU LES WILIS. By Vernoy de St. Georges Gautier and Coraly. Translated by Cyril W. Beaumont. London, The Dance Journal Oct. 1925.
Demy 8vo (8·3 × 5·2 ins.). pp. 78–80 and 126. Orig. dec. wrapps.
The Dance Journal Vol. I Nos. 4 and 7. I do not believe the synopsis was ever completed in its translation.

BEAUMONT (CYRIL W.). GRAND BALLET DE MONTE CARLO. London, Ballet Oct. 1948.
Demy 8vo (8.3 × 5·2 ins.). pp. 13–20, 56 illus. Orig. dec. wrapps.
An article in *Ballet* Vol. 6 No. 1. See also *Bibliography*, Part I, Beaumont and also Detaille & Mulys.

BEAUMONT (CYRIL W.). LE GRAND BALLET DE MONTE CARLO. London, Ballet Aug. 1949.
Demy 8vo (8·3 × 5·2 ins.). pp. 12–23 illus. Orig. dec. wrapps.
An article in *Ballet* Vol. 8 No. 2. This is of course the De Cuevas Company.

BEAUMONT (CYRIL W.). THE GROWTH OF STYLE IN ENGLISH BALLET.
Roy. 4to (13 × 8 ins.). 3 pp.
An article in original typescript produced by Central Office of Information (C.O.I.) for the British Council. Unpublished.

BEAUMONT (CYRIL W.). THE HAUNTED BALLROOM.
London, The Dance Journal June 1934.
 Demy 8vo (8·3 × 5·2 ins.). pp. 136–138. Orig. dec. wrapps.
 The Dance Journal Vol. VI No. 2. A review of the de Valois ballet *The Haunted Ballroom*.

BEAUMONT (CYRIL W.). HAUNTING DISCLAIMED.
London, Ballet March 1952.
 Demy 8vo (8·3 × 5·2 ins.). pp. 34–35. Orig. dec. wrapps.
 A letter in *Ballet* Vol. 12 No. 2 in which the author denies haunting the premises of the Nicholas Legat School of Ballet.

BEAUMONT (CYRIL W.). A HISTORY OF BALLET IN RUSSIA. I. From 1613–1674. London, The Dancing World March 1923.
 Cr. 4to (10·7 × 8·3 ins.). pp. 30, 31 illus. Orig. dec. wrapps.
 An article, later run in serial form in *The Dance Journal* and published in book form in 1930. Also *A Disappointment and a Surprise* (Julie Sedowa at the Coliseum and Massine and Lopokova at Covent Garden) (p. 23).

BEAUMONT (CYRIL W.). A HISTORY OF BALLET IN RUSSIA FROM 1613–1880. London, The Dance Journal Feb. 1929.
 Demy 8vo (8·3 × 5·2 ins.). pp. 8–14, 50–59, 76–85, 129–138, 243–250, 280–286, 303–308, 344–352, 451–458, 485–490, 492; 43–46, 81, 82, 252–256, 242, 293–296, 374–376, 349 illus. Orig. dec. wrapps.
 The Dance Journal issues from: Vol. II Nos. 1, 2, 3, 4, 5, 6, 7, 9, 10, 11, 12. Vol. III Nos. 1, 2, 4, 5, 6, 8. The publication of *A History of Ballet in Russia 1613–1880* in instalments stopped with Chapter IX partially completed.

BEAUMONT (CYRIL W.). HOEBRIDGE SCHOOL FOR BOYS. Report for Year Ending Christmas 1903.
 (4·7 × 8 ins.). 1 p. Xerox.
 Cyril Beaumont's yearly endeavour in the fourth form, first division was rewarded by a first in General Work, second in Conduct, first in English Examinations, and a third in Attendance. Signed by Harriet Baker, Principal.

BEAUMONT (CYRIL W.). HOMAGE TO DIAGHILEV (1872–1929). London, Columbia Gramophone Co.
Cr. 4to (10 × 7·4 ins.). 8pp. n.n. Orig. white wrapps.
A brochure accompanying Recordings of Ballet Music identified with the Diaghilev Company, Igor Markevitch conducting the Philharmonia Orchestra. Ten ballets are described.

BEAUMONT (CYRIL W.). HOMMAGE À JEANMAIRE. London, The Ballet Annual No. 4 1950.
Med. 8vo (9·6 × 7·2 ins.). pp. 67–74 illus. Orig. dec. cloth.
An article in *The Ballet Annual* No. 4. See also *Enciclopedia dello Spettacolo* Vol. VI for biographical information.

BEAUMONT (CYRIL W.). HORSE BALLETS. London, Ballet Oct. 1947.
Demy 8vo (8·3 × 5·2 ins.). pp. 19–28 illus. Orig. dec. wrapps.
An article in *Ballet* Vol. 4 No. 4.

BEAUMONT (CYRIL W.). HUGH STEVENSON. London, The Studio April 1944.
Cr. 4to (9·6 × 7·3 ins.). pp. 122–126 illus. some in colour. Orig. green wrapps.
An article about the designer Hugh Stevenson. See also Beaumont's *Ballet settings and costumes in recent Productions*.

BEAUMONT (CYRIL W.). IN MEMORIAM – GIUSEPPINA CECCHETTI. London, The Dance Journal, Dec. 1927.
Demy 8vo (8·3 × 5·2 ins.). pp. 77, 78. Orig. dec. wrapps.
The Dance Journal Vol. I No. 12.

BEAUMONT (CYRIL W.). INTERNATIONAL BALLET'S SWAN LAKE. London, Ballet May 1947.
Demy 8vo (8·3 × 5·2 ins.). pp. 13–16 illus. Orig. dec. wrapps.
Ballet Vol. 3 No. 4. Review of this company with Nana Gollner as *Odette-Odile*.

BEAUMONT (CYRIL W.). THE INTERNATIONAL BALLET. London, Ballet Dec. 1948.
Demy 8vo (8·3 × 5·2 ins.). pp. 6–8, 13–16 with one illus. Orig. dec. wrapps.

An article in *Ballet* Vol. 6 No. 3. See *Bibliography*, Part III, G. Handley-Taylor, *Mona Inglesby*.

BEAUMONT (CYRIL W.). AN INTERVIEW WITH STANISLAS IDZIKOWSKI. London, The Dancing World Oct. 1923.

Demy 4to (11 × 8·4 ins.). pp. 18, 19 with one full page photo. Orig. dec. wrapps.

An article. See also *Bibliography*, Part I, Beaumont, *The Art of Stanislas Idzikowski*.

BEAUMONT (CYRIL W.). JEAN TARGET. London, The Studio 1961.

Cr. 4to (9·6 × 7·2 ins.). 2pp. illus.

An illustrated article about the sculptor appearing in *The Studio* March 1961. See also Target, Jean, A Letter to Cyril Beaumont.

BEAUMONT (CYRIL W.). LE JUGEMENT DE PARIS. Ballet Héroique de Jean Georges Noverre. Translated by Cyril W. Beaumont. London, The Dance Journal March 1925.

Demy 8vo (8·3 × 5·2 ins.). pp. 31–32 and 46, 48. Orig. dec. wrapps.

Issues of *The Dance Journal* Vol. I Nos. 2, 3.

BEAUMONT (CYRIL W.). JULES PERROT. London, The Dance Journal 1939.

Demy 8vo (8·3 × 5·2 ins.). Vol. XI comprising 3 Nos. Illus. Orig. dec. wrapps.

An article in parts on Jules Perrot: Vol. I No. 1 (pp. 41–45, 57 with 1 illus.); Vol. I No. 2 (pp. 113–116, 111). Interrupted by the war, publication of this article was never resumed. Also in Xerox.

BEAUMONT (CYRIL W.). KIRSTEIN BALANCHINE AND OTHERS. [London], Tempo Autumn 1950.

Cr. 4to (10·1 × 7·1 ins.). pp. 9–15. Orig. dec. wrapps.

An article giving careful analysis of Balanchine's musicality, groupings and floor patterns, his abstraction and its probable influence on the N.Y.C. Ballet. Also appreciations of the leading members of this organization.

BEAUMONT (CYRIL W.). THE KURT JOOSS BALLET.
London, The Dance Journal March 1934.
Demy 8vo (8·3 × 5·2 ins.). pp. 65, 88. Orig. dec. wrapps.
The Dance Journal Vol. VI No. 1. Review of *The Green Table* and *Impressions of a Big City*.

BEAUMONT (CYRIL W.). LE LAC DES CYGNES AT COVENT GARDEN. London, Ballet Feb. 1937.
Demy 8vo (8·3 × 5·2 ins.). pp. 45–52 + illus. Orig. dec. wrapps.
Ballet Vol. 3 No. 2. A revival of this ballet with settings and costumes by Leslie Hurry. See also *Bibliography*, Part I, Hurry, Leslie.

BEAUMONT (CYRIL W.). THE LAST YEARS OF ISADORA DUNCAN. London, The Dance Journal April 1929.
Demy 8vo (8·3 × 5·2 ins.). pp. 314–318. Orig. dec. wrapps.
The Dance Journal Vol. II, No. 8. An unsigned review of *Isadora Duncan's Russian Days* by Irma Duncan and Allan Ross Macdougall.

BEAUMONT (CYRIL W.). LEONTINE BEAUGRAND.
London, The Dance Journal Sept. 1934.
Demy 8vo (8·3 × 5·2 ins.). pp. 170–176 illus. Orig. dec. wrapps.
The Dance Journal Vol. VI No. 3. See also *Bibliography*, Part I, Beaumont, *Three French Dancers of the 19th Century* and Fourcaud, *Léontine Beaugrand*.

BEAUMONT (CYRIL W.). A LETTER FROM ÉDITIONS HYPÉRION. Paris, Le 26 Decembre 1939.
Demy 4to (11 × 8·2 ins.). 1 p. Xerox.
A copy of a letter contract from *Editions Hypérion* setting forth conditions for the translation of a book on the dance in French. The mss was completed but the fee never paid and Mr. Beaumont could not remember the author. Very possibly it was a work of Pierre Tugal.

BEAUMONT (CYRIL W.). LETTERS TO DORIS NILES AND SERGE LESLIE. London, 1950–1976.
(A collection of letters of various sizes in a folio.)

Some 250 odd letters mostly typewritten to Doris Niles and Serge Leslie at 557 So. Coronado St. Los Angeles, California and 67 Redcliffe Gardens, London. See also *Bibliography*, Part I, Beaumont, *A Collection of Personal Letters to Serge Leslie*.

BEAUMONT (CYRIL W.). THE LIFE OF A BALLET GIRL IN THE 'SIXTIES'. London, Dec. 1924, The Dancing Times.
 Med. 8vo (9·2 × 6·4 ins.). pp. 371, 373, 375. Bound in Vol. for 1924. Orig. blue cloth.
 An unsigned article identified by a footnote. See also The Ballet Girl Then and Now in the July, August and September issues of *The Dancing Times* 1922.

BEAUMONT (CYRIL W.). THE LITERATURE OF THE BALLET. A Select Bibliography 1830–1948.
 Demy 4to (11 × 8 ins.). 5 pp. typescript.
 The original typescript of an article, The Literature of The Ballet published in *British Book News* 1949 (pp. 14–17).

BEAUMONT (CYRIL W.). THE LONDON ARCHIVES OF THE DANCE AND SOME OF ITS TREASURES. London, The Ballet Annual, Adam & Charles Black 1947.
 Med 8vo (9·6 × 7·2 ins.). pp. 108–111 with 2 illus. Orig. tan cloth.
 An article in *The Ballet Annual* first issue. Among the important holdings mentioned are The William Bolitho Collection of Ballet Scores and The Margaret Rolfe Collection of personal effects of Marie Taglioni, of which some are reproduced.

BEAUMONT (CYRIL W.). LONDON'S OVERDUE FESTIVAL OF BALLET. London, Opera & The Ballet Vol. 2 No. 8 Autumn 1924.
 F'cap 4to (8·2 × 6·4 ins.). pp. 8, 9, 41. Orig. dec. wrapps.
 An article. There are two further articles by the author: Pavlova (p. 10) and Pavlova's 'English Ballet' (pp. 11, 12) with one full page plate of Pavlova.

BEAUMONT (CYRIL W.). MADELEINE GUIMARD. London, The Dance Journal March 1934.

Demy 8vo (8·3 × 5·2 ins.). pp. 30–35, 60 illus. Orig. dec. wrapps.
The Dance Journal Vol. VI No. 1. See also Bibliography, Part I, Beaumont, Three French Dancers of the 18th Century and De Goncourt, La Guimard.

BEAUMONT (CYRIL W.) & IDZIKOWSKI (STANISLAS). A MANUAL OF THE THEORY AND PRACTICE OF CLASSICAL THEATRICAL DANCING (Méthode Cecchetti). With a Preface by Maestro Cav. Enrico Cecchetti and illustrations by Randolph Schwabe. New York, Dover Publications 1975.
Demy 8vo (8·3 × 5·2 ins.). 201 pp. + plates and Index. Orig. dec. wrapps.
The first time in soft covers, this is an unabridged reissue of the first 1922 edition. The Manual was revised in 1971, the basic change being a linking together of movements to be performed simultaneously by a vertical line, and some slight alterations in terminology. However, long time users of the Manual may still prefer the 1922 edition.

BEAUMONT (CYRIL W.) & IDZIKOWSKI (STANISLAS). A MANUAL OF THE THEORY AND PRACTICE OF CLASSICAL THEATRICAL DANCING. Revised edition 1977.
Demy 8vo (8·4 × 5·3 ins.). 272 pp. illus. with photogs. Orig. dec. wrapps.
The new edition has half-tone photographs replacing the Randolph Schwabe drawings and reflecting the increased plasticity and extension of more recent Cecchetti teaching. Naturally the photographs lack much of the conciseness of the Schwabe drawings. See Mary Skeaping's review of the Manual in *The Dancing Times* of July 1977.

BEAUMONT (CYRIL W.). MARGOT FONTEYN. London, The Ballet Annual No. 8 1954.
Med. 8vo (9·6 × 7·2 ins.). pp. 73–77 illus. Orig. cream cloth.
An article in *The Ballet Annual* No. 8. See also *Bibliography*, Part I, Beaumont, for a monograph on this artist, also Part II, Money, for other works.

BEAUMONT (CYRIL W.). MARIA MERCANDOTTI.
London, Ballet May 1948.
Demy 8vo (8·3 × 5·2 ins.). pp. 28-34 illus. Orig. dec. wrapps.
An article in *Ballet* Vol. 5 No. 5. See also *Bibliography*, Part I, Guest, *The Romantic Ballet in England*, Chapter VI.

BEAUMONT (CYRIL W.). MARIE SALLÉ. London, The Dance Journal June 1933.
Demy 8vo (8·3 × 5·2 ins.). pp. 108-112, 168-170 illus. Orig. dec. wrapps.
The Dance Journal Vol. V Nos. 3, 4, 5. See also *Bibliography*, Part I, Beaumont, *Three French Dancers of the 18th Century* and Part III, Migel, *Marie Sallé* and also W. E. Stanley Vince, *Marie Sallé*.

BEAUMONT (CYRIL W.). MARIE TAGLIONI by André Levinson. Translated by Cyril W. Beaumont. London, The Dance Journal June 1929.
Demy 8vo (8·3 × 5·2 ins.). pp. 325-328, 370-375, 466-474; 19-24, 61-67, 97-101, 140-144, 147, 273-276, 313-316, 356-361, 400-404, 440-442, 549-522; 627-629, 725-731, 883-884; 47, 48, 27 illus. Orig. dec. wrapps.
The Dance Journal issues from: Vol. II Nos. 9, 10, 11, 12. Vol. III Nos. 1, 2, 3, 4, 5, 6, 7, 8, 9, 10, 11, 12. Vol. IV Nos. 2, 4, 5, 6; Vol. V No. I (concluded). See *Bibliography*, Part I, Levinson, for publication in book form.

BEAUMONT (CYRIL W.). MARIE TAGLIONI AND LA SYLPHIDE. London, The Dancing World Dec. 1923.
Demy 4to (10·7 × 8·3 ins.). pp. 33-36 with illus. Orig. dec. wrapps.
An article. See also Haskell, *Ballet Annual* first issue, *Bibliography*, Part I, and Beaumont, *Extracts from the Diary of a Pupil of Marie Taglioni*, Part III. This issue also contains another article by Beaumont, *The Sakharoffs: The Blue Bird Theatre* (p. 21).

BEAUMONT (CYRIL W.). MARIUS PETIPA. Based on a Monograph by D. L. Leshkov. London, The Dance Journal June 1937.
Demy 8vo (8·3 × 5·2 ins.). pp. 100-105, 302-304; 40-42, 64, 121-124, 311, 312, 141, 157, 167, 218. Orig. dec. wrapps.
The Dance Journal Vol. IX Nos. 2, 4. Vol. X Nos. 1, 2, 3. Published in 1971 with added Appendices.

BEAUMONT (CYRIL W.). MARKOVA AND DOLIN IN GISELLE. London, Ballet July 1948.
 Demy 8vo (8·3 × 5·2 ins.). pp. 30–37 illus. Orig. dec. wrapps.
 An article in *Ballet* Vol. 5 No. 7. See also Beaumont, *The Autobiography of a Premier Danseur.*

BEAUMONT (CYRIL W.). MARY WIGMAN. London, The Dance Journal June 1932.
 Demy 8vo (8·3 × 5·2 ins.). pp. 692, 693. Orig. dec. wrapps.
 The Dance Journal Vol. IV No. 3. A review of a Mary Wigman performance during her three-matinée stay at the Globe Theatre in May 1932.

BEAUMONT (CYRIL W.). THE MASSINE BALLET. London, The Dancing World May 1922.
 Demy 4to (11 × 8·4 ins.). pp. 14, 15 incl. one full page plate. Orig. dec. wrapps.
 An article. Review of the first weeks performance at the Royal Opera House beginning April 3rd, 1922.

BEAUMONT (CYRIL W.). MENU-DINNER TO CELEBRATE THE COMING OF AGE OF CYRIL WILLIAM BEAUMONT. [London], Friday Nov. 1st, 1912.
 (5·5 × 3·7 ins.). 4 pp. Xerox.
 The printed menu of a dinner given at the Restaurant d'Italie, which is autographed by the guests.

BEAUMONT (CYRIL W.). MICHEL FOKINE & HIS BALLETS. London, C. W. Beaumont 1945.
 Demy 8vo (8·4 × 5·2 ins.). 170 pp. with 33 illus. incl. frontis. Orig. black cloth.
 This second edition has the same text as that of the 1935 edition, but with a short Preface and three photographs added, including one of the last to be taken of Fokine who died August 22nd 1942.

BEAUMONT (CYRIL W.). MICHEL FOKINE. A Record of His Choreographic Achievements. London, The Dance Journal Feb. 1933.
 Demy 8vo (8·3 × 5·2 ins.). pp. 19–24, 62–70, 132–136, 158–163, 268–267, 316–320; 84–88, 141–143, 147, 150,

191–195, 242–274, 362–368, 313; 47–52, 43, 128–132, 112; 167–172, 193, 233, 258, 351–356; 48–56, 91–98, 231–234, 176, 279–282, 261, 240; 41–44, 40 illus. Orig. dec. wrapps.
The Dance Journal Vol. V Nos. 1, 2, 3, 4, 5, 6; Vol. VI Nos. 1, 2, 3, 4; No. VII Nos. 1, 2, 3, 4; Vol. VIII Nos. 1, 2, 3, 4; Vol. IX No. 1. These instalments include the entire 1935 publication on Michel Fokine with the exception of the Appendices.

BEAUMONT (CYRIL W.). MR. BEAUMONT'S BOOKS. Hurst, Reading, Berkshire, G. F. Sims.

Demy 8vo (8·5 × 5·5 ins.). 25 pp. Orig. white printed wrapps.
A Catalogue of Books From the Library of C. W. Beaumont. Catalogue No. 95. A selection of books from the personal library of Cyril Beaumont with items 20–42 being of the *Beaumont Press*. Many of the books contain a dedication from the author – Blunden, Davies, Drinkwater, Gibson, Haskell, Kirstein, Levinson, Masefield, Nichols, Lifar, Sitwell, Osbert and Sacheverell and others. There were few books on the ballet, since most of Mr. Beaumont's ballet collection went to the Victoria & Albert Museum for further distribution. The catalogue numbered 396 items, including books from other sources.

BEAUMONT (CYRIL W.). A MIRROR FOR WITCHES. London, Ballet Today May 1952.

Cr. 4to (9·6 × 7·2 ins.). pp. 6–8 illus. Orig. dec. wrapps.
An article in *Ballet Today* Vol. 5 No. 5 in which the ballet is described and commented upon by the author. The choreography and scenario is by Andrée Howard.

BEAUMONT (CYRIL W.). MR. SERGE DIAGHILEV REQUESTS THE HONOUR OF THE COMPANY OF MR. BEAUMONT to assist at the Final Rehearsal of Igor Stravinsky's Renard. London, Royal Opera House July 15th.

Cr. 8vo (7·6 × 5 ins.). 1 p. in Xerox.
An invitation to the final rehearsal of *Renard*, previous to its first presentation in England.

BEAUMONT (CYRIL W.). MORE LIGHT ON GISELLE. London, The Dancing Times May 1945.

Demy 8vo (8·4 × 5·2 ins.). pp. 346 + illus. Orig. dec. wrapps.

An article in issue No. 416 of *The Dancing Times*. See also Beaumont, Cyril W., *Four Giselles* and *Carlotta Grisi and Giselle*. Also *Bibliography*, Part I, Beaumont, *The Ballet Called Giselle*, *Dancing under my lens*.

BEAUMONT (CYRIL W.). MORE TAGLIONI TREASURES. London, The Dancing Times Dec. 1966.

Demy 4to (11·4 × 9 ins.). pp. 132, 133, 152 with 6 illus. Orig. dec. wrapps.

An article in Vol LVII No. 675. See also Beaumont, *Taglioni Treasures*, Vol. LVI No. 672 of *The Dancing Times*.

BEAUMONT (CYRIL W.). MUSINGS FROM NEAR THE MUSEUM. London, The Dancing Times March 1967.

Demy 4to (11·4 × 9 ins.). p. 309 with 1 illus. Orig. dec. wrapps.

An article in Vol. LVII No. 678 of *The Dancing Times*. Near the Museum of course refers to 68 Bedford Court Mansions, the residence of Mr. Beaumont.

BEAUMONT (CYRIL W.). MUSINGS FROM NEAR THE MUSEUM. London, The Dancing Times Nov. 1967.

Demy 4to (11·4 × 9 ins.). pp. 74, 75 with 1 illus. Orig. dec. wrapps.

An article in *The Dancing Times*, Vol. LVIII No. 686. Recollections of the Kirov Ballet and also of Rosita Mauri.

BEAUMONT (CYRIL W.). THE NATIONAL BALLET OF LITHUANIA. London, The Dance Journal Mar. 1935.

Demy 8vo (8·3 × 5·2 ins.). pp. 29–31. Orig. dec. wrapps.

The Dance Journal Vol. VII No. 1. Review of a short season of this ballet company at the Alhambra Theatre, with artists Vera Nemchinova, Nicholas Zverev and Anatole Obukhov.

BEAUMONT (CYRIL W.). NEW YORK CITY BALLET: TWO OF ROBBINS. Ballet, Aug. 1952.

Demy 8vo (8·3 × 5·2 ins.). pp. 10–12 illus. Orig. dec. wrapps.

An article in *Ballet* Vol. 12 No. 8. Review of *The Cage* and *The Pied Piper*. See also *Sunday Times* reviews for July 20th and 27th 1952.

BEAUMONT (CYRIL W.). NICHOLAS GRIGORIEVICH SERGEYEV. London, The Ballet Annual No. 6. 1952.
> Med. 8vo (9·6 × 7·2 ins.). pp. 56–59 illus. Orig. dec. cloth.
> An article in *The Ballet Annual* No. 6. An estimate of this Artist-Regisseur and his contributions of choreographic reproductions, particularly in Western Europe.

BEAUMONT (CYRIL W.). THE NIJINSKY GALAS. London, Ballet Jan. 1950.
> Demy 8vo (8·3 × 5·2 ins.). pp. 30–36 illus. Orig. dec. wrapps.
> An article in *Ballet* Vol. 9 No. 1 analyzing several attempts to raise money for the benefit of Vaslav Nijinsky by combining well known dancers with dancing schools or smaller ballet companies.

BEAUMONT (CYRIL W.). NOT ALTHOUGH, BUT BECAUSE: A Dialogue with Michel Fokine, trans. by C. W. Beaumont. London, The Dance Journal 1934.
> Demy 8vo (8·3 × 5·2 ins.). pp. 126–129, 125. Orig. dec. wrapps.
> An article in *The Dance Journal* Vol. VI No. 2. This Dialogue was recorded by Dr. Pierre Tugal and first published in French in the *A.I.D.* Jan. 1934.

BEAUMONT (CYRIL W.). A NOTE ON LÉON BAKST. London, Opera & The Ballet June 1924.
> F'cap 4to (8·2 × 6·5 ins.). pp. 22, 26 with 3 illus. Orig. dec. wrapps.
> An article. There is also a second one: *A Burmese Pwè at Wembley* (pp. 21, 30) which is continued in the July issue of Opera & The Ballet.

BEAUMONT (CYRIL W.). NOTES ON THE CHANGES IN DANCE IN FIFTY YEARS. London, The Dancing Times Oct. 1950.
> Demy 8vo (8·3 × 5·2 ins.). pp. 17 + illus. Orig. dec. wrapps.
> An article in No. 481 of *The Dancing Times*.

BEAUMONT (CYRIL W.). LE NOUVEAU BALLET DE MONTE CARLO. London, Ballet Aug. 1946.
> Demy 8vo (8·3 × 5·2 ins.). pp. 18–24 + illus. Orig. dec. wrapps.

An article in *Ballet* Vol. 2 No. 3. See also *Bibliography*, Part I, Detaille & Mulys, *Les Ballets de Monte-Carlo*.

BEAUMONT (CYRIL W.). L'OISEAU DE FEU. London, C. W. Beaumont 1912.

Cr. 4to (10·3 × 8 ins.). 6pp. typescript. Plain wrapps.

An original typescript on *The Firebird*, his first essay on this ballet which he later published in 1919 in the *Impressions of the Russian Ballet* series. Written in 1912 or 1913 according to author.

BEAUMONT (CYRIL W.). ON EXAMINATIONS IN THE CECCHETTI SYLLABUS. London, The Dance Journal Feb. 1927.

Demy 8vo (8·3 × 5·2 ins.). pp. 43, 44, 41. Orig. dec. wrapps. *The Dance Journal* Vol. I No. 9.

BEAUMONT (CYRIL W.). ON THE TEACHING OF DANCE HISTORY. London, The Dance Journal June 1927.

Demy 8vo (8·3 × 5·2 ins.). pp. 49, 50. Orig. dec. wrapps. *The Dance Journal* Vol. I No. 10.

BEAUMONT (CYRIL W.). ON THEATRICAL DANCING. New York, Theatre Arts Dec. 1928.

Demy 4to (11 × 8 ins.). pp. 885–90 illus. Orig. dec. wrapps.

An illustrated article about Lambranzi. See also *Bibliography*, Part II, Lambranzi, Gregorio.

BEAUMONT (CYRIL W.). THE ORIGIN OF THE TAGLIONI CAKE CEREMONY.

Roy. 4to (12·6 × 8·2 ins.). 3pp. Typescript.

A Xerox copy of an article explaining how the Taglioni Cake Ceremony came into being on June 22, 1957. The ceremony is held annually in the green room of the Royal Opera House and Alicia Markova cut the cake in the inaugural year. See also *Ballet Today* (Sept./Oct. 1966) p. 3 for an account and photograph of Mr. Beaumont with Anton Dolin assisted by Ninette de Valois.

BEAUMONT (CYRIL. W.). OUR FIRST NATIONAL SCHOOL OF DANCING. London, The Dancing Times Aug. 1967.

Demy 4to (11·4 × 9 ins.). pp. 588, 589 with 1 illus. Orig. dec. wrapps.

An article in *The Dancing Times* Vol. LVII No. 683. The Directress of this early national school was Mme. Katti Lanner.

BEAUMONT (CYRIL W.). THE PASSING OF A GREAT ARTIST. Maestro Enrico Cecchetti. Florence, The Mask 1928.

Demy 8vo (8·7 × 6·2 ins.). pp. 146–153 with a frontis. of Cecchetti. Orig. dec. wrapps.

An article in the Oct.–Nov. issue of *The Mask*. See also *Bibliography*, Part III, Beaumont; Part II Racster; and Part III Celli.

BEAUMONT (CYRIL W.). PAULINE DUVERNAY. London, The Dance Journal June 1935.

Demy 8vo (8·3 × 5·2 ins.). pp. 95–104. Illus. Orig. dec. wrapps.

The Dance Journal Vol. VII No. 2. See also *Bibliography*, Part I, Beaumont, *Three Dancers of the 19th Century*, also Guest, *The Romantic Ballet in England*, Chapter X.

BEAUMONT (CYRIL W.). PAVLOVA. London, Opera & The Ballet Autumn 1924.

F'cap 4to (8·2 × 6·5 ins.). pp. 10 + 1 full page plate. Orig. dec. wrapps.

An article in *Opera & The Ballet* Vol. 2 No. 8.

BEAUMONT (CYRIL W.). PAVLOVA LOPOKOVA AND "HASSAN". London, The Dancing World Oct. 1923.

Demy 4to (11 × 8·4 ins.). pp. 13, 14 with 1 full page photo. Orig. dec. wrapps.

An article which concludes with an appreciation of Fokine's *Hassan*. Also in this issue *An Interview with Stanislas Idzikowski* (pp. 18, 19) including a full page photograph.

BEAUMONT (CYRIL W.). PETIT'S BALLABILÉ. London, Ballet June 1950.

Demy 8vo (8·3 × 5·2 ins.). pp. 7–9 illus. Orig. dec. wrapps.

An article in *Ballet* Vol. 9 No. 6. The first ballet to be arranged for the Sadler's Wells Ballet by a French Choreographer.

BEAUMONT (CYRIL W.). PETRUSHKA IN LONDON. London, W. W. Norton & Co. 1967.

Demy 8vo (8·1 × 6 ins.). pp. 190–194. Orig. dec. wrapps.

An article on *Petrushka* edited by Charles Hamm which gives an analysis of the complete score with further essay, views and comments. See also *Some Memorable Occasions* and *Bibliography*, Part I, Beaumont, *Impressions of the Russian Ballet, Petrouchka.*

BEAUMONT (CYRIL W.). A POLISH DANCER NEW TO LONDON. London, The Dancing World June 1923.

Demy 4to (11·2 × 8·6 ins.). p. 20 with 1 illus. Orig. dec. wrapps.

An article about Melle. Peppi Ptaszynsky, from the Royal Opera House, Budapest, who made her debut at the Coliseum on May 14, 1923.

BEAUMONT (CYRIL W.). THE PRACTICE OF BALLET CRITICISM. London, Adam & Charles Black. 1950.

Demy 8vo (8·4 × 5·4 ins.). pp. 13–21. Orig. blue cloth.

An article appearing in *Dancers and Critics*, edited by Cyril Swinson. The article is dedicated to Margot Fonteyn.

BEAUMONT (CYRIL W.). PROGRAMME OF DANSE-DIVERTISSEMENTS. The Duke's Rehearsal Theatre Nov. 29, Dec. 2, 1926. London, Novello Printers.

Demy 4to (10·4 × 8·2 ins.). 4 pp. Orig. dec. wrapps.

A joint programme of The Mayfair Co. of English Dancers and the Cremorne Co. with Frederick Ashton and Harry Webster. A number of items on the programme were arranged by Cyril Beaumont and he appeared in *Circus* as *Ringmaster* and in *Bal Mabille* as a *Dandy* or *Fop*.

BEAUMONT (CYRIL W.). PROGRAMME OF A GRAND MATINEE DEVOTED TO BALLET DIVERTISSEMENTS & SONG SCENAS. Presented by the Cremorne Company on March 11, 1926. London, New Scala Theatre.

Cr. 4to (9·6 × 7·4 ins.). 8 pp. Orig. printed wrapps.

Featured in this Programme were two ballets by Cyril Beaumont: *The Christmas Tree*, ballet in one act and *Circus* A Burlesque Ballet in three scenes. See Payne, Wyndham for the costume designs and also *Dance and Dancers* for Dec. 1961, where there is some description of the performances of these pieces.

**BEAUMONT (CYRIL W.). THE PROMISE OF SVET-
LANA BERIOSOVA.** Kingston, Ballet Today June 1955.
  Cr. 4to (9·6 × 7·2 ins.). pp. 16–17 illus. Orig. dec. wrapps.
  See also *Bibliography*, Part I, Franks, and Part II, Swinson, for other monographs on this artist.

**BEAUMONT (CYRIL W.). PUSHKIN AND HIS IN-
FLUENCE ON RUSSIAN BALLET:** 1. London, Ballet Dec. 1947.
  Demy 8vo (8·3 × 5·2 ins.). pp. 56–60 with one dec. Orig. dec. wrapps. Part 1 of a 2-part article in *Ballet* Vol. 4 No. 6.

**BEAUMONT (CYRIL W.). PUSHKIN AND HIS IN-
FLUENCE ON RUSSIAN BALLET:** 2. London, Ballet Jan. 1948.
  Demy 8vo (8·3 × 5·2 ins.). pp. 39–46 illus. Orig. dec. wrapps.
  Ballet Vol. 5 No. 1. The second part. See also Elyash and Slonimsky.

BEAUMONT (CYRIL W.). THE RED SHOES. Picture Parade No. 12. (LTS).
  Roy. 4to (12·7 × 8 ins.). 4pp. Xerox.
  A corrected typescript of a dialogue concerning the merits of the film *The Red Shoes*, by Cyril Beaumont and Dilys Powell.

BEAUMONT (CYRIL W.). THE RETURN OF BALLET THEATRE. London, Ballet Nov.–Dec. 1950.
  Demy 8vo (8·3 × 5·2 ins.). pp. 14–26 illus. Orig. dec. wrapps.
  An article in *Ballet* Vol. 10 No. 3. See also Beaumont, *The Ballet Theatre* and *Bibliography*, Part III, Cohen & Pischl, *The American Ballet Theatre*.

**BEAUMONT (CYRIL W.). THE RETURN OF LOPOK-
OVA.** London, Dancing Life No. 1 Nov. 1921.
  Demy 4to (11·2 × 8·6 ins.). p. 3. Orig. illus. wrapps.
  The first number of *Dancing Life* which later became *Dancing World*. Cyril Beaumont's *The Art of Lydia Lopokova* was published in 1920 and *Lydia Lopokova* in 1922.

OF DANCING BE 67

BEAUMONT (CYRIL W.). THE RETURN OF MARKOVA AND DOLIN. London, The Ballet Annual 1949.
Med. 8vo (9·6 × 7·2 ins.). pp. 53–55 with 2 illus. Orig. cream cloth stamped in red.
An article in *The Ballet Annual* No. 3. Return of Markova and Dolin in *Giselle*, appearing with the Sadler's Wells Ballet.

BEAUMONT (CYRIL W.). ROLAND PETIT'S BALLETS DE PARIS. London, Ballet April 1949.
Demy 8vo (8·3 × 5·2 ins.). pp. 33–41 illus. Orig. dec. wrapps.
An article in *Ballet* Vol. 7 No. 4. See also Beaumont, *Les Ballets des Champs-Elysées*.

BEAUMONT (CYRIL W.). THE ROMANTIC BALLET. London, Time and Tide 4 Dec. 1954.
Roy. 4to (13 × 8·2 ins.). 2pp. Xerox.
A Xerox copy of a two page article on Ivor Guest's *The Romantic Ballet in England*, Phoenix House 1954.

BEAUMONT (CYRIL W.). ROSS'S CAPRICHOS. London, Ballet Jan.–Feb. 1951.
Demy 8vo (8·3 × 5·2 ins.). pp. 26–28 illus. Orig. dec. wrapps.
An article in *Ballet* Vol. II No. 1.

BEAUMONT (CYRIL W.). THE ROYAL DANISH BALLET. London, Ballet Aug. 1953.
Cr. 4to (9·6 × 7·2 ins.). pp. 9–10 illus. Orig. dec. wrapps.
An article in *Ballet Today* Vol. 6 No. 7. Besides the standard classics for which this company is known, Harald Lander's ballet *Qaartsiluni* and Birger Bartholin's *Romeo and Juliet* were given.

BEAUMONT (CYRIL W.). THE RUSSIAN BALLET 1921–1929. By W. A. Propert. London, Art Work No. 28 Winter 1931.
Demy 4to (11·1 × 8·1 ins.). pp. 299–300. Orig. printed wrapps.
An article reviewing Propert's second book, *The Russian Ballet 1921–1929*. See *Bibliography*, Part II, Propert for comment on *The Russian Ballet in Western Europe 1909–1920* and also this present volume.

BEAUMONT (CYRIL W.). THE SAKHAROFFS: THE BLUE BIRD THEATRE. London, The Dancing World Dec. 1923.

Cr. 4to (10·7 × 8·3 ins.). p. 21. Orig. dec. wrapps.

An article reviewing performances of Alexandre and Clotilde Sakharoff and also the Jasha Jushny Blue Bird Theatre. For the Sakharoffs, see also *Bibliography*, Part I, Brandenberg, H., *Der Moderne Tanz* and Part II, Levinson, André, *Les Visages de la Danse* (pp. 277–280 illus.).

BEAUMONT (CYRIL W.). SALLY GILMOUR. London, Ballet June 1947.

Demy 8vo (8·3 × 5·2 ins.). pp. 20–24 + illus. Orig. dec. wrapps.

Ballet Vol. 3 No. 5. An account of Sally Gilmour, her studies and roles with the Ballet Rambert.

BEAUMONT (CYRIL W.). SCHOOLS & METHODS OF DANCE TRAINING. London, World Ballet News. Tuesday Nov. 20, 1947.

Roy. 4to (13·4 × 9·7 ins.). pp. 4, 5. Orig. newsprint.

An article on *The Cecchetti Method of Training in Classical Ballet* as it derives from the first pedagogue Carlo Blasis.

BEAUMONT (CYRIL W.). SEE HOW THEY DANCE. London, Royal Albert Hall 1961.

Cr. 4to (9·4 × 7·4 ins.). p. (i). Orig. dec. wrapps.

A Foreword in a Programme of Festival of National Dances given at Royal Albert Hall March 18, 1961.

BEAUMONT (CYRIL W.). SERGE DIAGHILEV. London, The Dancing Times Nov. 1929.

Med. 8vo (9·2 × 6·4 ins.). pp. 155–59. Orig. dec. wrapps.

An article in this issue. See also *Bibliography*, Part I, Beaumont, *The Diaghilev Ballet in London* and *Serge Diaghilev* and *Bookseller at the Ballet*.

BEAUMONT (CYRIL W.). SERGE GRIGORIEV 1883–1968. London, The Dancing Times Nov. 1968.

Demy 4to (11·1 × 8·5 ins.). pp. 68, 69 illus. Orig. dec. wrapps.

An article. See also *Bibliography*, Part III, Grigoriev, Serge and Part I Belknap *Guide to Dance Periodicals* Vol. I and following.

BEAUMONT (CYRIL W.). SIMON SLINGSBY. London, Ballet Nov. 1947.
Demy 8vo (8·3 × 5·2 ins.). pp. 13–19 with 1 illus. Orig. dec. wrapps.
An article in *Ballet* Vol. 4 No. 5. See also *Bibliography*, Part I, Fletcher, Ifan Kyrle & Cohen, Selma Jean, *Famed for Dance*.

BEAUMONT (CYRIL W.). THE SLEEPING PRINCESS. London, Dancing Life No. 2 Dec. 1921.
Demy 4to (11·2 × 8·6 ins.). pp. 28, 29 incl. 1 plate of Egorowa. Orig. dec. wrapps.
An article reviewing *The Sleeping Princess* as represented Nov. 2nd at the Alhambra Theatre. See also the author's *The Sleeping Princess* in 2 parts (*Impressions of the Russian Ballet*), *Impressions of the Sleeping Beauty*, *Ballet* Vol. I No. 5 (p. 2) and *The Sleeping Beauty as presented by the Sadler's Wells Ballet* (Beaumont & Mandinian 1946).

BEAUMONT (CYRIL W.). SOME CLASSIC DANCES OF JAPAN. London, The Dance Journal Mar. 1934.
Demy 8vo (8·3 × 5·2 ins.). pp. 15–17. Orig. dec. wrapps.
The Dance Journal Vol. VI No. 1. Report of a Lecture Demonstration given by Rikhuhei Umemoto. See also *Bibliography*, Part II, Umemoto, Rikhuhei.

BEAUMONT (CYRIL W.). SOME DANCERS OF THE DIAGHILEV BALLET. London, Ballet Sept. 1949.
Demy 8vo (8·3 × 5·2 ins.). pp. 16–22 illus. Orig. dec. wrapps.
An article in *Ballet* Vol. 8 No. 3. Most of the issue is devoted to Diaghilev and his company.

BEAUMONT (CYRIL W.). SOME DANCERS OF THE SADLER'S WELLS THEATRE BALLET. Parts I & II. London, Foyer Autumn and Winter Numbers.
Roy. 4to (12 × 9 ins.). Part II. pp. 53, 54, 56, 58, 60 illus. Orig. dec. wrapps.
A Xerox copy of the original article in two parts. This is part two.

BEAUMONT (CYRIL W.). SOME MEMORABLE OCCASIONS. London, [Tempo] Summer 1948.
Cr. 4to (10·2 × 7·1 ins.). pp. 9–14 with 2 plates. Orig. dec. wrapps.
An article devoted to Strawinsky and his ballets. The issue is called the *Strawinsky Number* and also contains articles by Tamara Karsavina, Henry Boys, Eric Walter White and others. *Tempo No. 8* Summer 1948.

BEAUMONT (CYRIL W.). SOME NEW PAINTINGS OF THE RUSSIAN BALLET. London, The Dancing World June 1922.
Demy 4to (11 × 8·4 ins.). pp. 22, 23 with 4 illus. Orig. dec. wrapps.
An article on the Laura Knight Exhibition. The text of the article is damaged by water stain, but is accompanied by the original typescript.

BEAUMONT (CYRIL W.). SOME NOTES ON THE BALLET-SHOES WORN BY ANNA PAVLOVA. London, The Dance Journal April 1932.
Demy 8vo (8·3 × 5·2 ins.). pp. 634, 635 with 1 illus. Orig. dec. wrapps.
An article in *The Dance Journal* Vol. IV No. 2.

BEAUMONT (CYRIL W.). SOME OBSERVATIONS ON THE PRODUCTION OF SWAN LAKE. London, The Dancing Times Feb. 1964.
Demy 4to (11·4 × 9 ins.). pp. 236, 263 with 1 illus. Orig. dec. wrapps.
An article in Vol. LIV No. 641. See also Beaumont, *Le Lac des Cygnes at Covent Garden*, *Swan Lake at Covent Garden* and *Swan Lake at Stockholm*.

BEAUMONT (CYRIL W.). SOME POSTCARDS OF THE IMPERIAL RUSSIAN BALLET. London, Ballet April 1948.
Demy 8vo (8·3 × 5·2 ins.). pp. 19–24 illus. Orig. dec. wrapps.
An article in *Ballet* Vol. 5 No. 4 with interesting illustrations.

BEAUMONT (CYRIL W.). SOME PRINTS OF THE ROMANTIC BALLET. London, Print Collectors Quarterly July 1931.
Roy. 4to (12·4 × 10 ins.). pp. 885–890. Orig. dec. wrapps.
An illustrated article in Vol. 18 No. 3 of *The Print Collectors Quarterly*.

BEAUMONT (CYRIL W.). SOME RECENT REVIVALS BY THE ORIGINAL BALLET RUSSE. London, Ballet Sept. 1947.
Demy 8vo (8·3 × 5·2 ins.). pp. 16–24 illus. Orig. dec. wrapps.
An article in *Ballet* Vol. 4 No. 3. See also *Bibliography*, Part I, De Basil.

BEAUMONT (CYRIL W.). SOME STAGES IN THE DEVELOPMENT OF THE ACADEMIC BALLET. London, Aug.–Sept. 1922. The Dancing World.
Demy 4to (10·7 × 8·3 ins.). pp. 24, 25, with 2 illus. Orig. dec. wrapps.
An article. Also in this issue: *The Art of Maud Allan* by Cyril Beaumont and *Fanny Elssler and the Famous Forties* by McL Yorke (pp. 28, 29), both illustrated.

BEAUMONT (CYRIL W.). SPEECH FOR THE CRITIC'S CIRCLE by Cyril W. Beaumont. London.
Roy. 4to (13 × 8·2 ins.). 4 pp. Xerox.
A Xerox copy of an article in typescript in which the author defends the art of criticism and also welcomes the guests present at the *Critic's Circle* annual function.

BEAUMONT (CYRIL W.). STAGE DECORATIONS AND THE DANCE. London, The Dancing World July 1922.
Demy 4to (10·7 × 8·3 ins.). pp. 18, 19 with 4 illus. Orig. dec. wrapps.
An article concerning the exhibition of Theatrical Art held at the Victoria & Albert Museum. There is also a second article, *The Art of Ruth St. Denis*, by Mr. Beaumont.

BEAUMONT (CYRIL W.). SUR LES POINTES. London, The Dance Journal June 1925.
    Demy 8vo (8·3 × 5·2 ins.). pp. 42, 48. Orig. dec. wrapps.
    The Dance Journal Vol. I No. 3.

BEAUMONT (CYRIL W.). SWAN LAKE AT COVENT GARDEN. London, Ballet June 1948.
    Demy 8vo (8·3 × 5·2 ins.). pp. 49–54 with 2 pen drwgs. Orig. dec. wrapps.
    Ballet Vol. 5 No. 6. A revival of *Swan Lake* with Fonteyn as *Odette-Odile* and Somes as *Prince Siegfried*.

BEAUMONT (CYRIL W.). SWAN LAKE AT STOCKHOLM. New Ideas in Production. Kingston, Ballet Today May 1953.
    Cr. 4to (9·6 × 7·2 ins.). pp. 8–11 illus. Orig. dec. wrapps.
    This number contains a second article, *Les Sylphides Televised*, by Beaumont.

BEAUMONT (CYRIL W.). THE SWEDISH BALLET. London, Ballet May 1951.
    Demy 8vo (8·3 × 5·2 ins.). pp. 18–27 illus. Orig. wrapps.
    An article in *Ballet* Vol. II No. 4. See also Idestam, Bengt, *Svensk Balett* and *Bibliography*, Part III, Skeaping, Mary, *Ballet under Three Crowns*.

BEAUMONT (CYRIL W.). LA SYLPHIDE 1832–1947. London, Ballet July 1947.
    Demy 8vo (8·3 × 5·2 ins.). pp. 16–24 illus. Orig. dec. wrapps.
    An article in *Ballet* Vol. 4 No. 1. See also Beaumont – *Marie Taglioni*, and *Marie Taglioni and La Sylphide*.

BEAUMONT (CYRIL W.). LES SYLPHIDES TELEVISED. Kingston, Ballet Today May 1953.
    Cr. 4to (9·6 × 7·2 ins.). p. 7 with 1 illus. Orig. dec. wrapps.
    An article in *Ballet Today* Vol. 6 No. 4.

BEAUMONT (CYRIL W.). TAGLIONI. Cyril W. Beaumont makes another discovery about the Taglioni Family. London, Dance and Dancers 1963.

Demy 4to (11 × 8·4 ins.). pp. 34, 35 incl. 1 plate. Orig. dec. wrapps.

An article in the May 1963 issue of *Dance and Dancers* concerning Angelo Inganni's painting, captioned *La Danzatrice Maria Taglioni*. See also *Bibliography*, Part III, Beaumont, *Extracts from the Diary of a Pupil of Marie Taglioni*. Also Part IV, Beaumont, *Taglioni Treasures*, *More Taglioni Treasures*, and *La Sylphide*.

BEAUMONT (CYRIL W.). TAGLIONI TREASURES.
London, The Dancing Times Sept. 1966.

Demy 4to (11.4 × 9 ins.). pp. 632, 633 with 8 illus. Orig. dec. wrapps.

An article in Vol. LVI No. 672 of *The Dancing Times*.

BEAUMONT (CYRIL W.). A TERPSICHORE OF THE EIGHTEENTH CENTURY MADELEINE GUIMARD (1743–1816). London, The Dancing World Feb. 1923.

Demy 4to (11 × 8·4 ins.). pp. 26, 27 with 1 illus. Orig. dec. wrapps.

An article. See also *Bibliography*, Part I, Beaumont, *Three French Dancers of the 18th Century*, and also De Goncourt, *La Guimard*.

BEAUMONT (CYRIL W.). THREE DANCE PERFORMANCES. London, The Dance Journal Feb. 1931.

Demy 8vo (8·3 × 5·2 ins.). pp. 335, 336, 327. Orig. dec. wrapps.

The Dance Journal Vol. III No. 7. Performances of Lydia Lopokova & Co., Melusine Wood & Co., and The Camargo Society.

BEAUMONT (CYRIL W.). THREE POLISH DANCERS. London, Adam & Charles Black 1940.

Med. 8vo (9·5 × 7·1 ins.). pp. 29–32. Orig. dec. cloth.

An article in *Ballet to Poland*, edited by Arnold Haskell, in which the three dancers discussed are, Nijinsky, Idzikovsky and Woizikovsky. See also Beaumont, *A Polish Dancer New to London* (Melle. Peppi Ptaszynsky).

BEAUMONT (CYRIL W.). THREE STUDIES IN CHARACTER. London, Ballet Jan. 1949.

Demy 8vo (8·3 × 5·2 ins.). pp. 31, 32. Orig. dec. wrapps.

An article in *Ballet* Vol. 7 No. 1. Studies of three artists appearing with the International Ballet who have given the author much pleasure in performance: Wanda Evina, Errol Addison, and Joan Tucker.

BEAUMONT (CYRIL W.). A TRIBUTE TO CECCHETTI. London, The Ballet Annual 1955.

Med. 8vo (9·6 × 7·2 ins.). pp. 124–125. Orig. cream cloth stamped in blue.

An article in *The Ballet Annual* No. 9. The full title is *A Tribute to the Memory of Cecchetti*. In this issue Beaumont also contributed to a Symposium – *The Russian Dancer in London*.

BEAUMONT (CYRIL W.). TRIBUTE TO FOKINE. [Paris], Editions du Trident.

Roy. 4to (12·1 × 9·3 ins.). 16 pp. n.n. illus. Orig. dec. wrapps.

A splendid article with fine photographs appearing in *Dance Art Beauty*. The issue is devoted to the dance and the following have contributed: Barrault, Senghar, Honneger, Hall, Hastings, Tugal, Peter, and Toumanova. See also Beaumont, C. W., *Fokine's Ballets*; *Michel Fokine*; and *Michel Fokine and His Ballets*.

BEAUMONT (CYRIL W.). A TRIBUTE TO NIJINSKY. London, Ballet May 1950.

Demy 8vo (8·3 × 5·2 ins.). pp. 21 + illus. Orig. dec. wrapps.

An article in *Ballet* Vol. 9 No. 5. See also Beaumont, *The Funeral of Nijinsky, Garland for Nijinsky, The Nijinsky Galas* and *The Wedding of Nijinsky*.

BEAUMONT (CYRIL W.). A TRIBUTE TO WANDA EVINA. London, The Dancing Times Feb. 1967.

Demy 4to (11·4 × 9 ins.). pp. 248, 251 with 2 illus. Orig. dec. wrapps.

An article in *The Dancing Times* Vol. LVII No. 677. Wanda Evina was a dancer and long time accompanist for the classes of Stanislas Idzikovski.

BEAUMONT (CYRIL W.). TRUE CECCHETTI. London, The Dancing Times Oct. 1970.

Demy 4to (11·1 × 8·5 ins.). p. 22. Orig. dec. wrapps.

A letter to the editor replying to Derra de Moroda's criticism of current teaching of Cecchetti which appeared in the September issue of *The Dancing Times*.

BEAUMONT (CYRIL W.). THE TRUTH ABOUT THE DIAGHILEV COMPANY. London, The Dancing World Aug.–Sept. 1923.
Demy 4to (10·7 × 8·3 ins.). p. 27. Orig. dec. wrapps.
An article.

BEAUMONT (CYRIL W.). TWO MASSINE BALLETS. London, Ballet Mar.–Apr. 1947.
Demy 8vo (8·3 × 5·2 ins.). pp. 29–42, 63. Orig. dec. wrapps.
An article in *Ballet* Vol. 3 No. 3 concerning *The Three Cornered Hat* and *La Boutique Fantasque*.

BEAUMONT (CYRIL W.). TWO SHOWS. London, The Dance Journal April 1933.
Demy 8vo (8·3 × 5·3 ins.). pp. 94–96. Orig. dec. wrapps.
The Dance Journal Vol. V No. 2. Review of a show at the Coliseum including *The Debutante* with Phyllis Bedells and Harold Turner, and Teachers of the Revived Greek Dance at Rudolf Steiner Hall.

BEAUMONT (CYRIL W.). THE TYPESCRIPT OF COMPLETE BOOK OF BALLETS. London, C. W. Beaumont 1930–1937.
Roy. 4to (13 × 8 ins.). 14 folders containing typescript.
The original text of the *Complete Book of Ballets* as typewritten, corrected and edited by Beaumont. There are also many ballet synopses and press criticisms in pencil by the author's own hand. This majestic work was first published in 1937 by Putnam and consisted of 1,100 pages. Other editions followed rapidly.

BEAUMONT (CYRIL W.). A VALUABLE CONTRIBUTION. London, The Dancing Times Dec. 1964.
Demy 4to (11·4 × 9 ins.). p. 133 with 1 illus. Orig. dec. wrapps.
An article in Vol. LV No. 651. A Review of Joan Lawson's *A History of Ballet and its Makers*.

BEAUMONT (CYRIL W.). VERLEDEN HEDEN EN TOEKOMST VAN HET SADLER'S WELLS BALLET. Nederlands, Dans Kroniek Nos. 6–7.

Roy. 4to (12·1 × 9 ins.). pp. 108–118 illus. Orig. dec. wrapps.
An article, text in Dutch.

BEAUMONT (CYRIL W.). THE WEDDING OF NIJINSKY. London, The Dancing Times July 1964.
Demy 4to (11·6 × 9 ins.). pp. 523, 524 illus. Orig. dec. wrapps.
The translation of an article appearing in *La Gaceta de Buenos Aires*, Jueves II de Septiembre de 1913.

BEAUMONT (CYRIL W.). A WREATH FOR MONTIE. London, The Dancing Times Oct. 1966.
Demy 4to (11·4 × 9 ins.). pp. 20, 21 with 1 illus. Orig. dec. wrapps.
An article in Vol. LVII No. 673 on William Beaumont Morris. Morris was a remarkable collector of ballet material and much of his collection figured in a Sotheby sale.

BEAUMONT (CYRIL W.). THE YEAR IN BALLET. London, The British Council 1950–1951.
Med. 8vo (9·2 × 6 ins.). pp. 35–41 with 1 illus. in colour. Orig. dec. wrapps.
An article in *The Year's Work in the Theatre* 1950–1951, recording the increased interest in ballet in Britain, which Beaumont attributes to the film *The Red Shoes*, explanations of ballet technique on television and the activities of ballet clubs. An important event was the founding of The Festival Ballet. Visiting companies included the New York City Ballet, the American National Ballet Theatre, the Ny Norsk Ballet and Teresa and Luisillo's Company. The year was marked by the award of the DBE to Ninette de Valois and the CBE to Frederick Ashton.
The illustration is Osbert Lancaster's design for *Pineapple Poll*.

BEAUMONT (CYRIL W.). YVETTE CHAUVIRÉ AS PRINCESS AURORA. London, Ballet Today Nov. 1958.
Demy 4to (11 × 8·4 ins.). p. 8. Orig. dec. wrapps.
An article in *Ballet Today* Vol. II No. 9. See also Beaumont – *Four Productions of Giselle*, in which an account is given of Chauviré's appearance with the Nouveau Ballet de Monte Carlo, in *Bibliography*, Part I, Beaumont, *Dancers under my Lens* (pp. 80–87), and Chauviré, *Je suis Ballerine*. Also Shoviré.

BEDNÁŘ (KAMIL). LE LAC DES CYGNES. Illustré par Ludmila Jirincová. Paris, Gründ. 1968.
Demy 4to (11 × 8 ins.). 64 pp. illus. in colour. Orig. buckram.
The story of *Swan Lake* in French for the young.

BEGICHEV (V. P.) & GELTSER (V. F.). LEBEDINOE OZERO, Balet v 4 Aktakh. Moskva, Nemirovich-Dantchenko. [1964].
Demy 8vo (8·3 × 5·5 ins.). 3 pp. Orig. white printed wrapps.
A programme with the cast and artist list for *Swan Lake* as performed by the Nemirovich-Dantchenko Company with Violetta Bovt and Sofia Vinogradova alternating the role of *Odette-Odile*.

BEGICHEV (V. P.) & GELTSER (V. F.). SWAN LAKE. Ballet in four acts. London, Royal Opera House 1970.
Med. 8vo (9 × 5·6 ins.). 22 pp. Orig. red wrapps.
The house programme for American Ballet Theatre Sat. Aug. 1st, 1970, which gives the synopsis and cast for David Blair's production of *Swan Lake*.

BEISWANGER (GEORGE). MARTHA GRAHAM. Three New Dances. New York, Theatre Arts Jan. 1945.
Demy 4to (10·7 × 8 ins.). pp. 51–55 ilus. Orig. dec. wrapps.
An article in *Theatre Arts* for January 1945.

BEISWANGER (GEORGE), HOFMANN (WILFRED), LEVIN (DAVID MICHAEL). THREE ESSAYS IN DANCE AESTHETICS. New York, Dance Perspectives, Autumn 1973.
Med. 8vo (9 × 7·3 ins.). 48 pp. illus. Orig. dec. wrapps.
Issue No. 55 of *Dance Perspectives*.

BELKNAP (S. YANCEY). GUIDE TO DANCE PERIODICALS. Vol. 8 1957–1958. New York, The Scarecrow Press 1960.
Demy 8vo (8·4 × 5·2 ins.). pp. n.n.
In this 8th volume the text is no longer set in double columns, nor are the titles of articles in capitals. Orig. green paper boards.

BENESH (RUDOLF AND JOAN). READING DANCE. The Birth of Choreology. London, A Condor Book Souvenir Press Ltd. 1977.
 Med. 8vo (9·2 × 6 ins.). xvi + 139 pp. Illus. with a frontis. and drwgs. Orig. grey cloth.
 A book about the beginnings and uses of Choreology (Benesh Method) which is now the well established method used by the Royal Ballet for preserving its repertory. See also *Bibliography*, Parts I and III, Benesh, Rudolf and Joan.

BENOIS (ALEXANDRE). LA FAMILLE BENOIS. A Christmas Exhibition of the work of Alexandre Benois and seven members of his family. 15th December–7th January 1960–1961. London, Arthur Tooth & Sons Ltd.
 Demy 8vo (8·3 × 6·2 ins.). 1 fold (4 pp). Orig. pink cartoline.
 The members represented were: Alexandre, Lela Clement, Nadia and Nicholas Benois, Aina and Catherine Serbriakova, Alexandre Tcherkessoff and Peter Ustinov.

BENOIS (ALEXANDRE). A LETTER TO CYRIL BEAUMONT. Paris, 2 Rue Auguste Vitre Apr. 4, 1938.
 Cr. 4to (10·4 × 8·1 ins.). 2 pp. Xerox.
 A copy of a letter in French concerning *Petrouchka*. See also Schwarz, Edith, *Petrouchka*.

BENOIS (ALEXANDRE). A LETTER TO CYRIL W. BEAUMONT. Paris, le 6 Janvier 1947.
 Cr. 4to (10·7 × 8·2 ins.). 2pp. Xerox.
 A letter concerning *Petrouchka*.

BENOIS (ALEXANDRE). A LETTER TO CYRIL W. BEAUMONT. Paris, le 21 Janvier 1947.
 Cr. 4to (10·7 × 8·2 ins.). 1 p. Xerox.
 A copy of a letter thanking Mr. Beaumont for the magazine *Ballet*.

BÉRARD (CHRISTIAN). AN EXHIBITION OF PAINTINGS AND DECORS. [London], The Arts Council 1950.
 Roy. 4to (12 × 8·4 ins.). 16 pp. n.n. with reproductions of 2 pen sketches. Orig. dec. wrapps.
 A catalogue listing 70 of Bérard's works with a Foreword by Philip James and an Appreciation of Bérard by Cecil Beaton.

BETZ (RUDOLF). DYNAMISCHES BALLETT. Folge I.
Keller Verlag [Munchen 1961].
 Demy 4to (11·6 × 9·2 ins.). 28 pp. illus. Orig. boards.
 An album of 26 photographs and (2 pp.) text by the photographer Rudolf Betz.

BIBLIOGRAFIA ZAGADNIEŃ SZTUKI TANECZNEJ z lat 1945-1955. Warszawa, Centralna Poradnia Amatorskiego Ruchu Artystycznego 1959.
 Demy 4to (11·3 × 8 ins.). 123 pp. Mimeograph. Orig. dec. wrapps.
 A Bibliography of the Problems of the Art of Dancing. A list containing 761 items related to dancing that were printed in Poland. Divided into two basic sections: Folk Dance, and Artistic and Classical Dance. Perhaps inspired by Belknap's *Guide to Dance Periodicals*, it usually gives a two line description of the article or book which Belknap does not.

BIBLIOGRAFIA ZAGADNIEŃ SZTUKI TANECZNEJ z lat 1958-1960. Opracowala Irena Ostrowska. Warszawa, Centralna Poradnia Amatorskiego Ruchu Artystycznego 1962.
 Demy 4to (11·3 × 8 ins.). 154 pp. Mimeograph. Orig. dec. wrapps.
 Zeszyt (Part III) of the Bibliografia contains 1242 items of which 35 are books on Dance and Music. There are now Indexes.

BIBLIOGRAFIA ZAGADNIEŃ SZTUKI TANECZNEJ z lat 1961-1962. Opracowala Irena Ostrowska. Warszawa, Centralna Poradnia Amatorskiego Ruchu Artystycznego 1964.
 Demy 4to (11·3 × 8 ins.). 110 pp. incl. indexes. Orig. dec. wrapps.
 Zeszyt IV containing 683 items of which 32 are books either on the dance or music. Important among the authors are: Mieczyslaw Banaszyński, Ludwig Erhardt, Sygietyński, Irena Turska and Tacjanna Wysocka.

BIBLIOGRAFIA ZAGADNIEŃ SZTUKI TANECZNEJ z lat 1963-1964. Opracowala Roderyk Lange. Warszawa, Centralna Poradnia Amatorskiego Ruchu Artystycznego 1969.
 Med. 8vo (9·3 × 6·2 ins.). 190 pp. Mimeograph. Orig. dec. wrapps.

Zeszyt V containing 1283 items of which 22 books are on the dance or music. Important among the authors are: Elzbieta Darewska, Jaroslaw Iwaszkiewicz and Irena Ostrowska.

BIBLIOGRAFIA ZAGADNIEŃ SZTUKI TANECZNEJ z lat 1965–1966. Opracowla Irena Ostrowska. Warszawa, Centralna Poradnia Amatorskiego Ruchu Artystycznego 1968.

Med. 8vo (9·3 × 6·2 ins.). 176 pp. Mimeograph. Orig. dec. wrapps.

Zeszyt VI containing 640 items of which 28 are books on the dance or music. Important among the authors are: Maria Drabeca, Jadwiga Hryniewicka, Janina Pudelek (items 510, 511, 514). In the last two parts (V & VI) comment has increased from two or three lines to a usual five or six and sometimes as many as fifteen lines.

BIE (OSKAR). DER TANZ. Zweite Erweiterte und zum Zahlreiche Neue Bilder Verbesserte Auflage. Mit Hundert Kunstbeilagen. Buchausstattung von Karl Walser. Berlin, Im Verlag von Julius Bard. [1919].

Med. 8vo (9 × 6·4 ins.). 394 pp. with 100 illus. incl. some in colour. Orig. dec. boards and fabric spine.

The second enlarged edition. Contents: I. Rhythmische Künste. II. Das Fest der Elemente. III. Der Tanz im Dienst. IV. Der Gesellschaftlicher Verkher. V. Der Gesellschaftanz. VI. Das Kunstwerk des Tanzes. VII. Das Ballett. Die Musik. Der Nachtrag.

BINNEY (EDWIN 3rd). ROYAL FESTIVALS AND ROMANTIC BALLERINAS 1600–1850. Washington, D.C. [Smithsonian Institute] 1971.

Ob. Cr. 4to (7 × 10 ins.). 32 pp. n.n. illus. Orig. dec. wrapps.

A catalogue of items selected from the collection of Edwin Binney, circulated by the Smithsonian Institute 1971–1973 for display, with Introduction and Notes by Edwin Binney. See also *Bibliography*, Part III, Binney.

BITOV (B[ORIS LEONIDOVICH]). DVENADCHAT MESYATSEV. Balet. Leningrad, Sovetskii Kompozitor 1958.

12 mo (5·4 × 4·3 ins.). 17 pp. Orig. pink wrapps.

The synopsis only. *Dvenadchat Mesyatsev* (Twelve Moons?) is in the repertory of the Malyi Operni Teatr (see *Bibliography*, Part III) where eight full pages are shown of this ballet.

BITOV (B[ORIS LEONIDOVICH]). GAVROSH. Balet. Leningrad, Sovetskii Kompozitor 1925.
12 mo (5·4 × 4·3 ins.). 16 pp. Orig. rose wrapps.
The synopsis only. *Gavrosh* was first performed in the Malyi Operni Teatr, with music by Bitov and choreography by Vladimir Varkovitsky, Feb. 28, 1948.

BLAND (ALEXANDER). THE NUREYEV IMAGE. London, Studio Vista [1976].
Demy 4to (11·7 × 8·3 ins.). 288 pp. illus. Orig. green cloth.
With over 300 illustrations this must certainly be the most complete record in photographs of Nureyev to date. For ample criticism of this book and also the one by John Percival, see the November issues of *Dance and Dancers* and *The Dancing Times*.

BLASIS (CARLO). THE CODE OF TERPSICHORE. A Practical, and Historical Treatise on The Ballet. Translated by R. Barton. London, James Bulcock 1828. [N.Y. Dance Horizons 1975].
Demy 8vo (8 × 5·2 ins.). (vi) + 548 pp. with a frontis. and 16 plates + 22 pp. of music. Orig. printed wrapps.
An unabridged republication of this work, the earliest edition. The first Edward Bull edition was published in 1830, the second (titled, *The Art of Dancing*) in 1831. Preliminaries excepted, this *Code of Terpsichore* has the same pagination as the first Edward Bull edition of 1830.

BLAZISA (SOCH. KARLA). Tantsi Voobshe. BALETNIYA ZNAMENITOSTI I NATSHIONALNIE TANTSI. Baletmeistera Imperatorskikh Moskovskihh Teatrov, Professora, Tantsovalnik i Mimisheski Uchilitsi, Avtora Sochineii ob Izyashnkh Iskusstvakh i Literatura Iroch., Izdainikh na Yazikakh Frantsuzskom, Italyanskikh i Anglieskom, Chlena Mnogikh Artisticheskikh Literaturnikh Obshestiv. Moskva vb Tipografii Lazarevsk. Instituta Vostochn Yazikovb 1864.
Demy 8vo (8·5 × 5·5 ins.). 225 pp. Orig. green printed wrapps.
Listed in Magriel's *Bibliography* (pp. 26, 29) as *Les Danses en Général, les Célébrités du Ballet et les Danses Nationales*. Moscou, Imp.

de l'Institut Lazarev 1864. See Chapter 8 (p. 66) for mention of Flora Fabbri, Amalia Ferraris, Baderna, Ramachini and others. See also *Bibliography*, Parts I and III, for other works by Carlo Blasis.

BLUM (ODETTE). DANCE IN GHANA. Introduction by Kobla Ladzekpo. New York, Dance Perspectives Winter 1973.

Cr. 4to (9 × 7·4 ins.). 57 pp. illus. Orig. dec. wrapps.

Issue No. 56 of *Dance Perspectives* which concludes with some Ghanaian movements in Laban notation.

BOAS (FRANZISKA). THE FUNCTION OF DANCE IN HUMAN SOCIETY. A Seminar Directed by Franziska Boas. Brooklyn, Dance Horizons 1972.

Demy 8vo (8 × 5·2 ins.). (x) + 63 pp. illus. Orig. dec. wrapps.

A seminar with contributions by Franziska and Franz Boas, Geoffrey Gorer, Harold Courlander and Claire Holt.

BOCCACCIO (GIOVANNI). LA COMMEDIA UMANA. Teatro dei Parchi di Nervi. Genova 1960.

Roy. 4to (12·2 × 9 ins.). 19 pp. with 3 illus. in colour and 11 full page plates. Orig. dec. wrapps.

Leonide Massine's ballet presented at the Ve Festival Internazionale del Balletto (listed only in *Friedrich's Ballettlexikon*). Other ballets by Massine performed during this Festival were: *Bal des Voleurs*, *Choreartium*, *Le Beau Danube*, and *Il Barbière di Siviglia* (Opera). All have synopses and are illustrated.

BOCHARNIKOVA (Z.). STRANA VOLCHEBNAYA BALET. Moskva, Detskaya Literatura 1974.

F'cap 4to (8·1 × 6·3 ins.). 188 + (iv) pp. illus. Orig. dec. boards with fabric spine.

The book contains an interesting selection of teachers and balletmasters (E. Legat, Semonova, Litovkina, Messerer and others).

BOLSHOI BALLET. BOLSHOI BALLET. London, Dance Books Ltd. [1974].

Demy 4to (11·4 × 8·2 ins.). pp. n.n. with 97 numbered illus. Orig. dec. wrapps.

A book of photographs with a short introduction by Roberta and John Lazzarini. This served as a souvenir book for the Bolshoi's 1974 visit to London's Coliseum Theatre.

BOLSHOI TEATR. BOLSHOI TEATR. Soyza SSR. Moskva, Izdanie Gosudarstvennogo Ordena Lenina Akademicheskogo Bolshogo Teatra SSSR 1947.
Demy 4to (11·3 × 8·6 ins.). 321 + (iii) pp. illus. Orig. grey cloth.
Soderjanie: 1825–1946 (str. 23). B. V. Asafiev, Bolshoi Teatr (29). Y. A. Bakhrushin, Balet Bolshogo Teatr (Istoricheskaya Spravka) (161). A very interesting book on the Bolshoi Theatre and Ballet with many little known illustrations. Bakhrushin, author of the section on the Bolshoi Ballet, has autographed this copy to Cyril Beaumont.

BOLSHOI TEATR. SEGODNYA NA STSENE BOLSHOGO TEATR 1776–1976. Moskva, 'Iskusstvo' 1976.
Demy 4to (11·4 × 8·5 ins.). 208 pp. illus. Orig. red leatherette, boxed.
Twelve operas and twelve ballets, each with a scene in colour and text mostly by different authors. Ballets less commonly known are: *Asel*, *Anna Karenina*, and *Ivan Groznii*. A very beautifully produced book. See also *Bibliography*, Part I, Bolshoi, The and Part IV *Bolshoi Ballet*, and *Bolshoi Teatr*.

BOLSHOI TEATR SSSR. OPERA. Kniga Pervaya. Pod Redaktsiei V. A. Boni. Moskva 'Planeta' 1976.
Roy. 4to (13 × 10·1 ins.). About 280 pp. n.n. profusely illus. in colour (small, half, full-page and double page) and many in black and white. Orig. dec. rose cloth.
This is Book 1 of a 2 book set. Book 1 contains 33 Operas from the repertory of The Bolshoi Theatre. The following Operas have either dancing scenes or ballroom scenes: *Ruslan i Liudmila; Evgenii Onegin; Pikovaya Dama; Knyaz Igor; Khovanshtsina;* and *Voina i Mir* (War and Peace). Apart from a short history of The Bolshoi Theatre by B. Pokrovskii, the book consists of very beautiful illustrations set in this pattern: the first Opera is *Ivan Susanin* and its history is traced from 1842 by means of 37 photographs from O. A. Petrov 1842 (*Ivan Susanin*) to M. C. Reshetin (*Ivan Susanin*) 1962. This is followed by important artists of today, scenes, paintings, etc., many in colour and double page panorama. This pattern is continued throughout Book II. Balet.

BOLSHOI TEATR SSSR. BALET. Kniga Vtoraya. Pod Redaktsiei V. A. Boni. Moskva 'Planeta' 1976.
Roy. 4to (13 × 10·1 ins.). About 220 pp. n.n. illus. as the above. Orig. dec. blue cloth.

This is Book 2 of a 2 book set. Beginning with a short Preface by Yuri Grigorovich the following Ballets from the repertory of The Bolshoi Theatre are shown with splendid photography in colour and black and white: *Jizel* (Giselle); *Tshtsetnaya Predostrojnost* (Vain Precautions); *Konek-Gorbonok* (Little Hump-Backed Horse); Don Quixot; *Lebedinoe Ozero* (The Swan Lake); *Spyashtsaya Krasavitsa* (The Sleeping Beauty); *Raimonda; Bayaderka; Shelkunchik* (The Nutcracker); *Krasni Mak* (The Red Poppy); *Shopeniana* (Chopiniana); *Plamya Parija* (Flames of Paris); *Bakhchisaraiskii Fontan; Zolushka* (Cinderella); *Romeo i Djulietta; Shurale; Laurencia; Spartak; Leili i Medjnun; Legenda o Liubi* (Legend of Love); *Vesna Svyashtsennaya* (The Rites of Spring); *Asel; Karmen-Suita; Anna Karenina*; and *Ivan Groznii* (Ivan The Terrible). 25 ballets with their history and principal interpreters traced through small photographs to those of today's dancers in lavish colour. Perhaps the finest book of photography issued on the Bolshoi Theatre. See also *Bibliography*, Part I, *The Bolshoi Theatre*.

BOND (CHRYSTELLE T.). A CHRONICLE OF DANCE IN BALTIMORE 1790–1814. New York Dance Perspectives Summer 1976.

Cr. 4to (9 × 7·3 ins.). 49 pp. illus. Orig. dec. wrapps.
Number 66 and the final one of *Dance Perspectives*.

BOURCIER (PAUL). NOTRE DAME DE PARIS. Paris, L'Opéra de Paris 1966.

Demy 4to (11 × 8·2 ins.). pp. 23–29 illus. Orig. dec. wrapps.
An article on Roland Petit's ballet *Notre Dame de Paris*. Also in this issue No. XXIV of L'Opéra are: A Propos de *Coppélia* by A.N., Le Spectacle Strawinsky by Claude Samuel and Ballets sur Deux Scènes by Maurice Tassart.

BOURNONVILLE (AUGUSTE). NAPOLI. Spëlaret 1973–74. Premiär den 1 December. Göteborgs Teater -och Konservaktiebolag.

Cr 8vo (7·7 × 4·7 ins.). 20 pp. illus. Orig. wrapps.
A synopsis for a new production of *Napoli* with choreography by Elsa Marianne von Rosen. The brochure also contains articles: *Bournonville Traditionen* by Von Rosen and *August Bournonville* by Allan Fridericia.

BOWDEN (NANCY). CYRIL BEAUMONT. A Birthday Tribute. London, The Dancing Times Nov. 1972.

Demy 4to (11·2 × 8·5 ins.). pp. 79–81 with 1 illus. Orig. dec. wrapps.

I appreciate Nancy Bowden's words, 'Without him the literature and teaching of the dance would have had a very different structure'. Beautifully and simply expressed in less than twenty words.

BOWERS (FAUBION). THEATRE IN THE EAST. A Survey of Asian Dance and Drama. New York Grove Press. [1960].
 Roy. 8vo (10 × 6·4 ins.). x + 374 pp. incl. Index. with 4 sections of photogs. Orig. dec. wrapps.
 A reprint of The Thomas Nelson edition published in 1956. See *Bibliography*, Part III, Bowers, Faubion.

BRINSON (PETER) & CRISP (CLEMENT). THE INTERNATIONAL BOOK OF BALLET. New York, Stein and Day. [1971].
 Demy 8vo (8·1 × 5·4 ins.). xvi + 304 pp. illus. Orig. fabric spine and boards.
 Principally a collection of 115 ballets and their synopses, with comment by the authors. See also *Bibliography*, Part III, Brinson, Peter.

BRITISH SOVIET FRIENDSHIP SOCIETY. SOVIET DANCERS IN BRITAIN. In Action Photographs. London, The British Soviet Friendship Society 1953.
 Cr. 4to (9·4 × 7·2 ins.). 8 pp. n.n. illus. Orig. wrapps.
 A pamphlet marking the second visit of Soviet Dancers to England since 1917. See also Lawson, Joan, *Ballet in the U.S.S.R.*

BRODOVITCH (ALEXEY) & DENBY (EDWIN). BALLET. 104 Photographs by Alexey Brodovitch, Text by Edwin Denby. New York, J. J. Augustin. [1945].
 Ob. Demy 4tol (8·3 × 11 ins.). 143 pp. incl. Index. with 104 photogs. Orig. boards.
 From the text: 'Brodovitch's photographs look strangely unconventional – blurred, distorted, too black and spectral, or too light and faded looking'. These are intentional effects, but the results must mean more to the photographer than the viewer.

BROWN (IAN F. Editor). THE AUSTRALIAN BALLET 1962–1965. A record of the Company, its Dancers and its Ballets. [Australia], Longmans. [1967].

Cr. 4to (9·1 × 7·1 ins.). 154 pp. with frontis. in colour and other illus. Orig. blue cloth.
See *Bibliography*, Part III, Bellew, Peter, Van Praagh, Peggy and also Hall, Hugh P.

BRUCE (H. J.). SILKEN DALLIANCE. London, Constable. [1947].
Demy 8vo (8·4 × 5·2 ins.). vii + 183 pp. with a frontis. and 5 other illus. Orig. blue cloth.
For other memoirs by Karsavina's husband, see also Bruce, *Thirty Dozen Moons*, *Bibliography*, Part I.

BRUHN (ERIK) & MOORE (LILLIAN). BOURNON-VILLE & BALLET TECHNIQUE. Studies and Comments on August Bournonville's Études Chorégraphiques. Brooklyn. A Dance Horizons Republication.
Demy 8vo (8 × 5·3 ins.). 70 pp. + 16 numbered illus. Orig. dec. wrapps.
See *Bibliography*, Part I, Bruhn & Moore, for comment on the original edition.

BUCKLE (RICHARD). HOMAGE TO THE DESIGNERS OF DIAGHILEV (1909–1929). Venice, Palazzo Grassi June 15–Sept. 14, 1975.
(8·5 × 9·3 ins.). xv + 41 + 16 pp. of plates. Orig. illus. wrapps. (Picasso).
A catalogue made on behalf of the Theatre Museum, London by Richard Buckle.

BUCKLE (RICHARD). NIJINSKY. New York, Simon & Schuster. [1971].
Med. 8vo (9·1 × 6 ins.). xiv + 482 pp. illus. with photogs. and line drwgs. Orig. cloth.
The American edition. See *Bibliography*, Part III, for the first English edition.

BUCKLE (RICHARD). NIJINSKY. [London], Penguin Books. [1975].
Cr. 8vo (7·6 × 8·1 ins.). xxxii + 592 pp. illus. Orig. dec. wrapps.
The Introduction to this, the second edition, announces it

contains a little new material, and many corrections. The illustrations are fewer than in the first edition (59 on 32 pp.) and are necessarily reduced in size.

BULLETIN DES LOIS. (FRANCE). Partie Supplémentaire. No. 1261.
Demy 8vo (8·4 × 5·5 ins.). pp. 853-872.
Décret Impérial No. 20,792, qui approuve 4 liquidations de Pensions Civiles du 6 Octobre 1866. Listing of Pensionnaires with date of birth, grade, nature of services and amount of Pension.
Under Decret 20,806 Georges Jacobi was given permission to reside in France in 1866. He became conductor of Bouffe-Parisiennes in 1872 and musical director of the Alhambra Theatre, London until 1898. He married Maria Pilatte. See *Bibliography*, Part III, *Théâtre Impérial de L'Opéra*.

BURCHENAL (ELIZABETH).. FOLK-DANCES AND SINGING GAMES. Twenty-Six Folk Dances. Revised Edition. New York, G. Schirmer. [1938].
Demy 4to (11·7 × 9 ins.). 83 pp. illus. with photogs. diags. and music. Orig. dec. boards.
First published in 1913, this is the new edition. See *Bibliography*, Part I, for other works by Burchenal.

BURCHENAL (ELIZABETH). FOLK-DANCES FROM OLD HOMELANDS. A Third Volume of Folk-Dances and Singing Games. New York, G. Schirmer. [1922].
Demy 4to (11·7 × 9 ins.). (x) + 85 pp. illus. with photogs. diags. and music. Orig. dec. wrapps.
The original edition containing Thirty-Three Folk Dances.

BUREAU OF MUSICAL RESEARCH. MUSIC AND DANCE IN THE NEW ENGLAND STATES INCLUDING MAINE, NEW HAMPSHIRE, VERMONT, MASSACHUSETTS, RHODE ISLAND & CONNECTICUT. New York Bureau of Musical Research 1953.
Med. 8vo (9 × 5·7 ins.). 332 pp. illus. Orig. black cloth.
For information on Edwin Binney 3rd see Alicia Langford, wife and associate in *Alicia Langford Ballet Group* (p. 229). Edited by Sigmund Spaeth with William Perlman as director and managing editor.

BUREAU OF MUSICAL RESEARCH. MUSIC AND DANCE IN PENNSYLVANIA, NEW JERSEY AND DELAWARE. New York Bureau of Musical Research 1954.
Med. 8vo (9 × 5·7 ins.). 339 pp. illus. Orig. brown cloth.
A book about Regional Music and Dance edited by Sigmund Spaeth with William Perlman as director and managing editor. See also *Bibliography*, Parts I and III, *Bureau of Musical Research*, for other regions.

BURIAN (K. V.). THE STORY OF WORLD OPERA. London, Peter Nevill. [1961].
Demy 4to (10·4 × 9·2 ins.). 294 pp. with 364 illus. Orig. dec. blue cloth.
Contains plates of dancing scenes from *Orfeo, Le Triomphe de l'Amour, Le Nozze di Peleo e di Teti, Il Pomo d'Oro, Ercole in Tebe* and other Operas. See also *Bibliography*, Part I, Burian, K. V., *The Story of World Ballet*.

CALDWELL (HELEN). MICHIO ITO. The Dancer and His Dances. Berkeley, University of California Press. [1977].
Cr. 4to (9·1 × 7·5 ins.). 184 pp. illus. Orig. black cloth.
A biography of Michio Ito, dancer from Japan, who became enamoured of the modern dance of the West and included it in many of his performances. Appendices give roles, date of performance, and Theatre. Appendix 4 shows motion picture film stills of sequences of Ito's ten basic arm movements (Gestures).

CANCIONES Y DANZAS DE ESPANA 9. a edición. Seccion Feminina de F.E.T.Y. las J.O.N.S.
Roy 4to (12·7 × 9·5 ins.). 36 pp n.n. + 4 pp. illus. in colour. Orig. dec. wrapps.
Songs and Dances from: Andalucia, Vascongadas, Galicia, Canarias, Baleares, Castilla la Nueva, Extramadura, Leon, Castilla la Vieja, Aragon, Cataluña, Asturias, Murcia, Valencia. See also *Bibliography*, Part I, Busquets-Llobet, *Bailes Tipicos y Escudos de Espana y sus Regiones*.

CANYAMERES (FERRAN) I (IGLÉSIES, Josep). LA DANSARINA ROSETA MAURI (1850–1923). I. Reus, Asociacion de Estudios Reusenses 1971.
Roy. 8vo (10 × 6·7 ins.). In 2 parts: Vol. I. 164 pp. with XIII plates and 11 pp. text. Vol. II. 170 pp. XIII plates with 12 pp. text. Orig. printed wrapps.

The first full length work on Rosita Mauri who left her mark at the Paris Opera with creations of *La Maladetta, La Korrigane, Les Deux Pigeons* and others as well as operas *Le Cid, Polyeucte, Faust* in which she did not create the dancing role. The text is mostly in Catalan, but the criticisms, assembled by the authors, concerning these pieces in which she appeared are mainly in French. Léandre Vaillat in his *Ballets de L'Opéra de Paris* 1947 gives the date of her birth as 15 September 1856. The present work after examining many documents settles on 15 Sept. 1849, as does Sebastiano Gasch in his *Diccionario del Ballet y de la Danza*. Edition limited to 530 copies of which this is No. 46.

CAPMANY (AURELIO). UN SIGLO DE BAILE EN BARCELONA. Que y Donde Bailaban los Barceloneses el Siglo XIX. Barcelona, Ediciones Libreria Milla. 1947.

Demy 8vo (8·1 × 5·6 ins.). 93 pp. illus. Orig. paper boards.

A Century of Dancing in Barcelona: Dances, Balls and Masquerades, well illustrated. See also Capmany, *Bibliography*, Parts I and III.

CARRAFFA (ARTURO GARCIA). MALIA MOLINA. Madrid, Saez Hermanos y Compania 1916.

F'cap 8vo (6·6 × 4·3 ins.). 182 pp. + Index. Orig. brown cloth.

A résumé of the career of Malia Molina, singer and dancer. Divided into parts: I. Biography. II. Poems about her. III. Criticisms. Text in Spanish.

CARTER (HUNTLY). THE NEW SPIRIT IN DRAMA AND ART. New York & London, Mitchell Kennerley 1913.

Cr. 4to (9·7 × 7·4 ins.). x + 270 pp. incl. Index. illus. with some in colour. Orig. dec. cloth.

For information on the Russian Ballet in London see: *Schéhérazade, Pavillon d'Armide, Carnaval, Prince Igor* (pp. 19–28). In Paris: *Schéhérazade, Cléopâtre, Narcisse, Martyre de St. Sebastien* (pp. 54–58). On Jaques Dalcroze in Dresden (pp. 120–127). Particularly interesting for a study of contrasts in lighting and production in London and Paris.

CASTIGLIONI (VITTORANGELO). MARIO E IL MAGIO. Azione Coreografica di Luchini Visconti dal Racconto di Thomas Mann. Coreografico di Leonida Massine.

Milano, Teatro alla Scala Stagione Lirico 1955–1956.
Med. 8vo (9·4 × 6·4 ins.). pp. 282–289 illus. Orig. dec. wrapps.
An article on this ballet, principally concerned with the music of Franco Mannino. There are 6 scene designs by Lila de Nobili. *Friedrich's Ballettlexikon* seems to have the only listing of *Mario e il Magio*.

CASTLE (IRENE). CASTLES IN THE AIR. As Told to Bob and Wanda Duncan. Garden City, Doubleday & Co. 1958.
Demy 8vo (8·2 × 5·4 ins.). 264 pp. with about 50 illus. Orig. fabric spine and boards.
The story of Irene and Vernon Castle. See also *Bibliography*, Part I, Castle, Vernon, *Modern Dancing*.

CAVLING (VIGGO). BALLETTENS BOG. Ballettkunstens Udvikling Fortalt I Billeder. Kobenhavn, Alfred G. Hassings Forlag 1941.
Cr. 4to (10·2 × 7·6 ins.). 120 pp. n.n. illus. Orig. green cloth.
A useful picture book, mainly about the Danish Ballet, to be added to the works of Elith Reumert and Svend Kragh-Jacobsen. There is however material on the Diaghilev and Swedish Ballets and other companies. The book bears the signature of Adeline Genée.

CECCHETTI SOCIETY, THE. THE CONSTITUTION AND ACTIVITIES OF THE CECCHETTI BRANCH OF THE IMPERIAL SOCIETY OF TEACHERS OF DANCING. London, 70 Gloucester Place W.1.
Cr. 8vo (8·1 × 5 ins.). 8 pp. Orig. illus. wrapps.
A pamphlet concerned also with the origin of *The Cecchetti Society*.

CHABUKIANI (VAKHTANG). OTELLO. Tbilisi, Ministerstvo Kulturi CCR 1958.
Med. 8vo (9·5 × 6·4 ins.). 10 pp. + 21 full page plates. Orig. dec. red wrapps.
A synopsis of the ballet *Othello* with both cast and artists listed, and more and larger photographs than in the item below.

CHABUKIANI (VAKHTANG). OTELLO. Balet. Tbilisi, Gosdarstvennoe Izdatelstvo Sabochta Sakartvelo 1958.
Demy 8vo (8 × 4·7 ins.). 56 pp. with photogs. and mus. ex. Orig. dec. wrapps.

A synopsis of the ballet *Othello* in 6 acts with music by Macavariani. First performed at Tiflis Nov. 29, 1957 with Chabukiani (*Othello*) and Vera Shignadze (*Desdemona*).

CHENEY (SHELDON). THE THEATRE. Three Thousand Years of Drama, Acting and Stagecraft. New York Tudor Publishing Co. 1935.

Med. 8vo (9 × 6·1 ins.). ix + 558 pp. incl. Index. Illus. Orig. red cloth.

See, Dancing forerunner of the theatre (pp. 11–29). Consult Index under Ballet Opera etc.

CHEREKHOVSKAYA (R. L.). TANTSEVAT MOGUT VSE. Izdatelstvo 'Narodnaya' Asveta, Minsk 1973.

Demy 8vo (8·3 × 6·3 ins.). 189 pp. + (iii) illus. Orig. fabric spine and dec. boards.

Classic ballet exercises for the young, followed by light character dances and social or ballroom dances for two. Text in Russian.

CHERVINSKII (N.) RODNYE POLYA. Leningrad, Sovetskii Kompozitor 1958.

12mo (5·5 × 4·2 ins.). 18 pp. with 1 illus. Orig. green wrapps.

The synopsis of the ballet *Rodnye Polya* (Native Fields), first performed at the Kirov June 4, 1953 with choreography by A. Andreyev.

CHRISTOUT (MARIE FRANÇOISE). THE COURT BALLET IN FRANCE 1611–1641. New York, Dance Perspectives 1964.

Med. 8vo (9 × 7·4 ins.). 37 pp. illus. Orig. dec. wrapps.

Issue No. 20 of *Dance Perspectives*, shared with Saint Hubert. See also *Bibliography*, Part II, Saint Hubert, *How to Compose a Successful Ballet*.

CHRISTOUT (MARIE-FRANÇOISE). LE MERVEILLEUX ET LE THÉÂTRE DU SILENCE. En France à Partir du XVII Siècle. La Haye, Paris, Editions Mouton 1965.

Cr. 4to (9·6 × 7 ins.). 447 pp. incl. Indexes and Tables. Illus. Orig. dec. black cloth.

The Marvellous and the Silent Theatre. I feel that the drawings by

Monique Lancelot in the opening pages of the book, and the space given to the ballets of modern composers (particularly those of Serge Lifar, of which there are some 30 examples), are misplaced in a book of this title. The text of Hannah Winter's *Theatre of Marvels* is much more simple and straightforward, as true mystery should be, and her choice of illustrations is far richer.

CHUDNOVSKY (M.). FOLK DANCE COMPANY OF THE U.S.S.R. Igor Moiseyev Art Director. Moscow, Foreign Languages Publishing House 1959.

F'cap 4to (8·4 × 6·4 ins.). 104 pp. illus. Orig. dec. wrapps.

The title on the front cover is *Dancing To Fame*. See also Sheremetyvskaya — *Rediscovering the Dance, Bibliography*, Part III, for another work on the Moiseyev Company.

CHUJOY (ANATOLE) & MANCHESTER (P. W.). THE DANCE ENCYCLOPEDIA. Revised and Enlarged Edition. New York, Simon and Schuster.

Med. 8vo (9 × 6 ins.). xii + 992 + (iii) pp. illus. Orig. dec. wrapps.

A soft covered edition issued by Touchstone. See also *Bibliography*, Parts I and III, for other editions.

CHURKO (YULIKA). BELO RUSKII BALET. Izdatelstvo 'Nauka i Tekhnika', Minsk 1966.

F'cap 4to (8 × 6·4 ins.). 125 pp. + (iii) pp. illus. Orig. dec. boards.

The White Russian Ballet at the Minsk Opera House. Little known artists of this company, such as A. Nikolaeva and S. Drechin in *Arlekinada*, and *Solovei* (The Nightingale). Others include I. Savleva and V. Davidov.

CLARK (BARRET H.). A NOTE ON THE SWEDISH BALLET. Chicago, The Drama 1922.

Demy 4to (12 × 9 ins.). pp. 303–305 with 3 illus. Orig. dec. wrapps.

An illustrated article in the June–July–August issue of *The Drama*. This, I believe, was prefatory to the Jean Borlin and Les Ballets Suedois de Rolfe de Maré's first visit to America.

CLARKE (ASHLEY). ENRICO CECCHETTI.

Roy. 4to (13 × 8 ins.). 3 pp. typescript + a letter.

An article in Italian on Cecchetti by Ashley Clarke of The British Embassy, Rome. There is also a letter to Cyril Beaumont by Clarke. This article appeared in *Dance Journal*.

CLARKE (MARY). C. W. BEAUMONT GIVES UP HISTORIC LONDON BOOKSHOP. New York, Dance News Dec. 1965.
Imp. 4to (16·4 × 11·2 ins.). p. 7 with 1 illus.
An article marking the closing of the bookshop which Beaumont had kept since 1910, under the sign, *At the Sign of the Harlequin's Bat*.

CLARKE (MARY). MARGOT FONTEYN. [Brooklyn, New York Dance Horizons 1976].
Med. 8vo (9 × 7 ins.). 20 + (iv) pp. incl. both wrapps. Illus.
A monograph with photographs by Anthony Crickmay. One of *Dance Horizons Spotlight Series*. See also Forrester, *Ballet in England* and Belknap, *Guide to Dance Periodicals* (all volumes) for considerable listing of books and articles about Fonteyn.

CLARKE (MARY). THE SADLER'S WELLS THEATRE BALLET. Boston, Chrysalis 1951.
Cr. 8vo (8 × 5·2 ins.). 14 pp. with 3 illus. Orig. dec. wrapps.
An issue of *Chrysalis* 1951 Vol. IV Nos. 7, 8. See also *Bibliography*, Part I, Clarke, Mary, *Sadler's Wells Ballet*.

CLARKE (MARY) & CRISP (CLEMENT). BALLET. An Illustrated History. London, Adam and Charles Black. 1973.
Cr. 4to (9·5 × 7·2 ins.). 245 pp. Profusely illus. Orig. blue cloth.
The following 10 chapters are all preceded by text and followed by a list of works consulted. 1. How it all Began (p. 23). 2. The Age of Reason and Technique (p. 42). 3. The Romantic Movement (p. 63). 4. Marius Petipa and the Imperial Russian Ballet (p. 92). 5. Emigrés: Diaghilev and Pavlova (p. 112). 6. Bridging the Gap: The Baby Ballerinas (p. 149). 7. Building of British Ballet (p. 163). 8. America: Two kinds of Dancing (p. 189). 9. Soviet Ballet: Vaganova and Her Pupils (p. 206). 10. Today's Ballet (p. 222).

CLARKE (MARY) & CRISP (CLEMENT). MAKING A BALLET. [London], Studio Vista [1974].
Cr. 4to (9·5 × 7·3 ins.). 160 pp. illus. Orig. paper boards.

Interesting conversations with Paul Taylor, David Blair, Christopher Bruce, Peter Darell, Norman Morrice and other choreographers. The Appendices on Notation: Petipa's notes for *The Sleeping Beauty* and *The Nutcracker*; Bronislav Nijinska's for *Les Noces* and Natalia Roslavleva's on *The Bronze Horsemen* are most happily collected together in one book.

CLENDENEN (F. LESLIE). CLENDENEN'S TREATISE ON ELEMENTARY AND CLASSICAL DANCING. Technical terms criticized by Prof. Louis Kretlow. Davenport, Instructor Publishing Co. 1903.

Cr. 8vo (7·6 × 5 ins.). 174 + (ii) pp. Illus. with photogs. and drwgs. Orig. red cloth.

A most interesting book which gives some idea of the American dancer in recital and on the stage. Clendenen has shared the book with some of his colleagues and their pupils – H. Layton Walker, H. N. Grant and Peter D. Findlay. A pupil of Findlay is shown in a long coat, top hat and tights poised on the neck of a bottle on the right toe, with left leg crossed above right knee. If not a trick photograph, a very interesting stunt indeed. See also *Bibliography*, Part I, Clendenen, for another work.

COCTEAU (JEAN). A CALL TO ORDER. Translated from the French by Rollo H. Myers. London, Faber and Gwyer 1926.

Cr. 8vo (7·3 × 4·7 ins.). viii + 248 pp. with a frontis. Orig. brown cloth with label.

Pungent remarks about *Parade, Les Biches, Les Fâcheux*, and other Diaghilev ballets. Included in Ifan Fletcher's *Books Relating to the Diaghilev Ballet*.

COHEN (SELMA JEANNE). DANCE AS A THEATRE ART. Source Readings in Dance History from 1581 to the Present. New York, Dodd Mead 1974.

Med. 8vo (9 × 6 ins.). viii + 224 pp. illus. Orig. dec. wrapps.

A good but rather rapid survey of the period, with naturally many omissions. Marie Sallé (p. 219) is mentioned as the only ballerina who merited a biography: this of course overlooks Letainturier-Fradin's *La Camargo* and De Goncourt's *La Guimard*. Also I would prefer the spelling of Lalla Roock as *Lalla Rookh* as both Beaumont in *Complete Book of Ballets* (p. 264) and the author of *Lalla Rookh*, Thomas Moore use that spelling.

COLE (JACK). THE JACK COLE DANCE AND THEATRE COLLECTION. Los Angeles.
(14 × 8·2 ins.). 62 pp. A Xerox copy. Brown wrapps.

A remarkable collection assembled by Jack Cole and divided into five main Parts. I. Books Libretti and Mss. (Nos. 1–2,796). This section is confused; Nos. 1229–1534 do not exist, and there are several hundred lightweight biographies (cinema and theatre) which should be listed elsewhere. Nos. (2,796–6,082) are Dance Periodicals. II. Archival Material Nos. (6,083–6,912) Scrapbooks, Souvenir Programs, Newspaper articles etc. III. The Jack Cole Collection (6,913–8,401) Musical Scores, Set Designs, Photographs, Costumes etc. IV. The Jean Cocteau Collection (8,402–8,505) Scrap Books, Mss, Drawings, Books etc. V. Ruth St. Denis Collection (8,506–10,652) Photographs, Negatives, Letters, Scrapbooks, etc. Miscellaneous (10,653–11,946). Original Art (11,947–12,003). The real prize is of course Part I, Books, Libretti, and Mss. The book section of the Part I in printed works of the 16th to 18th century is outstanding. It is perhaps better to list a few important books of these centuries that the collection lacks – originals of *Ballet Comique de la Reine, Orchesography* (both Arbeau and Weaver), Negri, *Nuove Inventioni di Balli*, Kellom-Tomlinson, *The Art of Dancing* and Minguet *Arte de Danzar a la Francesa* – than to try to select a few of the many included. There are some 600–800 important libretti, good but far from exhaustive.

COLL (CHARLES J.) & ROSIERE (GABRIELLE). DANCING MADE EASY. New and Revised Edition. New York, Edward J. Clode. [1922].

Cr. 8vo (7·2 × 4·7 ins.). 277 pp. illus. with drwgs. and diagrams. Orig. cloth.

A manual aiming for correct social dancing with considerable attention paid to the Cotillion and its figures (pp. 195–227).

COLLINS (RICHARD). BEHIND THE BOLSHOI CURTAIN. London, William Kimber. [1974].

Med. 8vo (9·2 × 6 ins.). 238 pp. with 16 illus. Orig. red cloth.

The story of a young dancer Richard Collins, who trained and danced four years with the *Bolshoi Ballet*.

CONYN (CORNELIUS). DARJA COLLIN EN EDMEE MONOD. Holland, De Fakhel Sept. 1941.

Cr. 4to (10 × 6·6 ins.). pp. 7 incl. 2 illus. A Xerox copy.

An article on the Dutch dancer Darja Collin. See also Koegler *Friedrich's Ballettlexikon* for brief biographical details.

CONYN (CORNELIUS). HET WEZEN VAN DEN SPAANSCHEN DANS.
Demy 4to (11·6 × 8·7 ins.). pp. 20–28 with 6 illus. Plain wrapps.
An extract from *Elsevier's Magazine* (n.d.). The photographs are of: Argentinita, Manuela del Rio, Escudero, Carmita Garcia, Laura de Santelmo, La Joselita and La Argentina. See also *Bibliography*, Parts I and III, Conyn, Cornelius.

COOMARASWAMY (ANANDA K.). THE DANCE OF SHIVA. Revised Edition. New York, The Noonday Press. [1957].
Demy 8vo (8 × 5·3 ins.). 182 pp. Illus. Orig. dec. wrapps.
The illustrations precede the title page in this edition. See also *Bibliography*, Part I, Coomaraswamy, Ananda K.

COOPER (DOUGLAS). PICASSO THEATRE. Paris, Editions Cercle d'Art, 1967.
Large sq. 4to (11·5 × 9·5 ins.). 364 pp. with 62 illus. in colour (32 full page). Orig. dec. cloth.
The first edition in French. See *Bibliography*, Part III, Cooper, Douglas for the English edition and comment.

CORNELL (JOSEPH). A LETTER TO CYRIL BEAUMONT. Flushing New York, June 7, 1948.
Imp. 4to (15·3 × 9 ins.). Xerox of 1 typewritten page with cutout dec. Signed.
A letter of appreciation to Beaumont, having as a heading a cutout of Lucile Grahn in *Eoline*, showering golden stars over the page. The figure of Grahn is decorated with small fragments actually taken from costumes worn by Markova and Toumanova. See also *Bibliography*, Part I, Cornell, Joseph.

COSMAN (MILEIN). STRAVINSKY AT REHEARSAL. A sketchbook by Milein Cosman with text by Hans Keller. London, Dennis Dobson. [1962].
Demy 8vo (8 × 6 ins.). (iv) + 15 pp. + plates. Orig. cloth.
Milein Cosman was also a contributor to *The Ballet Annual*.

COTON (A. V.). WRITINGS ON DANCE 1938–1968. Selected and Edited by Kathrine Sorley Walker and Lilian Haddakin. Foreword by Martin Cooper. London, Dance Books. [1975].
Demy 8vo (8·3 × 5·4 ins.). xv + 174 pp. with a frontis. Orig. dec. wrapps.
Contents: I. The Critic's Function (p. 3); II. Looking Back and Around (p. 13); III. English Ballet (p. 41); IV. Foreign Ballet (p. 89); V. Modern Dance (p. 135); VI. What's the use of Critics (p. 159). See also *Bibliography*, Parts I and III, Coton, A. V.

CRAFT (ROBERT). STRAVINSKY. Chronicle of a Friendship 1948–1971. New York, Alfred A. Knopf 1972.
Med. 8vo (9·2 × 6·1 ins.). xvi + 424 + xvi pp. incl. index. Illus. Orig. brown cloth.
See also Stravinsky and Craft.

CRAFT (ROBERT). STRAVINSKY. The Chronicle of a Friendship 1948–1971. London, Victor Gollancz 1972.
Med. 8vo (9·2 × 6·1 ins.). xvi + 424 + xvi pp. incl. Index. Illus. Orig. brown cloth.
Like the American edition, but with a third block of photographs added (p. 412).

CRAIG – RAYMOND (PETER). ROLAND PETIT. Surbiton, Surrey, Losely Hurst. [1959].
Med. 8vo (9·6 × 7·3 ins.). 44 pp. n.n. Illus. Orig. dec. wrapps.
See also *Bibliography*, Part II, Lidova, Irène, *Roland Petit*.

CRAWFORD (CAROLINE). FOLK DANCES AND GAMES. New York, A. S. Barnes & Co. 1909.
Demy 4to (11·1 × 8·2 ins.). ix + 82 pp. with a frontis. and num. mus. airs. Orig. green cloth.
The contents include: Finnish, Swedish, Scotch, English, German, French and Bohemian Dances.

CRISP (CLEMENT). BALLERINA. Portraits and Impressions of Nadia Nerina. London, Weidenfeld & Nicolson. [1975].

Roy. 4to (12 × 8·6 ins.). pp. n.n. illus. Orig. cloth with boards.

A work edited by Clement Crisp with contributors: David Blair, Margaret Dale, Peter Darrell, Natalya Dudinskaya, Arnold Haskell, Robert Helpmann, Eileen Keegan, Leo Kersley, Nadia Nerina, Peggy Van Praagh, Alexis Rassine, Natalia Roslavleva, Konstantin Sergueyev, Ninette de Valois. Many excellent photographs. See also *Bibliography*, Part II, Swinson, Cyril.

CRISP (CLEMENT), SAINSBURY (ANYA), WILLIAMS (PETER). 50 YEARS OF BALLET RAMBERT. Great Britain, The Scolar Press 1976.

Roy. 4to (12·4 × 9·3 ins.). 64 pp. illus. Orig. dec. white wrapps.

See also *Bibliography*, Part I, Bradley, *16 Years of Ballet Rambert* and Haskell, *The Marie Rambert Ballet*. Part III Clarke, *Dancers of Mercury*; also *Dance Magazine Portfolio* for Feb. 1973.

CRISP (CLEMENT) & CLARKE (MARY). MAKING A BALLET. New York, Macmillan Publishing Co. [1974].

Med. 8vo (9·5 × 7·3 ins.). 160 pp. with many illus. Orig. black cloth.

A pleasant book mainly comprising accolades for fellow authors and artists. The Appendices are of real value: Appendix B, *The Sleeping Beauty* is a translation of Petipa's scenario with his original notes. (Joan Lawson first published these notes in *The Dancing Times* Dec. 1942 and Jan., Feb., Mar. 1943.) See also *Bibliography*, Part I, Conyn, *Three Centuries of Ballet*, Chapter XIII (p. 103).

CROCE (ARLENE). THE FRED ASTAIRE & GINGER ROGERS BOOK. New York, Galahad Books. [1972].

F'cap 4to (8·1 × 7 ins.). 191 pp. illus. Orig. yellow boards.
See also *Bibliography*, Part III, Astaire, Fred, *Steps in Time*.

CROWLE (PIGEON). MOIRA SHEARER. Portrait of a dancer. London, Faber & Faber Ltd. 1949.

Med. 8vo (9·7 × 7·2 ins.). 80 pp. with a frontis. and 46 plates. Orig. cloth.

The first edition. See also *Bibliography*, Part II, Swinson, Cyril and Tennent, Rose and Part III Gibbon, Monk, *The Red Shoes Ballet* and *Tales of Hoffmann* for other books about Shearer. See also Shearer, Moira, *A Letter to Cyril Beaumont*.

CROXTON (ARTHUR). CROWDED NIGHTS – AND DAYS. An Unconventional Pageant. London, Sampson Low Marston & Co. [1930].
Demy 8vo (8·6 × 5·3 ins.). xviii + 398 pp. with a frontis. Orig. black cloth.
See Chapter XVII Great Farewells and a Return for information on Genée, and Chapter XXV Diaghilev and the Russian Ballet and Chapter XXVI Re-enter Diaghilev.

CROZIER (GLADYS BEATTIE). THE TANGO AND HOW TO DANCE IT. London, Andrew Melrose. 1913.
Cr. 8vo (7·3 × 4·6 ins.). 152 pp. + 32 full page plates. Orig. cloth.
See also Petermann, *Tanzbibliografie*, Lieferung 24, 25, 26.

CUNNINGHAM (KITTY). WATCHING BOURNON-VILLE. New York, Ballet Review Vol. 4 No. 6 1974.
Demy 8vo (8·4 × 6·6 ins.). pp. 24–31. Orig. dec. wrapps.
See also Antoine and Auguste Bournonville; Terry, *Blithe Spirit and Bournonville Bounce* and *Theatre Research Studies, Bibliography*, Part III.

DAGUERRE (PIERRE). LE MARQUIS DE CUEVAS. Paris, Editions Denöel. [1954].
Cr. 8vo (7·7 × 5·7 ins.). 162 pp. with illus. throughout the text. Orig. dec. wrapps.
Le Marquis de Cuevas (1885–1961) founder of *Le Grand Ballet du Marquis de Cuevas* which began its existence as *Ballet International*. The book contains biographical information on de Cuevas, listing of repertory of his company, and short biographical notes on important members of the company.

DANCE AND DANCERS. Peter Williams, Editor, David Raher Assistant Editor. Jan. 1950 Vol. I No. 1. London, Dance and Dancers.
Cr. 4to (10·5 × 8 ins.). 156 Nos. of this magazine. Illus. 4 vols. bound, the rest in binders or unbound.
Thirteen years of this magazine which began with Caryl Brahms, Evan Senior, Tatlock Miller and Howard Byrne (Photographer) as contributors. Clive Barnes joined the staff in May 1950 and his articles entitled *Ballet Perspectives* from Sept. 1956 to Dec. 1964 were perhaps his most important European contributions.

DANCE BOOKS LTD. CATALOGUES OF DANCE BOOKS LTD. NEW BOOKS AND ADDITIONS TO STOCK APRIL 1977. Directors: John O'Brien and David Leonard. London, 9 Cecil Court.
Demy 4to (11·5 × 8·2 ins.). 6 pp.
Formerly called *Ballet Bookshop Ltd*. These book lists with price, ample description and evaluation, do not mention publisher and represent but a fraction of the very important material that flows through their hands. Dance Books now has a growing list of books and pamphlets they reprint and in some cases publish for the first time.

DANCE MAGAZINE. DANCE MAGAZINE 1949–1979. New York, Dance Magazine.
Demy 4to (11 × 8·3 ins.). 372 numbers illus. Orig. dec. wrapps.
In 1968 with the October number, Dance Magazine began including a centre fold, usually of about 16 pages, printed on tinted art paper. This was called *Dance Magazine Portfolio*. These articles were perhaps not always the best or most interesting, but collectors found they could usually be extracted from the text of the issue without carrying with it material belonging to the preceding or following article. The art work is mostly by Herbert Migdoll.

DANCE MAGAZINE. DANCE MAGAZINE PORTFOLIO. 1968–1979. New York, Dance Magazine.
Demy 4to (11 × 8·3 ins.). 96 portfolios with orig. dec. wrapps of the issue.
A collection of 90 articles extracted from the monthly issues of *Dance Magazine*. In general the articles fall into three categories: Artists, Ballet Companies, and Ballets.

DANCE MART (THE). CATALOGUES. Brooklyn New York 1966–1975.
(8·4 × 3·6 ins.). Orig. wrapps.
Catalogues from 1966–67, 1967–68, 1968, 1969, 1970 (2), 1971, 1972, 1973 (2), 1974 (2), (1975) (2), 1977 (2), 1978 (2). Also *Ballet* (18 pp.). Later catalogues are illustrated and contain some very rare books.

DANCE MART (THE). THE DIAGHILEV BALLET. New York, The Dance Mart.
(8·4 × 5·4 ins.). 10 pp. mimeograph.

A catalogue containing about 150 items on this company, representing Critical Works, The Dancers, Choreographers, Ballets, Designers, Composers and Souvenir Programs. See also Fletcher, Ifan Kyrle, *Books Relating to the Diaghilev Ballet.*

DANCE PERSPECTIVES. ALL THAT STRANGE AND MYSTERIOUS FOLK. Studies in Ballet Supernaturals. New York, Dance Perspectives Spring 1975.

Cr. 4to (9 × 7·3 ins.). 49 pp. illus. Orig. dec. wrapps.

Number 61 of *Dance Perspectives*. A selection of three articles: Neidish, Juliet, *Whose Habitation is in the Air*, Sticklor, Susan Reimer, *Angel with a Past*, and Au, Susan, *Prints of a Parisian Peri*.

DANCE PERSPECTIVES. DANCE PERSPECTIVES 1972 –1976. New York, Dance Perspectives.

Med. 8vo (9 × 6 ins.). Sizes vary somewhat.

See *Bibliography*, Part III, for listing of first 50 numbers. 51. *The Dance in the Philippines.* 52. *The Dance, The Dancer, and the Poem.* 53. *Sixty Years of Italian Dance Prints 1815–1875.* 54. *Entries from an Early Diary.* 55. *Three Essays in Dance Aesthetics.* 56. *Dance in Ghana.* 57. *In the Shadow of the Swastika.* 58. *The Beautiful Danger.* 59. *Shorashim.* 60. *Three Years with Charles Weidman.* 61. *All that Strange and Mysterious folk.* 62. *Les Fées des Forêts de St. Germain, Ballet de Cour 1625.* 63. *The Art of the Sleeve in Chinese Dance.* 64. *Prechistenka: The Isadora Duncan School in Russia.* 65. *Rural Felicity: Social Dances in 18th Century Connecticut.* 66. *A Chronicle of Dance in Baltimore 1780–1814. Dance Perspectives* ceased publication with issue number 66.

DANCING TIMES (THE). CANADA LAND OF PROMISE. London, The Dancing Times 1960.

Med. 8vo (9·1 × 6 ins.). 20 pp. illus. Orig. dec. green wrapps.

A brochure about the Canadian Ballet and opportunities for dancers in various Canadian Cities. Issued as a Special Supplement of *The Dancing Times.*

DANCING TIMES (THE). THE DANCING TIMES Oct. 1951 to Sept. 1962. London, The Dancing Times.

Med. 8vo (9·1 × 6·1 ins.). Orig. illus. wrapps.

A run from No. 492 (Oct. 1951) to No. 624 (Sept. 1962), 132 Nos. in all. P. J. S. Richardson editor.

DANCING TIMES (THE). THE DANCING TIMES Oct. 1962 to Sept. 1978. London, The Dancing Times.

Demy 4to (11·2 × 8·4 ins.). Orig. illus. wrapps.

The issue No. 625 represents the change in format from Med. 8vo (9·1 × 6·1 ins.) to Demy 4to (11·2 × 8·4 ins.). A. H. Franks was the editor until 1963; upon his death Mary Clarke took over his post. Numbers 625 to 816 a total of 191 numbers.

DANILOVA (ALEXANDRA). THE ART OF ALEXANDRA DANILOVA. Boston, Chrysalis 1959.

Cr. 8vo (8 × 5·2 ins.). 20 pp. Orig. illus. with white wrapps.

An issue of *Chrysalis* Vol. XII Nos. 1–4 with text by B. H. Haggin and Edwin Denby. See also *Bibliography*, Part II, Twysden and Part III, *Ballet Review*.

DANILOVA (ALEXANDRA). CHOURA. Biannual Journal of the Alexandra Danilova Fan Club.

Med. 4to (11 × 8·4 ins.). 10 pp. mimeograph with 1 photo. and 3 line drwgs. Orig. illus. wrapps.

Contents: Backstage with Alexandra Danilova by Rosario Hudson (p. 1); Picture Page (p. 6); This and That (p. 7). See also *Dance Magazine Portfolio* for Oct. 1977 (pp. 55–70), article by Anthony Fay.

LA DANZA. REVISTA ESPANOLA DEL MONDO DEL BALLET. No. 1. Junio 1972. Madrid.

Demy 4to (11·4 × 8·3 ins.). 42 pp. illus. Orig. dec. wrapps.

Marcos Menkes was Editor for the first two issues. He was succeeded by Luis F. Solar Garcia. To date there have been 13 or 14 numbers published, a few of them double numbers. The first seven issues contained a number of *Letters of Noverre* translated into Spanish. Number 12–13 announced the publication of these in book form.

DARLING (AMANDA). LOLA MONTEZ. New York, Stein & Day 1972.

Med. 8vo (9·1 × 6 ins.). 240 pp. with a frontis. Orig. two-tone cloth.

A pleasantly written addition to the long line of books about Lola Montez. See also *Bibliography*, Part II, Q (Charles G. Rosenberg), *Lola Montez* (p. 98).

DAUBERVAL (JEAN). LA FILLE MAL GARDÉE. Ballet, in two acts. Scenery and costumes by Osbert Lancaster. London, Royal Opera House, Matinee 24 June 1972.
Demy 8vo (9 × 5·2 ins.). 26 pp. n.n. illus. Orig. red wrapps.
A house programme with synopsis for *La Fille Mal Gardée* as performed by The Royal Ballet School with choreography by Frederick Ashton. For further study see Ivor Guest, *La Fille Mal Gardée* and Lanchbery & Guest, *The Scores of La Fille Mal Gardée*, *Bibliography*, Parts I & III.

DAUBENY (PETER). STAGE BY STAGE. London, John Murray [1952].
Demy 8vo (8·4 × 5·3 ins.). 162 pp. incl. Index. Many illus. Orig. rose cloth.
See Stage Four: International, for information on Rosario and Antonio, Pilar Lopez, Carmen Amaya, The Marquis de Cuevas Company and The Yugoslav Company.

DAVIDSON (GLADYS). MORE BALLET STORIES FOR YOUNG PEOPLE. London, Cassell. [1961].
Cr. 8vo (7·5 × 5·1 ins.). x + 205 pp. illus. Orig. red cloth.
Illustrated by Lotte Reiniger. See also *Bibliography*, Part III, Davidson, Gladys.

DAVIES (ELINOR). COPPÉLIA A Storïau Eraill O'r Falé. [England], Gwasg Gomer 1965.
Cr. 8vo (7 × 4·6 ins.). 105 pp. illus. with photogs. and drwgs. Orig. light blue cloth.
Stories of the following ballets with text in Welsh: *Coppelia, Le Lac des Cygnes, Y Brydferth Ynghwsg* (Sleeping Beauty), *Giselle, La Boutique Fantasque, Le Coq d'Or, Romeo and Juliet, Le Tricorne, Petrouchka* and *La Fille Mal Gardée*.

DAVIS (MIKE). PRINCESS BALLET BOOK No. 4. London, Fleetway Publications.
Med. 8vo (9·5 × 6·7 ins.). 128 pp. Profusely illus. Orig. dec. boards.
See *Bibliography*, Part III, for Book I.

DAVIS (MIKE).   PRINCESS BALLET BOOK No. 5. [London, Fleetway Publications Ltd. 1964].
   Cr. 4to (10·7 × 7·7 ins.). pp. n.n. illus. in colour and black and white. Orig. dec. boards.
   The Annual for 1964.

DAVIS (MIKE).   PRINCESS TINA BALLET BOOK No. 6. Text: H. Shirley Long. London, IPC Magazines 1973.
   Roy. 4to (11·6 × 9·1 ins.). 69 pp. illus. in colour. Orig. dec. boards.
   The Annual for 1973.

DAVIS (MIKE).   PRINCESS TINA BALLET BOOK No. 7. Text: Robin May. London, IPC Magazines Ltd. 1974.
   Roy. 4to (11·6 × 9·1 ins.). 70 pp. illus. in colour. Orig. dec. boards.
   The Annual for 1974.

DAVIS (JESSE).   PRINCESS TINA BALLET BOOK No. 8. Text: Robin May. London, IPC Magazines Ltd. 1975.
   Roy. 4to (11·6 × 9·1 ins.). 71 pp. illus. in colour. Orig. dec. boards.
   The Annual for 1975.

DAVIS (JESSE).   PRINCESS TINA BALLET BOOK No. 9. Text: Robin May. London, IPC Magazines Ltd. 1976.
   Roy. 4to (11·6 × 9·1 ins.). 71 pp. illus. in colour. Orig. dec. boards.
   The Annual for 1976 and the final one, I believe.

DEAKIN (IRVING).   THE CRITICISM OF BALLET. Boston, Chrysalis 1956.
   Demy 8vo (8·1 × 5·2 ins.). 19 pp. with 3 illus. Orig. illus. white wrapps.
   This article in Vol. IX Nos. 3, 4 is excerpted from *At the Ballet*.

DEAKIN (IRVING).   TO THE BALLET. An Introduction to the Liveliest of the Arts. With a Foreword by John Van Druten. George Allen & Unwin Ltd. [1936].
   Cr. 8vo (7·6 × 5 ins.). 176 pp. incl. Index. with 8 plates incl. the frontis. Orig. cloth with labels.

The English edition. The plates differ from the American in that they are slightly larger, and printed on one side of the paper only; also the Diaghilev plate has been replaced by one of Irving Deakin with Toumanova and Danilova. See *Bibliography*, Part I, for the first edition.

DE GAMEZ (TANA). ALICIA ALONSO. At Home and Abroad. With an Appreciation of the Artist by Arnold L. Haskell. New York, The Citadel Press. [1971].

Demy 8vo (10·7 × 8·3 ins.). 189 pp. + (ii) with many illus. Orig. rose cloth.

This is primarily a book of photographs. For biographical details see Chujoy & Manchester, *The Dance Encyclopedia*, and for full documentation on her Ballet Theatre roles see Cohen & Pischl, *The American Ballet Theatre* 1940–1960. Also *Dance Magazine Portfolio* Aug. 1971, Maria Horosko, *Alicia Alonso*.

DEGEN (A.) & STUPNIKOV (I.). MASTERA TANTSA. Materali k Istorii Leningradskogo Baleta 1917–1973. Izdatelstvo 'Muzika' Leningradskoe Otdelenie 1974.

F'Cap 8vo (6·4 × 4·1 ins.). 246 + (ii) illus. Orig. dec. boards with fabric spine.

A Dictionary of soloists, balletmasters, pedagogues and orchestra conductors appearing with the Leningrad Ballet between 1917 and 1973. Biographical material (books and articles) is also listed under each entry when available, and there is a fine listing of authors who have written about the Leningrad Ballet and its artists (pp. 226–242).

DE LAJARTE (THÉODORE). BIBLIOTHÈQUE MUSICALE DU THÉÂTRE DE L'OPÉRA. Catalogue historique, chronologique, anecdotique. Hildesheim, Georg Olms. 1969.

Demy 8vo (8·3 × 5·6 ins.). 2 vols. illus. with engravings by Le Rat. 374 pp. (1). 350 pp. (2). Orig. full rose cloth.

An excellent reprint of a most valuable catalogue of the Paris Opera from *Pomone* 1671 to *Sylvia* 1876. Complete repertory of this institution which has occupied 13 theatres and has had almost as many titles (Académie Royale, Académie Impériale, Académie Nationale etc.) in its unbroken line of performances. See *Bibliography*, Part I, De Lajarte, Théodore, for the first edition published in 1878.

DELARUE (ALLISON). FANNY ELSSLER IN AMERICA. With an Introduction and Notes by Allison Delarue. New York, Dance Horizons 1976.

Med. 8vo (9·5 × 8·2 ins.). (viii) + 219 pp. illus. Orig. dec. red cloth.

Contents: Historical Background to America's Elsslermania. I. *Memoir of Fanny Elssler.* 2. Libretto for *La Tarantule.* 3. *No Slur, Else-Slur.* A Dancing Poem. 4. *La Déesse an Elssler-atic Romance.* 5. *A Short and Correct Sketch of the Life of Mad'lle. Fanny Elssler.* 6. *The Letters and Journal of Fanny Elssler.* 7. *Sad Tale of the Courtship of Chevalier Slyfox-Wikof.* The reissuing of these seven important pamphlets as a collection in a very attractive binding is most welcome indeed; however the use of a grey background to the text is a serious mistake.

DEMENŸ (G.) & SANDOZ (A.). DANSES GYMNASTIQUES. Composées pour les établissements d'enseignment primaire et secondaire de Jeunes Filles. Avec dessins de M. Demenÿ. Paris, Librairie Vuibert 1920.

F'cap 8vo (6·7 × 4·3 ins.). (iii) + 122 pp. illus. with line drwgs. and mus. ex. Orig. ½ shagreen.

Contents: Indications générales des termes et notations. II. Séries de danses gymnastiques avec musique.

DE MILLE (AGNES). SPEAK TO ME, DANCE WITH ME. Boston, Little Brown & Co. [1973].

Demy 8vo (8·1 × 5·2 ins.). 345 pp. incl. Index. Many illus. in halftone. Orig. cloth.

Further autobiographical writings by Agnes de Mille. See also *Bibliography*, Parts I and III, De Mille.

DE VALOIS (NINETTE DE). STEP BY STEP. The Formation of an establishment. London, W. H. Allen 1977.

Demy 8vo (8·3 × 5·1 ins.). 204 pp. illus. Orig. maroon cloth.

Interesting portions of the book are Two Studies: John Cranko and Kenneth Macmillan, also that concerning the foundation of The Turkish State Ballet. For the latter see also And, Metin, *Turkish Dancing.*

DE VERE BEAUCLERK (HELEN). THE TALE OF IGOR. Adapted from the old Russian Legend with six illustrations

designed and hand-coloured by Michel Sevier. London, C. W. Beaumont 1918.
  Demy 8vo (8·6 × 5·6 ins.). 23 pp. illus. Orig. buckram spine and boards with label.
  One of 100 copies on antique paper signed by Michel Sevier. Copy No. 30.

DEVI (RAGINI). DANCE DIALECTS OF INDIA. Printed in India, Vikas Publications [1972].
  Demy 4to (10·6 × 8·4 ins.). 227 pp. incl. Appendices and a bibliography. Many illus. some in colour. Orig. cloth.
  An excellent study with very expressive, strong hand symbols, and excellent photographs of Indrani Rahman, the daughter of Ragini Devi. See also *Bibliography*, Part II, Ragini, Sri, *Nritanjali*.

DICKENS (CHARLES). MEMOIRS OF JOSEPH GRIMALDI. With illustrations by George Cruikshank. Edited by Richard Findlater, with new notes and Introduction. London, Macgibbon & Kee. [1968].
  Demy 8vo (8·3 × 5·3 ins.). 311 pp. incl. Index. With frontis. in colour and 9 other illus. Orig. boards.
  First published in 1838 as *Memoirs of Joseph Grimaldi*, edited by 'Boz'.

DJAVRISHVILI (D. D.). GRUZINSKIE NARODNIE TANTSI. II Izdanie. Tbilisi, Izdatelstvo 'Ganatleba' 1975.
  Demy 8vo (8·3 × 6·2 ins.). 278 + (ii) pp. illus. with drwgs., diags., and music. Orig. dec. boards with fabric spine.
  Georgian Folk Dances published at Tiflis. Six dances amply described, with arm movements, steps, floor patterns, music and costume.

DOBBS (BRIAN). DRURY LANE. Three Centuries of the Royal Theatre Royal 1663–1971. London, Cassell. [1972].
  Med. 8vo (9 × 6·4 ins.). xiv + 226 pp. incl. Index. Illus. Orig. turquoise cloth.
  See Noverre's *The Chinese Festival* (pp. 105–106).

DOBROVOLSKAYA (G.). TANETS PANTOMIMA BALET. Iskusstvo Leningradskoe Otdelenie 1975.
  Cr. 8vo (7·7 × 5·4 ins.). 123 + (iv) pp. with 72 illus. Orig. dec. black boards with fabric spine.

A book in Russian on Dance Pantomime and Ballet. The author has also written a short biography on Vladlen Semenov, see Chistyakova, *Leningradskii Balet Segodnya* Part 2.

DOLIN (ANTON). MARKOVA. Her Life and Art. London, White Lion Publishers. 1973.

Demy 8vo (8·4 × 5·2 ins.). 294 pp. incl. Index. Cloth.

A republication of the W. H. Allen 1953 edition. See also *Bibliography*, Parts I and III, Dolin, Anton.

DOLIN (ANTON). OLGA SPESSIVTZEVA. The Sleeping Ballerina. With a Foreword by Dame Marie Rambert. London, Dance Books Ltd. [1974].

Demy 8vo (8·2 × 5·3 ins.). xv + 130 pp. incl. Index. Illus. Orig. brown cloth.

A republication of the Frederick Muller edition of 1966. See also *Bibliography*, Part II, Shaikevitch, André, *Olga Spessivtzeva* and Vaillat, Léandre, *Olga Spessivtzeva Ballerine*.

DOLMETSCH (ARNOLD). THE INTERPRETATION OF THE MUSIC OF THE XVIIth and XVIIIth CENTURIES. London, Novello & Co.

Demy 8vo (8·3 × 5·1 ins.). 493 pp. incl. Index and mus. notation. Orig. blue cloth.

See (pp. 44–52), The Tempo of Dance Movements. See also *Bibliography*, Part I, Dolmetsch, Mabel.

DORCY (JEAN). THE MIME. And essays by Etienne Decroux, Jean Louis Barrault and Marcel Marceau. London, White Lion Publishers. 1975.

Cr. 8vo (7·6 × 5 ins.). xxv + 116 pp. illus. Orig. purple cloth.

See also *Bibliography*, Part I, Dorcy, *J'Aime la Mime*.

DORRIS (GEORGE). THE LEGACY OF HUROK. Brooklyn, New York, Ballet Review 1975–1976.

Med. 8vo (9 × 6 ins.). pp. 78–88. Orig. dec. wrapps.

An article in *Ballet Review* Vol. 5 No. 1 1975–76. The author feels that Hurok's fostering of the full-evening's ballet of the great classics has been detrimental to smaller companies. In some instances this is possibly so, but in the main it has strengthened ballet all over the world. How long could Opera have survived with continual performances of *Cavalleria Rusticana* and *Pagliacci* or similar pairings? See also *Bibliography*, Part III, Hurok, Sol, *Impressario*.

DOUGHTY (JOHN CARR). AN EXHIBITION OF COSTUME AND SET DESIGNS CHIEFLY FOR THE DIAGHILEV'S BALLETS, DRAWN FROM THE COLLECTION OF JOHN CARR DOUGHTY. London, Arts Council 1967.
(9·4 × 4·7 ins.). 19 pp. incl. 6 plates. Orig. dec. wrapps.
A catalogue. See also Parke Bernet and Sotheby's, *Bibliography*, Part III.

DRABECA (MARIA). TAŃCE HISTORYCZNE. Zeszyt I. Kurant, Menuet, Sarabanda. Warszawa, Centralna Poradnia Amatorskiego Ruchu Artystycznego 1966.
Med. 8vo (9·2 × 6·3 ins.). 281 pp. illus. with line drwgs. mus. ex. and Laban Kinetograms. Orig. dec. wrapps.
Historical Dances with examples taken from Kellom-Tomlinson, Feuillet, Rameau, and Gottfried Taubert. Also interleaved are 10 plates of Laban Kinetograms: *Kuranta* by G. Reber, *Menueta* by I. Danker, *Sarabandy* by I. Bartenieff. There is a good bibliography (pp. 275–280).

DRABECA (MARIA). TAŃCE HISTORYCZNE. Zeszyt 2. Pawana, Galiarda, Wolta. Warszawa, Centralna Poradnia Amatorskiego Ruchu Artystycznego 1968.
Med. 8vo (9·2 × 6·3 ins.). 226 pp. illus. with line drwgs. and mus. ex. Orig. illus. wraps.
Vol. 2 of Historical Dances. The Laban Kinetograms are now in a separate booklet. The bibliography with some exceptions is the same as in Vol. 1. Unknown to me were: Felippo degli Alessandri *Discorso sopra il Balle*, Terni 1620. Livio Lupi da Caravaggio, *Mutanze di Gagliarda, Tordiglioni, Passi e Mezzo, Canari e Passeggi* – Palermo 1600. Prospero Lutti, *Opera Bellissima nella quale si Contengono molte Partite et Passeggi di Gagliarda*, Perugia 1589.

DRABECA (MARIA). TAŃCE HISTORYCZNE. Zeszyt 2 Pawana, Galiarda, Wolta Kinetogramy. Warszawa, Centralna Poradnia Amatorskiego Ruchu Artystycznego 1968.
Med. 8vo (9·2 × 6·3 ins.). 26 pp. of Kinetography. Orig. white wrapps.

Examples in Labanotation from: T. Arbeau, *Orchesografie*, P. Lutti, *Opera Bellissima* and Cesare Negri, *Nuove Inventioni di Balli*.

DRABECA (MARIA). TAŃCE HISTORYCZNE. Basse Danse. Ballo. Branle. Zeszyt 3. Warszawa, Centralny Ośrodek Metodyki Upowszechniania Kultury 1971.
Med. 8vo (9·2 × 6·3 ins.). 194 pp. illus. with line drwgs. and diags. Orig. illus. wrapps.

Under *Basses Danses* the mss of the House of Burgundy (see Closson, *Bibliography*, Part I), Antoniuza de Areny and Thoinot Arbeau are consulted. Under *Balli*, Domenica z Biacenzy and Gugielmo Ebreo. Under *Branles*, Thoinot Arbeau and Franziska de Lauze. There is also a bibliografia.

DRABECA (MARIA). TAŃCE HISTORYCZNE. Muzyka Kinetogramy Zeszyt III. Warszawa, Centralny Ośrodek Metodyki Upowszechniania Kultury 1971.
Med. 8vo (9·2 × 6·3 ins.). 73 pp. of Kinetography and mus. ex. Orig. illus. white wrapps.

Examples in Labanotation of *Basses Danses, Balli,* and *Branles*.

DROMGOOLE (NICHOLAS). SIBLEY AND DOWELL. Photographs by Leslie Spatt. London, Collins 1976.
Demy 4to (10·7 × 8·1 ins.). 223 pp. illus. Orig. rose cloth.

An important study of these artists. See also Harris, Dale, *Antoinette Sibley* and Rosen, Lillie, *Anthony Dowell*, for separate short biographies. See also *The Dancing Times* of Jan. 1977 for review of the book. Dromgoole is dance critic for the *Sunday Telegraph*.

DUKE (VERNON). LISTEN HERE. A Critical Essay on Music Depreciation. New York, Ivan Oblensky. [1963].
Demy 8vo (8·3 × 5·4 ins.). (v) + 406 pp. incl. Index. Orig. red cloth.

See Chapter V. The Deification of Stravinsky and IX. Opera and Ballet U.S. Style. See also *Bibliography*, Part III, Duke, Vernon, *Passport to Paris*.

DUNCAN (ISADORA). THE ART OF THE DANCE. ISADORA DUNCAN. Edited with an Introduction by Sheldon Cheney. New York, Theatre Arts MCMXXVIII.

Cr. 4to (10·4 × 7·5 ins.). (x) + 147 pp. illus. with drwgs. and photogs. Orig. buckram spine and boards.
The original, limited edition. See *Bibliography*, Part III, Duncan, Isadora, *The Art of the Dance*, for the second edition and comment.

DUNN (BERYL). DANCE. Therapy for Dancers. Introduction by Dame Margot Fonteyn. Foreword by H. Jackson Burrows. London, Heinemann Health Books. [1974].
Med. 8vo (9·6 × 6 ins.). xiii + 98 pp. incl. index. Illus. Orig. boards.
See also Como, William and Sparger, Celia, *Bibliography* III.

DUNTON (JAMES). THE TRUTH ABOUT NIJINSKY. New York, Dance Magazine Oct. 1928.
Roy. 4to (12·6 × 9·4 ins.). pp. 18, 19, 68 illus. Orig. dec. wrapps. (Doris Niles).
An article in the Oct. 1928 issue of *Dance Magazine*, with the second instalment appearing in the Nov. issue. Not listed in Belknap, *Guide to Dance Periodicals*.

DUNTON (JAMES). THE TRUTH ABOUT NIJINSKY. New York, Dance Magazine Nov. 1928.
Roy 4to (12·6 × 9·4 ins.). pp. 32, 33, 64 illus. Orig. dec. wrapps. (Evelyn Law).
Part II, the final article on *The Truth about Nijinsky*. See *Bibliography*, Part II, Reiss, Françoise, *Nijinsky ou la Grace* (pp. 113–116), for an important listing of books and articles about Vaslav Nijinsky.

EGLEVSKY (ANDRÉ) & GREGORY (JOHN). NICOLAS LEGAT. Heritage of a Ballet Master. [Brooklyn, New York]. Dance Horizons 1977.
Demy 4to (11 × 8·4 ins.). ix + 114 pp. illus. Orig. blue cloth.
Divided in two parts: I. Nicolas Legat 1869–1937; II. Seven Classes by Nicolas Legat. A very nice book, but regarding the lessons the same sparcity of instruction prevails as in Legat's *Ten Variegated Class Lessons in Operatic Dancing*. (Perhaps Ana Roje would be the one to achieve a successful manual of Legat's method.) See also Leslie, Serge *Seven Leagues of a Dancer*, Legat (pp. 134, 164, 165, 166, 173), *Bibliography* III.

EHM-SCHULZ (ROSEMARIE) & PETERMANN (DR. KURT). GRUNDLAGEN DER STRUKTUR UND FORMANALYSE DES VOLKSTANZES. IFMC 1976.
Demy 8vo (8·2 × 5·5 ins.). 23 pp. illus. with symbols. Orig. dec. wrapps.
A study of the foundation and structure of Folk Dances by means of symbols. See also Petermann, Kurt.

ELYASH (NIKOLAI). AVDOTIYA ISTOMINA. Izdatelstvo Iskusstvo, Leningradskoe Otdelenie 1971.
F'cap 8vo (5·4 × 4 ins.). 187 + (iv) pp. illus. Orig. white cloth.
The first biography, I believe, on Avdotiya Istomina, one of Russia's foremost dancers during the second quarter of the 19th century. A pupil of Didelot, her important ballets were *Zephyr and Flora, Prisoner of the Caucasus* and *Apollon and Mysis*. See also *Bibliography*, Part I, Beaumont, *History of Ballet in Russia*. Part III, Swift, *A Loftier Flight* and almost any Russian work on the ballet which includes the 19th century.

ELYASH (NIKOLAI). PUSHKIN I BALETNII TEATR. Moskva, Izdatelstvo Iskusstvo 1970.
Cr. 8vo (7·6 × 5 ins.). 343 + (i) pp. with many illus. Orig. white cloth.
Pushkin and the Ballet Theatre. See also Slonimsky, Yuri – *Baletnie Stroki Pushkina* and Beaumont, Cyril W., *Pushkin and his Influence on Russian Ballet*. *Bibliography*, Part III, lists other works by Elyash.

ELYASH (NIKOLAI). ZRITELU O BALETE. Izdatelstvo 'Znanie' Moskva 1963.
Demy 8vo (8·3 × 5·4 ins.). 47 + (i) pp. Orig. dec. wrapps.
Zritelu o Balete (Spectator at the Ballet). Contents: V Tantse, Dusha Naroda (Soul of the People); Slojnii Teatraliyi Janr (Complex Theatrical Style); Sovetskaya Khoregrafiya – Iskusstvo Mnogonashionalnoe (Choreographic Counsel – Art of Many nationalities).

EMMANUEL (MAURICE). THE ANTIQUE GREEK DANCE, After Sculptured and Painted Figures. Translated by Harriet Beauly. London, John Lane Co. 1927.
Med. 8vo (9·6 × 6·4 ins.). xxvii + 304 pp. with 5 plates and over 600 line drwgs. Orig. grey cloth.

The second English edition. See *Bibliography*, Part I, Emmanuel, for the first French and American editions.

ENKELMANN (S.). BALLETT. Text René Drommert. Hamburg, Verlag Hans Hoeppner. [1962].
Roy. 4to (14·2 × 10·4 ins.). (iv) + 32 plates + (ii) pp. Orig. dec. boards.
An album of photographs. See also *Bibliography*, Parts I and III, Enkelmann, S.

ENTERS (ANGNA). PRESS MATERIAL. Management, Metropolitan Musical Bureau, Inc. New York 1938.
Imp. 4to (14·3 × 10·7 ins.). 24 pp. illus. Orig. dec. wrapps.
Printed reproductions of tour notices for 1937–1938. See also *Bibliography*, Part III, Enters, Angna.

EPSTEIN (ALVIN). THE MIME THEATRE OF ETIENNE DECROUX. Boston, Chrysalis 1949.
Cr. 8vo (8 × 5 ins.). 14 pp. with 2 photogs. and 3 line drwgs. Orig. dec. white wrapps.
An issue of *Chrysalis* for 1949, Vol. II Nos. 11–12. The booklet bears a short foreword by Decroux.

EPSTEIN (ALVIN). THE MIME THEATRE OF ETIENNE DECROUX. Boston, Chrysalis 1958.
Cr. 8vo (8 × 5·2 ins.). 16 pp. with 1 illus. in text. Orig. dec. white wrapps.
An issue of *Chrysalis* Vol. XI Nos. 1–2. This seems to be a textual reprint of the 1949 edition with only one photograph and without the line drawings.

ERNST (EARLE). THE KABUKI THEATRE. New York, Grove Press [1956].
Roy. 8to (10·6 × 6·4 ins.). xxiii + 296 pp. with 58 half-tone illus. Orig. dec. wrapps.
See also *Bibliography*, Part I, Mishima, Y. Part II Miyake, S. Part III Toita, Y and Yoshida, C.

ESCUDERO (ROSARIO). METODO DE CASTAÑUELAS. Primera Edicion. San Sebastian 1959.
Demy 8vo (8·2 × 5·4 ins.). 29 + (i) pp. illus. with line drwgs. Orig. dec. wrapps.

A simple but effective method for noting elementary castanet rhythms. See also *Bibliography*, Part I, Florencio, *Crotalogia* and Barbieri, *Las Castañuelas*. Part II, Wright, *Notations of Ten Castanet Solos* and Part III Matteo, *Woods that Dance*.

EVANS (EDWIN). THE MARGIN OF MUSIC. London, Oxford University Press 1924.

Cr. 8vo (7·6 × 5·4 ins.). 71 pp. Orig. marbled boards with fabric spine.

See *The Choreographic Age* (pp. 39–43). See also *Bibliography*, Part I, Evans, Edwin.

EVANS (EDWIN). STRAVINSKY. The Fire-Bird and Petrushka. London, Oxford University Press. [1945].

F'cap 8vo (6·4 × 4 ins.). 44 pp. illus. with mus. ex. Orig. printed wrapps.

See also Beaumont, *Petrushka in London*.

FAIER (YURI). YURI FAIER o Sebe o Muzike o Balete. Moskva 1970. Vsesouznoe Izdatelstvo Sovetskii Kompozitor.

F'cap 8vo (6·5 × 5 ins.). 571 pp. + (iv) illus. Orig. grey cloth.

Yuri Faier, About Myself, About Music, About Ballet. Faier, perhaps the best known conductor of the Bolshoi Ballet, has made many visits to the West. The photographs are interesting, particularly those following p. 320: Tikhomirov, Margarita Kandaurova, Viktor Smoltsov, Viktorina Kriger, Mariya Reisen, Anastasiya Abramova, and Lubov Bank.

FAIZIE (A.). SHURALE. Balet v 3-k Deistviyak. Moskva 1955.

F'cap 4to (8·3 × 6·6 ins.). Illus. with frontis. photo and drwgs. Orig. dec. wrapps.

The libretto of this ballet with choreography by Leonid Yacobson. Chujoy's *Encyclopedia* gives the date of June 28, 1950 as the first performance at the Kirov but Slonimsky's *Vse o Balete* mentions an earlier one. Dudinskaya (*Suimbike*) and Sergeyev (*Ali-Batyr*) were featured in the 1950 performance.

FAUST (EDWARD). A TREATISE ON THE PRINCIPLES AND EVOLUTION OF THE PORT DE BRAS. Butler University 1972.

Demy 4to (11 × 8·4 ins.). Mimeograph of 112 pp. illus. Bibliography.

A thesis for a dance research project presented to the faculty of Jordan College of Music, Butler University. A considerable number of excellent source materials are presented, but the evolution needs further clarification.

FEUILLET (RAOUL AUGER). CHOREGRAPHIE OU L'ART DE DÉCRIRE LA DANSE. A Facsimile of the 1700 Paris Edition. New York, Broude Brothers. [1968].

Demy 4to (11·3 × 7·7 ins.). (viii) + 106 pp. illus. by Caracters, Figures et Signes Demonstratifs. Orig. cream buckram.

Bound up with *Choregraphie* are: *Recueil de Danses* composées par M. Feuillet (84 pp.), and *Recueil de Danses* composées par M. Pecourt (72 pp.). See *Bibliography*, Part I, where an edition of (84 pp.) is described. To my knowledge these books are the finest and clearest facsimiles of Feuillet that exist. They are complete with reproductions of the original title pages as well as the modern.

FISHER (HUGH). ALICIA MARKOVA. London, Black. [1954].

Cr. 4to (10 × 7·4 ins.). 32 pp. with 39 illus. Orig. grey cloth.

The first edition. See *Bibliography*, Part III, for the second edition. Text and illustrations differ in both editions.

FISHER (HUGH). MARGOT FONTEYN. London, Adam & Charles Black. 1957.

Cr. 4to (10 × 7·4 ins.). 32 pp. illus. Orig. grey cloth.

This is the second edition, revised by Cyril Swinson in 1957. See *Bibliography*, Parts I & III, Fisher, for other editions.

FISHER (HUGH). THE STORY OF THE ROYAL BALLET. Revised Edition with 40 illustrations. London, Adam & Charles Black. [1959].

Demy 8vo (8 × 5·4 ins.). 81 pp. + (ii) with Index. Illus. Orig. yellow cloth.

First published in 1954 as *The Story of the Sadler's Wells Ballet*, reprinted with corrections in 1956, revised edition as *The Story of The Royal Ballet* in 1959. See also Fisher, *Bibliography*, Parts I and III.

FLEET (SIMON). SOPHIE FEDOROVITCH. A Biographical Sketch. Privately printed by the Grovely Press, Wilton, nr Salisbury 1955.

Cr. 8vo (7·4 × 4·6 ins.). 20 pp. Orig. dec. wrapps.

This biographical sketch was written as an Introduction to the book *Sophie Fedorovitch*, Tributes and Attributes, but did not reach the publisher in time. See *Bibliography*, Part I, Fleet, Simon.

FLETCHER (IFAN K.). BIBLIOGRAPHICAL DESCRIPTIONS OF FORTY RARE DANCE BOOKS. Relating to the Art of Dancing. In the collection of P. J. S. Richardson. London, Dance Books Ltd. 1977.

Med. 8vo (9·4 × 6·5 ins.). 23 pp. illus. Orig. printed green wrapps.

A reprint by Dance Books Ltd. of this very carefully and competently described list first published by *The Dancing Times* in 1954.

FLETCHER (IFAN K.). BOOKS RELATING TO THE DIAGHILEV BALLET. London, The Observer 1954.

Demy 4to (11 × 8·4 ins.). pp. 68–70. Orig. dec. wrapps.

A check list of material, principally books relating to The Diaghilev Ballet, in both the Edinburgh and Forbes House catalogues. See Buckle, Richard, *The Diaghilev Exhibition, Bibliography* III.

FLETCHER (IFAN K.). DANCE. Rare Books, Prints Autograph Letters Music Programmes and a Statuette. Catalogue 3. London, Ifan Kyrle Fletcher, 26 Old Bond Street.

Demy 8vo (8·3 × 5·4 ins.). 16 pp. Orig. illus. wrapps.

A very early catalogue issued when Fletcher was at Old Bond Street. The front cover bears a reproduction of the statuette of Flora Fabbri as *La Sylphide* by J. A. Fauginet.

FLEURY (COMTE). JEAN-ETIENNE DESPRÉAUX. Chansonnier Maître des ballets de la Cour sous Louis XVI, Maître à danser de Marie-Louise. Paris, Revue de la France Moderne Juin 1900.

Med. 8vo (9 × 6 ins.). pp. 411–432. Orig. printed wrapps.

An article. See also *Bibliography*, Part I, Despréaux, Jean-Etienne for other sources of information.

FOKINE (MICHEL). IS MODERNISM MODERN? New York, Dance Magazine Mar. 1931.

Roy. 4to (12·4 × 9·4 ins.). pp. 21, 49, 50, 51 with 2 illus. Orig. dec. wrapps. (Franz Felix).
An illustrated article in the March 1931 issue of *Dance Magazine*.

FOKINE (MICHEL). LIFAR – HIS BOOK AND THEORIES. A Reply by Michel Fokine. London, The Dancing Times Aug. 1938.
Med. 8vo (9·1 × 6 ins.). pp. 518–520. Orig. dec. wrapps.
An article replying to some of the statements made by Lifar in his book, *La Danse: Les Grands Courants de la Danse Académique*. A second thorough review by Edouard Zamba, on this book, is also in this issue (pp. 532–535).

FOKINE (MICHEL). MICHEL FOKINE DANCE STUDIOS. Four Riverside Drive, New York City.
Med. 8vo (9 × 6 ins.). 12 pp. illus. Orig. dec. wrapps.
An illustrated brochure concerning Fokine's school in the mid 1920's. Doris Niles is in a group photograph (page 5).

FONTEYN (MARGOT). MARGOT FONTEYN. Autobiography. London, W. H. Allen 1975.
Demy 8vo (8·3 × 5·2 ins.). 284 pp. illus. Orig. cloth.
See Peter Williams in the November 1975, *Dance and Dancers*, for a review.

FONTEYN (MARGOT). Autobiography. New York, Alfred A. Knopf 1976.
Med. 8vo (9·2 × 6·1 ins.). xii + 266 + ix pp. illus. with 80 pp. of photographs. Orig. black cloth.
The American edition. See also *Bibliography*, Part II, Money, Keith and *Dance Magazine Portfolio*, July 1973.

FOX (GRACE) & MERRILL (KATHLEEN GRUPPE). FOLK DANCING IN HIGH SCHOOL AND COLLEGE. Drawings by Charlotte St. John.
Demy 4to (11 × 8·3 ins.). ix + 89 pp. illus. with drwgs. and mus. airs. Orig. black cloth.
Dances from Russia, England, Sweden, Ireland, Bohemia, Lithuania, Moravia, Finland, Latvia, and Switzerland, concluding with a section of American Square Dances.

FRANGINI (GUALTIERO). LE CREATURE DI PRO-METEO. Firenze, XIX Maggio Musicale Fiorentino 1956.

Cr. 4to (10·5 × 7·3 ins.). 10 pp. illus. Orig. printed wrapps.

An article in *Balletti* issued for the XIX Maggio Musicale Fiorentino. The choreography is by Aurel Milloss and there is, besides the list of artists, a synopsis in Italian, French, English and German. Added are 3 photographs of scenes from the ballet. The issue also contains articles by Frangini on *Le Quattro Stagioni*, and *La Leggenda di Giuseppe*, complete with synopses. All choreography by Aurel Milloss.

FREEDLY (GEORGE) & REEVES (JOHN A.). A HISTORY OF THE THEATRE. With hundreds of Illustrations from Photographs, Playbills, Contemporary Prints etc. New York, Crown Publishers 1941.

Med. 8vo (9·3 × 6·3 ins.). xvi + 688 pp. incl. Index. Orig. red cloth.

See also *Bibliography*, Part I, Freedly, George.

FRIDE (V.). E. P. EDUARDOVA. Kotkritif chetvertago uchebnago goda eya baletnoe shkola. Jar Ptitsa 1923.

Roy. 4to (12·2 × 9·4 ins.). pp. 26–32 with 1 illus. Orig. dec. wrapps.

An article in *Jar Ptitsa* (Firebird) about Eugenia Platonowa Eduardova. For a short resumé of her career see either Chujoy, Friedrichs or Wilson. See also *Bibliography*, Part I, Grunenberg, *Figuren*, for a fine drawing of her.

FROSTICK (MICHAEL) & SWINSON (CYRIL). MARGOT FONTEYN IN AUSTRALIA. London, J. C. Williamson Theatres and James Laurie & Associates. 1957.

Demy 4to (11·4 × 9·2 ins.). 36 pp. illus. Orig. dec. wrapps.

A souvenir booklet about Fonteyn's 1957 visit to Australia and the Borovansky Ballet, with her colleagues Michael Somes, Rowena Jackson and Brian Ashridge.

FUCHS (THEODORE). STAGE LIGHTING. London, George Allen & Unwin Ltd. 1929.

Med. 8vo (9·2 × 6 ins.). viii + 500 pp. illus. Orig. blue cloth.

Basically a technical book. Chapter II concerns the History of Stage Lighting.

FÜHMENN (FRANZ). GALINA ULANOVA. Berlin, Henschelverlag 1961.

Demy 8vo (8·3 × 5·5 ins.). 82 pp. illus. Orig. boards with fabric spine.

See also *Bibliography*, Part II, Soviet Ballet and Part III, Lvov-Anokhin, B. and Ulanova, Galina.

FULLER (LOIE). FIFTEEN YEARS OF A DANCER'S LIFE. With an Introduction by Anatole France. New York, Dance Horizons.

Cr. 8vo (6·7 × 5·2 ins.). xiii + 288 pp. with 16 illus. Orig. printed wrapps.

A republication of the 1913 edition. See also *Bibliography*, Part I, Fuller, Loie.

FÜLÖP-MILLER (RENÉ) & GREGOR (JOSEPH). THE RUSSIAN THEATRE. Its Character and History. Translated by Paul England. London, George G. Harrap. 1930.

Roy. 4to (12·2 × 9·1 ins.). 136 pp. + 405 numbered plates. Orig. dec. red buckram.

The work contains 48 illustrations in colour and 557 in half-tone. The section on the *Ballet* is relatively short (pp. 106–111), but the illustrations are profuse: Léon Bakst (Nos. 82–104); Russian Ballet Performers (Nos. 105–132); Bakst's Successors (Nos. 133–182). Edition limited to 650 copies for England and 350 for U.S.A. See also Gregor, Joseph.

GABOVICH (MIKHAIL). MIKHAIL GABOVICH. Stati vospominaniya o M. M. Gaboviche. Moskva, Iskusstvo 1977.

Demy 8vo (8·4 × 6·4 ins.). 237 + (ii) pp. illus. Orig. white cloth.

A collection of short articles by Gabovich and a series of reminiscences about Gabovich by Slonimsky, Ulanova, Messerer, Liepa and others. See also *Bibliography*, Part II Soviet Ballet, *Mikhail Markovich Gabovich* and Roslavleva, *Era of the Russian Ballet*.

GABRIEL (JOHN). BALLET SCHOOL. [London], Faber & Faber [1947].

Cr. 4to (10·6 × 8·1 ins.). 128 pp. profusely illus. with photogs. Orig. black cloth.

The first English edition which was later published in New York by Pitman in 1951. See *Bibliography*, Part I, Gabriel, John for comment.

GALMES (ANTONIO). MALLORCAN FOLK DANCES. Palma, Galerias Costa 1953.
F'cap 8vo (6·5 × 4·6 ins.). 16 pp. with illus. and mus. ex. Orig. dec. wrapps.
The English version by Beltram Galbraith.

GARFIAS (ROBERT). GAGAKU. The Music and Dances of the Japanese Imperial Household. Edited and with an Introduction by Lincoln Kirstein. New York, Theatre Arts Books 1959.
(11 × 6·7 ins.). 40 pp. illus. Orig. dec. wrapps.
See also *Bibliography* III, Togi, Masataro.

GARLING (JEAN). AUSTRALIAN NOTES ON THE BALLET. Studies by Daryl Lindsay and William Constable. Sydney, The Legend Press.
Demy 8vo (7 × 8·3 ins.). 40 pp. illus. in colour and black and white. Orig. green and black cloth.
See also *Bibliography*, Part III, Lindsay, Daryl and Part IV, Hall, Hugh P.

GELTSER (YEKATERINA). THE WAY OF A BALLERINA. Moscow, Soviet Travel 1934.
Demy 4to (11·2 × 8·3 ins.). pp. 53–56 illus. Orig. dec. wrapps.
An article in *Soviet Travel*, Special Theatre No. 3. See also O. Martynova's book *Yekaterina Geltser* and *Comoedia Illustré* No. 18, June 15, 1910. Also Yuri Bakhrushin, Balet Bolshogo in *Bolshoi Teatr* (pp. 192–199).

GEORGE (WALDEMAR). MICHEL LARIONOV. Oeuvres Anciennes et Récentes. Du 25 Mai au 13 Juin 1956. Paris, Galerie de l'institut.
Demy 8vo (8·5 × 6·1 ins.). 8 pp. + 8 full page plates. Orig. grey wrapps.
A catalogue of an exhibition which bears a 5 line inscription to Doris Niles and Serge Leslie. See also *Bibliography*, Part II, Leslie,

Serge, *The Seven Leagues of a Dancer*, chapter 8, Nathalie Gontcharova and Michel Larionov.

GEORGE (WALDEMAR). NATHALIE GONTCHAROVA. Oeuvres Anciennes et Récentes. Du 4 au 23 Mai 1956. Paris, Galerie de l'institut.

Demy 8vo (8·5 × 6·1 ins.). 8pp. + 8 full page plates.

A catalogue of an exhibition which bears a 6 line inscription to Doris Niles. See also *Bibliography*, Part I, Gontcharova and Part II, Larionov.

GEVA (TAMARA). SPLIT SECONDS. A Remembrance. New York, Harper & Rowe 1972.

Demy 8vo (8·2 × 5·4 ins.). iv + 358 pp. Orig. cloth.

The autobiography of Tamara Geva who left Russia with Balanchine, Danilova, Efimov and unfortunate Leda Ivanova. Parting from Diaghilev in turn she joined the Chauve Souris to tour America until she found her place in American musicals. See also *Dance Magazine* for Jan. 1973.

GIANELLA (A. M.). PICCOLA STORIA DELLE MASCHERE ITALIANE. Torino-Milano Firenze, G. B. Paravia & Co. 1923.

Med. 8vo (9·3 × 6·3 ins.). 83 pp. with 17 illus. in colour. Orig. dec. wrapps.

Short sketches of the following characters of the Italian Comedy, each accompanied by a coloured drawing (with the exception of Pulcinella): Il Ruzzante, Arlecchino, Brighella, Trivellino, Meo Pataca, Il Capitano, Pagliaccio, Peppe Nappa, Pantalone, Il Dottor Baloardo o Balazone, Stenterello, Meneghino, Gianduja, Pasquariello, Franca Trippa e Fritellino, Coviello, Tartaglia, and Pulcinella. The designs are by Attilio Mussino.

GILBERT (MELVIN BALLOU). THE DIRECTOR. Dancing Deportment Etiquette Aesthetics Physical Training. Portland, Melvin Ballou Gilbert. Brooklyn, New York, Dance Horizons.

Cr. 4to (10·6 × 7·7 ins.). 306 pp. illus. with photogs. line drwgs. and diags. Orig. buckram spine and dec. boards.

A very attractive reissue of *The Director*, published between Dec. 1897 and Nov. 1898 by the editor Melvin Ballou Gilbert who also wrote other books, *Round Dancing* amongst them. It was not however the first American magazine devoted to dance. E. Woodworth Masters published *The Galop* from 1884 until at least 1897, which had as its title page or frontispiece Canova's *Terpsichore*. See *Bibliography*, Part I, Galop, The.

GILBERT (RICHARD). MUSIC FOR THE BALLET. On Victor Records. Printed in U.S.A.

Med. 8vo (9·3 × 6·7 ins.). 23 pp. illus. Orig. dec. wrapps.

An outline of Ballet History and a Guide to Victor Recordings of Ballet Music. The closing discography lists only 23 recordings, but the description is rather fuller than most listings.

GLUSZKOVSKII (A. P.). VOSPOMINANIYA BALETMEISTERA. Leningrad-Moskva, Gosudarstvennoe Izdatelstvo 1940.

Med. 8vo (9·6 × 7 ins.). 246 + (ii) pp. illus. Orig. stamped blue cloth.

The Memoirs of a Ballet Master, Gluszkovskii, edited and prepared from the original Russian by Slonimsky. Gluszkovskii was Didelot's closest Russian disciple and was reputedly the first to use Pushkin's poems in ballet subject matter rather than foreign literature.

GOLDNER (NANCY). THE STRAVINSKY FESTIVAL OF THE NEW YORK CITY BALLET. Written and Edited by Nancy Goldner with Photographs by Martha Swope and others. New York, The Eakins Press. [1973].

F'cap 8vo (5·4 × 6·7 ins.). 303 pp. illus. Orig. red cloth.

Contents: I. Dance and Music; II. The Stravinsky Festival; III. Reviews; IV. Preparation: June 1971–June 1972; V. Beginnings: 1890–1972. Thirty-one ballets to music by Stravinsky, twenty-one prepared for the occasion, performed in one week June 1972.

Few artists or musicians of the 20th century have had such a tribute paid to them.

GOLDOVSKY (BORIS) & HASTINGS (BAIRD). STRAVINSKY AND THE STAGE. Boston, Chrysalis 1951.

Demy 8vo (8 × 5·2 ins.). 19 pp. illus. Orig. dec. wrapps.

Vol. IV Nos. 11, 12 of *Chrysalis*. See also Stravinsky and Craft.

GOLDRON (ROMAIN). A LA RECHERCHE D'UN LANGAGE. Lausanne, Les Editions Rencontre 1966.

Demy 8vo (8·2 × 7·2 ins.). 128 pp. illus. in black and white and colour. Orig. dec. boards.

Primarily a book about musicians: Fauré, Debussy, Ravel, Roussel, De Falla, Schoenberg, Von Webern, Berg, Stravinsky and Bartok, with many photographs of dancers and designs in colour by Bakst, Picasso, Leo Rath, Degas and Helmut Jürgens.

GOLDSCHMIDT (AENNE). VOKABULAR DEUTSCHER VOLKSTANZSCHRITTE. Teil I. Die Konzertanzschritte. Leipzig, Zentralhaus fur Kulturarbeit der DDR 1974.
Demy 8vo (8 × 5·7 ins.). 42 pp. incl. mus. ex. Orig. printed wrapps.
A Vocabulary of Steps used in German Folk Dances. Text in German Part I. See also Ehm-Schulz, Rosemarie and Petermann, Dr. Kurt.

GOLDSCHMIDT (AENNE). VOKABULAR DEUTSCHER VOLKSTANZSCHRITTE. Teil II. Leipzig, Zentralhaus fur Kulturarbeit der DDR 1975.
Demy 8vo (8 × 5·7 ins.). 54 pp. + a 28 pp. booklet of mus. Orig. wrapps.
A Vocabulary of Steps used in *Ländler-Walzer* and *Mazurka*. Part II. Text in German.

GOLDSCHMIDT (AENNE). VOKABULAR DEUTSCHER VOLKSTANZSCHRITTE. Teil III. Die Typen des Geh-, Lauf-, Hupf-, Nachstell-und Wechselschrittes in den geradtakigen Tanzen. Leipzig, Zentralhaus fur Kulturarbeit der DDR 1976.
Demy 8vo (8 × 5.7 ins.). 59 pp. with ex. of time values and rhythm. Orig. wrapps.
Text in German. There is also a 24 page booklet containing 27 musical airs.

GOLUBOV (V.). GALINA ULANOVA. Moskva, Teatr 1945.
Med. 8vo (9·6 × 6·5 ins.). pp. 141–155 with 4 illus. Orig. printed grey wrapps.
An article in the Russian periodical *Teatr* for 1945. See also Bogdanov-Beresovsky, V. Fühmann, Franz. Kahn, Albert. Lvov-Anokhin, B. and Sizova, M. I.

[GOLUBOV (I. V.)]. MUZIKA I KHOREOGRAFIYA SOVREMENNOGO BALETA. Sbornik Statei. Leningradskoe Izdatelstvo Muzika 1974.

Demy 8vo (8·4 × 5·4 ins.). 296 pp. illus. Orig. white boards with fabric spine.
Soderjanie: Problemi Baletnogo Teatr (p. 7). Muzika v Balete (p. 109). Mastera Sovetskogo Baleta (p. 157). Ot Prostlogo k Nastoyastemu (p. 235). 19 Soviet writers have contributed including Slonimsky, Petrov, Lopukov and Krasovskaya.

[GOLUBOV (I. V.)]. MUZIKA I KHOREOGRAFIYA SOVREMENNOGO BALETA. Sbornik Statei Vipusk 2. Leningradskoe, Izdatelstvo Muzika 1977.
Demy 8vo (8·4 × 5·5 ins.). 238 + (ii) pp. illus. Orig. red dec. boards with cloth spine.
The second part of the above. Many articles of importance including Slonimsky's *Vigano and his Vestale* (pp. 224–233).

GOMEZ (E.). SEVILLA Y LA SEMANA SANTA. Sevilla, E. Gomez 1928.
Demy 8vo (8·2 × 6·1 ins.). 128 pp. + (ii) illus. incl. plates in colour tipped in. Bound in full violet chagrin.
A book on Holy Week in Seville with many illustrations of religious paintings and costumes of the various *Penitentes* in colour.

GOODMAN (WALTER). AN ENGLISH BALLET IN SPAIN. London, The Theatre Nov. 1, 1885.
Med. 8vo (9 × 5·7 ins.). pp. 241–248 unbound.
An article concerning a British Ballet appearing in 1862 at the *Teatro del Circo*, Barcelona, in a piece called *Apolo en el Jardin de Terpsichore*. See *Bibliography*, Part III (p. 17), Artis, *Ricardo Moragas*, where this piece is listed.

GORDON (JOHN). ISAMU NOGUCHI. Published for the Whitney Museum of American Art. New York, Frederick A. Praeger 1968.
(9 × 9 ins.). 68 pp. illus. Orig. tan cloth.
A monograph which concludes with a Selected Bibliography. See also Tobias, Tobi.

GRAHAM (MARTHA). THE NOTEBOOKS OF MARTHA GRAHAM. With an Introduction by Nancy Wilson Ross. New York, Harcourt Brace Jovanovich, Inc. [1973].
Demy 4to (10·7 × 8·3 ins.). xvi + 464 pp. illus. Orig. blue cloth.

Technically Graham's notes are often little more than sparse movement instructions such as one might find on an opera score: these will undoubtedly mean more to those who have been in her company or classes. However, there are excellent photographs which illustrate the action of these instructions.

GRAY (PAUL). U.S. BALLET SOARS. And in model roles, the model is high-flying Gelsey Kirkland. New York, Time Magazine May 1, 1978.

Demy 4to (10·7 × 8·1 ins.). pp. 82–88 illus. Orig. dec. wrapps. (Gelsey Kirkland).

An article in the May 1st 1978 issue of *Time*. See also *Dance Magazine* for Dec. 1971, Goodman, Saul, *Gelsey Kirkland*.

GREBENSHIKOV (S. M.). STSENICHESKIE BELORUS-SKIE TANTSI. Minsk, Izdatelstvo 'Nauka i Tekhnika' 1974.

Demy 8vo (8·3 × 6·4 ins.). 328 pp. illus. Orig. grey cloth.

Stage Dances from White Russia, illustrated with diagrams figures and music. See also Churko, *Belo Russkii Balet*.

GRECO (JOSÉ). THE GYPSY IN MY SOUL. Garden City, Doubleday & Co. 1977.

Demy 8vo (8·1 × 5·2 ins.). (v) + 279 pp. illus. Orig. black cloth.

An autobiography written in collaboration with Harvey Ardman. To round out the activities of this dancer one might consult the dozen or more American souvenir programs of José Greco and His Company.

GREGOR (JOSEPH) & FÜLÖP-MILLER (RENÉ). DAS RUSSISCHE THEATER. Sein Wesen un seine Geschichte mit besonderer Berucksichtigung der Revolutionsperiode. Mit 48 bunten und 357 einfarbingen Bildern. Zurich Leipzig Wien. Amalthea-Verlag [1928].

Roy 4to (12·2 × 9·1 ins.). 138 pp. + 405 num. plates 48 illus. in colour and 357 black and white. Orig. dec. light brown cloth.

The German edition and the first of *The Russian Theatre*. See also Fülöp-Miller, René, for the London edition.

GREGORY (JOHN). DIAGHILEV'S OVERSIGHT. And the Aftermath. Foreword by Sir John Anderson Bart. London, The Federation of Russian Classical Ballet. [1954].

Med. 8vo (9·3 × 6 ins.). 18 pp. Orig. dec. white wrapps.

The title undoubtedly refers to Diaghilev's failure to establish a school to produce the dancers required for his company. The pamphlet traces briefly the elements that made the Diaghilev Company possible, the role of the Monte Carlo Ballet following the disbandment of it, and several solid ideas for the future of ballet in general.

GREGORY (JOHN). LIGHT ON A SYSTEM OF CLASSICAL DANCE. Foreword by Prof. Hugo Fischer. Cover drawing by Peter Revitt. London, The Federation of Russian Classical Ballet. [1950].

Med. 8vo (9·4 × 6·2 ins.). 16 pp. n.n. Orig. dec. wrapps.

A lecture on Nicholas Legat and the Russian Classic Ballet, given at the Annual Conference of the National Association of Teachers of Dancing, London July 4, 1950.

GRIGOROV (S.). BALETNOE ISKUSSTVO I S. V. FEDOROVA 2-ya. Opit sb Desyatvf Portretami Moskva 1914.

Demy 8vo (8 × 6 ins.). 76 + (iv) pp. with 10 illus. Orig. dec. wrapps.

Sophie Vasilievna Fedorova, 1879–1963, created the role of the *Povlovtsian Girl* in Prince Igor for Diaghilev. The photographs are mainly of her roles with the Bolshoi and the two from *La Fille de Pharaon* show her feet in one line, a position associated with Nijinsky and the *Afternoon of a Faun*. See also Stals, Georgs, *Das Lettische Ballett der Rigaer Oper* (plate V).

GROSS (REV. J. B.). THE PARSON ON DANCING. As it is taught in the Bible, and as it was Practiced among the Ancient Greeks and Romans. New York, Dance Horizons.

Demy 8vo (8 × 5·3 ins.). 98 pp. Orig. wrapps.

One of the few published religious tracts or books sympathetic to the dance and dancing. See bibliography in *The Mathers on Dancing* for many books and articles that are not.

GRUEN (JOHN). THE PRIVATE WORLD OF BALLET. Penguin Books. 1976.

Cr. 8vo (7·6 × 5 ins.). xv + 464 pp. incl. Index. Illus. Orig. dec. wrapps.

Contents: 1. Looking Back; 2. The Current Scene; 3. Looking

Ahead. The book is a series of interviews with artists principally from The Royal Ballet, The Stuttgart Ballet, Les Ballets du XXeme Siècle, American Ballet Theatre, N.Y.C. Ballet and City Center Joffrey Ballet. The weakest section seems to be the final one, Looking Ahead.

GUEST (IVOR). LE BALLET DE L'OPERA DE PARIS. Trois Siècles d'Histoire et de Tradition. Traduction Paul Alexandre. Paris, Théâtre National de L'Opéra. 1976.

Demy 8vo (8·2 × 5·5 ins.). (ii) + 349 pp. illus. Orig. dec. wrapps.

Although too incomplete to be a definitive study of the Paris Opera Ballet, this work nevertheless has the Guest stamp for care and accuracy. Writing as a historian (for I do not believe Mr. Guest saw the Lifar Period, at least not the first years 1930–1945) he has to some extent penetrated the pink cloud of eulogy and extravagant acclaim which resisted most attempts at criticism, even constructive. There are accounts and photographs of Solange Schwarz, Suzanne Lorcia, Marie-Louise Didion, Serge Peretti and many others who have never really had their appreciation even in French publications.

One thing more: since the book begins with the Louis XIV period and cites pieces even earlier (*Ballet Comique* 1581), why not begin with Campra and Lulli and list all works? Castil-Blaze, De Lajarte, and Prodhomme have all begun their lists of repertory from the earliest pieces performed at the Paris Opera and it would have been nice if Mr. Guest had done the same.

GUEST (IVOR). THE BALLET OF THE SECOND EMPIRE. London, Pitman Publishing. Middletown: Wesleyan University Press. [1974].

Demy 8vo (9 × 6 ins.). xiv + 279 pp. incl. index. Illus. Orig. red cloth.

The combined edition of the two volume study of the Second Empire. See *Bibliography*, Part I, Guest, for comment on the two first editions.

GUEST (IVOR). CARLOTTA ZAMBELLI. Part I. New York, Dance Magazine 1974.

Demy 4to (11 × 8·4 ins.). pp. 51–66 illus. Orig. illus. wrapps. (Bejart).

An article (Part I) in *Dance Magazine Portfolio* for Feb. 1974. See also *Bibliography* Part III, Guest, Ivor, *Carlotta Zambelli*.

GUEST (IVOR). CARLOTTA ZAMBELLI. Part II. New York, Dance Magazine 1974.

Demy 4to (11 × 8·3 ins.). pp. 43–58 illus. Orig. dec. wrapps. (Zambelli).

An article (Part II) in *Dance Magazine Portfolio* for March 1974.

GUEST (IVOR). THE DIVINE VIRGINIA. A Biography of Virginia Zucchi. New York, Marcel Dekker. 1977.

Med. 8vo (9 × 6 ins.). xv + 188 pp. illus. Orig. dec. yellow boards.

Few paintings demonstrate the strength, artistry, and sensuousness of a subject as George Clairin's portrait of Zucchi in *Sieba* does. Mr. Guest brings these qualities to life, and it is one of his best biographies. For a resumé of *The Divine Virginia* see *The Dancing Times* of Feb. 1977.

GUEST (IVOR). FANNY CERRITO. The Life of a Romantic Ballerina. With a frontis. and 48 monochrome plates. London, Dance Books Ltd. [1974].

Demy 8vo (8·2 × 5·3 ins.). 176 pp. incl. index. Illus. Orig. blue cloth.

This is a second revised edition published by Dance Books Ltd. 1974. To the very fine Bibliography which follows the text one might add notes from Karla Blazisa, *Baletniya Znamenitosti I Natshionalvnie Tantsi* (p. 72), and text and illustration from André Levinson's *Mastera Baleta* (op. pp. 84, 86 and 130).

GUILLOT (GENEVIEVE) & PRUDHOMMEAU (GERMAINE). THE BOOK OF BALLET. Translated by Katherine Carson. New Jersey, Prentice Hall. [1976].

Med. 8vo (9·1 × 6·7 ins.). vi + 418 pp. illus. Orig. yellow fabric.

The English version of *Grammaire de la Danse*. See *Bibliography*, Part III, for comment.

GUITRY (SACHA). DEBURAU. Illustrations de Jean Boullet. Cannes, Raoul Solar, Editeur. [1950].

Demy 8vo (8·2 × 6·2 ins.). 202 + (iii) pp. illus. with woodcuts. Orig. dec. wrapps.

A play in 4 acts about the famous mime Deburau with Guitry playing the title role. See also Winter, Marian Hannah, *That Magnificent Mute*.

GÜNTHER (DOROTHEE). DER TANZ ALS BEWE-GUNGSPHÄNOMEN. Wesen und Werden. Rowohlt 1962.
Cr. 8vo (7·3 × 4·3 ins.). 230 pp. illus. Orig. dec. wrapps.
The dance as a phenomenon of movement. Text in German.

GUTHRIE (JOHN). HISTORICAL DANCES FOR THE THEATRE. The Pavan and the Minuet. Worthing, Aldridge Bros. 1950.
Cr. 4to (9·5 × 7·2 ins.). vii + 79 pp. illus. with choreographic plates and Music. Orig. dec. red cloth.
Concentration on two dances, the *Pavan* and the *Minuet* with steps, choreographic symbols and music. The work closes with a short bibliography. See also Drabeca, Maria, *Tańce Historyczne*.

HACHETTE (DÉPARTEMENT ÉTRANGER). BALLET ET DANSE. Paris Hachette.
Demy 8vo (8·3 × 5·3 ins.). 8 pp. Orig. illus. wrapps.
A catalogue listing 73 books on the dance and ballet in French.

HÄGER (BENGT). SJU DANSKONST-NÄRER. Stockholm 1949.
Demy 4to (10·7 × 8·3 ins.). 8 pp. n.n. illus. Orig. dec. wrapps.
Illustrated sketches of Birgit Åkesson, Elsa Mariane von Rosen, Björn Holmgren, Birgit Cullberg, Ivo Cramér och Tyyne Talvo and Per-Arne Qvarsebo.

HAGGIN (B. H.). VIOLETTE VERDY. Photographs by Martha Swope. New York, Dance Horizons Spotlight Series.
Med. 8vo (9 × 7 ins.). 24 pp. illus. Orig. illus. wrapps.
A monograph. See also *Dance Magazine Portfolio* for Feb. 1972, *Violet Verdy* by Marcia Marks.

HALFORD (AUBREY S. & GIOVANNA M.). THE KABUKI HANDBOOK. A Guide to Understanding and Appreciation, with Summaries of Favorite Plays, Explanatory Notes and Illustrations. Rutland Vermont, Tokyo, Japan, Charles E. Tuttle Co. [1974].
Cr. 8vo (7·1 × 4·2 ins.). xxi + 487 pp. illus. with line drwgs. Orig. dec. wrapps.

Contents: Foreword by Faubion Bowers (p. xi); Author's Preface (p. xv); Summaries of Plays (p. 1); Notes (p. 389); Bibliography (p. 477); Index (p. 479).

HALL (HUGH P.). BALLET IN AUSTRALIA. From Pavlova to Rambert. Melbourne, Georgian House. [1948].
Imp. 4to (10·5 × 14·6 ins.). 211 pp. incl. index to all photogs. Profusely illus. Orig. blue buckram.
Contents: 1. Introduction (pp. 7–15); 2. Pavlova –1926 and 1929 (pp. 16–19); 3. Col. de Basil's Monte Carlo Ballet Company (pp. 21, 22–51); 4. Col. de Basil's Covent Garden Russian Ballet 1938–1939 and 1939–1940 (pp. 53, 54–163); 5. The Kirsova Ballet (pp. 164, 165–169); 6. Borovansky Australian Ballet Company (pp. 171, 172–195); 7. Ballet Rambert (pp. 197, 198–210); 8. Index to all photographs (p. 211). An excellent album of photographs with much little known material and good ballet groupings.

HARLEQUINADE. SECOND HAND & ANTIQUARIAN BOOKS. SPECIALIST SUBJECT BALLET. Elstree Herts, Mrs. Cynthia Morris.
Demy 8vo (8·2 × 5·7 ins.). 16 pp. illus. Orig. dec. wrapps.
Catalogue No. 15 on *Dance and Drama* issued by Mrs. Cynthia Morris. Most of the 15 Bulletins now published are on *Dance and Drama* and related subjects. Description of books and condition consistently good.

HARPER (RAY) MILADY OF MILAN. New York, The Dance Magazine Feb. 1928.
Roy. 4to (12·4 × 9·6 ins.). pp. 15, 60 with 2 illus. Orig. dec. wrapps (Vanessi).
An illustrated article about Rosina Galli, Première Danseuse at the Chicago Opera 1911–1912, 1912–1913; Première Danseuse at the Metropolitan Opera 1914 and Ballet Mistress 1919–1935. See also Metropolitan Opera House, *The Golden Horseshoe* (pp. 118, 122, 124, 159, 173). Also Kolodin, Irving, for numerous references to Rosina Galli.

HARRÉ (T. EVERETT). NIMURA – DANCER OF THE SAMURAI. New York, The Dance Magazine Oct. 1931.
Roy. 4to (12·6 × 9·6 ins.). pp. 39, 40, 51 illus. Orig. dec. wrapps. (des. by W. Stuart Leech).

An illustrated article. See also Koegler, *Concise Oxford Dictionary of Ballet*, for short biographical information.

HARRIS (DALE). ANTOINETTE SIBLEY. Brooklyn, New York, Dance Horizons 1976.
   Med. 8vo (9 × 7 ins.). 19 + (v) pp. illus. Orig. dec. wrapps.
   A monograph with photographs by Anthony Crickmay, one of *Dance Horizons Spotlight Series*. See also Dromgoole, Nicholas.

HARRIS (JOHN), ORGEL (STEPHEN), STRONG (ROY). THE KING'S ARCADIA: INIGO JONES AND THE STUART COURT. London, Arts Council of Great Britain 1973.
   Cr. 4to (9·2 × 7 ins.). 232 pp. with many illus. Orig. dec. wrapps.
   A catalogue of a Quatercentenary Exhibition held at the Banqueting Hall, Whitehall from July 12th to Sept. 2nd 1973. *The Royal Masques* occupy (pp. 165–184).

HARRIS (LEON). THE RUSSIAN BALLET SCHOOL. With photographs by the author. New York, Atheneum 1970.
   Med. 8vo (9·2 × 6·6 ins.). (iv) + 60 pp. illus. Orig. cloth.
   One thing is evident from the photographs of the students at practice: the turn-out is more pronounced than in most schools of the West.

HASKELL (ARNOLD L.). BALLET. A Complete Guide to Appreciation History Aesthetics Ballets Dancers. Harmondsworth Middlesex, Penguin Books [1949].
   Cr. 8vo (7·1 × 4·2 ins.). 217 pp. incl. index. Illus. Orig. dec. wrapps.
   Revised edition of 1949. Chapter 6 concludes with ballet No. XXV *The Green Table* and the section of photographs begins with Anne Heaton and concludes with Irène Skorik.

HASKELL (ARNOLD L.). BALLET. A READERS GUIDE. London, Published for the National Book League 1947.
   Demy 8vo (8·4 × 5·3 ins.). 12 pp. Orig. dec. blue wrapps.
   A slender pamphlet compiled by W. A. Munford who remarks

'It makes no claim to be comprehensive, and many good books have been necessarily omitted'. The pamphlet is however scarce.

HASKELL (ARNOLD L.). BALLET DANCING. Introduction by Marie Rambert. London, The New Era Publishing Co. [1951].
    Med. 8vo (9·7 × 7·2 ins.). pp. 178–215 illus. Orig. green cloth.
    An article with interesting illustrations in *Theatre and Stage* Vol. I, Edited by Olin Downes. See also Haskell, *Bibliography*, Parts I and III.

HASKELL (ARNOLD L.). BALLETOMANIA THEN AND NOW. New York, Alfred A. Knopf 1977.
    Med. 8vo (9·3 × 6·1 ins.). xiv + 304 pp. illus. with line drwgs. Orig. fabric spine and dec. boards.
    Part 1. Balletomania, The Story of an Obsession. Part 2. Balletomania Now. The chapters in Part 1 bear Postscripts and Part 2 is dedicated to Galina Ulanova 'The miracle woman who rekindled my dormant balletomania'. The book is entirely illustrated by line drawings by Natalie Gontcharova and Michel Larionov. They were very close friends and Larionov possessed several of Haskell's original typescripts. I believe *Balletomania* was among them.

HASKELL (ARNOLD L.). DANCING AROUND THE WORLD. New York, Dodge Publishing Co. [1938].
    Demy 8vo (8·4 × 5·4 ins.). xiv + 288 pp. incl. Index. Orig. tan cloth.
    First published by Gollancz in 1937. This is the American edition.

HASKELL (ARNOLD L.). PRELUDE TO BALLET. An Analysis and a Guide to Appreciation. London, Thomas Nelson & Sons 1947.
    Cr. 8vo (7·1 × 4·5 ins.). viii + 119 pp. illus. with woodcuts. Orig. black cloth.
    The new and revised edition, also with Doboujinsky decorations.

HAYDEN (MELISSA). MELISSA HAYDEN OFF STAGE AND ON. Photographs by Fred Fehl. New York, Doubleday & Co. [1963].

Med. 8vo (9·1 × 5·6 ins.). 127 pp. illus. in halftone. Orig. two-tone cloth.

Known as Mildred Herman at the beginning of Ballet Theatre's 1945–1946 season, she changed her name to Melissa Hayden. For salient points in her career see Chujoy, *The Dance Encyclopedia* (rev. ed.). See also *Dance Magazine* for Nov. 1970 and Aug. 1973.

HAYS (DAVID). PAINTERS IN THE THEATRE. Stage Designs of Chagall Roualt Berman Berard and Leger. Boston, Chrysalis 1952.

Cr. 8vo (8 × 5·2 ins.). 18 pp. with 5 illus. Orig. dec. white wrapps.

An issue of *Chrysalis* Vol. VI Nos. 3–4. See also Jeudwine, Wynne.

HEATH (CHARLES). BEAUTIES OF THE OPERA AND BALLET. New York, Da Capo Press 1977.

Roy. 8vo (10 × 6·7 ins.). 160 pp. with 10 portraits on steel and numerous woodcuts. Orig. rose cloth.

A welcome republication as many of the original copies have become spotted. See *Bibliography*, Part I, Gautier & Others, and Heath, Charles for original French and English editions.

HEDGCOCK (FRANK A.). DAVID GARRICK AND HIS FRENCH FRIENDS. London, Stanley Paul & Co. 1911 c.

Demy 8vo (8·5 × 5·4 ins.). 442 pp. illus. Orig. green cloth.

See Chapter IV. Jean-Georges Noverre (pp. 127–168) with 2 illustrations. Contains the account of Noverre's ballet *Les Fêtes Chinoises*, drawn from *Le Nouveau Calendrier des Spectacles*, Paris 1775.

HENRY (LUIGI). AMLETO. Nel Gran Teatro la Fenice il Carnovale dell'Anno 1828. Venezia dalla Tipografia Casali.

F'cap 8vo (6·4 × 4·2 ins.). 11 pp. Unbound.

A synopsis for the ballet *Hamlet* with Luigi Henry (*Amleto*) Maria Queriau (*Geltrude*) Effizio Catte (*Claudio*) and Luigia Demartini (*Ofelia*). Henry first produced this ballet for the Porte St. Martin, Paris le 28 Février 1816.

HERZFELT (FRIEDRICH). IGOR STRAVINSKY. Berlin, Rembrandt Verlag 1961.

Cr. 8vo (7·2 × 5·4 ins.). 64 pp. illus. Orig. dec. boards. Text in German. See also Stravinsky and Craft.

HEYWORTH (ANITA) & POWELL-TUCK (KATHLEEN M.). CURIOUS CHARACTER DANCES.
Adapted from a Book on Dancing by Gregorio Lambranzi published in 1716. Music arranged by K. M. Wollaston. Leeds, E. J. Arnold & Son Ltd. n.d.
Cr. 4to (9·6 × 7·2 ins.). 44 pp. incl. 5 plates, diags. and music. Also includes an 8 pp. music supplement. Orig. fabric spine and boards.

Five dances from Lambranzi: The Two Blacksmiths, The Platter Dance, The Gondolier and his Wife, The Cook's Dance, and The Peasant Man, with the music harmonized and simple but effective steps arranged after studying Lambranzi's Notes and the Johann Georg Puschner engravings. See also *Bibliography*, Parts II and III, Lambranzi.

HILLESTRÖM (GUSTAF). THEATER UND BALLETT IN SCHWEDEN.
Ubersetzung Manfred Grabs. Stockholm, Schwedisches Institut 1956.
Cr. 8vo (7·7 × 5·2 ins.). pp. n.n. with many illus. Orig. dec. wrapps.

Theatre and Ballet in Sweden. Principally a book of photographs with the theatre having the lion's share. Text in German. There is an edition in English.

HILLESTRÖM (GUSTAF). THEATRE AND BALLET IN SWEDEN.
Stockholm, The Swedish Institute 1953.
Cr. 8vo (7·7 × 5·4 ins.). 88 pp. illus. Orig. printed tan wrapps.

I believe this is the first English edition translated by Anne Bibbey. It has fewer pages than the German edition and the section on Ballet has 6 fewer photographs. Most interesting are plates 1 and 2 of *Orpheus and Euridice* 1775 and *Atys* 1785, which show flight from the tonnelet, that dress reform so ardently desired by Noverre.

HIRSCHORN (CLIVE). GENE KELLY.
Chicago, Henry Regnery & Co. [1974].
Demy 8vo (8·5 × 5·7 ins.). 335 pp. incl. Index. With 2 blocks of illus. Orig. cloth.

A biography with Foreword by Frank Sinatra.

HOBBIES. THE DANCE IN ART AND HISTORY.
Chicago, Hobbies Nov. 1975.
Demy 4to (11·4 × 8·4 ins.). pp. 105, 108 illus. Orig. dec. wrapps.
An article in the magazine *Hobbies*, concerning sculpture in the collections of George Chaffee and Conrad Waldstein. See also Belknap's *Guide to Dance Periodicals* under Sculpture.

HOLLINSHED (MARJORIE). SOME PROFESSIONAL DANCERS OF, OR FROM QUEENSLAND, and Some Teachers of the Past and Present. Brisbane, W. R. Smith & Patterson Ltd. 1963.
Demy 8vo (8·3 × 5·3 ins.). 92 pp. illus. Orig. dec. cloth.
A Dictionary of Professional Dancers and Teachers from Queensland which is Part 3 of an as yet unpublished mss called 'In Search of Ballet'. Marjorie Hollinshed (Lucas) has signed the flyleaf.

HOLMES (MARTIN). SHAKESPEARE & HIS PLAYERS.
[London], John Murray [1972].
Demy 8vo (8·4 × 5·2 ins.). x + 212 pp. with IV plates and 16 figures in text. Orig. red cloth.
See William Kemp (pp. 47–49) plus one illustration. See also *Bibliography*, Part III, Kemp, *Kemp's Nine Daies Wonder*, also Sorell, *The Dancers Image* (pp. 297–304).

HOOREMAN (PAUL). DANCERS THROUGH THE AGES. Translated by Susan Bellamy. Milan, The Uffici Press n.d.
Cr. 8vo (7·6 × 5·3 ins.). 64 numbered plates. Orig. illus. boards.
A short resumé of the Dance Through the Ages followed by illustrations with captions. The 20th Century is represented by one painting and one water colour: Xavier Nogues, *The Sardana in Banyoles* 1907 and José-Marie Sert, *Pas de Deux* 1920.

HOPE-WALLACE (PHILIP). THE YEAR IN BALLET.
London, The British Council 1949.
Med. 8vo (9·2 × 6 ins.). pp. 42–47 with 1 illus. Orig. dec. wrapps.
An article in *The Year's Work in the Theatre* 1948–1949. There is also a second article, The Sadler's Wells Ballet by Ninette de Valois

(pp. 38–41). The issue also contains 3 plates in colour from *Apparitions, A Midsummer Night's Dream,* and *Job.*

HOPE-WALLACE (PHILIP). THE YEAR IN BALLET. London, The British Council 1949–1950.
> Med. 8vo (9·2 × 6 ins.). pp. 42–46 with 1 illus. (frontis. in colour). Orig. dec. wrapps.
> An article in *The Year's Work in the Theatre 1949–1950* which has a colour plate of Harold Turner's costume in *Don Quixote.*

HORGAN (PAUL). ENCOUNTERS WITH STRAVINSKY. A Personal Record. London, The Bodley Head. [1972].
> Demy 8vo (8·4 × 5·2 ins.). 224 pp. incl. Index. Illus. Orig. boards.
> An abridgement of the original American edition.

HORST (LOUIS). PRE-CLASSIC DANCE FORMS. Brooklyn, New York, A Dance Horizons Republications. [1972].
> Cr. 8vo (7·7 × 5·3 ins.). xii + 140 pp. illus. Orig. dec. wrapps.
> A compilation of text and illustration from Playford, Lambranzi, Guillaume, Desrat, Ardern Holt and others. See *Bibliography*, Part I, for the first edition.

HUMPHREY (DORIS). DORIS HUMPHREY: AN ARTIST FIRST. An Autobiography edited and completed by Selma Jeanne Cohen. Introduction by John Martin, Foreword by Charles Humphrey Woodford, Chronology by Christena L. Schlundt. Middletown, Conn., Wesleyan University Press. 1972.
> Med. 8vo (9 × 6 ins.). xvi + 305 pp. illus. Orig. cloth.
> See also *Bibliography*, Part III, Humphrey, Doris and Belknap's *Guide to Dance Periodicals.*

HUROK (S.) & GOODE (RUTH). IMPRESARIO. A Memoir by S. Hurok in collaboration with Ruth Goode. New York, Random House 1946.
> Med. 8vo (9 × 5·7 ins.). (ix) + 291 pp. with 40 illus. Orig. blue cloth.

The American edition. At least 20 of the illustrations are of dancers. See *Bibliography*, Part III, Hurok, S., *Impresario* for the English edition.

HUTCHINSON (ANN). A THIRD READER. Classical Ballet Technique (Cecchetti Method) Grade Three. New York, Dance Notation Bureau Inc. [1966].

Demy 4to (11 × 8·4 ins.). 19 pp. of Labanotation. Orig. white wrapps.
Contents: Keys and Abbreviations, Theory, Exercises at the Barre, Center Practice, Adage, Allegro, Enchainments. See also *Bibliography*, Parts I and III, Hutchinson, Ann.

IDAYATZADE (L.), SLONIMSKOGO (Y.), RAKHMANA (S.). SEM KRASAVITS. Balet v 3 Deistviyak 9 Kartinakh. Moskva Mai 1959.

Med. 8vo (9 × 6·2 ins.). 16 pp. illus. Orig. dec. wrapps.
A booklet of the ballet *Sem Krasavits* (Seven Beauties) with cast, libretto, and artists, well illustrated. The music is by Kara Karaev and the choreography by P. Gusev.

IDESTAM-ALMQUIST (BENGT – 'Robin Hood'). SVENSK BALETT. With English text, The Ballet in Sweden. Upsala, Bokforlaget Orbis 1951.

Demy 4to (11·4 × 8·4 ins.). 106 pp. incl. index. Illus. Orig. dec. wrapps.
In a plea for better understanding of the Swedish Ballet, the author points out that performances were held in Stockholm as early as 1638; that Jean Baptiste Landé was head of the Bollus Theatre in the 1720s and that Antoine Bournonville had been premier danseur and choreographer in Stockholm for 13 years. There is a list of dance books published in Sweden (p. 90). See also Bibliography, Part III, Skeaping, Mary, *Ballet under Three Crowns*.

IMPERIAL SOCIETY (THE). BACKGROUND TO A GREAT SOCIETY. London, Imperial Society of Teachers of Dancing 1960.

Demy 8vo (8·6 × 5·7 ins.). 30 pp. illus. Orig. illus. wrapps.
A brochure issued as a supplement in *The Dancing Times* with notes on Ballroom, Latin American, Classical Ballet, Greek, Historical, National, Natural Movement, Scottish Country and Stage departments. See also *Bibliography* Parts I & III, *Imperial Society, The*.

INGBER (JUDITH BRIN). SHORASHIM. The Roots of Israeli Folk Dance. New York, Dance Perspectives Autumn 1974.
Med. 8vo (9 × 7·4 ins.). 60 pp. illus. Orig. dec. wrapps.
Issue No. 59 of *Dance Perspectives* which closes with an important bibliography on the subject.

JACKSON (B. T.). THE BEAUMONT PRESS 1917–1931. The Story of a Collection. London, The Private Library, Spring 1975.
Demy 8vo (8·4 × 5·4 ins.). pp. 4–38 illus. Orig. red wrapps.
This splendid article, which includes among its illustrations one of the Albion Press, used for printing *The Beaumont Press books*, carefully describes the twenty-six works of *The Beaumont Press* in their various states which amount to 61 editions.

JEUDWINE (WYNNE). STAGE DESIGNS. London, The Hamlyn Publishing Group 1968.
Med. 8vo (9 × 6·3 ins.). 64 pp. with 44 plates. Orig. dec. wrapps.
Reproductions of 16th–19th century stage designs, particularly of the Italian School with representatives of the Bibiena Family having the largest number of drawings. See also Hays, David; Polunin, Vladimir; Rowell, Kenneth, and Zinkheisen, Doris.

JO. (COUNT GUIDO SATELLI). A TAYLE OF YE DANSE. Walsall, W. Henry Robinson 1879.
Demy 8vo (8·3 × 5·3 ins.). 12 pp. Orig. printed wrapps.
A poem concerning the domestic difficulties of Count Guido Satelli, which were resolved by giving a sumptuous ball.

KAPRELIAN (MARY H.). AESTHETICS FOR DANCERS: A SELECTED ANNOTATED BIBLIOGRAPHY. [Washington, National Dance Association 1976].
Demy 4to (11 × 8·4 ins.). vii + 87 pp. Orig. dec. wrapps.
The first Bibliography to be concerned with dance aesthetics. The Preface (p. vii) bears a statement which is largely true: 'The average dancer does not seem to have a background in traditional aesthetic theory and not many aestheticians understand dance'. One hopes this list will encourage both groups to enlarge their reading habits.

KARIMOVA (R.). FERGANSKII TANETS. Metodicheskoe Posodie. Izdatelstvo Literatur i Iskusstva Imeni Gafura Gulyama Tashkent 1973.

Demy 8vo (8·3 × 6·4 ins.). 222 pp + (ii) illus. with photogs. drwgs. and music. Orig. grey fabric.

Eleven dances of the *Uzbegs*, Peoples of the USSR with steps, costumes, and some musical examples.

KARP (P.). O BALETE. Izdatelstvo Iskusstvo, Moskva 1967.

F'cap 8vo (6·3 × 4·6 ins.). 225 + (iii) pp. Orig. black cloth.

See p. 180 and following which deal with Balanchine and others (Balanchin i Drujbje).

KARPELES (MAUD). THE LANCASHIRE MORRIS DANCE. Collected and Edited by Maud Karpeles. London, Novello & Co.

Cr. 8vo (7·1 × 4·6 ins.). 44 pp. with mus. ex. Orig. blue cloth.

See also Beaumont, *Bibliography*, Sharp (p. 159).

KARSAVINA (T. P.). TEATRALINAYA ULITSA. Leningradskoe Otdelenie Izdatelstvo 'Iskusstvo' 1971.

Demy 8vo (7·6 × 5·6 ins.). 246 + (ii) pp. with about 50 illus. Orig. cloth.

Tamara Karsavina's *Theatre Street* in Russian with an excellent Introduction by Natalia Krasovskaya, and many little known photographs of Karsavina and her fellow artists. For other important works about this artist see *Bibliography*, Part I: Bruce, J. H.; Gir, C.; Barbier, G.; Haskell, A. L.; Karsavina, T.; Part II: Svetlov, V.

KARTSEVA (S. A.). MUZIKALNAYA FONETEKA V Shkola (I–III Klassi) is opita Raboti Moskva, 'Prosveshtsenie' 1976.

Demy 8vo (8·3 × 5·5 ins.). 144 pp. Orig. dec. wrapps.

Musical Phonetics in School, grades I to III, text in Russian. Considerable attention is paid to the ballet.

KERENSKY (OLEG). ANNA PAVLOVA. With an Introduction by Sir Frederick Ashton. London, Hamish Hamilton. 1973.

Cr. 8vo (7·3 × 5·2 ins.). xvi + 160 pp. incl. Index. Illus. Orig. green cloth.

The book concludes with an Appendix of the main sources used in the compilation of this work.

KERENSKY (OLEG). THE WORLD OF BALLET. New York, Coward-McCann Inc. 1970.
Demy 8vo (8·2 × 5·4 ins.). xiv + 302 pp. incl. Index. Illus. Orig. green cloth.
Contents: Part 1. What is Ballet; 2. How is it Done? and 3. The Appeal of Ballet.

KERSLEY (LEO) & SINCLAIR (JANET). BALLET VAN A TOT Z. Antwerpen, Prisma-boeken. [1961].
Cr. 8vo (7 × 4·1 ins.). 158 + (i) pp. illus. with drwgs. Orig. dec. wrapps.
Text in Dutch. A *Dictionary of Ballet Terms* which is considerably enlarged over their English edition of 1953.

KERSLEY (LEO) & SINCLAIR (JANET). A DICTIONARY OF BALLET TERMS. Drawings by Peter Revitt. London, Adam & Charles Black. [1973].
Cr. 8vo (7·6 × 4·7 ins.). 112 pp. incl. Index. Illus. with drwgs. Orig. red cloth.
The third edition. See also *Bibliography*, Part II, Sinclair, Janet.

KHVOROST (I. M.). BELORUSSKIE TANTSI. Minsk 'Belarusi' 1977.
Demy 8vo (7·6 × 5·5 ins.). 149 pp. + (iii) illus. with Drwgs. diags. and mus. Orig. dec. wrapps.
The following dances from White Russia with explanatory text, drawings, diagrams and music: Vishtsenka (p. 3); Krijachok (p. 26); Podushechka (p. 51); Taukachiki (p. 96); Mikita (p. 96); Kotchinskaya Kadril (p. 127). See also *Stenicheskie Belorusskie Tantsi*.

KIDSON (FRANK) & NEAL (MARY). ENGLISH FOLK-SONG AND DANCE. Cambridge: at the University Press 1915.
Cr. 8vo (7·4 × 4·7 ins.). vii + 178 pp. incl. Index with 6 illus. Orig. dec. cloth.
Divided in two parts: The Dance section (pp. 95–176, including a bibliography) contains information on The Sword Dance, The Furry Dance; The Country Dance, and The Present Day Revival of

The Folk Dance. For other works on folk dance consult the index of all volumes of the *Bibliography* under Folk, National and Ethnological Dance.

KILIAN (HANNES). MARCIA HAYDÉE. Porträt einer grossen Tänzerein. Mit Textbeiträgen von Heinz-Ludwig Schneiders Horst Koegler und John Percival. Jan Thorbecke Verlag. [1975].
Demy 4to (11·5 × 9 ins.). 34 pp. of text with frontis. in colour and 103 num illus. in black and white. Orig. grey buckram.
An album of photographs chosen and reproduced with great care. This does not however obviate the need of a smaller work which would reach many more who would like to read about Marcia Haydée. See also Horst Koegler's *Ballett*, Nos. from 1965 to date for information on Haydée and other members of The Stuttgart Ballet.

KINNEY (TROY). ANNA PAVLOVA — A VOTIVE OFFERING. New York, The Dance Magazine Jan. 1929.
Roy. 4to (12·4 × 9·6 ins.). pp. 18, 19, 49 with 5 illus. Orig. dec. wrapps. (Pavlova).
An illustrated article. See also *Selected Letters of Troy Kinney to Doris Niles* for plates of Pavlova in *Gavotte Pavlova* and *Amarilla*.

KINNEY (TROY). THE DANCE OF SPAIN. New York, The Dance Magazine March 1929.
Roy. 4to (12·4 × 9·6 ins.). pp. 18, 19, 56 illus. Orig. dec. wrapps. (Helen Macfadden).
An illustrated article which concludes with an appreciation of Doris Niles and her performances for the King of Spain, Alfonso XIII.

KINNEY (TROY). A DEVOTÉE OF THE ORIENT. New York, The Dance Magazine July 1928.
Roy. 4to (12·4 × 9·6 ins.). pp. 31, 54 illus. Orig. dec. wrapps.
An illustrated article about Vera Mirova and her oriental dances.

KIRCHMEYER (HELMUT). STRAVINSKYS RUSSISCHE BALLETTE. Der Feuervogel Petruschka Le Sacre du Printemps. Mit 76 Notenbeispielen. Stuttgart Philipp Reclam jun. [1974].

Demy 8vo (8·3 × 5·6 ins.). 128 pp. with 76 mus. ex. Orig. dec. red wrapps.
See also Siohan, Robert and Stravinsky and Craft. Text in German.

KIROVA (S. M.). TEATR OPERI I BALETA. Izdatelstvo 'Muzika' Leningradskoe Otdelenie 1976.
Cr. 4to (10·2 × 8 ins.). 160 pp. illus. Orig. dec. boards.
A cleanly printed book about Opera and Ballet at the Leningrad Kirov Theatre. Opera by A. P. Konnov and Ballet by I. V. Stupnikov. Of the ballets, those less often reproduced are *Ikar* (Icare) and *Sotborenie Mira* (Creation of the Universe). See also Degen, A. & Stupnikov, I., *Mastera Tantsa*.

KIRSTEIN (LINCOLN). ENTRIES FROM AN EARLY DIARY. For John Martin. [New York, Dance Perspectives Summer 1973].
Med. 8vo (9 × 7·3 ins.). 56 pp. illus. Orig. dec. wrapps.
Issue No. 54 of *Dance Perspectives* contains a number of Pavel Tchelitchev drawings.

KIRSTEIN (LINCOLN). THE MONUMENT OF DIAGHILEV. New York, Dance News Sept. 1954.
Imp. 4to (16·4 × 11·2 ins.). pp. 7, 8, illus. Orig. wrapps.
An article concluding with a list of dancers from the Diaghilev Ballet now living in America at this period (1954). See also *Bibliography*, Part III, Barzel, Ann, *European Dance Teachers in The United States*.

KIRSTEIN (LINCOLN). THE NEW YORK CITY BALLET. Photographs by Martha Swope and George Platt Lynes. New York, Alfred A. Knopf 1973.
Sq. (12 × 12 ins.). 261 + (i) pp. with more than 250 photogs. 32 in full colour. Orig. black fabric.
This attractive but rather unwieldy album gives the History and Repertory of the New York City Ballet in the various stages of its being: The American Ballet, Ballet Caravan, American Ballet Caravan, Ballet Society, and finally The New York City Ballet. See also *Bibliography*, Part I, Chujoy, *The New York City Ballet*.

KIRSTEIN (LINCOLN). NIJINSKY DANCING. With Essays by Jacques Riviere and Edwin Denby. Photographs by

Bert, de Meyer, Druet, Roosen, White and others. London, Thames & Hudson [1975].
Imp. 4to (12 × 13·1 ins.). 177 + (1) pp. profusely illus. Orig. fabric spine and black boards.
Contents: 1. Personality – Personification – Impersonation (p. 16); 2. Before Nijinsky-Russian Ballet 1850–1900 (p. 20); 3. Marius Petipa 1856–1900 (p. 24); 4. Michel Fokine 1900–1912 (p. 28); 5. Isadora Duncan 1900–1905 (p. 34); 6. The Siamese Court Dancers 1900 (p. 38); 7. Nijinsky 1912–1916 (p. 40); Chronology (p. 44). An album of the best that exists of photographs of Nijinsky; however it could be that due to the cumbersome format important parts of the text will pass unread.

KIRSTEIN (LINCOLN). THE SCHOOL OF AMERICAN BALLET INC. 1934–1944. New York School of American Ballet. n.d.
Demy 8vo (9 × 6 ins.). 51 pp. illus. Orig. printed wrapps.
A brochure on this organization, with a short preface by Lincoln Kirstein, Policy and Program, Chronological listing of Productions, Direction, Faculty and An Album of Distinguished Artists, Friends of the School of American Ballet. See also Chujoy, Anatole, *The New York City Ballet*, Howard, Ruth, *The American Ballet* and Hazan, *Dictionary of Modern Ballet* in *Bibliography*, Part I.

KISSELGOFF (ANNA). HELGI TOMASSON. Brooklyn, New York, Dance Horizons 1976.
Med. 8vo (9 × 7 ins.). 24 pp. incl. both wrapps. Illus.
A monograph with photographs by Martha Swope issued by *Dance Horizons Spotlight Series*. See also Gruen, John, *The Private World of Ballet* (pp. 312–318).

KISSELGOFF (ANNA). VLADIMIR VASILIEV. Brooklyn, Dance Horizons 1975.
Med. 8vo (9 × 7 ins.). 23 pp. illus. Orig. dec. wrapps.
A monograph in the *Dance Horizons Spotlight Series* with photographs by Mira. See also Bolshoi Teatr – *Segodnya na Stsene 1776–1976* for photographs of Vasiliev in *Romeo i Djulietta* (Romeo and Juliet), *Spartak* (Spartacus), *Ivan Groznii* (Ivan the Terrible), *Shelkunchik* (The Nutcracker), *Spyashtsaya Krasavitsa* (The Sleeping Beauty), and *Don Kixot* (Don Quichotte).

KNIGHT (JUDITH). BALLET AND ITS MUSIC. London, Schott Music 1973.

Roy. 4to (12·2 × 9 ins.). III pp. illus. with photogs. and mus. ex. Orig. black cloth.

As the author states in the Preface, this work only skims the surface of the subject; and although the 17 pieces of music from various ballets are of interest, wider knowledge on the subject may be obtained from either the Victor or Decca books on ballet and ballet music.

KNIGHT (LAURA). A LETTER TO CYRIL BEAUMONT. London, Aug. 7, 1967. 16 Langford Place, St. John's Wood.

Cr. 4to (10 × 8 ins.). 1 p. typescript.

A letter that confirms the fact that Cyril Beaumont and Laura Knight were the only visitors regularly allowed back-stage at the Diaghilev Ballet. A Xerox copy.

KNIGHT (LAURA). TWENTY-ONE DRAWINGS OF THE RUSSIAN BALLET. With an Introductory Note by P. F. Konody. London, Davis & Oroli 1920.

Imp. 4to (16 × 13 ins.). (iv) pp. + 21 plates. Orig. grey folio.

Limited edition of 350 numbered copies of which this is number 34. As Konody remarks in the Introductory Note, with the exception of the plate *Les Sylphides*, the drawings are of Massine, Karsavina and Lopokova. Further reproduction of her designs may be found in June Knight's article *The Dancers of Laura Knight*, in *The Dance* Dec. 1929 and Sotheby's *Catalogue of Diaghilev Ballet Material* June 13, 1967.

KOBBÉ (GUSTAV). KOBBÉ'S COMPLETE OPERA BOOK. Edited and Revised by The Earl of Harewood. London, Putnam & Co. [1974].

Demy 8vo (8·2 × 5·2 ins.). xvi + 1262 pp. incl. index. Illus. Orig. red cloth.

Not complete of course, but it does offer the libretto or synopsis of a great many Operas which should interest ballet masters or choreographers wishing to know (in a general fashion) where the ballet appears in *Faust, Les Huguenots, La Gioconda, Robert le Diable* and other Operas.

KOCHNO (BORIS). DIAGHILEV ET LES BALLETS RUSSES. Paris, Fayard 1973.

Roy. 4to (12·1 × 9·4 ins.). (x) + 294 pp. illus. many in colour. Orig. cloth. D.J. after Picasso's Parade.

Although the original edition of this book, published by Harper & Rowe, was designed by Bea Feitler, I find the larger type and 'Mise en page' superior in this, the French one, and with very few exceptions the colour plates are brighter and more effective. Definitely the finer of the two editions.

KOEGLER (HORST). BALLETT 1973. Chronik und Bilanz des Ballettjahres. [Hannover] Friedrich Verlag.

Oblong Cr. 4to (9·5 × 8·1 ins.). 124 pp. illus. Orig. dec. wrapps.

Inhalt: Hartmut Regitz: Im Schlagschatten des Todes von Cranko (p. 30). Noverre und Cranko – Horst Koegler über zwei Stuttgarter Beiträge zur Ballettgeschichte (p. 32).

KOEGLER (HORST). BALLETT 1974. Chronik und Bilanz des Ballettjahres. [Hannover] Friedrich Verlag.

Oblong Cr. 4to (9·5 × 8·2 ins.). 120 pp. illus. Orig. dec. wrapps.

Inhalt: Umfrage: Was halten Sie von der deutschen Ballettkritik (p. 35). Jens Wendland: John Cranko – eine Legende? (p. 51).

KOEGLER (HORST). BALLETT 1975. Chronik und Bilanz des Ballettjahres. [Hannover] Friedrich Verlag.

Oblong Cr. 4to (9·5 × 8·2 ins.). 116 pp. illus. Orig. dec. wrapps.

Inhalt: Horst Koegler: Yvonne Georgi (p. 14). Hartmut Regitz: Adèle Grantzow, eine Ballerina des 19 Jahrhunderts (p. 39).

KOEGLER (HORST). BALLETT 1976. Chronik und Bilanz des Ballettjahres. [Hannover] Friedrich Verlag.

Oblong Cr. 4to (9·5 × 8·2 ins.). 120 pp. illus. Orig. dec. wrapps.

Inhalt: Klaus Geitel: Die tänzerische Volksfront oder Der Historische Kompromiss (p. 19). Horst Koegler: Interview mit Birgit Keil (p. 40).

KOEGLER (HORST). BALLETT 1977. Chronik und Bilanz des Ballettjahres. [Hannover] Friedrich Verlag.

Oblong Cr. 4to (9·5 × 8·2 ins.). 120 pp. illus. Orig. dec. wrapps.

Inhalt: Klaus Geitel: Egon Madsen oder die Matamorphose des Harlekin (p. 32).

KOEGLER (HORST). THE CONCISE OXFORD DICTIONARY OF BALLET. London, Oxford University Press 1977.
Cr. 8vo (8 × 5 ins.). viii + 583 pp. Orig. black cloth.
An Anglo-American adaptation of *Friedrichs Ballettlexikon* with entries of interest only to German speaking peoples deleted. An interesting enough dictionary, but the biographical material seems to be lacking in choice and depth. See also *Bibliography*, Part III, Koegler, *Friedrichs Balletlexikon*.

KOEGLER (HORST). IN THE SHADOW OF THE SWASTIKA. Dance in Germany 1927–1936. New York, Dance Perspectives 1974.
Med. 8vo (9 × 6 ins.). 48 pp. illus. Orig. dec. wrapps.
Issue No. 57 of *Dance Perspectives*.

KOLODIN (IRVING). THE METROPOLITAN OPERA 1883–1935. New York, Oxford University Press 1936.
Med. 8vo (9 × 6 ins.). xix + 589 pp. incl. Index. Illus. Orig. brown cloth.
Consult the Index for ballets performed and artists engaged during this period. Diaghilev and his Company, Pavlova, and long time resident artists, Giuseppe Bonfiglio and Rosina Galli.

KOLODIN (IRVING). THE STORY OF THE METROPOLITAN OPERA 1883–1950. A Candid History. New York, Alfred A. Knopf 1953.
Med. 8vo (9·2 × 6·2 ins.). xx + 607 pp. + xxxviii pp. illus. Orig. buckram and cloth binding.
A continuation of *The Metropolitan Opera* 1883–1935, with many more illustrations although they are reduced in size.

KOROLEVA (E.). KHOREOGRAFISCHESKOE ISKUSSTVO MOLDAVII. Izadelstvo 'Kartya Moldovenyaskeh' Kishinev 1970.
F'cap 8vo (6·4 × 4·5 ins.). 185 + (iii) pp. illus. Orig. dec. wrapps.
Moldavian Choreographic Art. Among the interesting photographs are those of *Sestri* (The Sisters) and *Rassvet* (Dawn) both created at Kishinev. See *Bibliography*, Part III, Swift, M. G. *The Art of the Dance in the U.S.S.R.* (p. 178) for some account of both of these ballets.

KOROLEVA (E.). SPEKTAKL BALETMEISTER TANTSOVSHTSNIK. Izdatelstvo 'Literatura Artistike' Kishinev 1977.

F'cap 8vo (6·4 × 4·7 ins.). 164 pp. illus. Orig. dec. green fabric.

The repertory at the Kishinev theatre now seems mostly standard, with the exception of *Radde*, which apparently had little success. The work closes with an important bibliografiya which lists some 27 articles by Elfrida Aleksandrovna Koroleva.

KOSTROVITSKAYA (V.) & PISAREV (A.). SHKOLA KLASSICHESKOGO TANTSA. 'Iskusstvo' Leningradskoe Otdelenie 1976.

Demy 8vo (8·3 × 5·5 ins.). 270 + (ii) pp. illus. Orig. dec. purple cloth.

The second edition with additional material of *School of the Classic Dance*. See *Bibliography*, Part III, Kostrovitskaya for the first.

KRAGH-JACOBSEN (SVEND). BALLETTEN 1945–52. Areté 1953.

Cr. 8vo (8 × 4·1 ins.). 113 pp. illus. Orig. printed yellow wrapps.

Contains information on Birger Bartholin and Alexandre Volinine among others. See also *Bibliography*, Parts I and III, Kragh-Jacobsen, Svend.

KRAGH-JACOBSEN (SVEND). THE ROYAL DANISH BALLET. Drawings by Hans Bendix. [Copenhagen, The Royal Danish Ministry of Foreign Affairs. 1974].

Demy 8vo (8·2 × 4·7 ins.). 28 pp. n.n. with 11 pen sketches. Orig. white wrapps.

A booklet issued for the appearance of The Royal Danish Ballet at the London Coliseum April 1–6 1974.

KRASOVSKAYA (V.). NIJINSKII. Izdatelstvo Iskusstvo Leningradskoe Otdelenie 1974.

Cr. 8vo (7·7 × 5·4 ins.). 208 pp. illus. Orig. white cloth.

The text in Russian is illustrated with 67 numbered items after drawings, photographs etc.

KRASOVSKAYA (V. Editor). SOVETSKII BALETNI TEATR 1917–1967. Moskva, Iskusstvo 1976.

Cr. 8vo (7.7 × 5 ins.). 376 pp + large section of photogs. Orig. dec. white leatherette.

Soderjanie (Contents): E. Surich, Nachalo puti Balet Moskvi i Leningrada a 1917–1927 goda; N. Chernova, Balet 1930–1940 x godov; N. Cheremetevskaya, Molodie Baletnie Teatr; V. Krasovskaya, V. Seredine veka (1950–1960 godi); V. Berezkin, Khudojnik v Sovetskom Balete.

KRASOVSKAYA (V.). STATI O BALETE. [Iskusstvo Leningrad 1967].

F'cap 8vo (6.4 × 4.4 ins.). 337 + (iii) pp. illus. Orig. red cloth.

The illustrations include those of *Bereg Nadejdi* (Coast of Hope), and *Tropou Groma* (Path of Thunder) both after librettos by Slonimsky.

KRAUS (RICHARD). HISTORY OF THE DANCE IN ART AND EDUCATION. Englewood Cliffs, Prentice-Hall Inc. [1969].

Med. 8vo (9.2 × 6.2 ins.). xii + 371 pp. incl. Index. Orig. orange cloth.

A medium length history culminating with a study of College and University dance programmes, and the concern as to whether to point their effort towards developing individual skills among the students, or to seek to extend the knowledge and appreciation of dance among the wider public.

KRIEGSMAN (ALAN M.). SUZANNE FARRELL. Photography by Martha Swope. New York, Dance Horizons Spotlight Series.

Med. 8vo (9 × 7 ins.). 24 pp. illus. Orig. illus. wrapps.

A monograph. See also Koegler, *Dictionary of Ballet*, Farrell for listing of several articles about her.

LABAN (RUDOLF). THE LANGUAGE OF MOVEMENT. A Guidebook to Choreutics. Annotated and Edited by Lisa Ullmann. Boston, Plays Inc. [1966].

Cr. 4to (9.6 × 7.2 ins.). x + 214 pp. illus. with diags. Orig. green cloth.

The American edition of Laban's *Choreutics*. See also *Bibliography*, Parts II and III, Laban.

LANDER (HARALD). THI KENDES FOR RET – ?. Erindringer. Kobenhavn, Henning Branner's Forlag MCMLI [1951].
Cr. 4to (10·1 × 7·2 ins.). 147 pp. incl. Inhold. Orig. dec. wrapps.
Text in Danish. For other information on Harald Lander see: *Ballet Annual* No. 7, Royal Danish Ballet Festival (p. 113) and The Living Tradition in Denmark (p. 117); Chujoy, *The Dance Encyclopedia* (Rev. and Enl. edn.); Aschengreen, *Etudes*. Also *Ballet* Vol. II No. 7, Aug. 1951 for material on The Royal Danish Ballet and Harald Lander.

LANGDON-DAVIES (JOHN). DANCING CATALANS. London, Jonathan Cape [1929].
Cr. 8vo (7·5 × 4·7 ins.). 220 pp. Orig. cloth.
See Chapter II. The Dance (p. 29). Also Appendix: The Choreography of the Sardana (p. 213).

LANGE (RODERYK). DANCES FROM CUIAVIA KINETOGRAMS & MUSIC. Jersey, C.I., Centre for Dance Studies 1976.
Oblong (8 × 11·6 ins.). 15 pp. of kinetograms + 6 pp. of mus. Cream folder.
Laban kinetograms for the following dances from Poland: *Kujawiak, Chodzony, Dyna,* and *Czapnik*. For photographs of groups dancing the *Kujawiak* and *Chodzony* see Turska, Irena, *Taniec w Polsce*, also Raffé, W. G., *Dictionary of the Dance*, for definition of the Kujawiak.

LANGE (RODERYK). DANCE STUDIES. Les Bois, St. Peter, Jersey, C.I. 1976.
Cr. 8vo (7·7 × 5·7 ins.). vii + 87 pp. illus. Orig. wrapps.
Various short articles about Labanotation employing Laban Kinetograms from Roderyk Lange, Muriel Topaze, Billie Mahoney, Lisa Ullmann, Maria Drabeca, Mireille Backer and Jacqueline Challet-Haas.

LANGE (RODERYK). THE NATURE OF DANCE. An Anthropological Perspective. London, Macdonald & Evans. [1975].
Demy 8vo (8·4 × 5·2 ins.). xv + 142 pp. illus. Orig. orange boards.

A slender volume which might be considered a guide to the very large and important bibliography preceding the Index. The photographs are predominantly of aborigines and blacks, whose movements, like those of discotheque dancers, seem to use the head, arms, and legs as appendages to be flung about. Those of the Balinese, Cambodian, Indian etc., show these members closely integrated with body position and in general harmonious.

LANGLOIS (ROSE-MARIE). L'OPÉRA DE VERSAILLES. Paris, Pierre Horay 1958.
Demy 8vo (8·3 × 6·1 ins.). 153 + (iii) pp. illus. Orig. dec. blue wrapps.
The Opera de Versailles which came into being under Louis XV with Mariages Princiers, Bal Paré, Tragédie and Ballet. *La Tour Enchantée* was given on June 20, 1770. See *Bibliography*, Part I, Joliveau, for the original libretto. Falling into disuse L'Opéra was resuscitated and this book commemorates that fact.

LANSDALE (NELSON). THE BALLET: GOOD THING FOR PAINTERS. New York, Art News Oct. 1941.
Roy. 4to (13·3 × 10 ins.). pp. 14–17 illus. some in colour. Orig. dec. wrapps.
An article in the Oct. 1–14th issue of *Art News* concerning the 1941–42 season of Ballet Russe de Monte Carlo and Ballet Caravan.

LARIONOV (MICHEL). RETROSPECTIVE LARIONOV. Du Mardi 17 Juin au Samedi 27 Septembre 1969. Paris, Galerie de Paris.
Demy 8vo (8·2 × 5·7 ins.). 40 pp. n.n. incl. 62 items, 16 illus. in colour and many black and white. Orig. wrapps.
A catalogue with excellent illustrations in colour. See also *Bibliography*, Part III, Larionov.

LASSAIGNE (JACQUES). MARC CHAGALL. Dessins et Aquarelles pour le Ballet. Paris, XXe Siecle. [1969].
Roy. 4to (13·6 × 10·2 ins.). 155 pp. illus. principally in colour. Orig. cloth boxed.
A splendid volume of designs, mostly in colour, from *Aleko*, *L'Oiseau de Feu*, and *Daphnis et Chloé*. A book produced with care and suitably boxed. There is also an English edition.

LAUCHERY (HERRN). TAENZE MIT MUZIK. Contradanses, Quadrilles, Cotillon Ecossaise. Herausgegben von Herrn Lauchery, Konigl. Balletmeister und Solo-Tanzer in Berlin. [1823]

12 mo (4·4 × 3·3 ins.). 44 pp. diags. and music + 17 pp. Erklärung der Tänze. Lacks front end paper and board.

Albert Lauchery (1779–1853) was soloist at the Berlin Opera in 1803 and taught as head of the ballet school until 1846 at least.

LAVROVSKY (L. M.). ROMEO I DJULIETTA. Bolshoi Teatr.

Med. 8vo (9 × 6 ins.). 8 pp. with 1 illus. Orig. dec. wrapps.

A synopsis of the ballet *Romeo and Juliet* presented at the Kirov Jan 11, 1940 and at the Bolshoi Dec. 28, 1946. An insert programme of the second performance Jan. 7, 1947 is included with Ulanova (*Juliet*) and Gabovich (*Romeo*). Both versions were choreographed by Leonid Lavrovsky.

LAVROVSKY (L. M.). ROMEO I DJULIETTA. Izdanie Leningradskoe Gosud. Ordena Lenina Akad. Teatra Operi i Baleta im S. M. Kirova 1940.

Cr. 8vo (6·6 × 5·1 ins.). 19 + (ii) pp. with 3 illus. Orig. dec. wrapps.

A libretto in Russian for the ballet *Romeo and Juliet*, first performed by the Kirov Jan. 11, 1940 (with Ulanova and Sergeyev). See *Bibliography*, Part II, Roslavleva, *Era of the Russian Ballet* and Slonimsky, *The Bolshoi Ballet*.

LAWRENCE (D. H.). THE DANCE OF THE SPROUTING CORN. New York, Theatre Arts Monthly 1924.

Cr. 4to (9·8 × 7·4 ins.). pp. 447–457 with 4 illus. Orig. dec. wrapps.

An illustrated article in the July 1924 issue of *Theatre Arts Monthly*.

LAWSON (JOAN). BALLET IN THE U.S.S.R. S.C.R. London 1943.

Demy 8vo (8·2 × 5·2 ins.). 16 pp. illus. Orig. pink printed wrapps.

An early pamphlet produced by the Society for Cultural Relations between the Peoples of the British Commonwealth and the U.S.S.R.

LAWSON (JOAN). THE TEACHING OF CLASSICAL BALLET. Common Faults in Young Dancers and their Training. London, Adam & Charles Black [1973].
    Med. 8vo (9·5 × 7·2 ins.). 132 pp. with many illus. Orig. brown cloth.
    See also *Bibliography*, Part II, Lawson, Joan.

LAWSON (JOAN). TEACHING YOUNG DANCERS. Muscular co-ordination in Classical Ballet. With 140 photographs and 7 diagrams. London, Adam & Charles Black 1975.
    Cr. 4to (9·6 × 7·2 ins.). xi + 115 pp. illus. Orig. red fabric.
    A further work on muscular co-ordination in the vein of Gelabert and Sparger.

LEDERMAN (MINNA). STRAVINSKY IN THE THEATRE. Edited with an introduction by Minna Lederman. London, Peter Owen Ltd. [1951].
    Cr. 4to (9·5 × 7 ins.). (x) + 228 pp. illus. Orig. red cloth.
    This book represents a considerable enlargement on *Dance Index's* Stravinsky issue, and closes with an excellent bibliography divided in the following Sections: 1. Books Devoted to Stravinsky; 2. Special Periodical Issues devoted wholly to Stravinsky; 3. References to Stravinsky in other Books; 4. References to Stravinsky in Periodicals; 5. References to Specific Works by Stravinsky. A list of over 600 references without cross indexing.

LEDERMAN (MINNA). STRAVINSKY IN THE THEATRE. Edited with an introduction by Minna Lederman. [New York], Da Capo. [1975].
    Med. 8vo (9·7 × 6·2 ins.). (ix) + 228 pp. illus. Orig. dec. wrapps.
    This unabridged republication of the above 1949 edition contains the very important bibliography.

LEEPER (JANET). ENGLISH BALLET. London and New York, King Penguin Books 1944.
    F'cap 8vo (7·1 × 4·6 ins.). 31 pp. + 16 plates in colour. Orig. dec. boards.
    The first edition. See *Bibliography*, Part II, for the second revised edition. The drawings and plates remain the same in both editions.

LEHMANN (JOHN) & PARKER (DEREK). EDITH SITWELL. Selected Letters 1919–1964. New York, The Vanguard Press. [1970].
Med. 8vo (9 × 6 ins.). 264 pp. incl. Index. with 3 illus. Orig. brown cloth.
Includes interesting letters about *Facade* and Pavel Tchelitchew.

LENIN PRIZE WINNERS. SOVIET STARS. Theatre Music Art (1967–1970). Moscow, Progress Publishers. [1972].
Cr. 8vo (6·4 × 5 ins.). 304 pp. illus. Orig. dec. wrapps.
Important to the ballet are articles on *Spartacus* by Ulanova, Lvov-Anokhin, Dashieva, Lepeshinskaya, Grishina and Sobolev. These are most welcome and are fortunately the least tinged by propaganda. The 4th book in the series *'Soviet Stars'*.

LEONARD (RICHARD ANTHONY). A HISTORY OF RUSSIAN MUSIC. London, Jarrolds 1956.
Demy 8vo (8·3 × 5·2 ins.). 395 pp. incl. index. Orig. red cloth.
Also contains references to music by non-Russian composers, and many citations on Diaghilev. Consult the index.

LEONIDZE (G. D.) & VOLKOV (N.D.). SERDTSE GOR. Balet v 3 deistvniyakh i kartinakh. Izdanie Leningradskoe Gosud. Ordena Lenina Akad. Teatra Operi i Baleta im S. M. Kirova 1940.
Cr. 8vo (6·6 × 5·1 ins.). 12 + (ii) pp. with 3 illus. Orig. dec. wrapps.
A libretto in Russian for the ballet *Heart of the Hills*, Chaboukiani's first ballet with music by Balanchivadze. First performed by the Kirov June 28, 1938. See Roslavleva, *Era of Russian Ballet* (pp. 242–243). See also Slonimsky, *V Chest Tantsa* (plates between pp. 64–65).

LESLIE (SERGE). A BIBLIOGRAPHY OF THE DANCE COLLECTION OF DORIS NILES & SERGE LESLIE. Annotated by Serge Leslie. Edited by Cyril Beaumont Part III A–Z. London, C. W. Beaumont 1974.
Demy 8vo (8·4 × 5·4 ins.). Part III. 290 pp. incl. Index. Full Blue buckram.

The two previous parts were first published in 1966 and 1968 respectively.

Part III comprises mainly 20th century publications.

LESLIE (SERGE). CYRIL BEAUMONT. London, C. W. Beaumont 1958.

Demy 8vo (8·3 × 5·3 ins.). pp. 159–182 illus. Orig. red cloth.

Chaper IX of *The Seven Leagues of a Dancer*. See *Bibliography*, Part II, Leslie, Serge.

LESLIE (SERGE). CYRIL BEAUMONT. London, Theatre Notebook 1977.

Demy 8vo (8·4 × 5·2 ins.). pp. 4, 5. Orig. dec. wrapps.

A short appreciation of the literary accomplishments of Cyril Beaumont, particularly on the number and quality of articles he wrote. In *Theatre Notebook*, Vol. XXXI No. 1, 1977.

LEVINSON (ANDRÉ). BAKST. The Story of the Artist's Life. London, The Bayard Press 1923.

Imp. 4to (14·3 × 10·6 ins.). 240 pp. with text illus. + 68 plates full page of which 52 are in colour. Orig. dec. vellum.

This is copy No. 129 of an edition published by Alexander Kogan, *Russian Art*, Berlin and printed by Dr. Selle & Co. The entire edition is limited to 315 copies of which 15 were not for sale. See *Bibliography*, Parts II and III, Levinson for the French and German editions of this work.

LEVINSON (ANDRÉ). BERAIN AND THE FRENCH COSTUME TRADITION. New York, Theatre Arts Monthly 1926.

Cr. 4to (9·7 × 7·4 ins.). pp. 154–166 with 5 illus. Orig. dec. wrapps.

An illustrated article in the March 1926 number of *Theatre Arts Monthly*.

LEVINSON (ANDRÉ). A LETTER TO CYRIL BEAUMONT. Paris Le 1, Novembre.

Cr. 4to (10·2 × 8 ins.). 1 p. Xerox.

A copy of a letter to Cyril Beaumont concerning the mss of his work *Taglioni* and also one on Pavlova that he refused to allow to be sold.

LEVINSON (ANDRÉ). MARIE TAGLIONI (1804-1884). Translated by Cyril W. Beaumont. London, Dance Books Ltd. 1977.
 Demy 8vo (8·5 × 5·4 ins.). 111 pp. illus. Orig. red cloth.
 A textual reprint of the 1930 edition with the lovely head and tail pieces of Eileen Mayo. See also *Bibliography*, Part I, *Dollingen & Disderi*, for listing of other fine books about Taglioni.

LEVINSON (ANDRÉ). MASTERA BALETA. Ocherki Istorii i Teorii Tantsa. Izdanie N.V. Solovev Sanktpeterburg 1914.
 Demy 4to (11 × 7·5 ins.). 132 pp. + (iii) illus. with 2 plates in colour and 22 in black and white. Orig. dec. wrapps.
 The first edition of a fine book. Later published in German as *Meister des Balletts*, Potsdam 1923. See *Bibliography*, Part II, Levinson, André. One of Levinson's rarer works.

LEWIS (ARTHUR H.). LA BELLE OTERO. New York, Trident Press 1967.
 Demy 8vo (8·1 × 5·4 ins.). ix + 257 pp. illus. Orig. cloth with boards.
 See also *Bibliography*, Part II, Otero, Caroline.

LIBMAN (LILLIAN). AND MUSIC AT THE CLOSE. Stravinsky's Last Years. A Personal Memoir by Lillian Libman. London, Macmillan 1972.
 Demy 8vo (8·4 × 5·2 ins.). 400 pp. incl. Index. Illus. Orig. red cloth.
 The title is a trifle misleading, for the book contains numerous references to The Diaghilev Company, Diaghilev and Stravinsky's first ballets.

LIDO (SERGE). BALLETS ET DANSEURS DANS LE MONDE. Textes de Odon-Jerome Lemaitre, Peter Williams, Commentaires de Irène Lidova. Paris, Editions Vilo. [1973].
 Cr. 4to (10·1 × 8·4 ins.). (viii) + 80 plates + (vii pp.) of commentaires. Orig. illus. black boards.
 See also Lido, Parts II and III of the *Bibliography*.

LIDO (SERGE). BALLETT VON HEUTE. Berlin, Rembrandt Verlag [1966].

Demy 4to (11·6 × 9·3 ins.). 15 pp. + 167 of Photogs. and further text. Orig. rose cloth.
The translation into German of *Ballet d'aujourd'hui* by Klaus Geitel. See *Bibliography*, Part II, for the French edition under Lido.

LIDO (SERGE). LES ETOILES DE LA DANSE DANS LE MONDE. Textes de Marcel Schneider et de Irène Lidova. Paris, editions Vilo. [1975].
Cr. 4to (10·1 × 8·4 ins.). (viii) + 80 pp. of plates + (vii pp.) of Commentaires. Orig. illus. black boards.
Among some remarkable photographs I would choose plates 20, 21 of Maximova and Vasiliev for dramatic content and sheer beauty.

LIDOVA (IRENE). LE SECRET DE LA LIGNE PAR LA DANSE. 6 Lecons par 6 Etoiles. Paris, Rester Jeune No. 67.
Roy. 4to (12·3 × 9·6 ins.). 80 pp. n.n. illus. Orig. dec. wrapps.
Six Etoiles present six dancing lessons: Yvette Chauviré, Janine Charrat, Renée Jeanmaire, Ludmila Tcherina, Ethery Pagava, Janine Solane. Introduction by Lidova, photographs by Serge Lido.

LIFAR (SERGE). LE BALLET ET LA DANSE A L'ÉPOQUE ROMANTIQUE 1800–1850. Musée des Arts Décoratifs 1942.
Cr. 8vo (6·6 × 5·1 ins.). xvi + 120 + 12 pp. of illus. Orig. tan printed wrapps.
A catalogue of an Exposition organized by Serge Lifar and L'Union Centrale des Arts Decoratifs at the Musée des Arts Décoratifs Jan.–Avril 1942. 560 very well chosen items.

LIFAR (SERGE). BALLETS RUSSES DE DIAGHILEV 1909–1929. Musée des Arts Décoratifs. Paris, de Brunhoff 1939.
Cr. 4to (10·5 × 8·3 ins.). 39 + (i) pp. illus. Orig. dec. tan wrapps.
A catalogue of an exhibition organized at the Musée des Arts Decoratifs Avril–Mai 1939. At this time it was difficult to assemble a complete run of Diaghilev souvenir programmes for the Paris seasons. This item is listed in Ifan Kyrle Fletcher's *Books Relating to the Diaghilev Ballet*. See Buckle, *Bibliography*, Part I, *The Diaghilev Exhibition*.

LIFAR (SERGE). ISTORIYA RUSSKAGO BALETA. Ot XVII veka do 'Russkago Baleta' Dyagileva. Pariji 1945.

Med. 8vo (9·7 × 6·3 ins.). 302 pp. + (ii) illus. Orig. dec. wrapps.
This is the edition on finer hand made paper. See *Bibliography*, Part II, for the ordinary edition. Cyril Beaumont's personal copy autographed by Lifar.

LIFAR (SERGE). SERGE DIAGHILEV. His Life His Work His Legend. An intimate Biography. New York, G. P. Putnam's Sons. [1940].

Med. 8vo (9·1 × 6·1 ins.). xiv + 399 pp. incl. Index. Illus. with a frontis. and 65 other illus. Orig. red cloth.
Divided into two books: I. Diaghilev; 2. With Diaghilev. Book 1 is in three Parts: 1. The Young Diaghilev; 2. The World of Art Epoque; 3. The Russian Ballet.

LIFAR (SERGE). SUR LE PLATEAU. Paris, Formes et Couleurs.

Roy. 4to (12 × 9 ins.). 10 pp. with 6 illus. Orig. dec. wrapps.
An article in No. 5 XIeme série of *Formes et Couleurs*. The entire issue is devoted to L'Opéra de Paris and also has an article by Lycette Darsonval, *Reflections sur la Danse* (3 pp. with 3 illus.).

LIGHTFOOT (LOUISE). DANCE-RITUALS OF MANIPUR INDIA. An Introduction to 'Meitei Jagoi'. New Delhi, Ministry of Scientific Research and Cultural Affairs. [1959 c.].

Med. 8vo (8·3 × 5·3 ins.). 79 pp. with 19 illus. Orig. black paper boards.
Listed in Judy Van Zile's *Dance in India*.

LILLIESTAM (AKE). CHRISTIAN JOHANSSON OCH HANS BREV TILL AUGUST BOURNONVILLE. [Stockholm, Kungl. Boktr 1974].

Med. 8vo (9 × 5·7 ins.). pp. 75–103 illus. Orig. blue wrapps.
Sixteen letters from Christian Johansson (1817–1903) to August Bournonville (1805–1879). Reprinted from *Särtyck Personhistorisk tidskrift* Argång 69 1973. Text in Swedish, with a resumé on (p. 102–103). For further information on Johansson see: *Enciclopedia Dello Spettacolo* Vol. VI; Koegler, *Ballettlexikon* (p. 291); and Legat, *The Story of the Russian School*, Chapter V. The Class of Perfection.

LISTER (RAYMOND). THE MUSCOVITE PEACOCK. A Study of the Art of Léon Bakst. With a Memoir by Simon Lissim. Cambridge, The Golden Head Press 1954.

Demy 8vo (8·4 × 5·3 ins.). 52 pp. + a frontis. in colour and 11 plates in black and white. Orig. blue cloth with labels.

The strongest points in this delightful little book are the Study by Raymond Lister and the Memoir by Simon Lissim. The bibliography and even the Notes on Productions could well be amplified. Signed copy No. 105 of an edition of 150.

LITVINOFF (VALENTINA). THE USE OF STANISLAVSKY WITHIN MODERN DANCE. Drawings — Valentina Litvinoff. American Dance Guild, Inc. 1972.

Demy 8vo (9 × 6 ins.). 78 pp. illus. with line drwgs. Orig. dec. white wrapps.

This is the second printing.

LOBANOV-ROSTOVSKY (MR. & MRS. D.). RUSSIAN PAINTERS AND THE STAGE 1884–1965. Texas, The University of Texas at Austin 1977.

Demy 4to (11 × 8·3 ins.). 105 pp. illus. Orig. dec. wrapps. (Firebird).

A catalogue of an exhibition of Stage and Costume Designs held at the University Art Museum February 13–March 13 1977.

LOESER (NORBERT). HET BALLET. Haarlem-Antwerpen, Uitgeverij J. H. Gottmer. [1953].

Demy 8vo (8·3 × 5·2 ins.). 150 pp. illus. Orig. dec. soft paper boards.

Text in Dutch. Inhoud: I. De Oorzaken ven de Groeie ende Belangstelling voor de Dans; II. Het Wezen van de Dans; III. Een Stukje Geschiedenis; IV. De Dans in 20sts Eew; V. Het Tidjperk van Diaghilew. Kort Technisch Intermezzo; VI. De Moderne Dans en Het Jongste Verleden.

LONDON ARCHIVES OF THE DANCE (THE). LE LAC DES CYGNES. Catalogue of Exhibition held at The Ballet Guild Studio April 1945.

F'cap 8vo (6·4 × 4 ins.). 11 pp. mimeograph. Plain wrapps.

Reference Notes on the ballet *Le Lac des Cygnes*, and listing of different versions. Mention is made of a Mordkin production on Nov. 1938. I believe Mordkin also produced *Le Lac des Cygnes* for the All Star Russian Ballet appearing at the Metropolitan Opera House in 1911, and then again in his 1926-27 season, for which the programme contains a 4 pp. insert with a synopsis of *Lake of Swans* and photographs of himself and Makletzova. Neither Chujoy nor Wilson mention this one. *The Swan Lake* presented by Sadler's Wells in 1943 has perhaps the best documentation with Cyril Beaumont's *The Swan Lake*, Beaumont 1947 and *Ballet Designs of Leslie Hurry*, Faber & Faber 1946. The finest studies of the ballet itself are Beaumont's *The Ballet Called Swan Lake* and Slonimsky's *Lebedinoe Ozero*, Leningrad 1962.

LONGSTREET (STEPHEN). THE DANCE IN ART. Introduction by Stephen Longstreet. Alhambra, Borden Publishing Co. [1968].

Demy 4to (12 × 9 ins.). iv + 44 pp. of plates. Orig. dec. wrapps.

Reproductions of Degas, Tchelitchew, Picasso, Gir, Bakst and others. See also *Bibliography*, Part II, Lampkin, *The Dance in Art*; Lee-Elliot, *Paintings of the Ballet*, Moreck, *Der Tanz in der Kunst*.

LOPUKHOV (FEDOR). KHOREOGRAFICHESKIE OTKROVENNOSTI. [Moskva], Izdatelstvo Iskusstvo [1971].

Cr. 8vo (7·6 × 4·7 ins.). 214 + (ii) pp. illus. Orig. cream cloth.

This work in Russian is divided into two sections, both containing fine and little known photographs: 1. Khoreograficheskaya Kompozitsiya (Choreographic Compositions) and 2. Balet Meister i Ispolnitelv (Ballet Master and Executive). See *Bibliography*, Parts II and III, Lopukhov, Fedor for other works by this choreographer and author, also Swift, M. G., *The Art of the Dance in U.S.S.R.* for much information on Lopukhov.

LOPUKHOV (FYODOR) & ASAFIEV (BORIS). ANNALS OF THE SLEEPING BEAUTY. Brooklyn, New York, Ballet Review 1976.

Med. 8vo (9 × 5·6 ins.). pp. 21-43. Orig. dec. wrapps.

An article in *Ballet Review* Vol. 5 No. 4 in 2 parts: I. The Choreography; II. The Music. Lopukhov's analysis of various roles in *The Sleeping Beauty* give many clues into the secrets of Petipa's composing, and are written for the specialist, not the layman. These observations are extracted from his book *Khoreograficheskie Otkrovyennosti (Candid Reflections on Choreography)*, see entry above. II. Asafiev considers *The Sleeping Beauty* as a form of musical-choreographic action and pursues that train of thought. See also Asafiev, *Selected Works*, Moscow 1955.

Lopukhov (p. 23) observes that from 1917 to 1936 there were no new productions of *The Sleeping Beauty*. This of course ignores Alexandre Gorskii's productions for the Bolshoi in 1919 and 1934. See *Bolshoi Teatr SSSR, Spyashtsya Krasavitsa*.

LUTSKAYA (E.). ZHIZN V TANTSE. Izdatelstvo Iskusstvo, Moskva 1968.

Cr. 4to (10·2 × 8 ins.). 78 + (ii) pp. of text with 49 photogs., some d. page. Orig. dec. cream cloth.

There is a summary in both English and French for this story of the USSR Academic Ensemble of Folk Dance (Moiseyev). The dances are from many of the Soviet Republics.

LVOV-ANOKHIN (B.). MASTERA BOLSHOGO BALETA. Moskva, Iskusstvo 1976.

Cr. 8vo (7·7 × 5·5 ins.). 240 pp. + plates n.n. Orig. cream cloth.

Biographical material on the following: Grigorovich, Plisetskaya, Timofeeva, Maksimova, Vasiliev, Bessmertnova, Liepa, and Lavrovskii. Text in Russian. See also *Bibliography*, Parts II and III, Lvov-Anokhin, B.

MACDONALD (NESTA). DIAGHILEV OBSERVED. By Critics in England and the United States 1911–1929. Dance Horizons, New York and Dance Books Ltd., London. [1975].

Med. 4to (11·3 × 8·2 ins.). xvi + 400 pp. incl. index. Many illus. Orig. blue cloth.

A very important book containing mainly new material about the Diaghilev Ballet Company. Among the most valuable portions are: Russian Dancers in London Before Diaghilev (p. 16); Nijinsky at the Palace Theatre (p. 106); Background to the Tours in the U.S.A. (p. 128); *Till Eulenspiegel* (p. 182); *The Sleeping Princess* (p. 268). The last named includes photographs of Pavlova's *Sleeping Beauty* for the New York Hippodrome.

MACDONALD (NESTA). THE HISTORY OF THE PHEASANTRY CHELSEA 1776–1977. Privately Printed 1977.

Demy 8vo (8·2 × 5·7 ins.). 23 + (iii) pp. illus. Orig. tan dec. wrapps.

A history of this house and grounds which is particularly interesting to the dance enthusiast because of the biographical notes given about Princess Seraphine Astafieva, who lived and taught there from 1916–1934.

MACDONALD (NESTA). ISADORA REEXAMINED: Lesser Known Aspects of the Great Dancer's Life 1889–1900. New York, Dance Magazine July 1977.

Demy 4to (11 × 8·3 ins.). Part I pp. 51–67 illus. Orig. dec. wrapps. (Isadora Duncan).

An article in 6 Parts appearing in *Dance Magazine* from July 1977 through Dec. 1977. Part I is a *Dance Magazine Portfolio*; Parts II–VI are shorter in text and illustration.

MACKIE (JOYCE). BASIC BALLET. London, Imperial Society of Teachers of Dancing 1973.

F'cap 8vo (4·3 × 5·4 ins.). 120 pp. illus. with photogs. Orig. dec. wrapps.

A manual with positions demonstrated by Terri Mills and Trevor Wood.

MACMAHON (AUDREY). THE ART OF TROY KINNEY. New York, The Dance Magazine Nov. 1929.

Roy. 4to (12·6 × 9·4 ins.). pp. 34, 60 with 1 illus. Orig. dec. wrapps. (Helen Macfadden).

An article in the Nov. 1929 issue of *Dance Magazine* which contains a reproduction of an etching of Doris Niles. See also Kinney, Troy.

MACMILLAN (KENNETH). ANASTASIA. Royal Opera House, Friday 17, Jan. 1975.

Demy 8vo (9 × 5·2 ins.). 40 pp. n.n. illus. Orig. dec. wrapps.

A house programme containing the synopsis of this ballet. This is the 19th performance with Scenario and Choreography by Macmillan. See *About the House* Vol. III Nos. 9 and 10 for considerable information concering *Anastasia*.

MAGGS. MAGGS MUSICAL MISCELLANY No. 3. London, Nov. 1976.

Demy 8vo (8·3 × 5·4 ins.). 60 pp. illus. Orig. dec. wrapps.

A catalogue from the famous house of Maggs which contains 211 items under the heading Dance.

MAGRIEL (PAUL DAVID). A BIBLIOGRAPHY OF DANCING. A List of Books and Articles on the Dance and Related subjects. First Supplement 1936–37. New York, H. W. W. Wilson 1938.

Cr. 4to (10 × 6·4 ins.). 41 pp. incl. Index. Orig. red wrapps.

This is the First Supplement. See *Bibliography*, Part II, for Third and Fourth Cumulated Supplements.

MAGRIEL (PAUL Editor). NIJINSKY PAVLOVA DUNCAN. Three Lives in Dance Edited by Paul Magriel. New York, A Da Capo Paperback 1977.

Med. 8vo (9·2 × 7 ins.). 81 pp. + vi and 78 pp. + vii and 85 pp. all illus. and all with bibliographies. Orig. dec. wrapps.

A combined reprint of three works: Nijinsky 1946; Pavlova 1947; Duncan 1947; edited by Paul Magriel and published by Henry Holt, New York. See *Bibliography*, Part II, Magriel, Paul for the original editions.

MAKAROVA (DINA). NATALIA MAKAROVA. Photographs and text by Dina Makarova. Dance Horizons Spotlight Series.

Med. 8vo (9 × 6·7 ins.). 23 pp. illus. Orig. dec. wrapps.

A monograph on the artist who defected from the season of the Kirov Ballet in Royal Festival Hall 1970. See also Richard Austin, *Natalia Makarova* and *Dance Magazine Portfolio* for April 1977, and *Bibliography*, Part III, Chistyakovoi, *Leningradskii Balet Segodniya* first volume.

MAKYA (ALVIN JAMES). HOPI KACHINA ARTIST JAMES MAKYA. Arizona Highways, June 1973.

Roy. 4to (12 × 9 ins.). pp. 1–17 illus. Orig. dec. wrapps.

An article illustrated by 15 photographs in colour (4 full page) with captions identifying Hopi Indian singers and dancers.

MANCHESTER (P. W.). MERLE PARK. [Brooklyn, Dance Horizons 1976].

Med. 8vo (9 × 7 ins.). 16 + (viii) pp. incl. both dec. wrapps.

A monograph with photographs by Anthony Crickmay, one of *Dance Horizons Spotlight Series*. Merle Park was one of the first two *Princess Auroras* in The Royal Ballet's *The Sleeping Beauty* produced at Covent Garden October 14, 1977.

MANDELBERG (E. M.). LAURENCIA. Leningrad. Izdanie Leningradskogo Gosud. Ordena Lenina Akad. Teatra Operi i Baleta im S. M. Kirova 1940.
    F'cap 8vo (6·4 × 5·1 ins.). 16 pp. with 1 illus. Orig. dec. wrapps.
    A synopsis of the ballet first performed by the Kirov May 22, 1939 with music by Alexander Krein and choreography by Vakhtang Chabukiani. Principal dancers: Dudinskaya (*Laurencia*) and Chabukiani (*Frondozo*). See Slonimsky, Yuri, *Sovetskii Balet* (pp. 210–216), and Beaumont, *Supplement to Complete Book of Ballets*.

MANDER (RAYMOND) & MITCHENSON (JOE). PANTOMIME. A Story in Pictures. Foreword by Danny La Rue. London, Peter Davies 1973.
    Cr. 4to (9·6 × 7·2 ins.). (viii) + 56 pp. text + 249 num. illus. Orig. dec. leatherette binding.
    Introduction: The Story of Pantomime (p. 1); Pantomimes Illustrated (p. 50); Towns and Theatres represented (p. 53); Actors appearing in Pantomime (p. 53); Prints and Drawings (p. 54); Artists and Designers (p. 55). Individuals well represented pictorially are Joseph Grimaldi with 14 illustrations, and Dan Leno and John Rich with 10 each.

MARA (THALIA). DO'S AND DONT'S OF BASIC BALLET BARRE. [New York, Dance Magazine 1955].
    Demy 4to (11 × 8·3 ins.). 45 pp. illus. Orig. dec. boards.
    See also *Bibliography*, Parts II and III, Mara, Thalia for other books by this author.

MARG PUBLICATIONS. CLASSICAL AND FOLK DANCES OF INDIA. Marg Publications, Bombay 1963.
    Roy 4to (12·4 × 9·1 ins.). 6 sections, each containing articles profusely illus. by sketches and photogs., bound in full green silk.
    Contents: I. Bharata Natyam (pp. 1–58); II. Kathakali (pp. 1–54); III. Kathak (pp. 1–66); IV. Orissi Dance (pp. 1–52); V. Manipuri (pp. 1–64); VI. Folk Dances (pp. 1–78); Articles on many facets of the dance in India; Religious, Technical, Historical, Musical, all with interesting photographs and drawings. Under the heading of Kathakali there will be found a *Dictionary of Mudras*, 504 examples in paragraph form accompanied by a folding plate with descriptive drawings.

MARIEL (PIERRE) & TROCHER (JEAN). PARIS CAN-CAN. Translated by Stephanie and Richard Sutton. London, Charles Skilton 1961.

Med. 8vo (9·1 × 6·6 ins.). 112 pp. + a further 16 pp. of plates. Orig. red cloth.

Two short essays; Cancan Yesterday and Cancan Today, amply (and sometimes nudely) illustrated, but lacking a bibliography. Further reading might include: *Bal d'Etudiants* (Bullier); Blum, *Les Pieds qui remun't*; Caffin, *Dancing and Dancers Today: Conservatoire de la Danse Moderne* (*Bibliography* Part I); Revel, *Petits Mystères des Bals*; Vernier, *Rigolbrochmanie*; Warnod, *Bals de Paris* (*Bibliography* Part II).

MARKS (JOSEPH E. III). AMERICA LEARNS TO DANCE. A Historical Study of Dance Education in America before 1900. New York, Dance Horizons [1977].

Cr. 8vo (7·7 × 5·3 ins.). 133 pp. incl. index and bibliography. Orig. dec. wrapps.

The bibliography of 17 pp. indicates the amount of research given to this study. In America until the 19th century there were only a handful of books about the dance and the quotations from earlier literature usually amounted to from one to three lines; thus Mr. Marks' book follows a carefully quilted pattern. First published by *Exposition Press* in 1957, this is an unabridged republication.

MARKS (JOSEPH III). THE MATHERS ON DANCING. Including an Arrow against Profane and Promiscuous Dancing, Drawn out of the Quiver of the Scriptures by Increase Mather (1685). Also a Cloud of Witnesses, by Cotton Mather (c. 1700). With a Bibliography of Anti-Dance Books (1685–1963). Brooklyn, Dance Horizons 1975.

Demy 8vo (8·7 × 5·7 ins.). 99 pp. illus. Orig. mod. vellum.

The illustrations include title pages of the two works mentioned above and engravings of the two Mathers. The author mentions that the bibliography was begun by Paul Magriel and added to later. He asks for further additions, and two important ones come to mind: Boudet, Antoine, *Traité Contre les Danses et les Mauvaises Chansons*, Paris 1775 and Paradin, Guillaume, *Le Blason des Danses*, Paris 1830 (reprint of 1556 edition).

MARKS (J[OSEPH III]). A PICTORIAL HISTORY OF THE DANCE. [San Francisco, Contemporary Dance Foundation 1962].

Med. 8vo (9·2 × 6 ins.). (v) + 101 + (ii) pp. illus. Orig. dec. wrapps.
An edition limited to 1,000 copies of which this is No. 428 signed by the author.

MARSHALL (FRANCIS). BALLETTSTUDIEN. Musterschmidt, Gottingen.
Cr. 8vo (6·5 × 5·3 ins.). 64 pp. illus. Orig. blue cloth.
The German translation of *Sketching the Ballet*. See *Bibliography*, Part II, Marshall, Francis.

MARSHALL (NORMAN). THE OTHER THEATRE. London, Theatre Book Club [1950].
Demy 8vo (8·4 × 5·2 ins.). 240 pp. incl. index. Illus. Orig. rose cloth.
See Chapter 10: Ninette de Valois and the English Ballet.

MARTIN (ANDRÉ) & BERGAMIN (JOSÉ). CANTE HONDO. [France, Petite Planete 1957].
Demy 4to (10·6 × 8·3 ins.). (xxii) + 140 plates in halftone. Orig. black cloth.
An album of photographs by André Martin with text by José Bergamin recording the pageantry and savagery of the bullring and the dance at the festivals surrounding it.

MASON (RUPERT Editor). EXHIBITION OF DRAWINGS MASKS AND MODELS by Artists Contributing to Robes of Thespis. London, Ernest Benn 1928.
Demy 8vo (8·5 × 5·4 ins.). 10 pp. Orig. dec. wrapps.
A catalogue of 135 items by various artists. See *Bibliography*, Part II, Mason, Rupert, *Robes of Thespis*.

MASSINE (LEONIDE). MASSINE ON CHOREOGRAPHY. Theory and Exercises on Composition. London, Faber & Faber. [1976].
Demy 4to (10·6 × 8·4 ins.). 221 pp. illus. with line drwgs. and chor. symbols. Orig. blue cloth.
A note on p. 16 of the Introduction states, 'A System of Notation being indispensable, I have chosen and developed that of W. J. Stepanov (1891) which approximates to musical notation in

its symbols and their identical rhythmical value.' See also *Bibliography*, Part I, Anthony, Gordon, *Massine* and Part III, Massine, Leonide, *My Life in Ballet*.

MASSINE (LEONIDE). THEY'RE TURNING TO BALLET — ON ITS OWN TERMS. New York, Theatre Arts 1955.
Demy 4to (11·3 × 8·3 ins.). pp. 76, 77, 96 with 1 illus. Orig. dec. wrapps. (Massine).
An article in the May 1955 issue of *Theatre Arts*. See also Belknap, *Guide to Dance Periodicals* for many articles concerning Massine.

MATOS (M. GARCIA). DANZAS POPULARES DE ESPANA. Castilla la Neuva I. Dibujos por Fernando Lancho y Carlos Alfonso. Madrid, Seccion Femenina de F.E.T.Y. de Las J.O.N.S. 1957.
Roy. 4to (12·4 × 9·3 ins.). 192 + (ii) pp. with drwgs. photogs., mus. airs and 2 engravings in colour. Orig. blue cloth.

The first volume of a series which seems to me to be the finest exposition of any form of Spanish Dancing to date: Terminology, Castanet Playing, Figures (both diagrams and dancers in positions), and choreographic descriptions of the dances. Contents: Preambulo (p. 5); Introduccion (p. 7); Terminologia y signos convecionales de la coreografia (p. 13); Castilla la Nueva I. Seguidillas y Jotas (p. 23); Seguidillas manchegas de Ciduad Real (p. 33); Seguidillas meloneras de Ciudad Real (p. 51); Seguidillas de la Puebla de Almoradiel (Toledo) (p. 67); Seguidillas de Taracoń (Cuenca) (p. 85); Seguidillas madrileñas -de Escuela (p. 109); Seguidillas boleras y Jota de El Real de San Vicente (Toledo) (p. 135); Jota de Yuncler (Toledo) (p. 153); Jota de Montéjar (Guadalajara) (p. 173); Jota de Santa Maria de los Llanos (Cuenca) (p. 185).

MAYNARD (OLGA). THE CHRISTENSEN BROTHERS. New York, Dance Magazine 1973.
Demy 4to (11 × 8·3 ins.). pp. 43–58 illus. Orig. dec. wrapps. (Christensen brothers).
A *Dance Magazine Portfolio* for June 1973.

MCDONAGH (DON). THE COMPLETE GUIDE TO MODERN DANCE. Garden City, New York, Doubleday & Co. 1976.

Med. 8vo (9·1 × 6 ins.). x + 534 pp. incl. index and bibliography. Illus. Orig. dec. wrapps.

The analysis of over 225 dances, and lives and careers of more than 100 choreographers. Clear text and illustrations.

MCDONAGH (DON). MARTHA GRAHAM. A Biography. London, David and Charles [1974].
Med. 8vo (9·1 × 5·6 ins.). x + 341 pp. incl. index. Illus. Orig. red cloth.

See also *Bibliography*, Part III, Mcdonagh, Don also Leatherman, *Martha Graham*.

MENCHIKOV (L. N.). REFORMA KITAISKOI KLASSICHESKOI DRAMI. Moskva, 1959.
Cr. 8vo (7·7 × 5 ins.). 239 pp. + (iii) illus. with woodcuts. Orig. dec. wrapps.

Reform of the Classic Drama, translated from the Chinese. Text in Russian.

MEERLOO JOOST (A. M.). ALLE LEVEN DANST. Van primitieve dans tot Rock 'n' Roll en modern ballet. Amsterdam de Brugjambatan 1959.
Med. 8vo (9·7 × 7 ins.). 152 pp. with 91 num. illus. Orig. black cloth.

The first edition with text in Dutch. Translation of the original title, *Dance Craze and Sacred Dance*. See *Bibliography*, Part III, Meerloo Joost for the English edition.

MESKHETELI (V. E.). TATYANA. Balet i 3 Deistviyakh. Leningrad S. M. Kirova 1947.
Demy 8vo (8·6 × 6·1 ins.). 4 pp. Orig. dec. wrapps.

A synopsis of the ballet *Tatyana* first performed at the Kirov Theatre June 12, 1947. Choreographed by Burmeister and music by Krein. Tatyana Vetcheslova danced the role of *Tatyana*. See *Bibliography*, Part II, Vetcheslova, *Ya Ballerina* (op. p. 161), also Slonimsky, V. *Chest Tantsa* (op. p. 192), *Bibliography*, part III.

MESSERER (ASAF). CLASSES IN CLASSICAL BALLET. Translated by Oleg Briansky. New York, Doubleday & Co. 1975.

Med. 8vo (9·1 × 6 ins.). 494 pp. profusely illus. Orig. black cloth.

First one must say that this method, and others preceding it by Russians have produced for the Bolshoi and Leningrad ballets the most expansive and exciting style and quality of movement of any school in the world, and continue to do so. However for the smaller movements, *batterie, ronde de jambe* etc., I feel that certain of the former Russian schools (i.e. Volinine's) were superior. A musician might well be disconcerted to find the placement of middle C changed; and so might a dancer be who is given, as the first position, middle fifth, and the fifth as an approximation to what is, in most methods, the fourth. Moreover, there are six positions of the arms and only four of *arabesques*. Although second position of the arms (p. 32) seems correct enough there are examples of this position which show the arm in natural position with too much of the elbow exposed and the wrists higher than both shoulder and elbow. Blasis and Cecchetti would call these false positions.

In concluding, it is a great advantage to have such a large selection of Russian technique available; but for detailed explanation of how to actually perform the steps the palm must still go to the Cecchetti Method technical books with their explicit instructions.

METROPOLITAN OPERA HOUSE. THE GOLDEN HORSESHOE. The Life and Times of the Metropolitan Opera House. Editors Frank Merkling, John W. Freeman, Gerald Fitzgerald with Arthur Solin. Prologue by Eleanor R. Belmont. Epilogue by Anthony A. Bliss. New York, The Viking Press 1965.

Roy. 4to (12 × 9·1 ins.). 319 pp. incl. index. With over 400 photogs. Orig. dec. rose cloth.

A very fine picture book of the Metropolitan Opera House 1883–1966. The ballet plays a very important part and the Diaghilev and Pavlova appearances are featured. Unfortunately with shortened text, many fine opera singers and dancers were omitted. Giuseppe Bonfiglio is one of the dancers unlisted.

MICHALEK (ANTONI). OD KRAKOWIAKA DO POLKI.

A Xerox copy of an article on Beaumont's *The Romantic Ballet in Lithographs of the Time*. The extensive article is bordered by small wood blocks of the dancers.

MINISTRE DE L'INTERIEUR (FRANCE). CONSEIL D'ETAT. Extrait du Régistre des Délibérations. Séance du 2 Juin 1836.
Demy 4to (12 × 8 ins.). 3 pp. n.n. with seal. Engraved form filled in with pen.
A request by M. Sr. Pilatte that his pension as *Repetiteur des Ballets* and Artiste de L'Orchestre (Ier Violon) be returned to him, and that their annulment be voided. His case was won. See also *Bulletin des Lois* (France) for further information on French Civil Pensions. Could this be Pilati, a composer of *Les Farfadets*, 8 Mai 1841 Porte St. Martin?

MOLDON (PETER). YOUR BOOK OF BALLET. London, Faber & Faber 1974.
Demy 8vo (8·1 × 5·7 ins.). 77 pp. incl. index. Illus. with line drwgs. and photogs. Orig. dec. boards.
For the young reader.

MOLKENBUR (NORBERT), PETERMANN (KURT), SCHULTZ (JO). VOM HOPPELREI ZUM BEAT. Tanzimpressionen aus zwei Jahrtausenden. Berlin, VEB der Zeit-Musikverlag 1973.
Cr. 4to (10 × 8·5 ins.). 170 pp. illus. with some in colour. Orig. dec. yellow cloth.
A History of Social Dancing including dances of the Egyptians and Greeks, Court Dances and others. See also *Bibliography*, Part III, Franks, A. H., *Social Dance*.

MONAHAN (JAMES). THE NATURE OF BALLET. A Critic's reflections. [London], Pitman [1976].
Demy 8vo (8·4 × 5·2 ins.). v + 122 pp. incl. index. Orig. rose cloth.
See also *Bibliography*, Part II, Monahan, James.

MONDE DRAMATIQUE, LE. TOME Ier. Paris 1835.
Cr. 4to (10 × 6·4 ins.). 424 pp. illus. Unbound.
Contents: *Les Amours de Faublas*, Porte St. Martin (p. 72); *Melle Fanny Elssler* par Charles Romey (pp. 164–167) with lithograph; *Le Théatre Italien* (pp. 183–187) with lithograph; *L'Ile des Pirates* (pp. 198–200) with lithograph; *Melle Marie Taglioni* par Henri Blanchard (pp. 340–342) with lithograph.

MONEY (KEITH). FONTEYN. The Making of a Legend. London, Collins 1973.

Roy. 4to (12·2 × 9·7 ins.). 320 pp. incl. index. Illus. Orig. cloth.

A very attractive picture book which undoubtedly contains the greatest number of photographs yet assembled of this artist. See also Forrester, F. S., *Ballet in England* (pp. 130–133) for listing of 18 books and articles about Fonteyn.

MONEY (KEITH). THE ART OF MARGOT FONTEYN. With a commentary contributed by Ninette de Valois, Frederick Ashton, Keith Money and Margot Fonteyn herself. London, Dance Books. [1975].

Demy 4to (11 × 8·3 ins.). 272 pp. n.n. of plates with some captions and text. Orig. tan buckram.

A new edition well produced and strongly bound by Dance Books. See also *Dance Magazine Portfolio* for July 1973, Margot Fonteyn.

MONGOLIAN PEOPLES REPUBLIC (THE). KNIGHTS OF THE STEPPES. Moscow 1946.

Demy 4to (11 × 8·3 ins.). 11 pp. Orig. dec. wrapps.

The title of a film produced by Ulan Bator (The Mongolian Cinema Studies in 1945). Text in English and Russian.

MONGOLIAN PEOPLES REPUBLIC (THE). LIBRETTO OF THE CONCERT OF MONGOLIAN ART.

Demy 8vo (8 × 5·6 ins.). 15 pp. Orig. dec. wrapps.

A concert presented by Mongolian Singers, Dancers, Musicians, and Circus Performers. The Mongolian Ballet performed this year is *Mani-Bator*. Text in Russian and English.

MONGOLIAN PEOPLES REPUBLIC (THE). MONGOLIAN NATIONAL WRESTLING.

Med. 8vo (7·6 × 5·4 ins.). 4 pp. n.n. Orig. dec. wrapps.

Their national games '*Eryn Gurvan Nadom*' are three – Archery, Wrestling, and Horse-Racing.

MONGOLIAN PEOPLES REPUBLIC (THE). THE MONGOLIAN PEOPLES REPUBLIC. A Documentary Film. 1946.

Cr. 4to (10·4 × 7·4 ins.). 8 pp. n.n. Orig. dec. wrapps.
A film made in Ulan Bator, the capital of Mongolia. Libretto of the film in Russian and English.

MONTICINI (ANTONIO). GUSMANO D'ALMEIDA o sia Il Rinnegato Portoghese. Azione Mimico-Tragica in 5 atti. Milano per Gaspare Truffi.
F'cap 8vo (6·2 × 4 ins.). pp. 47—52. Orig. plain wrapps.
A synopsis of action with Marietta Monticini as Zulmira and Domenico Ronzi as Gusmano. This is bound up with *Adelaide e Comingio* a Melodramma Semiserio which bears the date of 1831 (pp. 1—46). See *Bibliography*, Part II, Monticini, Antonio for other ballets also Magriel, Bibliography (p. 162).

MOORE (EDWARD). 40 YEARS OF OPERA IN CHICAGO. New York, Horace Liveright 1930.
Med. 8vo (9·2 × 6·1 ins.). 430 pp. illus. Orig. cream cloth.
A history of the Chicago Opera from 1889—1928. There is no Index but the Statistical Resumé covers the period of Nov. 3, 1910 to March 26, 1929. During this period the following balletmasters held tenure: Luigi Albertieri (1910—1912, 1913); V. Romero (1914); Francois Ambrosini (1915—1917, 1919); Andreas Pavley (1919—1921); Serge Oukrainsky (1919—1921, 1924—1926); Adolph Bolm (1919, 1922, 1923); V. Swoboda (1926—1927).

MOORE (LILLIAN). ECHOES OF AMERICAN BALLET. A Collection of Seventeen Articles Written and Selected by Lillian Moore. Edited and with an Introduction by Ivor Guest. New York, Dance Horizons 1976.
Demy 8vo (9 × 6 ins.). vii + 165 pp. illus. Orig. fabric spine and boards.
See also *Bibliography,* Parts II and III, Moore, Lillian.

MOREAU DE SAINT MÉRY (M. L. E.). DANCE. An article drawn from the work by M. L. E. Moreau de Saint Méry entitled: Repertory of Colonial Information compiled alphabetically (1796). Translated and with an Introduction by Lily and Baird Hastings. Brooklyn, A Dance Horizons Publication. [1975].
F'cap 8vo (5·7 × 3·4 ins.). 73 pp. with 2 illus. Orig. dec. brown boards.

See also *Bibliography*, Part II, Moreau de St. Méry, where the French edition of 1802 and an Italian translation are listed. See also Moore, Lillian, *Dance Index* Vol. V No. 10, for further information.

MOUREY (GABRIEL). LES ROBES DE BAKST. Paris, Gazette de Bon Ton.

Cr. 4to (9·4 × 7·5 ins.). pp. 165–168 with 4 illus. in colour.

An illustrated article excerpted from *Gazette de Bon Ton*. Not listed in the bibliography included in Lister's *The Muscovite Peacock*.

MOYA (DON ALEJANDRO). EL TRIUNFO DE LAS CASTAÑUELAS, O Mi Viage a Crotalopolis. Barcelona: Por la Viuda Piferrer, vendese en su Libreria administrada por Juan Sellent.

F'cap 8vo (6·2 × 4·3 ins.). 128 pp. Orig. tan wrapps.

Bound up with Francisco Augustin Florencio, *Crotalogia* and Juanito Lopez Polinario, *Impugnacion Literaria a la Crotalogia Erudita*. The outside wrapps enclosing the three books are published by Baldomero Gual, Barcelona.

MUELLER (JOHN), FILMS ON BALLET AND MODERN DANCE. Notes and a Directory. New York, American Dance Guild 1974.

Demy 4to (11 × 8·4 ins.). 102 pp. + 6 addendum. Orig. orange wrapps.

More than a catalogue of Dance Films, it contains materials the author used in a course offered by the University of Rochester called *Dance as an Art Form*, and Part II lists books and articles.

MUZIKALNOE NASLEDIE CHAIKOVSKOGO. Iz Istorii ego Proizvednii Moskva, Izdatelstvo Akademii Nauk SSSR 1958.

Cr. 4to (10·1 × 7·5 ins.). 541 + (iii) pp. illus. Orig. light blue cloth.

A History of Tchaikovsky's Masterpieces. Text in Russian. See also Shaverdyana, Slonimsky, and Zhitomirsky, Bibls. III & IV.

NALBACH (DANIEL). THE KING'S THEATRE 1704–1867. London's First Italian Opera House. London, The Society for Theatre Research 1972.

Demy 8vo (8·3 × 5·2 ins.). xii + 164 pp. illus. Orig. blue cloth.

NEW YORK PUBLIC LIBRARY (THE). STRAVINSKY AND THE DANCE. A Survey of Ballet Productions 1910–1962. New York, The New York Public Library 1962.

(9 × 8·6 ins.). 60 pp. illus. with some in colour. Orig. dec. grey wrapps.

Contents include *Stravinsky and the Muses* by Herbert Read, *Ballet Productions 1910–1962* by Selma Jeanne Cohen, and the plates.

NEW YORK PUBLIC LIBRARY (THE). STRAVINSKY AND THE THEATRE. A Catalogue of Decor and Costume Designs for Stage Productions of his works. New York, The New York Public Library 1963.

(9 × 8·6 ins.). 57 pp. illus. with a frontis. in colour. Orig. dec. grey wrapps.

This volume is intended as a companion piece to *Stravinsky and the Dance*. See also *Bibliography*, Part II, Lederman, *Stravinsky in the Theatre*.

NEWS FROM HOME. ENCHANTED REALM. New York, Home Insurance Co. Vol. XIII No. 5, Holiday 1952.

Roy. 4to (12·1 × 9 ins.). pp. 9–13 illus. in colour. Orig. dec. wrapps.

Enchanted Realm, an article, is the most important of the several that grace this magazine. The subject is the Romantic Ballet with reproductions of both American and European lithographs.

NICOLL (ALLARDYCE). THE DEVELOPMENT OF THE THEATRE. A Study of Theatrical Art from the Beginnings to the Present Day. Fifth Edition Revised. London, George G. Harrap. [1966].

Cr. 4to (10·2 × 7·5 ins.). xix + 292 pp. with a frontis. and 278 num illus. Orig. blue cloth.

Contents: I. Introductory: Theatres of the Orient; II. The Greek Heritage; III. The Roman Theatre; IV. Performances in the Middle Ages; V. Renaissance Italy: Court Theatres and the Painted Scene; VI. Renaissance France, England and Spain; VII. The Baroque and its Legacy; VIII. The Theatre during the Nineteenth Century; IX. Theatres of the Twentieth Century; Appendix, Bibliography, Index. See Ballet, influence on scenic art and theatre design (pp. 220, 231, 240) and Bakst (pp. 217, 218, 220). See also *Bibliography*, Part III, Nicoll, for an earlier edition.

NICOLL (ALLARDYCE). MASKS MIMES AND MIRACLES. Studies in the Popular Theatre. With Two Hundred and Twenty-six illustrations. New York, Cooper Square Publishers 1963.
    Roy. 4to (12 × 8·3 ins.). 408 pp. incl. index. Illus. Orig. light green buckram.
    Contents: I. The Mimes (p. 17); II. The Heydey of Mimic Drama (p. 80); III. The Fate of the Mimes in the Dark Ages (p. 135); IV. The Commedia dell'Arte (p. 214); Appendix: The Commedia dell'Arte (p. 351). First published by Hartcourt Brace in 1931, this is a fine reprint.

NICOLL (ALLARDYCE). STUART MASQUES AND THE RENAISSANCE STAGE. With One Hundred and Ninety-Seven Illustrations. New York, Benjamin Blom 1968.
    Roy. 4to (12 × 8·3 ins.). 224 pp. incl. index. Illus. Orig. red cloth.
    Contents: I. This Insubstantial Pageant (p. 19); II. The Banqueting House (p. 28); III. The Prospectives (p. 54); IV. Chariots of Triumph and Diaphanal Glasses (p. 127); V. The Gaudy Scenes (p. 138); VI. Court Hieroglyphics (p. 154); VII. Onium Fere Gentium (p. 192); VIII. Knights of Apollo (p. 208). Appendix: List of Masques (1603–41) (p. 215). First published in 1938 by Harrap.

NICOLL (ALLARDYCE). THE WORLD OF HARLEQUIN. A Critical Study of the Commedia dell'Arte. Cambridge, At the University Press 1963.
    Cr. 4to (10·7 × 8·1 ins.). xvi + 243 pp. incl. index. With a frontis. in colour and 130 other illus. Orig. green cloth.
    Contents: Prologue-Hamlet and Harlequin (p. 1); The Comedy of Skill (p. 9); The Four Masks (p. 40); The Rest of the Cast (p. 95); The Comic Scene (p. 117); Triumph and Decline (p. 159); Bibliography (p. 224). One of the small number of truly fine books to be published about Harlequin during this 20th Century.

NIEHAUS (MAX). HEINZ BOSL. Mit Beiträgen von Emmy Bosl. Konstanze Vernon. Stefan Erler. Dieter Gackstetter. Max Niehaus and Dr. Gunther Rennert. Munchen, Sudwest Verlag [1975].
    Cr. 4to (10·4 × 8·2 ins.). 112 pp. illus. Orig. black dec. boards.

An album of photographs with tributes from the persons listed on the title page. Text in German.

NIJINSKY (ROMOLA). NIJINSKY. Foreword by Paul Claudel. New York, Simon & Schuster MCMXXXIV.
Med. 8vo (9·2 × 6·1 ins.). xvii + 447 pp. with a frontis. and 15 other illus. Orig. blue cloth.
The first edition and the finest. See also Krasovskaya, V., *Nijinskii*.

NIJINSKY (ROMOLA). NIJINSKY. By Romola Nijinsky his Wife. London, Victor Gollancz Ltd. [1942].
Demy 8vo (8·4 × 5·1 ins.). 416 pp. with a frontis. and 23 other full page plates. Orig. blue cloth.
First published by Gollancz Nov. 1933, this is the 10th impression of 1942.

NIJINSKY (ROMOLA). VIDA DE NIJINSKY. Barcelona, Ediciones Destino S.L. [1944].
Demy 8vo (8·2 × 5·3 ins.). 326 pp. + (iii) with 44 illus. Orig. cloth.
Although the work is announced as being translated from the original Hungarian by F. Oliver Brachfeld, the Table of Materials agrees with the Simon & Schuster edition of *Nijinsky*.

NURDJANOV (N.). TADZHIKSKII TEATR. Ocherk Istorii. Izdatelstvo 'Iskusstvo', Moskva 1968.
Cr. 8vo (7·6 × 4·7 ins.). 259 pp. + (iii) pp. illus. Orig. grey cloth.
The Tadzhikstan Republic's Theatre which includes some ballets with text and illustration: *Dve Rozi* (Two Roses) by Goleizovsky and *Lola* by Bourmeister, also *Leili i Medjnun* and *Tropou Groma*.

NUREYEV (RUDOLF). NUREYEV. An Autobiography with Pictures. Edited by Alexander Bland. [London], Hodder & Stoughton [1962].
Med. 8vo (9 × 5·7 ins.). 128 pp. + a 48 pp. section of photogs. Orig. black cloth.
The first English edition. See *Bibliography*, Part II, for the American edition. See also *Dance Magazine Portfolio* for May 1973.

NUREYEV (RUDOLF). NUREYEV. London, Dance Books Ltd. with Victor Hochhauser Ltd. [1976].
  Demy 4to (11 × 8·1 ins.). pp. n.n. illus. with 105 num. plates. Orig. illus. wrapps.
  An album of photographs with biographical text (uncredited, by David Leonard and Peter Moldon) and short captions. Salient points of Nureyev's career since his defection in Paris. See also Bland, Alexander; Percival, John; and Vollmer, Jurgen.

NUREYEV (RUDOLF). NUREYEV. London, Dance Books Ltd. in association with Victor Hochhauser Ltd. [1976].
  Demy 4to (11 × 8·1 ins.). pp. n.n. illus. with 105 num. plates. Orig. red cloth.
  The hard covered edition of the above.

O'MOORE (MARY Editor). A B C's OF DANCE TERMINOLOGY. Washington, Dance Masters of America. [1949].
  Demy 8vo (8·4 × 5·2 ins.). vii + 78 pp. illus. with diags. and line drwgs. Orig. red cloth.
  Contents: I. Acrobatic Terminology; II. Anatomy; III. Ballet Terminology; IV. History of Ballet; V. Ballroom Terminology; VI. Seventy Years of Ballroom Dancing; VII. Tap Terminology.

ORGEL (STEPHEN Editor). BEN JONSON: SELECTED MASQUES. New Haven and London, Yale University Press 1970.
  Demy 8vo (8 × 5·1 ins.). xii + 377 pp. with 3 illus. Orig. dec. wrapps.
  The selected Masques are: Hymenaei; The Masque of Queens; Oberon; Love Restored; Mercury Vindicated from the Alchemists at Court; The Golden Age Restored; The vision of Delight; Pleasure Reconciled to Virtue; News of the New World Discovered in the Moon; Pan's Anniversary; The Gypsies Metamorphosed; Neptune's Triumph for the Return of Albion; The Fortune Isles, and their Union; Love's Triumph through Callipolis; Clorinda. The work concludes with a select bibliography.

OULANOVA (GALINA). BALLETS SOVIÉTIQUES. Paris, Editions Cercle d'Art 1954.

Demy 4to (10·4 × 8·1 ins.). 62 + (ii) pp. illus. Orig. dec. wrapps.
The Study is divided in two parts: I. The Artists. II. Argument des Ballets. See also *Bibliography* Part II, *The Soviet Ballet*, and also *Bibliography*, Part III, Ulanova.

OVANESYANA (G. A.). SCHASTE. Balet v Trekh Aktakh i Shesti Kartin. Gosudarstvennoe Izdatelstvo Iskusstvo. Moskva 1939.
Demy 8vo (8·4 × 5·6 ins.). 35 + (iv) pp. illus. incl. 5 plates in colour. Orig. dec. wrapps.
A booklet in Russian concerning the ballet *Schaste* (Happiness) with music by Khachaturian and choreography by I. I. Arbatov. See Schneerson, Grigory, *Aram Khachaturian* also Slonimsky, Yuri, *Sovetskii Balet* (pp. 208, 209).

PAGE (RUTH). A LETTER TO CYRIL BEAUMONT. Paris, Thursday May 25, 1950.
Cr. 4to (10·2 × 8 ins.). 2 pp. a.l.s.
A letter concerning the reception of *Les Ballets Americains* at the opening of the May 1950 Season at the Théâtre des Champs-Elysées. Also in Xerox. See also *Bibliography*, Part II, Turbyfill, Mark, *The Art of Ruth Page* and of recent publication Martin, John, *Ruth Page*.

PALMER (STUART). 1200 BOOKS ON DANCING. New York, The Dance Magazine March 1929.
Roy. 4to (12·5 × 8·6 ins.). pp. 31, 54 illus. Orig. dec. wrapps. (Helen Macfadden).
An article 'A Visit to the Studio of W. B. Graham, Possessor of the World's Largest Known Collection of Volumes on the Rhythmic Art' (subtitle of the article). See also Troy Kinney, *The Dance of Spain* (pp. 18, 19, 56) with illustrations of dancers from the Doris Niles Ballet.

PANKRATOVA (ELENA ARKADEVNA). TEATRAL-NYI PORTRET. [USSR 1973].
Demy 4to (11·3 × 8·3 ins.). 23 pp. text + 51 plates, many in colour. Orig. cloth.
Includes interesting portraits of Pavlova, Karsavina, Nijinsky, and (plate No. 37) of Serge Diaghilev with his domestic, which is seldom reproduced in colour. Text in Russian and French. Le Portrait Théâtral fin du XIXe-début du XXe siècle.

PANTUKOVA (L.) LENINGRADSKOE GOSUDARSTVENNOE KHOREOGRAFICHESKIE UCHILISHCHE. Leningrad, Moskva, Iskusstvo 1948.

F'cap 8vo (6.5 × 5 ins.). 62 + (ii) pp. illus. Orig. printed yellow wrapps.

A booklet on the *Leningrad State School of Choreography*. Photographs show well known teachers, Vaganova, Charov, Bocharov, Tutina, Mei and others with their classes. See also Soviet Ballet, The *Programmi Spechilikh Distsiplin Khoreograficheskikh Uchilishche* Moskva 1947.

PARKER (DEREK Editor). SACHEVERELL SITWELL. A Symposium. Edited by Derek Parker. [London], Bertram Rota [1975].

Demy 8vo (8.3 × 5.3 ins.). xiv + 94 pp. with a frontis. Orig. tan cloth.

Contributors to the Symposium were: Georgia Sitwell, Cyril Connolly, C. P. Snow, Raymond Mortimer, Kenneth Clark, Denys Sutton, John Smith, Leonard Clark, William Walton, Humphrey Searle, Thornton Wilder, John Piper, John Rothenstein, Cyril Beaumont, Christian Hesketh, Diana Cooper, Geoffrey Elborn and Hugh MacDiarmid.

PASHKOV (L.) & PETIPA (M.). RAIMONDA. Balet, v 3-x Aktakh 6 Kartinakh. Leningrad 1972.

Demy 8vo (8.2 × 5.1 ins.). 5 pp. Orig. printed wrapps.

A cast and artist list for the ballet *Raimonda* (Raymonda) as performed by the Kirov Ballet with Irena Kolpakova (*Raimonda*) and Sergei Vikulov (*Jan de Brien*). See also *Bibliography*, Part I, Bellew for synopsis in English as performed by the Bolshoi. See also Abolimov, P. F., *Vasili Dmitrievich Tikhomirov* (pp. 64–65) for performances in 1908 with Geltsler.

PAVLOVA (ANNA). AN ALBUM OF ORIGINAL PHOTOGRAPHS.

Roy. 4to (10 × 11.5 ins.). Size of photographs mostly 9 × 7.6 ins. Orig. white buckram with Anna Pavlova stamped in gold on front cover.

1. Pavlova-Novikoff (Dionysus) signed. 2. Pavlova-Volinine (*Autumn Leaves*). 3. Pavlova (Ivy House, see Dandre p. 43). 4. Pavlova (Ivy House, another pose). 5. Pavlova (*Autumn Leaves*, with black veil). 6. Pavlova (at practice barre holding dog). 7. Pavlova

(seated on wicker basket with powder puff and mirror). 8. Pavlova (on wicker basket with dog at left). 9. Pavlova (at barre *en sous-sous* 5th pos.). 10. Pavlova (*Rondino*, 2nd costume) Becker & Maas. 11. Pavlova (study by Yarvroff, see Dandré p. 161). 12. Pavlova (seated on wicker basket with mirror on her knees). 13. Pavlova (*Old Russian Folk Dance*). 14. Pavlova (*Don Quixote*) by Abbé. 15. Pavlova (a draped costume with grapes and leaves head-dress, scarf on left wrist). 16. Pavlova (in *Christmas*) by d'Ora. 17. Pavlova (in wings with short classic costume, standing on r.l. hands together in 5th en bas). 18. Pavlova (a second pose in the above, this time *en sous-sous* 5th pos.). 19. Pavlova (in *Dionysus*). 20. Pavlova (3/4 length pose, metalique bodice, holding 2 white roses, hair soft without headdress). 21. Pavlova (a second pose in the same costume, nestling in the tulle). 22. Pavlova (in *Rondino*, the second costume: see Franks, Pavlova (op. p. 41). 23. Pavlova (in *Fairy Doll*, standing on r. toe, only hands of partner show).

PAVLOVA (ANNA). ANNA PAVLOVA ALBUM OF PRESS CUTTINGS.

Roy. 4to (9·4 × 11·6 ins.). 44 pp. n.n. of press cuttings. Orig. boards with ties.

An album belonging to Madame Pavlova, presented to Doris Niles by Cyril Beaumont. A season of 10 performances from May 3rd to 12th at Théâtre des Champs-Elysées. The cuttings contain announcements, articles, criticisms, drawings, and photographs. This season of May 1930 was Anna Pavlova's final appearance in Paris.

PAVLOVA (ANNA). ANNA PAVLOVA MISCELLANY.

(13·2 × 10·4 ins.). Black closed box with spring clip.

A collection of the following items: 8 Souvenir Programmes; 8 photographs (2 signed); 8 House Programmes (1 from Tokyo); Typescript of a B.B.C. Broadcast by Commander Ibbett; a large *affiche* in Russian announcing a lecture on Pavlova by O. Martynova.

PAVLOVA (ANNA). IVY HOUSE.

Sq. (8 × 8·7 ins.). pp. nn. Full violet marocain with dentelle interior; Ivy House stamped in gold on upper cover.

The Anna Pavlova Guest Album for Ivy House. The first signature is that of Theodore Stier, May 14, 1912 (former musical conductor for Pavlova) with the following inscription: 'May everyone who enters Ivy House bring joy and happiness to its adorable hostess'. From the Cyril Beaumont Collection, presented to Doris Niles.

PAYNE (WYNDHAM). THE CHRISTMAS TREE. A Fantastic Ballet in one Act by Cyril W. Beaumont. Music by Fred Adlington. Scenery and Costumes designed by Wyndham Payne. London, 1926.

Demy 4to (10 × 8 ins.). 20 original designs in colour on stiff cartoline. All signed by the artist.

First presented by the Cremorne Company on March 11, 1926 with Fred (Frederick) Ashton, Stanley Judson and Penelope Spencer in the cast. See Cyril Beaumont Anniversary Supplement of *Dance and Dancers* Dec. 1961 for comment, and also reproduction of Payne's design for the décor.

PAYNE (WYNDHAM). CIRCUS. A Burlesque Ballet in Three Scenes by Cyril W. Beaumont. London, 1926.

(2·6 × 2 ins.). 14 paper cutouts in colour mounted on small metal clasps.

The costume designs for *Circus* painted by Wyndham Payne. Frederick Ashton was a *Dervish Dancer* and Cyril Beaumont *The Ringmaster* with Penelope Spencer the *First Clown*. See programmes for Tuesday March 11th 1926, presented by the Cremorne Company.

PAYNE (WYNDHAM). LETTERS TO CYRIL BEAUMONT. Guilford, Waterden Cottage 1924–1925.

F'cap 8vo (6·7 × 4·4 ins.).

Six letters and four postal cards, some of them concerning the production of the ballet *The Christmas Tree*.

PEASE (ESTHER). MODERN DANCE. Dubuque, Wm. C. Brown Co. 1966.

Med. 8vo (9 × 6·2 ins.). 66 pp. illus. Orig. dec. wrapps.

A booklet about the Modern Dance with a list of Supplementary Reading (pp. 59–61).

PENROD (JAMES) & PLASTINO (JANICE GUDDE). THE DANCER PREPARES. Illustrations by Robert Carr. Palo Alto, National Press Books. 1970.

Med. 8vo (9 × 6 ins.). 58 pp. illus. with diags. line drwgs. and photogs. Orig. dec. wrapps.

Modern Dance for Beginners with important Chapters being: 3. Technique Analysis and 4. Anatomy, Injuries, Diet. Penrod has written another book, *Movement for the Performing Artist*.

PEOPLES REPUBLIC OF CHINA (THE). THE RED DETACHMENT OF WOMEN. China [1970].
Demy 8vo (8·1 × 5·5 ins.). 684 pp. profusely illus. with many in colour. Orig. dec. boards.
Text in Chinese. The most complete exposition of any ballet that I know of. The principal dancing scenes are in colour. The ballet is thoroughly diagrammed, the steps fully illustrated, accessories in colour, scenery in colour and in scale plans as well, and there is a lighting plot.

PERCIVAL (JOHN). NUREYEV. Aspects of the Dancer. New York, G. P. Putnam's Sons [1975].
Demy 8vo (8·2 × 5·3 ins.). 256 pp. illus. Orig. white cloth.
See also Nureyev and Vollmer.

PERCIVAL (JOHN). A REVITALIZED BALLET. The Royal Danish Ballet Assessed by the Ballet Critic of the Times. Copenhagen, Danish Foreign Office Journal, No. 62 1968.
Roy. 4to (12 × 7·4 ins.). pp. 29–31 illus. with pen sketches. Orig. illus. wrapps.
An article with pen sketches by Hans Bendix. See also *Bibliography*, Part III, Percival, John.

PERCIVAL (JOHN). THE WORLD OF DIAGHILEV. [London], Studio Vista [1971].
Cr. 8vo (7·2 × 4·6 ins.). 159 pp. illus. Orig. dec. wrapps.
Issued also in hardcover by Studio Vista. See *Bibliography*, Part III, Percival, John, *The World of Diaghilev* for table of contents.

PÉRES (LOUIS). AMERICAN BALLET THEATRE. Gala 35th Anniversary Performance Jan. 11, 1975.
Med. 8vo (9 × 6·7 ins.). 23 pp. illus. Orig. dec. wrapps.
A monograph on this company. See also Barnes, Clive, *Inside American Ballet Theatre* and *Bibliography*, Part III, *Dance Perspectives* No. 6 *The American Ballet Theatre: 1940–1960*.

PÉRES (LOUIS). CYNTHIA GREGORY. Photographs and text by Louis Péres. Dance Horizons Spotlight Series.

Med. 8vo (9 × 6·7 ins.). 23 pp. illus. Orig. dec. wrapps.
Cynthia Gregory, winner of the 1975 *Dance Magazine Award*.
See also Barnes, Clive, *Inside American Ballet Theatre* and Gruen, John, *The Private World of Ballet* (pp. 221–226).

PÉRES (LOUIS). IVAN NAGY. Photographs by Louis Péres. Text by Lillie F. Rosen. Dance Horizons Spotlight Series.
Med. 8vo (9 × 6·7 ins.). 23 pp. illus. Orig. dec. wrapps.
A monograph on Ivan Nagy who came to American Ballet Theatre by way of the Hungarian State Opera Ballet and the Washington D.C. Ballet Company. See also *Dance Magazine Portfolio* for July 1975, Maynard, Olga, *ABT's Ivan Nagy and Raymonda*.

PÉRES (LOUIS). MIKHAIL BARYSHNIKOV. Photographs by Louis Péres. Text by Patricia Barnes. Dance Horizons Spotlight Series.
Med. 8vo (9 × 6·7 ins.). 23 pp. illus. Orig. dec. wrapps.
A monograph on one of the greatest performing dancers of the 20th century. See also Baryshnikov, Mikhail.

PÉRES (LOUIS). RUDOLF NUREYEV. Photographs by Louis Péres. Text by Arthur Todd. Dance Horizons Spotlight Series.
Med. 8vo (9 × 6·7 ins.). 23 pp. illus. Orig. dec. wrapps.
See also *Bibliography*, Parts II and III, Nureyev, Rudolf.

PERRAULT (CHARLES). LA PRINCESA DURMIENTE. Gran Teatro del Liceo Sabado 9 de Mayo de 1953. Barcelona.
Cr. 8vo (7·2 × 5·1 ins.). 52 pp. illus. Orig. dec. wrapps.
An illustrated programme containing the synopsis of *The Sleeping Princess* as performed by The International Ballet with choreography by Marius Petipa reproduced by Nicolai Sergueff. See also *Bibliography*, Part I, Beaumont, *The Sleeping Beauty* and *The Sleeping Princess* and Part III, Krasovskaya, *Marius Petipa and The Sleeping Beauty*.

PERRAULT (CHARLES). THE SLEEPING BEAUTY. London, Festival Ballet Summer Season 1971.
Med. 8vo (9 × 5·2 ins.). 12 pp. illus. Orig. printed wrapps.

An illustrated programme for *The Sleeping Beauty* as performed by the London Festival Ballet Aug. 24th 1971 at Royal Festival Hall.

PERUGINI (MARK EDWARD). THE OMNIBUS BOX. Being digressions and asides on social and theatrical life in London and Paris 1830–1850. London, Jarrolds 1946. F'cap 8vo (6·6 × 4·3 ins.). 287 pp. incl. index. with 10 illus. Orig. brown cloth.
A sparkling little book with important chapters on the dance: XI. The Opera Revives; XII. A Philosopher in Front; XV. Behind the Scenes; XVI. Some Stars of the Ballet; XVII. Queens of Earth and Air; XIX. Fanny Arrives.

PETERMANN (KURT). TANZBIBLIOGRAPHIE. Verzeichnis der in deutscher Sprache veröfftlichten Schriften und Aufsätze zum Bühnen, Gesellschafts, Kinder, Volks-und Turniertanz sowie zur Tanzwissenshaft, Tanzmusik um zum Jazz. Herausgegeben vom Institut für Volkskunstforschung beim Zentralhaus für Kulturarbeit, Leipzig. Leipzig, VEB Bibliografisches Institut 1966.
F'cap 4to (8·6 × 6·1 ins.). 800 pp. Bound in full blue cloth.
A very important Bibliography of material printed in the German language which is issued in instalments (lieferung), which when completed purports to have all the material listed under the following headings: I. Nachschlagewerke (pp. 8–36); II. Periodica (pp. 37–52); III. Der Tanz in der Bildenden Kunst und Photographie (pp. 53–74); IV. Der Tanz in Gesellschaftlicher under Naturwiessenschaftlicher Sicht (pp. 75–439); V. Geschichte des Tanzes (pp. 440–751); VI. Der Volkstanz (pp. 752–1632); VII. Der Kindertanz; VIII. Der Gesellschaftstanz; IX. Der Turniertanz; X. Musik zum Tanz, Jazz; XI. Der Laientanz; XII. Der Bühnentanz; XIII. Sammlung von Programmheften; XIV Tanzrequisten; XV. Diskotek des Volks-, Turnier-und Bühnentanzes; XVI. Verzeichnis der Wichtigsten Tanz-Filme; XVII. Pantomime. This Vol. contains the works found in the first V and part of VI Material Headings.

PETERMANN (KURT). TANZBIBLIOGRAPHIE.
F'cap 4to (8·6 × 6·1 ins.). pp. 801–1632. Bound in full blue cloth.
This Vol. No. 2 completes Der Volkstanz beginning (p. 751) of Vol. 1. In Vols. 1 and 2 there are 9,511 numbered titles listed.

PETERMANN (KURT). TANZBIBLIOGRAPHIE. Verzeichnis des deutschprachigen Schrifttums über den Volks, Gesellschafts- und Bühnentanz. 21. Lieferung. Leipzig, VEB Bibliographisches Institut 1975.
Med. 8vo (9·1 × 6·4 ins.). pp. 1633–1712. Orig. dec. wrapps.
Instalment (Lieferung) No. 21 completes Part VI. Der Volkstanz and begins Part VII. Der Kindertanz. Item Nos. 9,512 to 9,764 are included in this instalment.

PETERMANN (KURT). TANZBIBLIOGRAPHIE. Verzeichnis des deutschsprachigen Schrifttums über den Volks-, Gesellschafts- und Bühnentanz. 22. Lieferung. Leipzig, VEB Bibliographisches Institut 1975.
Med. 8vo (9·1 × 6·4 ins.). pp. 1,713–1,792. Orig. dec. wrapps.
Instalment No. 22 (Lieferung) completes Part VII (I) Der Kindertanz and begins Part VII (2) Neue Tanze und Tanzspiele fur Kinder. Instalment No. 22 contains numbers between 9,765 and 10,189.

PETERMANN (KURT). TANZBIBLIOGRAPHIE. Verzeichnis des deutschsprachigen Schrifttums über den Volks-, Gesellschafts- und Bühnentanz. 23. Lieferung. Leipzig, VEB Bibliographisches Institut 1976.
Med. 8vo (9·1 × 6·4 ins.). pp. 1,793–1,872. Orig. dec. wrapps.
Instalment (Lieferung) No. 23 which completes Part VII (1 and 2) and begins Part VIII Der Gesellschaftanz. Instalment 23 contains numbers between 10,190 and 10,720.

PETERMANN (KURT). TANZBIBLIOGRAPHIE. Verzeichnis des deutschsprachigen Schrifttums über den Volks-, Gesellschafts- und Bühnentanz. 24. Lieferung. Leipzig, VEB Bibliographisches Institut 1976.
Med. 8vo (9·1 × 6·4 ins.). pp. 1,873–1,952. Orig. dec. wrapps.
Instalment (Lieferung) No. 24 which completes (1 and 2) of Part VIII and begins (3) Monographische Studien, Choreographien und

Aufsatze zu einzelen Gesellschaftstanzen. Instalment 24 contains numbers between 10,721 and 11,134.

PETERMANN (KURT). TANZBIBLIOGRAPHIE. Verzeichnis des deutschsprachigen Schrifttums über den Volks-, Gesellschafts- und Bühnentanz. 25. Lieferung. Leipzig, VEB Bibliographisches Institut 1977.
Med. 8vo (9·1 × 6·4 ins.). pp. 1,953–2,032. Orig. dec. wrapps.
Instalment (Lieferung) No. 25 which continues Part VIII (3) of Monographische Studien etc. Instalment contains numbers 11,135 to 11,635.

PETERMANN (KURT). TANZBIBLIOGRAPHIE. Verzeichnis des deutschsprachigen Schrifttums über den Volks-, Gesellschafts- und Bühnentanz. 26. Lieferung. Leipzig, VEB Bibliographisches Institut 1977.
Med. 8vo (9·1 × 6·4 ins.). pp. 2,033–2,112. Orig. dec. wrapps.
Instalment (Lieferung) No. 26 which concludes (3) of Part VIII and begins (4) of Part VIII – Beitrage uber die soziale Lage, Etc. Instalment contains numbers 11,636 to 12,186.

PETERMANN (KURT). TANZBIBLIOGRAPHIE. Verzeichnis des deutschsprachigen Schrifttums über den Volks-, Gesellschafts- und Bühnentanz. 27. Leiferung. Leipzig, VEB Bibliographisches Institut 1978.
Med. 8vo (9·1 × 6·4 ins.). pp. 2,113–2,192. Orig. dec. wrapps.
Instalment (Lieferung) No. 27 which concludes (4) of Part VIII and begins (5) Methodische und pädagogische Aufsätze zum Unterrichtsprogramm und zur Gestaltung von Tanzabenden. Instalment contains numbers 12,187 to 12,748.

PETIPA (MARIUS). MARIUS PETIPA MEISTER DES KLASSISCHEN BALLETTS. Selbstzeugnisse Dokumente Erinnerungen. Herausgegeben von Eberhard Rebling. Berlin, Henschelverlag 1975.
Med. 8vo (9·3 × 6·3 ins.). 430 + (i) pp. illus. Orig. blue cloth.
A fine book, the most comprehensive on Petipa's writings, ballets, and schematic choreography. Inhalt: Vorvort (Eberhard Rebling p. 6); Einleitung (Juri Slonimsky p. 10); Marius Petipa:

Memorien (p. 23); Marius Petipa: Tagebücher 1903–1905 (p. 63); Marius Petipa: Dokumente, Briefe, Interviews (p. 109); Marius Petipa: Musikalisch-szenische Pläne (p. 121); Marius Petipa: Choreographische Erläuterungen Mit Kommentaren von Fjodor Lopuchow (p. 141); Zur Biographie Marius Petipas (p. 211); Zum Werk Marius Petipas (p. 240); Erinnerungen an Marius Petipa (p. 273); Meinungen über Marius Petipa (p. 314); Inszenierungen Marius Petipa in Russland (p. 365); Ammerkungen (p. 380); Verzeichnis der Namen (p. 411). Translated from the Russian, *Marius Petipa, Materiali Wospominanija Stati*. Leningrad 'Iskusstvo' 1971.

PETIPA (MARIUS). 1822 CXXX 1947. Let so dnya rojdenya Baletmeistera Marius Petipa. Leningrad 1947.

Roy. 8vo (9·6 × 6·2 ins.). 8 pp. n.n. with portrait of Petipa. Orig. pale green wrapps.

A programme of *The Sleeping Beauty* commemorating the 125th Anniversary of Petipa. *Princess Aurora*, Semenova 1st act; Ulanova 2nd act; Dudinskaya 3rd act. *Prince Desiré*, Gabovich 2nd act; Sergeyev 3rd act. Marius Ivanovich Petipa 1822–1910.

PETIPA (MARIUS). THE NUTCRACKER. Decors and Costumes by Jürgen Rose. Toronto, The National Ballet Guild of Canada 1967.

Demy 8vo (8·7 × 5·6 ins.). 20 pp. n.n. Orig. dec. wrapps.

A house programme with synopsis and cast with choreography by Celia Franca, presented at O'Keefe Center Dec. 22–30 1967. Neither the name of Petipa nor Ivanov are mentioned on the title page nor in the synopsis used by The National Ballet of Canada. See *Dance Magazine Portfolio* for Dec. 1973, Maynard, Olga, *The Nutcracker* and *Bibliography*, Part III, Crowle, Pigeon, *The Nutcracker Ballet* also Swope, Martha, *The Nutcracker*.

PETIPA (MARIUS). THE NUTCRACKER. Ballet in 2 acts. Designer Suliko Virsaladze. Covent Garden, London, June 12–July 20 1974.

Med. 8vo (9 × 5·2 ins.). 20 pp. illus. Orig. black wrapps.

An illustrated house programme with synopsis for *The Nutcracker* as presented by The Bolshoi Ballet with choreography by Yuri Grigorovitch. The role of *Masha* was alternated between Maximova and Sorokina, that of *Nutcracker Prince* between Vasiliev and Vladimirov.

PETIPA (MARIUS) RAYMONDA. Brooklyn, New York, Ballet Review 1975-76.

Med. 8vo (9 × 6 ins.). pp. 38-44. Orig. dec. wrapps.

The scenario for *Raymonda* taken from Petipa's outline of the action for the 1898 production. Underlined are the actions of the characters and the amount and kind of music required. See also Beaumont, *Complete Book of Ballets*, for fuller scenario and *Bolshoi Teatr SSSR* book 2 Balet, Raimonda for at least eleven Russian ballerinas who have been cast as *Raymonda*.

PETIPA (MARIUS). SHELKUNCHIK. Balet v 2 Deistviyakh. Moskva, Bolshogo Teatr 1966.

Demy 8vo (8·1 × 5·5 ins.). 26 pp. illus. Orig. dec. wrapps.

A libretto for *The Nutcracker* containing articles by N. Shumskaya and B. Lvov-Anokhin.

PETIPA (MARIUS). SHELKUNCHIK. Moskva, Bolshoi Teatr 1973.

Demy 8vo (8·4 × 5·6 ins.). 4 pp. Orig. white wrapps.

A house programme for *The Nutcracker* at the Bolshoi, choreographed by Yuri Grigorovitch with Bessmertnova as *Masha* and Lavrovsky as *The Nutcracker Prince*. Date of performance Sept. 20, 1973. See *Bibliography*, Part I, Ivanov, *Shelkunchik* for a 1934 synopsis at the Leningrad (Kirov) Ballet. See also Slonimsky, *The Soviet Ballet* (pp. 204-207) and Slonimsky, *Writings on Lev Ivanov* (pp. 14-22) of *Dance Perspectives* No. 2.

PETIPA (MARIUS). SHELKUNCHIK. Moskva, Izdatelstvo 'Planeta' 1975.

(5·4 × 3·5 ins.). 12 postcards in folder. Orig. dec. folder.

A series of postcards of The Nutcracker (*Shelkunchik*) with Maksimova, Bessmertnova and Semenyaka in the role of *Masha* and Vasilev, Lavrovskii and Gordeev rotating in the role of the *Prints*. (Nutcracker Prince).

PETIPA (MARIUS). THE SLEEPING BEAUTY. War Memorial House, The Royal Ballet Nov. 4-13 1960. San Francisco.

Cr. 8vo (8·4 × 4·6 ins.). pp. n.n. Orig. dec. wrapps.

A house programme signed by Margot Fonteyn who danced *Princess Aurora* on Nov. 4th 1960; Annette Page danced the role on

Sat. Matinee Nov. 5th and Anya Linden the evening performance of Nov. 5th.

PETIPA (MARIUS). THE SLEEPING BEAUTY. Covent Garden, The Royal Ballet. London, Aug. 1958.
Cr. 8vo (7·3 × 4·7 ins.). 16 pp. Orig. printed white wrapps.
A house programme for Monday Aug. 18, 1958. Produced by Nicholas Serguyev after Petipa with Fonteyn and Somes. See also *Bolshoi Teatr SSSR* Book 2, *Balet* for *Spyashtsaya Karsavitsa* (The Sleeping Beauty).

PETIT TOUR. THE BULLETIN OF THE LONDON BALLET CIRCLE. Editor, Pamela Black, Vol. 2 No. 3 Jan. 1948.
Demy 4to (13 × 8·2 ins.). 10 pp. mimeograph. Orig. dec. wrapps.
The official magazine of the London Ballet Circle, with Honorary Members: Massine, Fonteyn, Helpmann, Grey, Alonso, Gilmour and Leo Kersley. Eight Nos. in all: Vol. 2 Nos. 3, 5, 7; Vol. 3 No. 3; Vol. 7 No. 4 and three others lacking a date. Not listed in Forrester's *Ballet in England*.

PETRIDES (THEODORE & ELFLEIDA). FOLK DANCES OF THE GREEKS. Origins and Instructions. Folkestone, Bailey Bros. & Swinfen [1974].
Cr. 8vo (7·7 × 5·2 ins.). 79 pp. illus. Orig. cloth.
See also Emmanuel, Maurice, *The Antique Greek Dance* and *Bibliography*, Part III, Crosfield, Domini, *Dances of Greece*.

PICASSO (PABLO). BALLETTZEICHNUNGEN. Mit einer Einleitung von Herbert Asmodi. [Munchen], Bucheim Verlag, Feldarfing [1956].
Cr. 8vo (7 × 4·4 ins.). 22 pp. + 14 plates of line drwgs. Also text illus. Orig. dec. boards.
A short text in German followed by 14 pages of pen sketches of dancers. See also *Bibliography*, Part III, Cooper, *Picasso Theatre*.

PICASSO (PABLO). PICASSO THEATRE. L'Avant Scène No. 500 Aout 1972.
Cr. 4to (10·4 × 7·1 ins.). 46 pp. illus. Orig. dec. yellow wrapps.

An issue of L'Avant-Scène devoted to Picasso's Le Désir Attrapé par la Queue and Les Quatres Petites Filles. See also Teatr Wielki, *Pozadanie* (Desiré) a ballet written by Picasso and performed at the Great Theatre, Warsaw.

PICKERSGILL (M. GERTRUDE). STAGE MOVEMENT AND MIME. London, The New Era Pub. Co. [1951].

Med. 8vo (9·7 × 7·2 ins.). pp. 1106–1127 illus. Orig. green cloth.

An illustrated article in *Theatre and Stage*, Vol. II, edited by Olin Downes. The author also has a book to her credit: *Practical Miming*, Pitman 1957.

PIERRE. LATIN AND AMERICAN DANCES FOR STUDENTS AND TEACHERS. London, 96 Regent St. 1948.

Demy 8vo (8·3 × 5·3 ins.). 86 pp. Orig. red cloth.
Contents: I. The Ballroom Rhumba; II. The Brazilian Samba; III. The Paso Doble; IV. American Swing; V. Clarification of Technique; VI. Some Prevalent Mistakes; VII. The Sistema Cubano. Appendix. See also Belknap, *Guide to Dance Periodicals* for ample listing of Latin American dancing.

PILCHER (VELONA). DANCING FROM BURMA. New York, Theatre Arts Monthly 1924.

Cr. 4to (9·7 × 7·4 ins.). pp. 673–678 with 3 drwgs. Orig. dec. wrapps.

An illustrated article in the Oct. 1924 No. of *Theatre Arts Monthly*. See also *Bibliography*, Part I, Beaumont, *A Burmese Pwè at Wembley*.

PIRROTA (NINO). COMMEDIA DELL'ARTE AND OPERA. New York, The Musical Quarterly, G. Schirmer 1955.

Med. 8vo (9·5 × 8·5 ins.). pp. 305–324 illus. Orig. printed yellow wrapps.

An article in the July 1955 issue of *The Musical Quarterly*, Vol. XLI No. 3. There is also a second article of interest: Musical Culture of the Arapaho by Bruno Nettl. See also Nicoll, Allardyce, *Masks Mimes and Miracles* and *The World of Harlequin*.

PISCHL (A. J.) & COHEN (BARBARA NAOMI) Editors. DANCE DATA. Number 1 in a series of Delvings into Dance History. Brooklyn, New York, Dance Horizons.

Demy 4to (11 × 8·5 ins.). 20 pp. illus. Orig. dec. wrapps.
 Dance Data No. 1 contains two charts by Joan Lawson. (1): The Development of Classical Ballet and the Various Types of Ballet; (2): A Chart for the History of Dance in Society and in the Theatre as Ballet.

PISCHL (A. J.) & COHEN (BARBARA NAOMI), Editors. DANCE DATA. Number 2 in a series of Delvings into Dance History. Brooklyn, New York, Dance Horizons.
 Demy 4to (11 × 8·5 ins.). 28 pp. illus. Orig. dec. wrapps.
 Dance Data No. 2 contains the following material: 1. The Borrowed Art of Gertrude Hoffmann by Barbara Naomi Cohen; 2. Album Souvenir de La Saison Russe; 3. On Your Toes – America. The Story of the First Ballet Russe. See also *Bibliography*, Part I, Caffin, *Dancing and Dancers of Today* and the souvenir programme for The Gertrude Hoffmann Company 1911.

PLAY PICTORIAL (THE). THE CLASSICAL BALLET. London, The Play Pictorial No. 109 Vol. XVIII.
 Demy 4to (11·6 × 8·6 ins.). viii + pp. 73–96 + xvi illus. Orig. dec. wrapps in colour.
 A splendid issue of *Play Pictorial* with one article by the editor B. W. Findon and excellent photographs of Kyasht, Bedells, Mossetti, Pavlova, Mordkin, Geltzer, Tichomiroff, Genée, Allan, Nijinsky, Fokine, Fokina and others, very well reproduced.

PLAYFORD (JOHN). JOHN PLAYFORD'S THE ENGLISH DANCING MASTER, or Plaine and easie Rules for the Dancing of Country Dances, with the Tune to each Dance. New York, Dance Horizons.
 Oblong Cr. 8vo (5·2 × 7·7 ins.). (xii) + 104 pp. illus. Orig. printed wrapps.
 A republication of the 1933 edition with Notes by Hugh Mellor and musical transcriptions by Leslie Bridgewater and reproduction of the frontispiece for the first edition by Wenceslas Hollar. See *Bibliography*, Part II, Playford, John.

PLESCHEEV (ALEKSANDR). M. I. PETIPA (1847–1907) k Shestidesyatiltu ego slujbi na Stsene Imperatorskikh Teatrov. s. dvumya Portretami i avtografom M. I. Petipa. S. Peterburg 1907.

Cr. 4to (10 × 6·6 ins.). 10 pp. with 2 illus. Orig. printed grey wrapps.
A monograph on Marius Ivanovich Petipa with a facsimile of his signature on first portrait. Very rare.

PLISETSKAYA (MAYA). MAYA PLISETSKAYA. Moscow Progress Pub. [1976].
Cr. 4to (10·1 × 6·4 ins.). 152 pp. with n.n. sections of photogs. preceding and following text. Orig. dec. boards.
A book of appreciations by Andrei Voznesensky, Andrei Vavra, Vadim Gayevsky, Viktor Komissarzhevsky, Boris Lvov-Anokhin, Yuri Tyurin, and George Shuvalov. The photographs range from her childhood and youth to the fulfilment of a long cherished dream – *Anna Karenina*. See also *Bolshoi Teatr SSSR*, Balet *Anna Karenina*.

POHL (ELSA). MANUAL OF DANCING STEPS. With a Compiled List of Technical Exercises (Russian School). New York, A. S. Barnes 1922.
Demy 4to (11 × 8·2 ins.). (v) + 63 pp. illus. with 39 line drwgs. Orig. tan printed cloth.
A manual of simple ballet and character dance steps illustrated with stick drawings and positions of the feet.

POHREN (D. E.). THE ART OF FLAMENCO. Moron de la Frontera, Society of Spanish Studies [1972].
Demy 8vo (8·2 × 6 ins.). 232 pp. incl. glossary and bibliography. Orig. red cloth.
The third edition revised and updated with 8 additional pages of photographs. See preface of the revised editions for differences in text and illustration. See also Puig, Alfonso, *el Arte del Baile Flamenco* and *Bibliography*, Part II, Niles, Doris, *El Duende* (In Defence of Flamenco).

POLINARIO (JUANITO LOPEZ). IMPUGNACION LITERARÍA A LA CROTALOGIA ERUDITA, Ó CIENCA DE LAS CASTAÑUELAS. Para Baylar el Bolero, Que en V. Reimpresiones ha dado a Luz El. Lic. Francisco Lopez Polinario. Barcelona, Por la Viuda Piferrer vendese en su Libreria administrada por Juan Sellent.
F'cap 8vo (6·2 × 4·3 ins.). 128 pp. Orig. tan wrapps.
Bound up with Francisco Augustin Florencio, *Crotalogia* and Don Alejandro Moya, *El Triunfo de las Castañuelas*, O Mi Viage a

Crotalópolis. See *Bibliography*, Part I, Florencia, Francisco Augustin for listing of 2 of these works. Also Barbieri, Francisco Asenjo, *Las Castañuelas*.

POLYAKOVA (LUDMILA). SOVIET MUSIC. Moscow, Foreign Languages Pub. House.
Demy 8vo (8·4 × 6·4 ins.). 183 + (i) pp. incl. index. Orig. cloth.
See Ballet Music (pp. 127–146), a well illustrated resumé of Soviet ballets from Gliere's *Red Poppy* to folklore legends: *Goldspinners* (Estonia), *Marmar* (Armenia), *Treasures of the Blue Mountain* (Georgia), and *Shuraleh* (Tartaria). See also *Bibliography*, Part III, Boleza, Igor, *Handbook of Soviet Musicians*.

POPOVA (E. Y.). OSNOVA OBUCHENIYA DISHANIYA v KHOREOGRAFII. Moskva, Izdatelstvo Iskusstvo 1968.
Cr. 8vo (7·6 × 5 ins.). 40 pp. illus. with pen drwgs. Orig. white wrapps.
A booklet concerning breathing and exercises for dancers. Text in Russian.

PORTER (KEYES). AS AN ORIENTAL LOOKS AT ART. New York, The Dance Magazine Jan. 1926.
Roy. 4to (12·4 × 9·6 ins.). pp. 33, 34, 35, 61, 62 illus. Orig. dec. wrapps. (des. by Carl Link).
An illustrated article on Michio Itow or Ito. See also Caldwell, Helen, *Michio Ito*.

PRUNIÈRES (HENRY). A NEW HISTORY OF MUSIC. The Middle Ages to Mozart. With an Introduction by Romain Rolland. New York, The Macmillan Co. 1946.
Demy 8vo (8·2 × 5·3 ins.). xv + 413 pp. incl. Index. Mus. ex. Orig. green cloth.
See chapter XV. The French School 1600–1700. Here Prunières gives an excellent definition of the court ballet, 'Born of an attempt to reconstitute the ancient tragedy with its recitations declaimed and sung, its choruses and its dances, the court ballet (*ballet de cour*) soon rejected the spoken word'. Also chapter XVI Lully, Ballets and comedies-ballets, and XVIII, The Opera and the Opera-Ballet from Lully to Rameau. See also *Bibliography*, Part II, Prunières, Henry.

PUIG (ALFONSO CLARAMUNT). EL ARTE DEL BAILE FLAMENCO. Con la colaboración técnica de Flora Albaicín. Prólogo de Sebastián Gasch. Illustraciones musicales de Ramón Vives. Barcelona, Ediciones Poligrafa, S.A. [1976].
Sq. (10·4 × 10 ins.). 325 pp. illus. with photogs. some in colour, mus. ex. and drwgs. Orig. full red buckram.
An art book on the Flamenco Dance, splendidly and honestly produced on heavy coated paper that brings out the richness of the illustrations. Alfonso Puig's essay about this art is personal rather than historical. He writes that many of the better flamenco dancers have migrated to the Continent and America, and that Spain has heavily commercialized flamenco at home. Towards the end of the essay Puig lists books and articles that he considers important on this subject; he considers *Tratado de Bailes* by José Otero to be one of the best. The text is in 4 languages; Spanish, English, French and German, which would have been better separated as it causes considerable page turning to follow the text. The book closes with the Metodo de Flora Albaicin: *Brazos; Zapateado; Escobillas; Vueltas,* etc. Alfonso Puig never saw the completion of his wonderful book; he died on February 2, 1976 and Flora Albaicin completed the task on which he had laboured so many years. See also *Bibliography*, Part II, Puig, Alfonso Claramunt.

RACSTER (OLGA). THE MASTER OF THE RUSSIAN BALLET. The Memoirs of Cav. Enrico Cecchetti. With an Introduction by Anna Pavlova. New York, E. P. Dutton & Co. 1923.
Med. 8vo (9·1 × 6·1 ins.). xiii + 301 + (ii) pp. with 8 illus. Orig. green cloth.
The American edition. See *Bibliography*, Part II, Racster, Olga for comment.

RAEDE (HARRY). AUSGEWÄHLTE PROBLEME DES TRAININGS IM TURNIERTANZ. Unter der Sicht des sportlichen Trainings (I).
Demy 8vo (8 × 5·7 ins.). 52 pp. Orig. grey wrapps.
Problems in training for Athletic Dances in Dance Competitions. Vol. I, text in German.

RAEDE (HARRY). AUSGEWÄHLTE PROBLEME DES TRAININGS IM TURNIERTANZ. Unter der Sicht des sportlichen Trainings (II).

Demy 8vo (8 × 5·7 ins.). 52 pp. Orig. tan wrapps.
Problems in training for Athletic Dances in Dance Competitions. Vol. II, text in German. Both Vols. published by Zentralhaus für Kulturarbeit der Deutschen Demokratischen Republik 1971 and 1972.

RAFFÉ (W. G.). DICTIONARY OF THE DANCE. Compiled, written and edited by W. G. Raffé assisted by M. E. Purdon. New York, A. S. Barnes [1975].
Cr. 4to (9·7 × 6·7 ins.). 583 pp. illus. Orig. black cloth.
A reissue of the 1964 Barnes publication. See *Bibliography*, Part III, Raffé, W. G. for the first edition and comment.

RAYE (ZELIA). AMERICAN TAP DANCING. Sketches by Lovell. London, The Dancing Times 1936.
Demy 8vo (8·4 × 5·3 ins.). xii + 50 pp. illus. with drwgs. and diags. Orig. dec. black cloth.
Contents: 1. Foreword; 2. An Appreciation; 3. Introduction; 4. Correct Footwear; 5. Tap Technique; 6. The Importance of Time and Rhythm; 7. Pattern and Direction; 8. Elementary Tap exercises; 9. Time Steps and Breaks; 10. Tap Routines. See *Bibliography*, Part II, Raye, Zelia for a second revised edition.

RAYE (ZELIA). A GLOSSARY OF TECHNICAL TERMS WITH ABBREVIATED DEFINITIONS TAP TECHNIQUE. [London], Imperial Society of Teachers of Dancing 1936.
F'Cap 8vo (5·6 × 3·4 ins.). 8 pp. Orig. printed tan wrapps.
A pamphlet.

REBLING (EBERHARD). BALLETT GESTERN UND HEUTE. Berlin, Henschelverlag Kunst und Gesellschaft 1957.
Med. 8vo (9·6 × 7·5 ins.). 415 pp. incl. Index. Profusely illus. Orig. grey cloth.
Ballet of Yesterday and Today. A general history of ballet with interesting illustrations. The section on the Swedish Ballet (pp. 124–136) is good; the reproductions are a little foggy.

REBLING (DR. E.). EEN EEUW DANSKUNST IN NEDERLAND. Met of 96 Illustraties. Amsterdam, N.V. EM, Querido's Uitgeversmaats maatschappij MCML.

Med. 8vo (9·4 × 6·4 ins.). 267 pp. incl. Indexes. Illus. Orig. boards with fabric spine.

Inhoud: Inleiding (p. 5); Opkomst en Eerste Bloei van Het Ballet in Nederland (p. 11); Een Eeuw Nederlands Ballet (p. 75); Ondergang en Nieuw Begin (p. 233). A most important history of the dance and ballet in Holland. *Ballet de la Paix, dansé par le Prince d'Orange* was presented à la Haye in 1668 and much attention is paid to Polly de Heus, perhaps Holland's greatest dancer of the first quarter of the 19th century. See also Hannah Winter's *Pre-Romantic Ballet* for information on this artist. See also *Bibliography*, Part III, Rebling, Eberhard for other works.

REGNER (OTTO FRIEDRICH). RECLAMS BALLETT-FÜHRER. Stuttgart, Reclams-Verlag 1956.

32mo (5·4 × 3·5 ins.). 430 pp. + (i) with 32 illus. Orig. grey cloth.

A book of Stories of the Ballet. See also *Bibliography*, Part III, Regner, Otto Friedrich for other books about the ballet.

REVITT (PETER). BALLET GUYED. Drawings by Peter Revitt, Introduction by Mary Clarke. London, Ballet Today 1949.

Med. 8vo (9·6 × 7·3 ins.). 46 pp. illus. Orig. dec. wrapps.

A book of caricature by Peter Revitt, well known illustrator for ballet books. See also *The Dancing Times* for April 1968, Mary Clarke, *Peter Revitt*. See also Nicholas Bentley, *Ballet-Hoo*, Alex Gard, *Ballet Laughs* and *More Ballet Laughs*, and Legat, *Russky Balet v Karikatura* for other works on ballet caricature.

REVUE CHOREGRAPHIQUE DE PARIS. LE DECALOGUE DE VICENTE ESCUDERO. Paris, Jacques Loyau Sept. 1952.

Cr. 4to (10·5 × 7·2 ins.). pp. 7–9 with 3 illus. Orig. dec. wrapps.

An article with drawings by Escudero. The issue (*Numero Special*) is devoted to La Danse Espanol featuring Escudero, Amaya, Rosario and Antonio. See also *Bibliography*, Part I, Escudero, Vicente and Leslie, Serge, *Seven Leagues of a Dancer* (pp. 35, 36–39).

REVUE CHORÉGRAPHIQUE DE PARIS. HOMMAGE À BALANCHINE. Paris, Jacques Loyau, Mai 1952.

Cr. 4to (10·5 × 7·2 ins.). 27 pp. illus. Orig. dec. wrapps.

An issue of *revue Chorégraphique* de Paris, largely devoted to Balanchine, with articles by Babilée, Balanchine, Lifar, Dinah Maggie and Jean Silvant.

REYNA (FERDINAND). CONCISE ENCYCLOPEDIA OF BALLET. Translated by André Gäteau. London, Collins [1974].

Demy 8vo (8·5 × 6 ins.). 250 pp. illus. Orig. cloth.

First published by Librairie Larousse in 1967. Although it has later material than Hazan's *Dictionnaire du Ballet Moderne* and Jacques Baril's *Dictionnaire de Danse* it is not conceived on the large scale of Wilson's *Dictionary of Ballet* or Koegler's *Friedrichs Ballettlexikon*.

RIBNIKOVA (M.). BALETI ASAFIEV. Poyachenie. Moskva Muzgiz 1956.

32mo (5·5 × 4·2 ins.). 64 pp. with frontis. of Asafiev. Orig. pink wrapps.

Discussion with synopses of *Plamya Parija* (Flames of Paris), *Bakhchisarai Fontan* (Fountain of Bakhchisarai), *Kavkazskii Plennik* (Prisoner of the Caucas), text in Russian. See also *Bolshoi Teatr SSSR* book 2 *Ballet, Plamya Pariji* and *Bakhchisarai Fontan*, and Golubov, *Muzika i Khoreografiya* for discussion and production of these ballets.

RICCO (EDWARD). THE SITWELLS AT THE BALLET. Brooklyn, New York, Ballet Review 1977–1978.

Med. 8vo (9 × 6 ins.). pp. 57–117 with 10 illus. Orig. dec. wrapps. (The Sitwells).

A very important article in *Ballet Review* Vol. 6 No. 1 which concludes with a fine Bibliography of all three of the Sitwells. It is difficult to exclude any of Sacheverell Sitwell's writings from this list because theatre, with all its children, is one of the springs of his literature. Thus in his accounts of Gothic Europe you may be surprised to find the *Dance of the Seises* in a Seville courtyard, or *Capitan Ceremonia* and *Signora Lavinia* along with *Riculina* and *Metzetin* in his *Southern Baroque Revisited*. Sacheverell confers real immortality on these figures as they appear in sunshine or rain, today or yesterday or even centuries ago.

RICHARDSON (PHILIP J. S.). STAGE DANCING. London, The New Era Publishing Co. 1951.

Med. 8vo (9·7 × 7·2 ins.). pp. 216–232 illus. Orig. green cloth.
An illustrated article in *Theatre and Stage* Vol. I edited by Olin Downes. Incidentally the first photograph of Alicia Markova is not an arabesque but rather 4th position *sur les pointes*.

ROOTZEN (KAJSA). DEN SVENSKA BALETTEN. Fran Stiernhielm till Brita Appelgren. Stockholm, Wahlstrom & Widstrand 1945.
Cr. 4to (10·2 × 8·1 ins.). 175 pp. + (i) illus. Orig. fabric spine and dec. boards.
Georg Stiernhielm (engraving on p. 10) produced his ballet *Den Fangne Cupido* in 1649, thus preceding Galeotti's *Whims of Cupid*. See also *Bibliography*, Part III, Häger, Bengt and Skeaping, Mary; also Idestam-Almquist, *Svensk Balett*.

ROSEN (LILLIE F.). ANTHONY DOWELL. [Brooklyn, New York, Dance Horizons 1976].
Med. 8vo (9 × 7 ins.). 21 + (iii) pp. incl. both wrapps.
A monograph with photographs by Anthony Crickmay, one of *Dance Horizons Spotlight Series*. See also Dromgoole, Nicholas, *Sibley and Dowell*.

ROSEN (LILLIE F.). JACQUES D'AMBOISE. [Brooklyn, New York, Dance Horizons 1976].
Med. 8vo (9 × 7 ins.). 22 + (ii) pp. illus. Orig. dec. wrapps.
A monograph with photographs by Martha Swope, one of *Dance Horizons Spotlight Series*. See also *Dance Magazine* for Oct. 1969 and Nov. 1970.

ROSLAVLEVA (NATALIA). PRECHISTENKA: The Isadora Duncan School in Moscow. New York, Dance Perspectives Winter 1975.
Cr. 4to (9 × 7·3 ins.). 48 pp. illus. Orig. dec. wrapps.
Number 64 of *Dance Perspectives*. Natalia Roslavleva, born *Natalia Rene* wrote extensively and well for *Dance and Dancers* as well as *The Dancing Times* for many years, sometimes writing on the same subject for both periodicals as in the case of Vinogradov's ballet *Asel* for which she wrote a review in *Dance and Dancers* Nov. 1967 and *The Dancing Times* Aug. 1967. Natalia Roslavleva had a lengthy

correspondence with Cyril Beaumont and often signed her letters *'The Lilac Fairy'*. See also *Bibliography*, Parts II and III, Roslavleva, Natalia.

ROSSI (LUIGI). IL BALLO ALLA SCALA 1778–1970. Milano, Edizioni della Scala [1972].
Med. 8vo (9·2 × 7·4 ins.). 211 pp. incl. index. Illus. Orig. dec. wrapps.
A cleanly printed book with well chosen illustrations, but an incomplete history of ballet at the Scala. Perusal of Indice dei Balli finds the following pieces missing: P. Taglioni, *Ellinor, ossia Vede Napoli e poi Mori* 1861–62; *Le Stelle* 1862–63; S. Taglioni, *Bianca di Messina* 1824; F. Romani, *Caterina di Cleves* 1841; *Gianni di Parigi* 1818; Merzagora, *Dai Natha* 1881–82; F. Romanelli, *Adelasia e Aleramo* 1807, to note but a few. There is no bibliography but the author quotes in footnotes Guest, Moore, Lifar, Vaillat and others. Interesting as they may be, it is the Italian sources for the romantic period that we need to know about.

ROURKE (CONSTANCE). TROUPERS OF THE GOLD COAST, OR THE RISE OF LOTTA CRABTREE. New York, Harcourt Brace & Co. [1928].
Demy 8vo (8·4 × 5·7 ins.). xiii + 262 pp. incl. index. Illus. Orig. red cloth.
Apart from the career of Lotta Crabtree, the notes on Lola Montez, Montplaisir and Rousset Ballet Troupes are of interest.

ROY (BASANTA KOOMAR). UDAY SHAN-KAR. The Spirit of the Hindu Dance. New York, Dance Culture Jan. 1933.
Roy. 4to (12·1 × 9·1 ins.). pp. 8, 9, 37 illus. Orig. dec. wrapps.
An article in *Dance Culture* Vol. I No. 1. The only issue published, I believe. See also Belknap, *Guide to Dance Periodicals* for listing of other articles about Shan-Kar.

ROYAL BALLET (THE). A TRIBUTE TO JOHN CRANKO. London, Sadler's Wells Theatre 3 Oct. 1973.
Demy 4to (11·6 × 8·1 ins.). 12 pp. illus. Orig. printed white wrapps.

A programme containing a tribute by Peter Rosenwald. Repertory performed: *The Lady and the Fool, Card Game, Pineapple Poll.* There is also a list of his own ballets from 1945 to 1973. See also Schafer, Walter Erick and *Bibliography*, Part III, Dominic, Zoe and Winkler-Betzendahl, Madeline, also Brinson & Crisp, *The International Book of Ballet* (pp. 161–176).

R.O.H. COVENT GARDEN. ABOUT THE HOUSE.
London, The Friends of Covent Garden, Vol. 4 No. 3 1973.
Demy 4to (11 × 8·4 ins.). 66 pp. illus. Orig. dec. wrapps.
Ballet: The Royal Ballet in South America (p. 8); *The Sleeping Beauty* (p. 18); Tilt and Twilight (p. 30); *Sacred Circles* (p. 36); Royal Ballet Choreographic Group (p. 42). See also *Bibliography*, Part III, R.O.H. Covent Garden for earlier numbers.

R.O.H. COVENT GARDEN. ABOUT THE HOUSE.
London, The Friends of Covent Garden, Vol. 4 No. 4 1973.
Demy 4to (11 × 8·4 ins.). 70 pp. illus. Orig. dec. wrapps.
Ballet: The Royal Ballet in Israel (p. 4); *The Seven Deadly Sins* (p. 12); Sword of Alsace (p. 22); Léon Bakst at Covent Garden (p. 26); Gala for John Cranko (p. 38); The Royal Ballet Choreographic Group (p. 50); Ballet for All-World of Harlequin (p. 52); Royal Ballet Matinee (p. 54).

R.O.H. COVENT GARDEN. ABOUT THE HOUSE.
London, The Friends of Covent Garden, Vol. 4 No. 5 1974.
Demy 4to (11 × 8·4 ins.). 70 pp. illus. Orig. dec. wrapps.
Ballet: Manon and the Abbé Prévost (p. 22); Manon in the 19th century ballet (p. 25); Manon and Massenet's music (p. 28); The Brontës (p. 40); Noverre and Cranko (p. 50); In the Night (p. 54).

R.O.H. COVENT GARDEN. ABOUT THE HOUSE.
London, The Friends of Covent Garden, Vol. 4 No. 6 1974.
Demy 4to (11 × 8·4 ins.). 69 pp. illus. Orig. dec. wrapps.
Ballet: Royal Foie Gras to the Sound of Trumpets (p. 16); *Manon* (p. 20); The Royal Ballet Choreographic Group (p. 38); *The Entertainers* (p. 54); *La Fête Étrange* (p. 55); Septet Extra (p. 56); *Charlotte Bronte* (p. 57).

R.O.H. COVENT GARDEN. ABOUT THE HOUSE.
London, The Friends of Covent Garden, Vol. 4 No. 7 1974.

Demy 4to (11 × 8·4 ins.). 68 pp. illus. Orig. dec. wrapps.
Ballet: Ragtime Reckoning (p. 12); *Elite Syncopations* (p. 17); Une Music Parfaitement Dansante . . .? Ravel (p. 36); The Royal Ballet in a Tent (p. 46); Unfamiliar Playground (p. 52).

R.O.H. COVENT GARDEN. ABOUT THE HOUSE.
London, The Friends of Covent Garden, Vol. 4 No. 8 Spring 1975.
Demy 4to (11 × 8·4 ins.). 70 pp. illus. Orig. dec. wrapps.
Ballet: *Four Schumann Pieces* (p. 14); Verdi's Ballets (p. 16); The Royal Ballet Choreographic Group (p. 42); *Shukumei* (p. 50); Recent Arrivals (p. 56); Anthony Dowell (p. 65).

R.O.H. COVENT GARDEN. ABOUT THE HOUSE.
London, The Friends of Covent Garden, Vol. 4 No. 9 Summer 1975.
Demy 4to (11 × 8·4 ins.). 64 pp. illus. Orig. dec. wrapps.
Ballet: The Royal Ballet in Korea and Japan (p. 4); *Four Seasons* (p. 12); The Royal Ballet Gala (p. 18); *The Concert* (p. 20); *Arpège* (p. 23); The Royal Ballet Choreographic Group (p. 32); *Coppelia* (p. 42); Ravel Centenary (p. 44); The Royal Ballet on Tour (p. 52); The Tent (p. 54).

R.O.H. COVENT GARDEN. ABOUT THE HOUSE.
London, The Friends of Covent Garden, Vol. 4 No. 10 Christmas 1975.
Demy 4to (11 × 8·4 ins.). 64 pp. illus. Orig. dec. wrapps.
Ballet: *L'Amour Brujo* (p. 24); *Symphony* (p. 32); *Checkmate* (p. 52).

R.O.H. COVENT GARDEN. ABOUT THE HOUSE.
London, The Friends of Covent Garden, Vol. 4 No. 11 Spring 1976.
Demy 4to (11 × 8·4 ins.). 70 + (ii) pp. illus. Orig. dec. wrapps.
Ballet: *A Month in the Country* (p. 22); The Russian Point of View (p. 27); *Pandora* (p. 30); *Rituals* (p. 38); Constant Lambert (p. 50); Martha Graham (p. 54).

R.O.H. COVENT GARDEN. ABOUT THE HOUSE.
London, The Friends of Covent Garden, Vol. 4 No. 12 Summer 1976.

Demy 4to (11 × 8·4 ins.). 70 + (ii) pp. illus. Orig. dec. wrapps.
Ballet: Letter from America (p. 10); Lincoln Kirstein Writes (p. 26); *Lulu* (p. 46); The Royal Ballet Choreographic group (p. 48); *Perfide Manon* (p. 56).

R.O.H. COVENT GARDEN. ABOUT THE HOUSE.
London, The Friends of Covent Garden, Vol. 5 No. 1 1976.
Demy 4to (11 × 8·4 ins.). 70 pp. illus. Orig. dec. wrapps.
Ballet: *Anastasia* (p. 13); Three Choreographers (p. 26); *Rashomon* (p. 36); *Summertide* (p. 42); *Onegin* (p. 50); The Sadler's Wells Royal Ballet (p. 54); Marius Petipa (p. 60).

R.O.H. COVENT GARDEN. ABOUT THE HOUSE.
London, The Friends of Covent Garden, Vol. 5 No. 2 1977.
Demy 4to (11 × 8·4 ins.). 74 pp. illus. Orig. dec. wrapps.
Ballet: The Royal Ballet Choreographic Group (p. 24); *Voluntaries* (p. 30); *Adagio Hammerklavier* (p. 38); *The Taming of the Shrew* (p. 52); Yuri Soloviev (p. 69).

R.O.H. COVENT GARDEN. ABOUT THE HOUSE.
London, The Friends of Covent Garden, Vol. 5 No. 3 1977.
Demy 4to (11 × 8·4 ins.). 70 + (ii) pp. illus. Orig. dec. wrapps.
Ballet: *The Sleeping Beauty* (p. 16); *The Fourth Symphony* (p. 26); *The Court of Love* in Rehearsal (p. 32); *The Court of Love* (p. 34); *Birdscape* (p. 35); Gemini (p. 40); Brenda Naylor Drawings (p. 48); *Gloriana Choral Dances* (p. 57); *Hamlet and Ophelia* (p. 57); Brenda Last (p. 58).

R.O.H. COVENT GARDEN. ABOUT THE HOUSE.
London, The Friends of Covent Garden Vol. 5 No. 4 Christmas 1977.
Demy 4to (11 × 8·4 ins.). 70 + (ii) pp. illus. Orig. dec. wrapps.
Ballet: *The Sleeping Beauty* (p. 10); *Mayerling* (p. 28); *Concerto Barocco* (p. 52); Sadler's Wells Royal Ballet Teheran and Salonika (p. 60).

R.O.H. COVENT GARDEN. ABOUT THE HOUSE.
London, The Friends of Covent Garden Vol. 5 No. 5 Spring 1978.

Demy 4to (11 × 8·4 ins.). 75 pp. illus. Orig. dec. wrapps. (Gontcharova Firebird).
Ballet: *Mayerling* (p. 10); *The Firebird* (p. 32); Sadler's Wells Royal Ballet (p. 42); John Weaver (p. 48).

ROZANOVA (Y.). SIMFONICHESKIE PRINTSIPI BALETOV CHAIKOVSKOGO. Moskva, 'Muzika' 1976.
Demy 8vo (8·3 × 6·3 ins.). 160 pp. illus. Orig. light blue printed wrapps.
Studies of *Swan Lake*, *Sleeping Beauty* and *Nutcracker* with considerable reproduction of musical fragments from both printed and mss scores. See also Zhitomirsky, *Baleti Chaikovskogo*, Moskva 1947.

RUSSIAN PAINTERS. RUSSIAN PAINTERS AND THE STAGE 1884–1965. A loan exhibition of stage and costume designs from the Collection of Mr. and Mrs. Nikita D. Lobanov-Rostovsky. Austin, University of Texas 1978–79.
Demy 4to (11 × 8·2 ins.). 105 pp. illus. Orig. dec. wrapps.
A catalogue of an exhibition lasting from Feb. 13 to Mar. 13, 1977. The Catalogue closes with a bibliography of which Parts V & VI (Catalogues of Exhibitions and Catalogues of Auctions) are of particular interest to the dance.

SACHS (CURT). WORLD HISTORY OF THE DANCE. Translated by Bessie Schonberg. New York, Bonanza Books.
Med. 8vo (9·1 × 6 ins.). xii + 469 pp. illus. Orig. two-tone cloth.
The second American edition. See also *Bibliography*, Parts II and III, for other editions.

SAMACHSON (DOROTHY). LET'S MEET THE BALLET. New York, Henry Schuman [1951].
Med. 8vo (9 × 5·6 ins.). (xviii) + 200 + (iv) pp. illus. Orig. blue cloth.
A slender book that tries to cover too much material. However interviews with Yurek Lazowsky, Alexandra Danilova and others are of interest.

SAMUEL (CLAUDE). PROKOFIEV. Translated by Miriam John, London, Calder and Boyars [1971].

Cr. 8vo (7·6 × 4·7 ins.). 192 pp. with mus. ex. and drwgs. Orig. cloth.

A monograph which has good descriptions of the ballet *Chout* and 9 full page drawings by Larionov of *Chout* taken from his sketchbook. See also *Bibliography*, Part II, Lifar, Serge, *La Musique par la Danse, de Lulli à Prokofiev* and Prokofiev, Serge, *Autobiography, Articles, Reminiscences.*

SAND (MAURICE). THE HISTORY OF THE HARLEQUINADE. New York, London, Benjamin Blom [1968].

Med. 8vo (9·1 × 6 ins.). In 2 vols.: 1. 311 pp. with 8 illus. 2. 311 pp. incl. Index with 8 illus. Orig. dec. mauve cloth.

A very clear reprint of the Martin Secker 1915 edition. See *Bibliography*, Part III, Sand. A very fine work which after offering an Introductory History of the Harlequinade continues with 16 biographies of the principal characters of the Italian Comedy beginning with Harlequin. See also Bibliography, Part I, Beaumont, *The History of Harlequin* and Part IV, Nicoll, *The World of Harlequin.*

SANDOZ (MAURICE). THE CRYSTAL SALT CELLAR. London, Guilford Press [1954].

Cr. 8vo (7·2 × 4·6 ins.). 125 pp. Orig. blue cloth.

See Chapter V. Serge de Diaghilev and VI. Vaslav Nijinsky. Published later in 1956 by Kamin, New York as *Diaghilev-Nijinsky and other Vignettes* with illustrations. See *Bibliography*, Part II, Sandoz.

SARINOVA (L[INDIYA] P[ETROVNA]). BALETNOE ISKUSSTVO KAZAKHSTANA. Alma-Alta 1976.

Demy 8vo (8·3 × 6·5 ins.). 175 pp. + plates and table. Orig. green fabric.

An Art Study of the Kazkhistan Ballet. Along with classic Russian repertory the ballets *Kambar i Nazim, Doktor Aibolit* and *Dorogoi Drujbje* (By the Friendship Road) are featured in photographs. The last, with music by Stepanov and Tlendeyev, and choreography by Kovalev, Zakharov and Abirov, was first given at the second dekada held in Moscow in 1958.

SASPORTES (JOSÉ). HISTÓRIA DA DANÇA EM PORTUGAL. [Lisboa], Fundação Calouste Gulbenkian [1970].

Demy 8vo (8·1 × 5·2 ins.). 450 pp. illus. Orig. dec. wrapps.
A very well documented history of the dance in Portugal, which has an excellent bibliography (pp. 417–430). Three very important 18th century books are listed: Natal Jácome Bonem, *Tratado dos Principaes Fundamentos da Dança*, Coimbra 1767; Julio Severim Pántezze, *Método ou explição par aprenaer com perfeição todas as dancas*, Lisboa 1750; and Joseph Thomas Cabreira, *Arte de Dançar à la Franceza*, Lisboa 1760. This last book of preliminaries is illustrated with woodcuts much in the manner of Ferriol's *Reglas Utiles para los aficionados a Danzar*, Napoles 1745. See also *Bibliography*, Part III, Sasportes, José, *The Dance in Portugal*.

SAVUCHKINA (N. I.). RUSKII NARODNII TEATR. Moskva, Izdatelstvo 'Nauka' 1976.

Cr. 8vo (7·7 × 4·7 ins.). 148 + (iv) pp. illus. Orig. dec. wrapps.
Russian National Folk Theatre. Text in Russian.

SAYLER (OLIVER M.). THE RUSSIAN THEATRE. New York, Bretano's 1923.

Demy 8vo (8·1 × 5·4 ins.). xvii + 346 pp. with 4 plates in colour and numerous in half-tone. Orig. blue cloth.
See chapter VII – The Russian Ballet in its own Home (pp. 95–118). Consult also the Index for numerous entries concerning the dance and ballet. Early photographs of Anderson, Kandaourova, Gorshkova, Mordkin, Froman, Zhukoff and Reyzen.

SAYRE (GWENDA). CREATIVE MIMING. London, Herbert Jenkins 1959.

Demy 8vo (8·3 × 5·2 ins.). 128 pp. incl. Index. Illus. with line drwgs. Orig. black cloth.
A handbook of simple body exercises for movement preparation, and suitable subjects to be transmuted into mime.

SCHAFER (WALTER ERICH). JOHN CRANKO. Gespräche mit Walter Erich Schafer über den Tanz. [Frankfurt am Main, S. Fischer 1974].

Cr. 4to (10·4 × 8·1 ins.). 126 pp. illus. Orig. black cloth.
See also Royal Ballet, The, *A Tribute to John Cranko*.

SCHLUNDT (CHRISTENA L.). THE PROFESSIONAL APPEARANCES OF RUTH ST. DENIS & TED SHAWN. New York, The New York Public Library 1962.
Cr. 4to (10 × 6·7 ins.). 85 pp. + (i) illus. Orig. dec. wrapps.
See also *Bibliography*, Parts II and III, Schlundt, Saint Denis and Shawn. See also *Dance Magazine Portfolio* for Feb. 1976.

SCHLUNDT (CHRISTENA L.). THE PROFESSIONAL APPEARANCES OF TED SHAWN & HIS MEN DANCERS. New York, The New York Public Library 1967.
Cr. 4to (9·7 × 6·7 ins.). 75 pp. illus. Orig. dec. wrapps.
See also *Bibliography*, Parts II & III, Shawn, Ted.

SCHLUNDT (CHRISTENA L.). TAMIRIS. A Chronicle of her Dance Career, 1927–1955. New York, The New York Public Library 1972.
Cr. 4to (10 × 6·7 ins.). 95 pp. illus. Orig. dec. grey wrapps.
See also Belknap, *Guide to Dance Periodicals, Bibliography*, Part I and Maynard, Olga, *American Modern Dancers*, Part III.

SCHMIDOVA (LIDKA). CESKOSLOVENSKY BALET. Praha, Orbis 1962.
Sq. (8·2 × 8·1 ins.). 57 pp. + 165 num. plates illus. with many in colour + (ii) pp. Orig. dec. white cloth.
A well illustrated book with many plates in colour shewing ballet in various cities. Much of the repertory is from Soviet Russia: *Fountain of Bakhchisarai, Spartacus, Gayane* etc., and there is little modern dance influence. See also *Bibliography*, Part II, Rey, Jan, *The World of Dance* and Part III Vasut, Vladimir, *Balet v Chekhoslovakii*.

SCHMIDT-GARE (HELMUT). BALLETT VOM SONNENKÖNIG BIS BALANCHINE. [Hannover], Friedrich Verlag [1966].
Cr. 8vo (7·1 × 5·2 ins.). 392 pp. inc. indexes. Illus. Orig. orange wrapps.
Ballet from the Sun-King (Louis XIV) to Balanchine with the major portion of the book devoted to Diaghilev and the following period.

SCHNEERSON (GRIGORY). ARAM KHACHATURYAN.
Moscow, Foreign Languages Publishing House 1959.
 Med. 8vo (8·4 × 6·4 ins.). 103 pp. illus. Orig. cloth.
 Listed among Khachaturyan's most important works are the three ballets: *Happiness* (Schaste). *Gayaneh*, and *Spartacus*. For information (including synopsis) on *Happiness* see Ovanesyana, G. A., *Schaste*, and for text and illustration, Slonimsky, Yuri, *Sovetskii Balet* (pp. 208, 209); for *Gayaneh* see Slonimsky, Yuri, *Sovetskii Balet* (pp. 257–260); for *Spartacus* see *Bolshoi Teatr SSSR* book 2 Balet, *Spartak* and Volkov, N., *Spartak*. Also see Balanchine, *Balanchine's Complete Stories of the Great Ballets* (new and rev. edn.). (pp. 571–575).

SCHOLTZE (JOHANNES). OPERNFÜHRER. Operette und Ballett mit einfuhrungen, geschichtlichen und biografischen mit teilungen und zahlreichen abbildungen. Berlin, Mode's Verlag 1927.
 Demy 8vo (8·1 × 5·1 ins.). pp. n.n. illus. Orig. dec. cloth.
 A collection of synopses for opera and ballet (mostly opera) with short cast lists.

SCHWARZ (EDITH). PETROUCHKA. Dans Kroniek. Amsterdam Juli 1950.
 Roy. 4to (12 × 9 ins.). pp. 103–106 with 4 illus. Orig. dec. wrapps.
 An article on the ballet *Petrouchka*. The entire issue is devoted to *Petrouchka* and Stravinsky, and includes a short article, *Reminiscences* by Cyril Beaumont. For illustrated synopses see *Bibliography*, Part I, Beaumont, Cyril W., *Petrouchka* and Part III, Lawrence, Robert, *Petrouchka*. See also Benois, Alexandre, A Letter to Cyril Beaumont.

SEARLE (HUMPHREY). BALLET MUSIC. An Introduction. Second revised edition. New York, Dover Publications [1973].
 Demy 8vo (8·3 × 5·3 ins.). xii + 256 pp. incl. index. Illus. Orig. dec. wrapps.
 First published in 1958, this is the second corrected edition with added Discography and Bibliography, the last of which might be extended considerably. See indexes of all vols. of the *Bibliography* under Music.

SELDES (GILBERT). THE 7 LIVELY ARTS. New York, Sagamore Press Inc. [1957].

Demy 8vo (8·1 × 5·3 ins.). x + 306 pp. Orig. cream cloth.
See They Call it Dancing (pp. 233–240).

SEREBRENIKOV (NIKOLAI). PAS DE DEUX. Translated by Elizabeth Kraft. New York, The Dance Magazine 1978.

Demy 4to (11 × 8·3 ins.). pp. 76, 77 illus. Orig. dec. wrapps.
An adaptation of Serebrenikov's *Pas de Deux* was begun in the Jan. 1978 issue of *Dance Magazine*.

SEREBRENNIKOW (NIKOLAI). PAS DE DEUX IM KLASSISCHEN TANZ. Herausgegeben von Werner Gommlich und Martin Puttke. Wilhelmshaven, Heinrichofen's Verlag [1976].

Demy 8vo (8·3 × 5·4 ins.). 173 + (i) pp. illus. with line drwgs. Orig. dec. grey cloth.
A translation into German of *Podderjka v Duztnom Tantse* by Boijidara Blaskova-Heyn and Klaus Trews.

SEREBRENNIKOV (N. N.). PODDERJKA V DUZTNOM TANTSE. Leningradskoe, Izdatelstvo Iskusstvo 1969.

Demy 8vo (8·3 × 5·4 ins.). 134 + (ii) pp. illus. with line drwgs. and photogs. Orig. dec. boards.
A book on Pas de Deux or Support, well illustrated. Text in Russian. See also *Bibliography*, Part I, Dolin, *Pas de Deux* also Ellis and Du Boulay, *Partnering*.

SERT (MISIA). TWO OR THREE MUSES. The Memoirs of Misia Sert. Translated from the French by Moura Budberg. London, Museum Press [1953].

Demy 8vo (8·4 × 5·2 ins.). ix + 216 pp. incl. index. With a frontis. and 18 other illus. Orig. cloth.
With the exception of The Fan (facing p. 33), the illustrations are the same as those in the American edition of *Misia and the Muses*. The portrait of Misia (facing p. 48) is attributed to Vuillard. In *Misia and the Muses* (3rd p. of plates) it is attributed to Bonnard.

SEYMOUR (MAURICE). BALLET PORTRAITS. New York, Pellegrini and Cudahay [1952].
    Roy. 4to (12 × 9 ins.). 165 pp. incl. index. With 145 photogs. Orig. buckram.
    A book of photographs with a Foreword by Arnold L. Haskell. See also *Bibliography*, Part III, for other volumes by Seymour and comment.

SHAKESPEARE (WILLIAM). ROMEO E GIULIETTA. Balletto in tre atti ed epilogo (dalla tragedia di W. Shakespeare). Musica di Sergei Prokofieff. Isola di San Giorgio, Teatro Verde 26–27–28 Luglio 1958.
    Demy 8vo (8·3 × 5·7 ins.). 32 pp. n.n. illus. Orig. dec. wrapps.
    A synopsis of the ballet in Italian, French and German with choreography by John Cranko and decorations by Nicola Benois. Cast: Fracci and Colombo (*Giulietta*); Pistoni and Perugini (*Romeo*). Neither Chujoy nor Wilson list this version, they refer to the Stuttgart production (1962) with decorations by Jürgen Rose and Marcia Haydée as *Juliet* and Barra as *Romeo*. See Stuttgart Ballet Souvenir Programmes for synopsis of this later edition.

SHAKESPEARE (WILLIAM). ROMEO E GIULIETTA. Balletto in tre atti e un epilogo di S. Radlov e S. Prokofiev dalla omonima tragedia di William Shakespeare. Prima Rappresentation a Milano 15 Gennaio 1959 Teatro alla Scala.
    Med. 8vo (9·4 × 6·6 ins.). pp. 137–166 with 10 plates. Orig. dec. wrapps.
    The booklet contains an important article by Luigi Pestalozza, cast, and several sketches by Nicola Benois not contained in above synopsis. Further performances of Cranko's ballet in Italy.

SHAKESPEARE (WILLIAM). THE TAMING OF THE SHREW. The Stuttgart Ballet, Royal Opera House Covent Garden. London, Royal Opera House 1974.
    Med. 8vo (9 × 5·2 ins.). 36 pp. illus. Orig. red wrapps.
    The house programme for July 1974 containing the synopsis of *The Taming of the Shrew*. See also the Stuttgart souvenir programme for the season 1969–1970. The world premiere of Cranko's ballet was on March 16, 1969.

SHARP (CECIL J.) & OPPÉ (A. P.). THE DANCE. An Historical Survey of Dancing In Europe. With a New Introduction by Richard Rastall. London, EP Publishing Ltd. 1972.

Demy 4to (11 × 8·6 ins.). xv + 54 pp. + 75 num. plates. Orig. red cloth.

This modestly priced republication is excellent value. Four plates printed in colour in the original edition are now in monochrome. See also *Bibliography*, Part II, Sharp.

SHEAD (RICHARD). CONSTANT LAMBERT. With a Memoir by Anthony Powell. London, Simon Publications. [1973].

Demy 8vo (8·3 × 5·3 ins.). 208 pp. incl. index. With a frontis. and 10 plates. Orig. black cloth.

Three Appendices include a list of compositions by Lambert, a very complete bibliography of articles and material appearing about him, also a discography. See also *Bibliography*, Part III, Lambert.

SHEARER (MOIRA). A LETTER TO CYRIL BEAUMONT. Sunday Aug. 7th 1953.

Cr. 8vo (7 × 5·5 ins.). 4 pp. in Xerox.

A letter from Moira Shearer, then residing at Flat E. 13 Melbury Road, Kensington W. 14, in which she thanks Mr. Beaumont for a copy of *The Sleeping Beauty* and laments the fact that no stage rehearsal is provided for her performance of *Aurora* at Covent Garden.

SHEARER (MOIRA). A LETTER TO CYRIL BEAUMONT. Thursday April 1954.

Cr. 8vo (7 × 5·1 ins.). 4 pp. Xerox.

A letter written after her performance as *Aurora* in *The Sleeping Beauty* in which she expresses her gratitude for his (Mr. Beaumont's) advice and help.

SHEARER (MOIRA). A LETTER TO CYRIL BEAUMONT. Sunday Jan. 4 1953.

Cr. 8vo (7 × 4·4 ins.). 2 pp. Xerox.

A letter written from 96 Stamford Court, thanking Mr. Beaumont for a copy of his translation of Gautier's *The Romantic Ballet*, which she finds tremendously interesting.

SHEARER (MOIRA). A LETTER TO CYRIL BEAUMONT. Wednesday Feb. 8th 1951.

Cr. 8vo (7 × 4·4 ins.). 2pp. Xerox.

A letter thanking Mr. Beaumont for 'a lovely Degas book' and inviting him, with Mrs. Beaumont, to attend her wedding on the 25th of February. She also writes that her charming little house is full of bookshelves.

SHENIN (A. S.). LEILI I MEDJNUN. Balet v 4 -kh deistviyakh, 6 kartinakh. Tadjinskii Gosudapstvennyi Ordena Lenina Teatr Oper i Baleta im Aini.

Cr. 8vo (7·6 × 5 ins.). 24 pp. illus. Orig. dec. wrapps.

A synopsis of the ballet. L. Zakidova and I. Savleva shared the role of *Leili* and M. Kabilov and V. Kormilin that of Käis (*Medjnun*). In 1964 Goleizovsky produced it for the Bolshoi with Bessmertnova and Vasiliev. See *Bolshoi Teatr SSSR*, book 2, *Balet, Leili i Medjnun*.

[SHERBAKOV (T. A.)]. MUZIKALINAYA KULTURA BELORUSSKOI SSR. Moskva, 'Muzika' 1977.

Cr. 8vo (7·6 × 4·6 ins.). 251 pp. + (iv), illus. Orig. white fabric.

Belo-Russian music and culture with a chapter, Belo-Russian ballet by K. Stepanskevich (pp. 69–92). See also Churka, Yulia, *Belo Russki Balet* and Grebeshnikov S. M., *Stsenicheskie Belorusskie Tantsi*. A collection of articles compiled by Sherbakov and edited by Glutsenko.

SHERIDAN (HOPE). ANDRÉ EGLEVSKY. The Great Classic Dancer. New York, Chrysalis.

32mo (4·1 × 5·4 ins.). 31 + (i) pp. Orig. illus. wrapps.

A monograph. See also Belknap, *Guide to Dance Periodicals* and Denby, Edwin, *Looking at the Dance* and only recently published Eglevsky and Gregory, *Nicolas Legat*.

SHKOLNIKOV (S. P.). ISKUSSTVO GRIMA. Minsk, 1964.

Demy 8vo (8·3 × 5·5 ins.). 134 + (ii) pp. illus. Orig. fabric spine and boards.

A book about make-up from the Roman times until today with very good examples of style, particularly in wigs and make-up for the 18th century. Text in Russian.

SHOSTAKOVICH (DMITRI) & OTHERS. RUSSIAN SYMPHONY. Thoughts about Tchaikovsky. New York, Philosophical Library [1947].
Demy 8vo (8·6 × 5·6 ins.). (iv) + 271 pp. with frontis. incl. index. Orig. paper boards.
A collection of essays about Tchaikovsky including one by Vasili Yakolev, The Ballets of Tchaikovsky (pp. 132–159). See also Rozanova, Y., *Simfonicheskie Printsipi Baletov Chaikovskogo.*

SHOVIRE (IVETT). YA BALERINA. Moskva 'Iskusstvo' 1977.
F'cap 8vo (6·4 × 5 ins.). 79 pp. + 30 plates of photographs in half-tone. Orig. white wrapps.
A translation into Russian of Yvette Chauviré's book *Je suis Ballerine.* See *Bibliography*, Part I, Chauviré, Yvette. Also Guest, Ivor, *Let Ballet de L'Opéra de Paris* (pp. 182–207, 216, 217, 240, 249, 280) and *Bibliography*, Part II, Nemenschousky, Léon, *A Day with Yvette Chauviré.*

SHUMILOVA (E[MILIYA IVANOVA]). PRAVDA BALETA. Moskva, Iskusstvo 1976.
Cr. 8vo (7·7 × 5·7 ins.). 151 pp. + a large section of plates. Orig. dec. wrapps.
Pravda Baleta, The Truth about Ballet is in 2 sections: Chast 1. Po Stranitsam Istorii (A Few pages from History); Chast 2. Sovremennie Balet (Contemporary Ballet).

SIDDONS (HENRY). PRACTICAL ILLUSTRATIONS OF RHETORICAL GESTURE AND ACTION. Second edition, first published London 1822, Reissued 1968. New York, Benjamin Blom.
Cr. 8vo (7·6 × 5 ins.). vi + 393 + xv pp. with 69 plates. Orig. blue cloth.
A modern reprint of the second improved edition first published in 1807. See *Bibliography*, Part I, Engel, and Part II, Siddons for comment on these earlier editions.

SIEGEL (MARCIA B.). AT THE VANISHING POINT. A critic looks at the Dance. New York, Saturday Review Press 1972.

Med. 8vo (9·2 × 6 ins.). ix + 320 pp. incl. index. Orig. two-tone cloth.
A critic with a rather strong bias toward the modern dance. See also *Bibliography*, Part III, Siegel, Marcia B.

SIGNORELLI (OLGA RESNEVEC). IL BALLETTO ITALIANO. Le sue caratteristiche nel passato e nel presente. Venezia XIII Festivale Internazionale di Musica Contemporeano 1950.
Med. 8vo (9·2 × 6·3 ins.). pp. 83–94 illus. Orig. dec. wrapps.
An article concluding with an appreciation of two new works, *Il Principe de Legno* and *Ballata Senza Musica*, with choreography by Aurel Milloss.

SILVANT (JEAN). DANSE. Paris, Intermède Printemps 1946.
Demy 4to (10·5 × 8·2 ins.). pp. 32–43 illus. Orig. dec. wrapps.
An article in Vol. No. I of *Intermède*, concerned mainly with the Diaghilev Ballet.

SIOHAN (ROBERT). STRAVINSKY. Translated by Eric Walter White. [1965].
Cr. 8vo (7·6 × 4·7 ins.). 192 pp. profusely illus. Orig. wrapps.
A monograph first published in French by Editions du Seuil in 1959 which concludes with a Chronology, A Selected Discography and A Selected Bibliography. See also Stravinsky and Craft.

SITWELL (EDITH). FACADE. Chamber orchestra conducted by Frederick Prausnitz Poems by Dame Edith Sitwell Music by William Walton.
Sq. (11·6 × 11·6 ins.). 8 pp. illus. with decorations. Wrapps.
A booklet accompanying Columbia record No. ML 5241 with music by William Walton. The verse is attractively printed; see also *Bibliography*, Part III, Sitwell, Edith, *Facade* and other Poems.

SITWELL (EDITH). THE RUSSIAN BALLET GIFT BOOK. Illustrated by I. de B. Lockyer. London, Leonard Parsons.

Cr. 4to (9·7 × 7·2 ins.). 77 + (i) pp. with 8 plates in colour. Orig. paper boards with fabric spine.

Following the Introduction are these short essays, each illustrated by a plate in colour: *The Dance Prelude; Kikimora; Kikimora's Dance; The Swan Princess; The Dragon-Fight; The Dragon's Funeral; Baba-Yaga*.

SITWELL (EDITH). TAKEN CARE OF. An autobiography. London, Readers Union Hutchinson 1966.

Demy 8vo (8·4 × 5·3 ins.). 192 pp. illus. Orig. black cloth.

See Tcheiitchew, Pavel (pp. 136, 137–41), also after p. 96 a portrait of Edith Sitwell.

SITWELL (OSBERT). C. W. BEAUMONT. London, Macmillan 1949.

Demy 8vo (8·5 × 5·4 ins.). pp. 36–37. Orig. red cloth.

An appreciation of the Cyril Beaumont Book Shop at 75 Charing Cross Road, contained in Sitwell's *Laughter in the Next Room*. See also Cecil Beaton, *The Monte Carlo Ballet Russe*; Nancy Bowden, *Cyril Beaumont*; Serge Leslie, *Seven Leagues of a Dancer*, and Peter Williams, *Between Heaven and Charing Cross* for other appreciations of Beaumont and the Charing Cross Road Shop.

SITWELL (OSBERT). GREAT MORNING. Being the third volume of Left Hand Right Hand. An Autobiography. London, Macmillan & Co. 1948.

Demy 8vo (8·5 × 5·4 ins.). viii + 324 pp. illus. Orig. red cloth.

Contains notes on Bakst, Cecchetti, Diaghilev, Nijinsky and others. Listed in the bibliographies included in Buckle's *Nijinsky* and Spencer's *Léon Bakst*.

SITWELL (OSBERT). LAUGHTER IN THE NEXT ROOM. Being the fourth volume of Left Hand Right Hand. An Autobiography. London, Macmillan & Co. 1949.

Demy 8vo (8·5 × 5·4 ins.). viii + 381 pp. illus. Orig. red cloth.

Contains notes on Bakst, The Coliseum Theatre, Diaghilev, Duncan, Nijinsky and many others. Listed in the bibliography included in Buckle's *Nijinsky*.

SITWELL (OSBERT). LEFT HAND RIGHT HAND. An Autobiography Vol. I: The Cruel Month. London, Macmillan & Co. 1945.

Demy 8vo (8·5 × 5·4 ins.). xvi + 272 pp. incl. index. Orig. red cloth.

Contains notes and material on Henriette d'Or, Mme. Taglioni and others.

SITWELL (OSBERT). NOBLE ESSENCES. A Book of Characters. New York, Grosset & Dunlap [1950].

Med. 8vo (8 × 5·3 ins.). 356 pp. incl. Index. Orig. dec. wrapps.

Contains material about Pavel Tchelitchew. Listed in the bibliography included in Parker Tyler's *The Divine Comedy of Pavel Tchelitchew.*

SITWELL (OSBERT). THE SCARLET TREE. Being the second volume of Left Hand Right Hand. An Autobiography. London, Macmillan & Co. 1946.

Demy 8vo (8·5 × 5·4 ins.). viii + 319 pp. illus. Orig. red cloth.

Contains notes and material on the ballet. Listed in the bibliography contained in Spencer's *Léon Bakst.*

SITWELL (SACHEVERELL). L'AMOUR AU THEATRE ITALIEN. [Brackley, Northants, Smart & Co. 1975].

Demy 8vo (8·3 × 5·3 ins.). 52 pp. Orig. pink wrapps.

A privately printed book of poems. Divided into (VI) sections. From (I) I chose: On a painted fan-leaf by Watteau; To the self-portrait of Watteau playing the hurdy-gurdy and (IV) Alhambra Theatre 2, November 1921 (*The Sleeping Princess*) and a memory of Nijinska and the finger variation.

SITWELL (SACHEVERELL). BADINERIE. [Smart & Co. (Printers). Brackley, Northants].

Demy 8vo (8·4 × 5·4 ins.). 8 pp. Orig. green wrapps.

Poems of great beauty including The Sylphide; A Memory of Nijinska in the Finger Variation; Pedrolino; and Ragonda.

SITWELL (SACHEVERELL). THE BRIDGE OF THE BROCADE SASH. Travels and Observations in Japan. Cleveland, The World Publishing Co. 1959.

Med. 8vo (9·1 × 6·1 ins.). 314 pp. illus. Orig. light green cloth.
Consult the Index for information on various dances and theatres unique to Japan.

SITWELL (SACHEVERELL). FOR WANT OF THE GOLDEN CITY. London, Thames and Hudson [1973].
Med. 8vo (9·2 × 6·1 ins.). 464 pp. incl. Index. Orig. blue cloth.
A beautiful book in which Ballets, Ballets Russes, Diaghilev, Elssler, Livry, Taglioni, Nijinsky, Vestris, Clara Webster and others are irradiated by the author's golden prose. The work is listed in a Bibliography concluding Edward Ricco's *The Sitwells at the Ballet* in *Ballet Review* Vol. 6 No. 1.

SITWELL (SACHEVERELL). GOTHIC EUROPE. London, Weidenfeld & Nicolson [1969].
Cr. 4to (9·5 × 6·7 ins.). xv + 192 pp. illus. with some in colour. Orig. brown cloth.
See Seville Dancers (*Dance of the Seises* pp. 132–34), plus a photograph of the ten dancers in a courtyard. See also *Bibliography*, Part I, Jobit, Pierre, *Le Ballet des Six* and Part III, Backman, E. Louis, *Religious Dances*.

SITWELL (SACHEVERELL). THE HUNTERS AND THE HUNTED. London, Macmillan 1947.
Demy 8vo (8·3 × 5·3 ins.). ix + 314 pp. with 16 illus. Orig. blue cloth with red label.
Divided into IV Books with III Entr'actes, II of the III Entr'actes are of interest to the dance: Bohemian Polka à la Smetana (pp. 89–92), and Harlequin and Columbine (pp. 239–258). See also Beaumont, *The History of Harlequin* for which Sacheverell wrote the Preface 'Concerning Harlequin in Art'.

SITWELL (SACHEVERELL). AN INDIAN SUMMER. Eight Poems on Indian Themes. [Brackley, Northants, Smart & Co.].
Demy 8vo (8·4 × 5·4 ins.). 31 pp. Orig. pink wrapps.
Longer and still more beautiful poems: Bacchus in India; Krishna with the Milkmaids; The Bayadères; Swinging Festival of The Brahmins project the golden imagery of the Dance. The first three were published in 1933, the last in 1972.

SITWELL (SACHEVERELL). LITTLE ITALY IN LONDON. [Brackley, Northants, Smart & Co. Printers].

Demy 8vo (8·3 × 5·3 ins.). 8 pp. Orig. printed light brown wrapps.

A tribute to the dancers and pantomimists of a forgotten golden age 1820–1850 in nostalgic verse: 'When you might see Chapino and Deulin who lodged with their Columbine wives near by, Running across to the theatre in the November rain with light from the new gas-lamps catching and diamonding their spangles'.

SITWELL (SACHEVERELL). SOUTHERN BAROQUE REVISITED. London, Weidenfeld and Nicolson. [1967].

Cr. 4to (9·5 × 6·7 ins.). xiii + 306 pp. illus. with many in colour. Orig. tan cloth.

See Jacques Callot's *Balli di Sfessania* (pp. 60, 61–65), and reproduction of 12 of the 24 plates from this ballet between pp. 252–259. See also Music Master to the Infanta Barbara: Domenico Scarlatti (pp. 240–279), and Scarlatti pieces selected for Diaghilev's ballet *The Good Humoured Ladies* (p. 283).

SITWELL (SACHEVERELL). TEMPLE OF SEGESTA. [Brackley, Northants, Smart & Co.].

Demy 8vo (8·3 × 5·3 ins.). 8 pp. Orig. light blue wrapps.

A privately printed poem. The Temple of Segesta stands; but its priests and acolytes are gone. Covent Garden and Drury Lane still stand, but where are Dan Leno, Grimaldi, George Wieland and Dicky Flexmore?

SITWELL (SACHEVERELL). TRUFFLE HUNT. London, Robert Hale Ltd. [1953].

Demy 8vo (8·3 × 5·2 ins.). x + 310 pp. incl. index. Illus. Orig. cloth.

A collection of short essays with several extended ones of which some twenty concern the dance and ballet. See Messrs Beaumont and Haskell (p. 85); *Pas de Deux* from *Don Quixote* with Mdlle Tamara Toumanova (pp. 301–303). Many of the essays are short but all are brilliant.

SLONIM (MARC). RUSSIAN THEATRE FROM THE EMPIRE TO THE SOVIETS. London, Methuen & Co. 1963.

Demy 8vo (8·5 × 5·3 ins.). 355 pp. incl. Index. Illus. Orig. dec. grey cloth.

See chapter 6 (pp. 171–181), The World of Art and Diaghilev: his renovation of the ballet.

SLONIMSKY (YURI). BALANCHINE: THE EARLY YEARS. Translated by John Andrews. Edited by Francis Mason. [Brooklyn, New York, 1976].

Med. 8vo (9 × 6 ins.). (iv) + 64 + (iv) pp. with 6 illus. Orig. dec. wrapps.

The complete issue of *Ballet Review*, Vol. 5 No. 3 devoted to Balanchine and his early years in Russia. See also Beaumont, *Balanchine's Ballet Imperial*, and *Bibliography*, Part III, Blackmur, R. P., *The Swan in Zurich*.

SLONIMSKY (YURI). BALETNIE STROKI PUSHKINA. Leningradskoe, Izdatelstvo Iskusstvo 1974.

Demy 8vo (8·4 × 5·4 ins.). 184 pp. illus. Orig. white cloth.

Text in Russian. See also *Bibliography*, Part IV, Beaumont, *Pushkin and his Influence on Russian Ballet*.

SLONIMSKY (YURI). DRAMATURGIYA BALETNOGO TEATR XIX VEKA. Ocherki Libretto Stsenarii. Moskva, 'Iskusstvo' 1977.

Cr. 8vo (7·7 × 5 ins.). 342 + (ii) pp. with about 80 illus. Orig. green cloth.

A collection of the synopses of the following ballets: *Dezertir; Zefir i Flora; Somnambula; Silfida; Jizel; Undina; Esmeralda; Katarina, doch Razboinika; Voinia Jenshtsin; Koppeliya; Spyashtsaya Krasavitsa*. Very nicely illustrated but unfortunately the quality of the off-set is very poor indeed.

SLONIMSKY (YURI). SEM BALETNIKH ISTORII. Rasskaz Stsenarista. Leningradskoe, Izdatelstvo Iskusstvo 1967.

Cr. 8vo (7·6 × 5·5 ins.). 254 + (vi) pp. illus. Orig. white cloth.

Seven Ballet Stories by Slonimsky with an Introduction by Yuri Grigorovich. The ballets are: *Yunost; Manon Lesko; Sem Krasavits; Leili i Medjnun; Tropou Groma; Vesennyaya Groza;* and *Bereg Nadejd*.

SLONIMSKY (YURI). SOVETSKII BALET. Materiali k Istorii Sovetskogo Baletnogo Teatra. Moskva-Leningrad 'Iskusstvo' 1950.

Cr. 4to (10·2 × 7·1 ins.). 365 + (iii) pp. illus. Orig. dec. brown cloth.

A very important book, one of Slonimsky's finest, concerned with ballet performed at Leningrad and Moscow theatres during 1917–1949. Many illustrations accompany a full text and many of these are seldom reproduced: *Tri Tolstyaka* (Three Fat Men); *Utrachennie Illusii* (Lost Illusions); *Mnimi Jenikh* (The False Bridegroom); *Skaza o Pope i ego Rabotnike Balda* (The Tale of a Priest and his Workman Balda); and many others. Not to be confused with *The Soviet Ballet* below. The book concludes with a list of first performances of all ballets given during this period of 1917–1949.

SLONIMSKY (YURI). THE SOVIET BALLET. By Yuri Slonimsky and others. New York, Da Capo Press 1970.

Roy. 8vo (9 × 5·7 ins.). xii + 285 pp. incl. Index. Illus. Orig. blue cloth.

A collection of articles on Soviet dancers, artists, teachers, choreographers etc., and the very extensive repertory of their ballet. This is a reprint of the edition first published in 1947.

SLONIMSKY (YURI). VESENNYAYA SKAZA. Voskresni 16 Marta 1947. Teatr Oper i Baleta S. M. Kirova.

Cr. 8vo (7·3 × 4·4 ins.). 6 pp. with 2 original photographs.

A house programme of the ballet *Vesennyaya Skaza* complete with cast and synopsis. The scenario is by Slonimsky, the music by Asafiev and the choreography by Fedor Loupokov. K. M. Sergeev is *Dobri Molodesh* and A. Shelest *Devisha-Krasa*. Two photographs accompany the programme, one of Sergeyev and Dudinskaya and the other of Scene No. 3. See Slonimsky, *Sovetskii Balet* (pp. 290–291 illus.).

SLONIMSKY (YURI). YUNOST. Balet v 3-k deistviyakh 8 kartinakh. Muzika M. I. Chulaki. Leningradskii, Malyi Opernii Teatr 1949.

Med. 8vo (9 × 5·3 ins.). 4 pp.

The house programme for the premier of Slonimsky's ballet *Yunost* (Youth), inspired by the Ostrovsky novel, *How the Steel was Tempered*. First performed Dec. 9, 1949 with the roles *Petya, Dima* and *Dacha* played by V. Tulubiev, F. Shishkin and G. Isayeva, choreography by Boris Fenster. See also, *Sem Baletnikh Istorii* (pp. 16–55).

SLONIMSKY (YURI) & ERMOLAEV (A. N.). SOLOVEĬ. Balet v 3 aktakh. Moskva, Dekada Belorusskogo Iskusstva 1940.

Demy 8vo (8·4 × 5·6 ins.). 8 pp. Orig. dec. wrapps.

A synopsis in Russian for the ballet *Soloveĭ* (The Nightingale) by Yuri Slonimsky and Alexandre Yermolaev. First performed in the Minsk Opera July 7, 1939. See Roslavleva, *Era of Russian Ballet* (pp. 268, 269). Music by Kroshner.

SLONIMSKY (YURI) & ERMOLAEV (A. N.). SOLOVEĬ. Balet v 3 aktakh. Gosudarstvennoe Izdatelstvo Iskusstvo, Moskva 1940.

Demy 8vo (8·5 × 5·6 ins.). 26 + (ii) pp. illus. with 2 plates in colour. Orig. dec. wrapps.

An illustrated booklet on the ballet *Soloveĭ* (The Nightingale) including the libretto and articles by Kroshner and Slonimsky. See the above synopsis for performing artists. See also Slonimsky, *Sovetskii Balet* (pp. 234–237 illus.).

SMIRNOV (IGOR). SAMPO. Balet v 3-kh Seistiyakh Dekada Karelskogo Iskusstva i Literaturi Avgust 1959.

Demy 8vo (8·7 × 5·6 ins.). 12 pp. Orig. white dec. wrapps.

A libretto for the ballet Sampo with music by Geltser Sinisalo. Text in Russian; see Slonimsky, *Vse o Balete*, for listing.

SNOW (LOIS WHEELER). CHINA ON STAGE. An American Actress in the Peoples Republic. New York, Random House [1972].

Med. 8vo (9·1 × 6 ins.). xv + 328 + (ii) pp. illus. Orig. blue cloth.

Chapter IV, Peasants and Soldiers in Ballet Shoes, contains the text for the ballet *Red Detachment of Women*, at present one of the two important ballets in modern China. The other is *The White Haired Girl*. See also *Bibliography*, Parts II and III, *Peoples Republic of China*.

SOLERTI (ANGELO). MUSICA, BALLO E DRAMMATICA ALLA CORTE MEDICEA DAL 1600 al 1637. Notizie tratte da un Diario con appendice di testi e rari. New York & London, Benjamin Blom 1968.
    Med. 8vo (9·1 × 6 ins.). xvi + 594 pp. incl. Index. Illus. Orig. red cloth.
    First published in Florence in 1905, reissued in 1968 by Blom.

SOLOVYOV-SEDOI (VASSILI). TARAS BULBA. Balet. Leningrad, Sovetskii Kompozitor 1959.
    Med. 16mo (5·4 × 4·2 ins.). 42 + (ii) pp. with one illus. Orig. green wrapps.
    A booklet about the ballet *Taras Bulba* with an appreciation of the composer Solovyov-Sedoi, and the libretto without cast or personnel. See Slonimsky, *Sovetskii Balett*, and Bolshoi Teatr *SSSR* book 2 Balet, *Taras Bulba* (pp. 239–246 illus.).

SORELL (WALTER. THE DANCE HAS MANY FACES. Second edition edited by Walter Sorell. New York, Columbia University Press 1966.
    Demy 8vo (9 × 6 ins.). x + 276 pp. illus. Orig. blue cloth.
    The second edition, revised with additions and deletions. See also *Bibliography*, Parts II and III, Sorell, Walter.

SOTHEBY & CO. BALLET AND THEATRE MATERIAL. Thursday June 5th 1975.
    Cr. 4to (9·5 × 7·1 ins.). 89 + (ii) pp. illus. with 8 in colour. Orig. dec. wrapps. (Bakst).
    An amply illustrated catalogue listing some 20 items of Bakst, 12 of Benois and 15 of Gontcharova. Important among the statuary were three by Jean-Auguste Barre (two of Elssler and one of Taglioni).

SOTHEBY & CO. BALLET AND THEATRE MATERIAL. Wed. 25th May 1977. London, Sotheby, Parke-Bernet.
    Cr. 4to (9·4 × 7 ins.). 85 pp. illus. some in colour. Orig. dec. wrapps.

A catalogue principally of designs by Bakst, Barbier, Gontcharova and Leger.

SOTHEBY & CO. DECOR AND COSTUME DESIGNS PORTRAITS MANUSCRIPTS AND POSTERS PRINCIPALLY FOR BALLET. Thursday 21st June 1973. London, Sotheby.

Cr. 4to (9·4 × 7 ins.). 77 pp. illus. Orig. dec. wrapps. (Cocteau).

A catalogue of 69 items, including 2 lots concerning Margot Fonteyn.

SOTHEBY PARKE-BERNET & CO. BALLET AND THEATRE MATERIAL. Day of Sale Wed. 17th May 1978. London, Sotheby's.

Med. 8vo (9·5 × 7·1 ins.). 74 pp. illus. Orig. dec. green wrapps.

This well illustrated catalogue includes 5 designs in colour; displays Costume and Decor designs, Books and Photographs. 142 numbered items of which Books and Photographs claim Nos. 127–142.

SOTHEBY PARKE-BERNET & CO. CATALOGUE OF THE HIGHLY IMPORTANT TOULOUSE-PHILIDOR COLLECTION of Manuscript and Printed Music and other Valuable Manuscripts and Printed Books. Day of Sale Monday June 26th, 1978. London, Sotheby's.

Cr. 4to (10·7 × 7·2 ins.). 87 pp. illus. with frontis. in colour. Orig. printed brown wrapps.

A splendid catalogue of mss and printed music of the late XVII and early XVIII century: mainly operas and ballets by Lully, Campra, Colasse, Couperin, Destouches, De La Coste. See lot 66 Lully, *Triomphe de L'Amour*, Paris Christophe Ballard 1707. See also *Bibliography*, Part II Quinault, Philippe, *Le Triomphe de L'Amour* for the original libretto of 1681.

SOTHEBY PARKE-BERNET INC. DANCE. THEATRE. OPERA. Costume and Decor Designs, Sculpture, Photographs and Books. Public Auction Dec. 15, 1977. New York, Sotheby Parke-Bernet Inc.

Sq. (9·1 × 8·7 ins.). pp. n.n. illus. with some in colour. Orig. dec. wrapps. (Bakst, La Boutique Fantasque).

A most attractive catalogue, mainly of Costume and Decor Designs, but with some rare books and souvenir programmes.

SOTHEBY PARKE-BERNET MONACO S.A. THE DIAGHILEV-LIFAR LIBRARY 28, 29, 30 Nov.–1er Dec. 1975.

Cr. 4to (9·5 × 7·2 ins.). 217 pp. illus. incl. a frontis. in colour. Orig. green dec. boards.

A catalogue splendidly illustrated and produced, of mainly non-theatrical books. However it must be stated that many of the books according to description were worn or incomplete or both.

SOTHEBY'S (SOTHEBY PARKE-BERNET & CO.). IMPRESSIONIST AND MODERN PAINTINGS DRAWINGS AND WATERCOLOURS AND BALLET AND THEATRE MATERIAL. Wednesday 20th Oct. 1976. London, Sotheby's.

Cr. 4to (9·5 × 7·1 ins.). 81 pp. illus. Orig. green wrapps.

Lots 186–227 contain the Ballet and Theatre Material. Pavel Tchelitchew is represented by lots Nos. 214–227.

SOTHEBY'S (SOTHEBY PARKE-BERNET & CO.). PRINTED & MANUSCRIPT MUSIC AUTOGRAPH LETTERS OF MUSICIANS & BOOKS ON MUSIC THE THEATRE AND DANCE. Days of Sale 8th & 9th Nov. 1976.

Cr. 4to (9·5 × 7·1 ins.). 110 pp. illus. Orig. printed wrapps.

The dance is represented by lots 166–201, not a large sale but some items reached astounding amounts: Blasis, *Delle Compozizoni Coreografiche* (£150); Caroso, *Il Ballarino* 1581 (£1,300); Feuillet, *Recueil de Danses* 1704 (£1,600); Levinson, *La Danse au Théâtre* (£130).

SOTHEBY'S (SOTHEBY PARKE-BERNET & CO.). SALE OF MATERIAL RELATING TO THE THEATRE OPERA BALLET MUSIC HALL AND CINEMA. Day of sale Monday Dec. 20th 1976. London, Sotheby's.

Demy 8vo (7·6 × 8·2 ins.). 89 pp. illus. Orig. printed red wrapps.

A sale at Sotheby's Belgravia in which 181 lots were sold. The ballet material consisted largely of a mixture of Souvenir Programmes, Photographs, and Press Releases for various American and European Ballet Companies. There were a few lithographs, and the album *Les Danseuses de L'Opéra* by Alophe.

SOVIET ART FESTIVALS. ART FESTIVALS USSR 1967. Ministry of Culture of the USSR.

Sq. (8 × 8 ins.). pp. n.n. illus. many in colour. Orig. dec. red wrapps.

Three Festivals in which the dance and ballet play an important part. The Festivals were: Moscow Stars May 5th–13th; White Nights June 21st–29th; and Russian Winter Dec. 25th–Jan. 5th 1968.

SOVIET BALLET (THE). BALET BOLSHOGO TEATR SSSR. Soviet USSR na Stroike.

Imp. 4to (15·5 × 11·6 ins.). 10 pp. n.n. illus. Unbound.

An article from the Soviet publication *U.S.S.R. na Stroike* No. 9, 1949, featuring Semenova, Struchkova, Messerer, Gabovich, Golovinka, Ulanova and others. See also Bakhrushin, Y. A. *Balet Bolshogo Teatr* in *Bolshoi Teatr* (pp. 161–284).

SOVIET BALLET (THE). KHUDOJESTVENNOE VOSPITANIE SOVETSKOGO SHKOLINKA Sbornik Statei i Materialov Vipusk I. Moskva, Institut Khudojestvennogo Vospitalniya Akademi Pedagogischeskikh Nauk 1947.

Cr. 4to (10·6 × 6·4 ins.). 182 + (ii) pp. Orig. wrapps.

A collection of eight articles including such figures as C. A. Apraksina; V. A. Bagadurov; A. A. Sergeev; G. V. Labunskaya; V. G. Shiryaeva; V. C. Kolesaev; Y. A. Bakhrushin and L. V. Bileeva. The Soviet Academy for Physical training. Text in Russian.

SOVIET BALLET (THE). PROGRAMMI SPETSIALNIKH DISTSIPLIN KHOREOGRAFICHESKIKH-UCHILISHCHE. Moskva Leningrad, Gosudarstvennoe Muzikalnoe Izdatelstvo 1947.

Cr. 8vo (7·5 × 5·4 ins.). 98 + (ii) pp. Orig. printed cream wrapps.

Programmed lessons in the Classic Dance, Historical Dance, Folk and Character Dance, Classical *Pas de Deux*, Rhythmic, Fencing, Make-up, Etc., in Eleven Programmed Lessons. See also Pantukova, *Leningradskoe Gosudarstvennoe Khoreografischeskoe Uchilits*.

SOVIET DANCE (THE). STSENICHESKIE BELORUSSKIE TANTSI. Izdatelstvo ['Belarusi' Minsk 1967].

Demy 8vo (8·3 × 6·5 ins.). 64 pp. illus. with drwgs., diags., and mus. Orig. dec. wrapps.

Three stage dances from White Russia. See also Churko, Yulia, *Belo Russki Balet*.

SOVIET DANCE (THE). SUJETNIE TANTSI. Izdatelstvo 'Iskusstvo' Moskva 1969.

Cr. 8vo (7·6 × 5 ins.). 80 pp. illus. with drwgs., diags., and mus. Orig. dec. wrapps.

Four Dances with subjects: *Doroga v Bessmertie* (Road to Immortality); *Stroiteli* (Builders of a New Life); *Voronyata* (Ravens); and *Pervaya Okhota* (Primitive Hunters). The drawings are simple but very descriptive.

SOVIET DANCE (THE). TANTSI NARODOV SSSR. Izdatelstvo 'Iskusstvo' Moskva 1964.

Cr. 8vo (7·6 × 5 ins.). 80 pp. illus. figures, line drwgs. and mus. Orig. dec. wrapps.

Editors for the following three dances, *Metelitsa, Molodejnaya Polka*, and *Vstrecha*, are: Stepanov for the choreography; P. Teplov for the music.

SOVIET DANCE (THE). TANTSI NARODOV SSSR. Vipusk 3 Izdatelstvo 'Iskusstvo' Moskva 1967.

Cr. 8vo (7·6 × 5 ins.). 68 pp. illus. with diags. line drwgs. and mus. Orig. dec. wrapps.

Editors for the following three dances, *Melnitsa, Strelutsa*, and *Bilkildak*, are: L. Stepanov for the choreography; P. Teplov for the music.

SOVIET DANCE (THE). TANTSI NARODOV SSSR. Vipusk IV. Izdatelstvo 'Iskusstvo' Moskva 1969.

Cr. 8vo (7·6 × 5 ins.). 64 pp. illus. with line drwgs., diags. and mus. Orig. dec. wrapps.

Editors for the following three dances, *Akbilek, Davluri-Mtiuluri*, and *Pailandjo*, are: P. Teplov for the music; L. Stepanov for the choreography.

SOVIET DANCE (THE). TRI SUJETNIKH TANTSA. Gosudarstvennoe Izdatelstvo 'Iskusstvo' Moskva 1961.

Cr. 8vo (7·6 × 5 ins.). 125 pp. illus. with drwgs., diags. and mus. Orig. dec. wrapps.
Three Dances with Subjects: *Ukhajer* (Courting Dance); *Shel so Slujbi Pogranichnik* (Dance of the Border Guards); and *Shesterka v Troikakh* (Troika for Six).

SPEED (JOHN F.). BACKGROUND TO A BALLET. A Record of the Sadler's Wells Ballet at Covent Garden. London, Louis Klemantaski Ltd. 1951
Demy 8vo (8·6 × 6·4 ins.). 32 pp. n.n. illus. Orig. dec. wrapps.
Sixty photographs by Louis Klementaski with captions by John F. Speed.

SPENCER (CHARLES). BAKST. An Exhibition at the Fine Arts Society 3 Dec.–4 Jan., 1974. London, The Fine Art Society.
Sq. (8·2 × 8·2 ins.). pp. n.n. illus. Orig. dec. wrapps.
A catalogue with a Prefatory note by Charles Spencer which contains descriptions of 144 numbered items, a Chronology of his life and a short Bibliography.

SPENCER (CHARLES). LÉON BAKST. London, Academy Editions [1973].
Roy. 4to (12 × 9 ins.). 248 pp. incl. bibliography and index. With 277 illus. incl. 32 in colour. Orig. cloth.
The book is a collage of other writers' works with an attempted analysis. In the matter of *The Sleeping Princess* (Chapter 8) I believe he errs in referring to a 'resounding commercial flop' (p. 189) and the 'Debacle of the *Sleeping Princess*' (p. 194). In theatrical parlance I take 'flop' to mean a short run of days or perhaps weeks: certainly not months. And can any ballet or opera prior to *The Sleeping Princess* boast of 105 consecutive performances? It is said (p. 205) that neither the designs nor the photographs of the production suggest that the subject was ideally suited to Bakst. The work might be considered a pastiche of ideas, and Harlequin and Columbine are perhaps copies from designs by an 18th century artist; but after seeing four or five other designers' attempts at *The Sleeping Princess* that of Bakst seems the definitive version.
The book could stand a further proof reading: Nemchinova not Netchinova (p. 230); Parke Bernet not Burnet (p. 230); Nijinska, not Nijinsky, version of *Bolero*; Bronislava Nijinska not Bratislava

(p. 153); Gabriel Astruc not Gabriele (p. 144); and (p. 38) Le Coeur de la Marquise not La Coeur. Finally, the colour reproductions are not of the standard of the Diaghilev Souvenir Programmes, and certainly not of the original Bakst editions of de Brunoff, The Fine Art Society etc.

SPENCER (CHARLES), DYER (PHILIP), BATTERSBY (MARTIN). THE WORLD OF SERGE DIAGHILEV. London, Paul Elek. 1974.

Cr. 4to (9·3 × 7·4 ins.). 173 pp. incl. Index. Orig. brown cloth.

Contents: Origin (p. 9); World of Art (p. 15); Widening Horizons (p. 29); The Ballets Russes – Early Years (p. 41); The Ballets Russes-Modernism (p. 93); Diaghilev's Heritage (p. 127); Diaghilev's Influence on Fashion and Decoration (p. 149). The illustrations are in the main well reproduced and the final chapters, Diaghilev's Heritage and Diaghilev's Influence on Fashion are the most interesting and contain the least hackneyed information.

STALS (GEORGS). DAS LETTISCHE BALLETT DER RIGAER OPER. Künstlerische Ausstattung von Prof. Ludolfs Liberts. Riga, J. Kadilis Verlag 1943.

Demy 4to (11·6 × 8·2 ins.). 53 pp. + 120 num. plates + 8 tipped-in coloured. Orig. dec. wrapps.

An excellent history of *Das Lettische Ballett der Rigaer Oper* (The Latvian Ballet of the Riga Opera House) with most interesting illustrations. Beginning in 1919 with 10 dancers and Voldemārs Komisārs as balletmaster, its history is documented in the list of repertory until 1941, during which time Sergeyev, Fedorowa, Fokin, Wilsak, Pianowski and finally Lēmanis held the post of balletmaster. Among these Fedorowa was one of the most important in forming its early classical ballets. It became part of the U.S.S.R. in 1940, during which years *Die Fontäne von Bachtschisarai* was presented.

STANISLAVSKI (CONSTANTIN). MY LIFE IN ART. Translated by J. J. Robbins. New York, Meridan Books [1959].

Med. 8vo (8 × 5·3 ins.). xi + 586 pp. incl. Index. Frontis. of the author. Orig. dec. wrapps.

See chapter LIV Isadora Duncan and Gordon Craig (pp. 505–524). While Isadora's early performances here are discussed, the article is mainly about Craig's production of Hamlet.

STEARNS (MARSHALL & JEAN). JAZZ DANCE. The Story of American Vernacular Dance. New York, The Macmillan Co. [1968].

Med. 8vo (9·3 × 6·1 ins.). xvi + 464 pp. illus. Orig. red and blue cloth.

The work is complete with selected Bibliography and List of Films as well as a glossary of Jazz Steps in Laban Notation. See also *Dance Magazine Portfolio* for Feb. 1968, Jazz-American Dance Machine.

STEEGMULLER (FRANCIS). 'YOUR ISADORA'. The Love Story of Isadora Duncan & Gordon Craig. Macmillan & The New York Public Library [1974].

Med. 8vo (9·1 × 6 ins.). vii + 399 + (i) pp. illus. Orig. black cloth.

Editor's Foreword: The chief content of the present volume is the major portion of more than two hundred letters from Isadora Duncan to Edward Gordon Craig. See also *Gordon Craig and the Dance, Bibliography*, Part III.

STEVENS (FRANKLIN). DANCE AS LIFE. A Season with American Ballet Theatre. New York, Harper & Row [1976].

Demy 8vo (8·2 × 5·3 ins.). viii + 190 pp. illus. Orig. black fabric spine and boards.

An author's experiences with various of New York City's ballet schools and companies, concluding with Ballet Theatre in which information is given about David Blair's *The Sleeping Beauty* and Baryshnikov's reception by the artists of the company.

STOKES (ADRIAN). A LETTER TO CYRIL W. BEAUMONT. Cornwall, May 22 [1944].

Demy 8vo (8·2 × 5·7 ins.). 2 pp. in Xerox.

A facsimile of a letter in which Stokes expresses his appreciation of Beaumont's *The Ballet Called Giselle*.

STOKES (SEWELL). RECITAL IN PARIS. A Novel. London, Peter Davies [1954].

Cr. 8vo (7·1 × 4·6 ins.). 250 pp. Orig. red cloth.

Author's Note: Anyone who identifies Sarah Menken with the late Isadora Duncan will not be altogether wrong. See also *Bibliography*, Part III, Stokes, Sewell.

STRATOU (DORA). LES DANSES GRECQUES. Lien Vivant avec La Grèce de l'Antiquité. Athenes 1967.
Med. 8vo (9·3 × 6·3 ins.). 49 pp. text with 114 num. photogs. Orig. dec. wrapps.
Text in French. See also Petrides, *Folk Dances of the Greeks*, where there are instructions for some of the dances herein described. See also *Bibliography*, Part III, Crosfield.

STRAUSS (GLORIA B.). THE ART OF THE SLEEVE IN CHINESE DANCE. New York, Dance Perspectives Fall 1975.
Med. 8vo (9 × 7·4 ins.). 48 pp. illus. Orig. dec. wrapps.
Issue No. 63 of *Dance Perspectives*.

STRAUSS (RICHARD). SCHLAGOBERS. Heiteres Wiener Ballett in Zwei Aufzügen. Berlin, Adloph Fürstner 1924.
Cr. 8vo (7 × 4·6 ins.). 18 pp. with 5 plates. Orig. dec. wrapps.
A synopsis of the ballet *Schlagobers* with illustrations by the designer Ada Nigrin. See also *Bibliography*, Part III, Rebling, *Ballet von A bis* and Schmidt-Garre, *Ballett vom Sonnenkönig bis Balanchine*. See also Beaumont, *Complete Book of Ballets* (pp. 615–619).

STRAUSS (RICHARD) & HOFMANNSTAHL (HUGO VON). A WORKING FRIENDSHIP. The Correspondence Between. Introduction by Edward Sackville-West. New York, Random House [1952].
Med. 8vo (9 × 6 ins.). xx + 558 pp. illus. Orig. red cloth.
Essential for information on the beginnings of *Josephlegende*. Nijinsky was the original choice for *Joseph*, and Karsavina finest of those who succeeded Marie Kussnetsoff as *Potiphar's Wife*.

STRAVINSKY (IGOR) & CRAFT (ROBERT). CONVERSATIONS WITH IGOR STRAVINSKY. London, Faber and Faber [1959].
Demy 8vo (8·4 × 5·3 ins.). 140 pp. incl. index. Illus. Orig. red cloth.
Contents: About Composing and Compositions; 2. About Musicians and Others; 3. About My Life and Times and Other Arts (Painters of the Russian Ballet); 4. About Music Today. The first of six books by Stravinsky and Craft written in dialogue form.

STRAVINSKY (IGOR) & CRAFT (ROBERT). DIALOGUES AND A DIARY. London, Faber and Faber [1968].
Demy 8vo (8·4 × 5·3 ins.). 328 pp. incl. index. Illus. Orig. rose cloth.
Contents: Scenes de Ballet (p. 48); The Flood (p. 72); The Rite (p. 81); Index of Works by Stravinsky (p. 313). These are the highlights of Vol. No. 4 of the 6 volume set.

STRAVINSKY (IGOR) & CRAFT (ROBERT). EXPOSITIONS AND DEVELOPMENTS. London, Faber and Faber [1962].
Demy 8vo (8·4 × 5·3 ins.). 168 pp. incl. index. Illus. Orig. green cloth.
Contents: 1. Expositions; 2. Developments; A check list of Tchaikovsky sources for *Le Baiser de la Fée* (p. 158). As the Table of Contents is sketchy consult the Index for information. The third volume.

STRAVINSKY (IGOR) & CRAFT (ROBERT). MEMORIES AND COMMENTARIES. London, Faber and Faber. [1960].
Demy 8vo (8·4 × 5·3 ins.). 183 pp. incl index. Illus. Orig. tan cloth.
Contents: I. Autobiographical; II. Portraits Memoires; III. Some Musical Questions; IV. Three Operas; Appendix. First Scenario for *The Rake's Progress*. The Autobiographical section contains A Russian Education; Diaghilev and his Dancers; Some Russian Composers. The second volume.

STRAVINSKY (IGOR) & CRAFT (ROBERT). RETROSPECTIVES AND CONCLUSIONS. New York, Alfred A. Knopf 1969.
Demy 8vo (8·3 × 5·4 ins.). ix + 350 + ix pp. incl. index. Orig. green cloth.
Contents: I. 1. Interviews; 2. Preface; 3. Reviews; II. From the Diaries of Robert Craft 1948–1968. This is volume No. 6 of the series.

STRAVINSKY (IGOR) & CRAFT (ROBERT). THEMES AND EPISODES. New York, Alfred A. Knopf 1967.
Demy 8vo (8·3 × 5·3 ins.). x + 352 pp. + xviii incl. index. Illus. Orig. black cloth.

Contents: 1. Contingencies; 2. Programme Notes; 3. Letters and Ripostes; 4. Interviews; 5. Obituary; 6. Book Reviews; 7. On Conductors and Conducting. II. From the Diaries of Robert Craft 1949–1966. Volume No. 5 of the 6 Vol. series. See also Craft, Robert.

STRAWINSKY (IGOR). ERINNERUNGEN. Zürich-Berlin, Atlantis-Verlag [1937].

Demy 8vo (8·7 × 5·4 ins.). 227 pp. incl. Table of Contents. Orig. black cloth.

The German translation of *Chroniques de Ma Vie*, illustrated with photographs and line drawings.

STRONG (ROY). SPLENDOUR AT COURT. Renaissance Spectacle and Illusion. London, Wiedenfeld and Nicolson 1973.

Cr. 4to (9·6 × 7·4 ins.). 287 pp. incl. index. Illus. with 16 pp. in colour and 200 others. Orig. red cloth.

Dr. Strong shows how, out of this art for the projection of power, almost by chance came our modern Opera and Ballet and the Theatre with the proscenium arch, which has lasted until our own day.

SUAREZ (VICENTE MARRERO). EL ACIERTO DE LA DANZA ESPAÑOLA. Esplandian 1952.

Cr. 8vo (7·5 × 4·4 ins.). 175 pp. illus. Orig. dec. red wrapps.

Text in Spanish. See also *Bibliography*, Part III, Vicente Marrero, *El Enigma de España en la Danza Española*.

SVETLOV (VALERIEN). ANNA PAVLOVA. Translated from the Russian by A. Grey. With 75 illustrations. New York, Dover Publications [1974].

Demy 4to (10·7 × 8·1 ins.). 194 pp. illus. with some in colour. Orig. dec. wrapps.

A republication of the de Brunhoff 1922 Paris edition. There were 22 full colour illustrations in that limited edition; the present contains 8. See *Bibliography*, Part II, Svetlov, Valerien, for the original editions.

SVĚTLOV (VALERIEN). ANTICKÁ CHOREOGRAFIE A ISADORA DUNCANOVÁ. Praha, Taneční Listy 18. 2. 1947.

Cr. 4to (9·7 × 7 ins.). pp. 100–105 illus. Orig. printed wrapps.

An article in *Tanečni Listy*, edited by Jan Rey. The issue is largely concerned with Isadora Duncan and the following writers have contributed: J. Rey; Claude-Roger Marx; Rozhor Hercem Sokolovem; M. de Saint-Marceau; M. A. Tymichová; M. Horová; J. Jěrábkova; Z. Urbanék and Dr. M. Vaněk. The illustrations are after Lafitte, José Clara, Rodin and Vera Fridrichova. See also *Bibliography*, Parts II & III, Svetlov, Valerien.

SVETLOV (VALERIEN). DIAGHILEV – THE TRAIL BLAZER. New York, The Dance Magazine Mar. 1931.

Roy. 4to (12·5 × 8·6 ins.). pp. 26, 27, 58, 59 illus. Orig. dec. wrapps. (Franz Felix).

The first of a four part article which contains a little known portrait of Vera Trefilova. See both Belknap, *Guide to Dance Periodicals* (Vol. I) and Magriel, *Bibliography*, for important listing of Svetlov's articles.

SVETLOV (VALERIEN). DIAGHILEV – THE TRAIL BLAZER. New York, The Dance Magazine April 1931.

Roy. 4to (12·5 × 8·6 ins.). pp. 15, 16, 49, 52, 53 illus. Orig. dec. wrapps.

Part Two of the four part article. See also portrait of Doris Niles (p. 22) in an article – The Treatment of Make-up. Valerien Svetlov also wrote the very fine articles that preceded each year of *Collection des Plus Beaux Numeros de Comoedia Illustré* et des Programmes. See *Bibliography* Part I, De Brunoff, Maurice.

SVETLOV (VALERIEN). DIAGHILEV – THE TRAIL BLAZER. New York, The Dance Magazine June 1931.

Roy. 4to (12·5 × 8·6 ins.). pp. 29, 30, 54 illus. Orig. dec. wrapps.

Part Four and the conclusion of *Diaghilev – The Trail Blazer*. Among the illustrations the Second Act of the ballet *Ode* is reproduced.

SVETLOV (VALERIEN). A LETTER TO CYRIL W. BEAUMONT. Paris, 22 Juin 1919.

Demy 8vo (8·2 × 5·3 ins.). 3 pp. in Xerox.

A copy of a letter by Svetlov proposing the mss. of Thamar Karsavina for publication. It was accepted and published by Beaumont in 1922. See *Bibliography* Part II Svetlov, Valerien, *Thamar Karsavina*.

SVETLOV (VALERIEN). LIGHTS THAT DANCE. New York, The Dance Magazine July 1929.
  Roy. 4to (12·5 × 8·6 ins.). pp. 43, 57 with 1 illus. Orig. dec. wrapps.
  An article in the July issue of *Dance Magazine*, crediting Loie Fuller for her early pioneering in matching Rhythmic Motion with Coloured Lights. See also *Bibliography*, Part I, Fuller, *15 Years of a Dancer's Life*.

SVETLOV (VALERIEN). VIRGINIA ZUCCHI. London, The Dancing Times Dec. 1930.
  Med. 8vo (9·6 × 8·5 ins.). pp. 278, 279 with 1 illus. Orig. dec. wrapps.
  An article in the Dec. 1930 issue of *The Dancing Times*. See also *Bibliography*, Part III, *Enciclopedia dello Spettacolo* Vol. IX, and Part II, Plescheev, *Nash Balet*. Also Guest, Ivor, *The Divine Virginia*.

SWIFT (MARY GRACE). A LOFTIER FLIGHT. The Life and Accomplishments of Charles-Louis Didelot, Balletmaster. London, Pitman [1974].
  Demy 8vo (8·7 × 5·7 ins.). x + 230 pp. incl. notes, index and illus. Orig. cloth.
  The first biography in English of Didelot. In spite of a discumbobulation (the author's word) or two and a slight tendency towards the vernacular it is a fine work. Other sources (some of which the author acknowledges) are Lawson's *History of Ballet and its Makers*, Roslavleva's *Era of the Russian Ballet*, and Slonimsky's *Didlot* and also his *Mastera Baleta*.

SWISHER (VIOLA HEGYI). TAMARA TOUMANOVA: A Unique Career. New York, Dance Magazine 1970.
  Demy 4to (11 × 8·3 ins.). pp. 44–63 illus. Orig. dec. wrapps. (Toumanova).
  A *Dance Magazine Portfolio* for September 1970. Since the mid-1930s there are few books on the ballet that do not contain material on Toumanova. To this must be added a large number of articles of which many are listed in Belknap's *Guide to Dance Periodicals*.

SWOPE (MARTHA). A MIDSUMMER NIGHT'S DREAM. The Story of the New York City Ballet's Production. Introduction by Lincoln Kirstein. Edited by Nancy Lassale. New York, Dodd Mead & Co. [1977].

(8·5 × 10·2 ins.). 64 pp. illus. Orig. lemon coloured cloth.
A ballet in two acts and six scenes with choreography by Balanchine. See also *Bibliography*, Part III, Balanchine, *New Complete Stories of the Great Ballets*, A Midsummer Night's Dream.

TAGLIONI (P[AUL]). LES PLAISIRS DE L'HIVER. Ou Les Patineurs. London, G. Stewart.

F'cap 8vo (6·7 × 3·7 ins.). 2pp. Mod. white boards folio with label.
A synopsis of the ballet which has a slightly different text from the synopsis in the Beaumont *Complete Book of Ballets*. The partial cast is the same with the exception of Madelle P. Stephan, who is added in capitals with C. Rosati and M. Charles deleting M. d'Or from the listing. A Note states that this ballet-divertissement was exhibited all over Germany in 1848 before it was introduced into Meyerbeer's *Le Prophète*. The music consisted of Hungarian and Polish national melodies.

TAGLIONI (CAV. PAOLO). SATANELLA. Gran Ballo Fantastico in Cinque Quadri Riprodotto dal Coreografo Mendez José. Al Teatro Regio di Torino 1873–1874. Torino, Tipografia Teatrale.

Cr. 8vo (7 × 4·4 ins.). 11 pp. Orig. dec. wrapps.
The synopsis with Carolina Pochini as *Satanella* and Ferdinand Pulini as *Carlo*. Created at Royal Theatre Berlin by Marie Taglioni II. See Edwin Binney, *A Century of Austro-German Dance Prints, Bibliography, Part III*, for reproduction of three lithographs of this artist.

TAGLIONI (PHILIPPE). LA GITANA. Ballet-Pantomime. Représenté pour la première fois sur le grand théâtre Impèrial de St. Petersbourg le 23 No. 1838. St. Petersbourg, Imprimerie J. Glasounoff et Cie.

Cr. 8vo (7·1 × 4·6 ins.). 33 pp. Unbound.
The original synopsis with all artists listed. At the time Cyril Beaumont published his *Complete Book of Ballets* this cast list was not available. Acte Premier: *Frédéric* Mr. Holz, *La Gitana* Melle

Taglioni, *Mina* Melle Télechowa 2e, *Don Alonzo* Mr. Spiridonoff. Performed later in London in 1839 shortly before Elssler appeared in *La Gypsy*.

TAGLIONI (SALVATORE). INES DE CASTRO. Ballo Storico in sei Atti. Nel Real Teatro di S. Carlo nell'autunno dell'anno 1831. Napoli, dalla Tipografia Flautina 1831.

Cr. 8vo (7 × 4·3 ins.). 16 pp. Orig. tooled red leather.

A synopsis with all the artists listed: *Don Pedro* Sig. Demasier, *Diego Lopez Pacheco* Sig. de Mattia, *Ines de Castro* Signora Porta, *Atto 30 Passo a Cinque* Signori Samengo, Ferrante e Rosati e dalle Signore Peraud-Taglioni e Brugnoli-Samengo.

TÁNCMÜVÉSZETI ÉRTESÍTÖ. A Magyar Táncmüveszek Szövetsgenek idószaki értesitöje gyanánt. Budapest 1966.

Med 8vo (9 × 6·2 ins.). 144 pp. Mimeograph. Orig. dec. wrapps.

Volume 1. Text in Hungarian. A catalogue of materials on the Hungarian dance and related subjects.

TÁNCMÜVÉSZETI ÉRTESÍTÖ. 1965. 3. Magyar Táncmüvészek Szövetsége. Budapest 1965.

Cr. 4to (10·7 × 7·7 ins.). 120 pp. Mimeograph. Orig. dec. wrapps.

Volume 3. Text in Hungarian.

TÁNCMÜVÉSZETI ÉRTESÍTÖ. 1965. 4. Magyar Táncmüvészek Szövetsége. Budapest 1965.

Cr. 4to (10·7 × 7·7 ins.). 193 pp. Mimeograph. Orig. wrapps.

Volume 4. Text in Hungarian.

TAPER (BERNARD). BALANCHINE. A Biography, revised and updated. New York, Collier Books [1974].

Med. 8vo (9 × 5·7 ins.). (ix) + 406 pp. incl. Index. Orig. dec. wrapps.

The book contains new material and 29 new photographs added to the original ones. See *Bibliography*, Part III, Taper, Bernard, for earlier edition.

TARASOV (N.). KLASSICHESKII TANETS. Shkola Mujskogo Ispotnitelstva. Moskva, Izdatelstvo Iskusstvo 1971.

Demy 8vo (8·4 × 5·4 ins.). 492 + (iii) pp. illus. Orig. black cloth.

A text book in Russian on the Classic Dance. The steps are listed under their French names and all the general headings are familiar with the exception of *Revoltade*. This step called *Revoltade*, *Riboulade* or *Rivoltade* by Kersley; *Rivoltade* by Wilson; *Riboulade* by Espinosa; and *Revolta* by Guillet and Prudommeau is actually a leap over an extended leg, with a half or sometimes a full turn. A good example of its use in 20th century choreography was in the *Danse des Bouffons* in Fokine's ballet *Don Juan*.

TARASSOW (NIKOLAI I.). KLASSISCHER TANZ. Die Schule des Tänzers. Wilhelmshaven, Heinrichofen's Verlag 1974.

Demy 8vo (8·4 × 5·7 ins.). 510 + (ii) pp. illus. with drwgs. and 16 pp. of photogs. Orig. light green cloth.

A translation into German of N. Tarasov's *Klassicheskii Tanets*. Moskva 1971 by Martin Puttke-Voss and the Fachschule für Tanz, Leipzig.

TARGET (JEAN). A LETTER TO CYRIL BEAUMONT. Paris 1961.

Cr. 4to (10·4 × 8·2 ins.). 3 pp. A signed letter.

A letter from Jean Target describing seven photographs of his works that Cyril Beaumont had requested. See also an article by Beaumont, *Jean Target. His Sculptures of the Dance*.

TEATR WIELKI. ETIUDY BALETOWE. Warszawa, Sala I. M. Emilia Mlynarskiego 1972.

(9·2 × 3·7 ins.). A folder containing 4 brochures, all illus. Orig. dec. wrapps in a grey folder.

Contents: II Koncert Brandenburski F-Dur (12 pp.); Cztery Sonety Milosne Pieśni Truwerów (16 pp.); Koncert H-Moll na Wiolonczele I Orkiestre (12 pp.); Salmo Gioiso (8 pp.). All brochures are illustrated and list choreographers and artists.

TEATR WIELKI. ETIUDY BALETOWE. Warszawa, Sala I. M. Emilia Mlynarskiego. 1971.

(9·2 × 3·7 ins.). A folder containing 5 brochures all illus. Orig. dec. wrapps. Orig. grey folder.

Contents: Ndege-Ptak (4 pp.); *Historia Zolnierza* (24 pp.);

Witold Lutoslawski (4 pp.); Metafrazy (8 pp.); Polymorphia (8 pp.). All brochures are illustrated and list choreographers and artists.

TEATR WIELKI. JEZORIO LABEDZIE. Warszawa 1973.

Med. 8vo (9·2 × 5·5 ins.). 48 pp. illus. Orig. white wrapps.

Swan Lake as presented at the Grand Theatre or Great Theatre Warsaw. Inserted in the booklet are a Russian translation (8 pp.) and a programme for the 25 Listopada 1973.

TEATR WIELKI. KRONIKA SEZONU 1970–1971. Teatr Wielki w Warszawa 1971.

Med. 8vo (9·1 × 5·6 ins.). 120 pp. with many illus. Orig. dec. wrapps.

The season of 1970–1971 at the Great Theatre of Warsaw. Ballets performed this season were: *Symfonia Fantastyczna; Danse Sacrée-Danse Profane*; and *Bolero*. See also *Bibliography*, Part III, Warsaw, *The Great Theatre*.

TEATR WIELKI. PIETRUSZKA. Warszawa 1973.

Med. 8vo (9·1 × 5·5 ins.). 56 pp. with many illus. Orig. white wrapps.

Petrouchka as presented at the Great Theatre with appreciations by Ludwik Erhardt, Paul Claudel, Stefan Wysocki and others. Inserted in booklet are Russian translation of synopsis (8 pp.), and programme for the 18 Marca 1973.

TEATR WIELKI. POŻADANIE. Warszawa 1973.

Med. 8vo (9·2 × 5·5 ins.). 24 pp. illus. Orig. white wrapps.

Pożadanie (Desire), a ballet written by Picasso and performed at the Great Theatre with appreciations by Grażyna Bacewicz, Tadeusz Zieliński and others. Inserts include synopsis in Russian, English and German and a programme for the 18 Marca 1973.

TEATR WIELKI. SPARTACUS. Warszawa 1968.

Med. 8vo (9·2 × 5·5 ins.). 64 pp. with many illus. Orig. white wrapps.

Spartacus as presented at the Great Theatre including inserts of Russian, English and German translations of the synopsis and a programme for the 28 Listopada 1968. See also Volkov, Nicolai.

TEATR WIELKI. 25 LAT OPERY WARSZAWSKIEJ W POLSCE LUDOWEJ 1945–1970. Warszawa, Teatr Wielki 1970.

Med. 8vo (9·2 × 6·2 ins.). 339 pp. with many illus. Orig. tan cloth.

Opera and Ballet for the years between 1945 and 1970 at the Great Theatre Warsaw. There is a most interesting section on Repertory, where the dust jackets encasing the Opera and Ballet Synopses are reproduced. Artists Cieliński, Januszewski, Srokowski, Tomaszewski and Ciéslewicz are among those included in the display of designs.

TEATR WIELKI. WIECZÓR BALETOWY. Warszawa 1966.

Med. 8vo (9·2 × 5·5 ins.). 64 pp. illus. Orig. white wrapps.

Karol Szymanoski's ballets *Nokturn I Tarantels; Mandragora; Harnasiach* (Harnasie) with text in Polish, Russian, French, English and German. The dust jacket of *Wieczor Baletowy* by Januszewski is reproduced on (p. 311) of 25 *Lat Opery Warszawski W Polsce Ludowej* 1945–1970. See Turska, Irena, *Taniec w Polsce* where illustrations of earlier performances of most of these ballets are recorded.

TEATRALNII KALENDAR. TEATRALNII KALENDAR na 1964 god. Leningrad-Moskva 'Iskusstvo' 1963.

F'cap 8vo (5·5 × 3·6 ins.). 167 + (i) pp. illus. Orig. dec. boards and fabric spine.

Theatre Calendar for 1964 with information on the following artists and ballet: Lev Ivanov, *Laurencia*, Maria Taglioni, Agrippina Vaganova, Vladimir Burmeister, Alexandre Gorskii, and Pavel Gerdt. In this year the photographs are inserted in sections between pp. 128–129.

TEATRALNII KALENDAR. TEATRALNII KALENDAR na 1966 god. Leningrad-Moskva 'Iskusstvo' 1965.

F'cap 8vo (5·4 × 4·1 ins.). 349 + (iii) pp. with small illus. Orig. dec. boards & fabric spine.

Theatre Calendar for 1966 presenting such diverse figures as L. Bakst, I. I. Valberg, E. M. Liukom, F. Ashton, Olga Lepesinskaya, Fedor Lopoukov, Ekaterina Geltser and Igor Moiseyev.

TEATRALNII KALENDAR. TEATRALNII KALENDAR na 1967 god. Leningrad-Moskva 'Iskusstvo' 1966.

F'cap 8vo (5·4 × 4·1 ins.). 334 + (ii) pp. illus. Orig. dec. boards.

Theatre Calendar for 1966 with information on I. Shoviré, A. Osipenko, A. Gribov, O. Jordan, G. Ulanova, T. Vecheslova and A. Shelest.

TEATRALNII KALENDAR. TEATRALNII KALENDAR na 1968 god. Leningrad-Moskva 'Iskusstvo' 1967.

F'cap 8vo (5·2 × 6·4 ins.). pp. n.n. illus. Orig. dec. boards.

Theatre Calendar for 1968 with the following artists and ballets: N. Dudinskaya in *Raimonda*, M. Liepa in *Tropu Groma*, *Plamya Parijii*, *Odinnadstatya Simfoniya*, Ninette de Valois, M. T. Semenova and V. Vasiliev.

TEATRALNII KALENDAR. TEATRALNII KALENDAR na 1969 god. Leningrad-Moskva 'Iskusstvo' 1968.

F'cap 8vo (5·4 × 4·1 ins.). pp. n.n. illus. Orig. dec. boards with fabric spine.

Theatre Calendar for 1969 with information on the following artists and ballets: *Legenda o Liubi*, Alla Shelest, I. Chernichev, *Laurencia*, Robert Helpmann, Martha Graham, M. Fonteyn, M. Marceau, K. Grisi, Mei Lan-Fan, A. A. Bakhrushin, P. Legat, N. Legat.

TEATRALNII KALENDAR. TEATRALNII KALENDAR na 1970 god. Leningrad-Moskva 'Iskusstvo' 1969.

F'cap 8vo (5·2 × 6·4 ins.). 218 + (vi) pp. illus. Orig. dec. boards.

Theatre Calendar for 1970 with the following artists and ballets: G. Ulanova, N. Kaye, O. Preobrajenskaya, *Lebedinoe Ozero*, E. Ermolaev, K. Konstantin, V. Chabukiani, *Pavilon Armida*, *Tri Mushketera*, *Esmeralda*, O. Spesivetseva, K. Blazis, A. Markova, *Jizel*.

TEATRALNII KALENDAR. TEATRALNII KALENDAR na 1971 god. Leningrad-Moskva 'Iskusstvo' 1970.

F'cap 8vo (5·2 × 6·4 ins.). 212 pp. + (iv). illus. Orig. dec. boards.

Theatre Calendar for 1971 with the following artists and ballets: S. Lifar in *Suite en Blanc*, O. Moiseev, Y. Soloviev, in *Legenda o Liubi*, N. Bessmertnova, A. Gorsky, S. Fedorova, A. Alonso, R. Rodrigo in *Karmen*.

TEATRALNII KALENDAR. TEATRALNII KALENDAR
na 1973 god. Leningrad-Moskva 'Iskusstvo' 1972.
F'cap 8 vo (5·2 × 6·4 ins.). 215 + (i) pp. illus. Orig. dec. boards.
Theatre Calendar for 1973 with the following artists and ballets: N. Dudinskaya in *Raimonda*, E. Vazem in *Trilbi*, G. Szmailova in *Zang*, V. I. Vainonen, G. K. Sabalyauskaite, Khoreograficheskogo Ansamblaya Berezka, Ninette de Valois, Z. Nasredtdinava, K. Safgulin in *Juravlinaya Pesnya*.

TEATRALNII KALENDAR. TEATRALNII KALENDAR
na 1974 god. Leningrad-Moskva 'Iskusstvo' 1974.
F'Cap 8vo (5·2 × 6·4 ins.). 239 + (ii) pp. illus. Orig. dec. boards.
Theatre Calendar for 1974 with the following artists: Roland Petit, Renée Jeanmaire, A. I. Istomina, V. P. Burmeister, M. A. Zsambaeva.

TEATRALNII KALENDAR. TEATRALNII KALENDAR
na 1975 god. Leningrad-Moskva 'Iskusstvo' 1974.
F'cap 8vo (5·2 × 6·4 ins.). 223 + (i) pp. illus. Orig. dec. boards.
Theatre Calendar for 1975 with the following artists and ballets: G. Almaszade and N. Urantses in *Deviche Bashnya*, I. Belskii in *Gayane*, V. M. Krasovskaya, R. Struchkova, P. V. Zakharov, V. Trefilova in *Don Quixot*, M. Plisetskaya.

TEATRALNII KALENDAR. TEATRALNII KALENDAR
na 1976 god. Leningrad-Moskva 'Iskusstvo' 1975.
F'cap 8vo (5·2 × 6·4 ins.). 165 + (iii) pp. Orig. dec. boards.
Theatre Calendar for 1976 with the following artists: V. I. Vainonen, V. D. Tikhomirov, E. V. Geltser.

TEATRALNII KALENDAR. TEATRALNII KALENDAR
na 1977 god. Leningrad-Moskva 'Iskusstvo' 1976.
F'cap 8vo (5·2 × 6·4 ins.). 189 + (iii) pp. illus. Orig. dec. boards.
Theatre Calendar for 1977 with the following artists and ballets: Y. Grigorovich, F. Lopoukhov *Ivan Groznii*, L. M. K. Velikova, Y. Slonimsky, J. J. Nover, V. Bovt, R. M. Gliere *Krasni Mak*. John Cranko *Ananasnaya Poll*. R. V. Zakharov.

TEATRALNII KALENDAR. TEATRALNII KALENDAR na 1978 god. Leningrad-Moskva 'Iskusstvo' 1977.

F'cap 8vo (5·2 × 6·4 ins.). 180 + (iv) pp. illus. Orig. dec. wrapps.

Theatre Calendar for 1978 with the following artists: Adelin Jene (Genée), R. Sen-Denis (St. Denis), Izadore Dunkan, Marina Timofeeva, Semonova, Erika Bruna (Eric Bruhn), Lidii Krupeninoi, A. Messerer and V. Viltsin.

TERRY (WALTER). ASSOLUTA: Alicia Alonso and her Ballet Nacional de Cuba. New York, Opera News 1978.

Demy 4to (10·7 × 8·3 ins.). pp. 12–18 illus. Orig. dec. wrapps. (Alicia Alonso).

An article in the June 1978 issue of *Opera News*. See also Gamez, T., *Alicia Alonso at Home and Abroad*.

TERRY (WALTER). BALLET GUIDE. Illustrated with Photographs. Background listings, Credits, and Descriptions of More than Five Hundred of the World's Major Ballets. New York, Popular Library [1977].

F'cap 8vo (6·6 × 4·1 ins.). (xviii) + 388 pp. illus. Orig. dec. wrapps.

While some ballets are favoured with considerable text, many are far too sparsely-treated to provide even a good guide to further research. For instance three ballets of Shostakovich, *Bolt* (Bolt); *Limpid Brook* (Svetli Rouchei or Bright Stream) and *Leningrad Symphony* (Sedmaya Simfoniya or Leningradskaya Simfoniya) will be found with fuller listing, and both Russian and English titles, in Koegler's *The Concise Oxford Dictionary of Ballet*.

TERRY (WALTER). FROM PAVLOVA TO ABT. An Informal Look at the Met's Pivotal Role in America's Colorful Dance History. New York, Opera News 1977.

Demy 4to (11 × 8·2 ins.). pp. 10–14 illus. Orig. dec. wrapps. An article in the June 1977 issue of *Opera News*.

TERRY (WALTER). LUDMILA SEMENYAKA. Brooklyn, Dance Horizons 1975.

Med. 8vo (9 × 7 ins.). 23 pp. illus. Orig. dec. wrapps.

A monograph in the *Dance Horizons Spotlight Series*. See also *Dance Magazine* for Aug. 1975, Bolshoi Profiles by Toni Tobias and

Bolshoi Teatr SSSR – *Spyashtsaya Krasavitsa* for further information on Ludmila Semenyaka.

TERRY (WALTER) & RENNERT (JACK). 100 YEARS OF DANCE POSTERS. [London], Michael Dempsey [1975].

Imp. 4to (16 × 11 ins.). 16 pp. text + 112 plates mostly in colour. Orig. dec. wrapps.

A selection of posters of artists appearing in Ballet, Music-Hall, Cabaret etc., some very well known, a few unknown. The colour is indifferent.

THEATRE ARTS. THEATRE ARTS ANTHOLOGY. New York, Theatre Arts April [1950].

Demy 8vo (8·2 × 5·3 ins.). xvi + 687 pp. incl. index. Orig. black cloth.

See chapter IV. Music and the Dance, for fine articles including Levinson's *The Spirit of the Classic Dance* (p. 117), and Argentina, *My Castanets* (p. 193).

TIGRANOV (G.). BALETI ARAMA KHACHATURYANA. Moskva, Sovetskii Kompozitor 1960.

F'cap 8vo (6·5 × 5 ins.). 158 pp. illus. + mus. ex. Orig. dec. wrapps.

Three ballets *Happiness* (Schaste), *Gayaneh* and *Spartacus* with photographs of the productions and musical examples. See also Schneerson, *Aram Khachaturyan* and Volkov, *Spartak*, *Bibliography*, Part IV.

TIHONOVS (J.). RIGAS BALETS. Izdevnieciba, 'Liesma' Riga 1967.

(9·3 × 8·3 ins.). 158 + (ii) pp. illus. Orig. cloth.

An album of photographs concerning the Latvian Ballet which are very interesting. Although the name of Tihonovs appears on the title page it is Irena Strode who has written the short history of the company in Latvian, Russian, English, French and German. The captions of the photographs are in Latvian and Russian.

TOBIAS (TOBI). ISAMU NOGUCHI. A Biography for Young People. Illustrated with Photographs. New York, Thomas Y. Crowell Co. [1974].

Sq. (8·6 × 8·6 ins.). 46 pp. + (i). Illus. Orig. orange cloth.

The life of a sculptor. See also Gordon, John.

TODD (ARTHUR). DAVID WALL. [Brooklyn, New York, Dance Horizons 1976].
Med. 8vo (9 × 7 ins.). 14 + (x) pp. incl. both wrapps.
A monograph with photographs by Anthony Crickmay. One of *Dance Horizons Spotlight Series*. See also *Dance Magazine* for Aug. 1974.

TODD (ARTHUR). A LETTER TO CYRIL BEAUMONT. New York, Sept. 12, 1968.
Demy 4to (11 × 8·4 ins.). 1 p. Xerox.
A letter from Arthur Todd to Cyril Beaumont explaining his legacy of dance books to the University of California, Los Angeles, and also a greeting from Ruth St. Denis accompanied by a signed photograph.

TODD (ARTHUR). PETER MARTINS. [Brooklyn, New York, Dance Horizons 1976].
Med. 8vo (9 × 7 ins.). 24 pp. incl. both illus. wrapps.
A monograph with photographs by Martha Swope, one of *Dance Horizons Spotlight Series*. See also Gruen, John, *The Private World of Ballet* (pp. 338–343).

TREND (J. B.). MANUEL DE FALLA AND SPANISH MUSIC. New York, Alfred A. Knopf 1934.
Demy 8vo (8 × 5·2 ins.). xvii + 184 + vi pp. Mus. ex. Orig. dec. yellow cloth.
Interesting for the study of the stories of *El Amor Brujo* and *The Three Cornered Hat* and of the musical themes.
It should be noted that *The Three Cornered hat* (p. 102) was not the first ballet decorated by Picasso and performed by the Diaghilev Ballet July 22, 1919 but rather *Parade* May 18, 1917.

TROWBRIDGE (CHARLOTTE). DANCE DRAWINGS OF MARTHA GRAHAM. With a Foreword by Martha Graham and a Preface by James Johnson Sweeney. New York, Dance Observer.
Cr. 4to (10 × 7·4 ins.). pp. n.n. illus. Orig. black cartoline.
Drawings of the following dances by Charlotte Trowbridge: *Letter to the World; El Penitente; Deaths and Entrances; Every Soul is a Circus; Appalachian Spring; Salem Shore;* and *Herodiade*. See also *Dance Magazine Portfolios* for July 1974 and March 1976.

TRUC (GONZAGUE). LA DANSE. Vingt Cinq Reproduction de Peintures, Gravures, Sculptures, Dessins, Accessoires dont une planche en couleurs. Paris, André Barry. n.d.
F'cap 4to (8·6 × 6·6 ins.). (iv) pp. introductory text + XIV plates. Orig. grey folio.
Fourteen plates containing 25 reproductions of which Plate No. X displays 2 bronzes by A. Barre, *Marie Taglioni* and *Fanny Elssler*.

TSIGNADZE (V.) & CHABUKIANI (V.). GORDA. Teatr Operi i Baleta im Z. Paliashivili. G. Tbilisi 1958.
Med. 8vo (9·4 × 6·4 ins.). 22 pp. illus. Orig. dec. wrapps.
A libretto for the ballet *Gorda* with choreography by Chabukiani and music by A. Toradze. First performed at Tiflis Dec. 30, 1950. See Swift, *The Art of the Dance in the U.S.S.R.* (p. 195).

TURBYFILL (MARK). BALLET – AMERICAN VERSION. New York, The Dance Magazine Sept. 1931.
Roy. 4to (12·5 × 8·6 ins.). pp. 24, 50 with 1 illus. Orig. dec. wrapps.
An article particularly on the Edna McRae studio of Chicago, Illinois. See also *Bibliography* Part II Turbyfill, Mark, *The Art of Ruth Page*.

TURSKA (IRENA). PRZEWODNIK BALETOWY. [Krakow], Polskie Wydawnictwo Muzyczne 1973.
F'cap 8vo (6·6 × 4·3 ins.). 412 pp. incl. indexes. Illus. orange cloth.
Stories of the ballets, mainly of the 20th century although *Giselle, Coppelia, Sylvia* among others are included. Dates of first performance and also first Polish performance with cast in both instances are given.

TURSKA (IRENA). TANIEC W POLSCE (1945–1960). Warszawa, Wydawnictwo Artystczno-Graficzne 1962.
Demy 4to (11 × 7·6 ins.). pp. n.n. illus. Orig. rose fabric spine and white dec. boards.
An important album of photographs on Folk and National Dancing (including Mazowsze and Slask), Nos. 1–86 and Ballet, Nos. 87–247. There is also a short historical resumé in Polish, English, and Russian which lists as important ballets: *Wedding at*

Ojcow (1823), *At the Billet* (1868), *Pan Twardowski* (1921), and *Harnasie* (1935), *Harnasie* was later (in 1936) produced at the Paris Opera. See also *Bibliography* Part III, Banaszyński, Mieczslaw; and Pudelek for other works on the Polish romantic ballet.

TWYSDEN (A. E.). ALEXANDRA DANILOVA. New York, Kamin Dance Publishers 1947.

Med. 8vo (9 × 6 ins.). 175 pp. incl. Index with 48 illus. incl. frontis. Orig. blue cloth.

See *Bibliography*, Part II, Twysden, for the English edition. See also *Dance Magazine Portfolio* for Oct. 1977, Anthony Fay, *Alexandra Danilova*, and *Bibliography*, Part III, *Ballet Review* Vol. 4 Nos. 4 and 5, *A Conversation with Alexandra Danilova*.

TYLER (PARKER). THE DIVINE COMEDY OF PAVEL TCHELITCHEW. A Biography. London, Weidenfeld and Nicolson [1967].

Cr. 4to (10 × 7 ins.). viii + 504 pp. illus. with some in colour. Orig. black cloth.

The work concludes with a Bibliography and an Index. The block of photographs following (p. 283) are mainly concerned with the dance. See also Buckle, *In Search of Diaghilev*; Coton, *A Prejudice for Ballet*; Duke, *A Passport to Paris*; Kirstein, *The Book of the Dance* and *Pavel Tchelitchew Drawings*; Sitwell, Osbert, *Noble Essences*; and Windham, *The Stage and Ballet Designs of Pavel Tchelitchew*.

ULANOVA, MOISEYEV, ZAKHAROV. ULANOVA, MOISEYEV, ZAKHAROV ON SOVIET BALLET. Edited by Peter Brinson, Foreword by A. H. Franks. London SCR, 14 Kensington Square 1954.

Demy 8vo (8·3 × 5·4 ins.). 48 pp. with 8 full page plates of photographs. Orig. dec. wrapps.

The contents include four short articles by Galina Ulanova and one each by Igor Moiseyev and Rotislav Zakharov.

UNESCO CATALOGUE. TEN YEARS OF FILMS ON BALLET AND CLASSICAL DANCE. Unesco 1968.

Demy 8vo (8·2 × 5·2 ins.). 105 pp. Orig. illus. wrapps.

Following a short Preface by Gerhard Brunner, 23 countries from Argentina to the United States of America are represented. See also *Bibliography*, Part III, Brinson, Peter, *A Catalogue of 120 Dance Films*.

UVAROVA (E. D. Editor). RUSSKAYA SOVETSKAYA
ZSTRADA 1917–1929. Ocherki Istorii. Moskva, Izdatelstvo
1976.
    Demy 8vo (8·3 × 6·3 ins.). 406 + (ii) pp. illus. Orig. red cloth.
    See *Tanets na Zstrada* by N. E. Sheremetevskaya (pp. 240–282) for information about Foregger and his *Ballet of Machines*, also Isadora Duncan and her probable influence on the Russian Dance if not the Ballet. See also *Bibliography*, Part III, Swift, Mary, *Art of the Dance in the USSR* for information on both Foregger and Duncan.

VAGANOVA (A.). LAS BASES DE LA DANZA CLÁSICA.
Buenos Aires, Ediciones Centurión [1945].
    Cr. 4to (10·2 × 7 ins.). 272 pp. + (ii) illus. with 120 drwgs. and 130 text + a frontis. Orig. yellow paper boards.
    A translation into Spanish of Vaganova's *Bases of the Classic Dance* (without musical examples). The work also contains three important Appendices: I. Evolución Histórica del Ballet by Demetrio Brazol; II. Breve Historia del Ballet Ruso by Victoria Tomina (fly leaf bears pen inscription to a friend); III. Vocabulario Técnico de la Danza Clasica by Esmée Bulnes. All are welcome, the last particularly so. What is a chassée? (a paso desplazado). A changement de pieds? (cambio de pies). The translations are excellent and ample.

VALERY (PAUL), COCTEAU (JEAN), LIFAR (SERGE).
PAGEOT-ROUSSEAUX (L.). SERGE LIFAR A L'OPERA.
Défini par Paul Valéry Parlé par Jean Cocteau Vécu par Serge Lifar Orné de croquis de movements par L. Pageot-Rousseaux. Paris, Thibault de Champrosay [1943].
    Roy. 4to (12·6 × 9·6 ins.). pp. n.n. illus. by black line drwgs. on various tinted papers. Orig. fabric spine and boards.
    With the *tirage* of 1,750 copies (limited in 4 states), and the collaboration of the above personalities, this should be a volume of considerable distinction. It seems to me to fall short: the Preface by Valery is too eulogistic, and the lines of Cocteau, which treat every ballet or divertissement by Lifar as a matched pearl of complete equality in perfection, are belied by the subsequent failure of most of these to find a permanent place in the repertory. The *croquis* are the weakest factor in the album; although the Lifar countenance in all roles, from *Les Créatures de Prométhée* to *L'Amour Sorcier*, is made manifest, the figure and the background seem more appropriate to poster display than an art book.

VAN DAMM (VIVIAN). TONIGHT AND EVERY NIGHT. With a Foreword by Emile Littler. London, Stanley Paul and Co. [1955].

Demy 8vo (8·2 × 5·2 ins.). 206 pp. incl. index, with 39 illus. Orig. red cloth.

Chapter IX: Ballet Throughout Britain is concerned with the formation of the Markova-Dolin Ballet, with Bronislava Nijinska as the principal choreographer.

VAN VECHTEN (CARL). THE DANCE WRITINGS OF CARL VAN VECHTEN. Edited, and with an Introduction by Paul Padgette. New York, Dance Horizons [1974].

Demy 8vo (8 × 5 ins.). xxi + 182 pp. with a frontis. and 17 other plates. Orig. violet cloth.

I find Van Vechten brilliant, thoughtful, and evocative; but he spreads his enthusiasm over so many varied kinds of dancing that there is sometimes an effect of superficiality. Also, like some other critics, he was unprepared for the technical feats of the classic dance: for instance, Nijinsky's *brisés volés*. Had he seen those of Alexandre Volinine, also a contemporary, they would not have seemed so unique an achievement. He finds Anna Pavlova superior to Adeline Genée, again as a classic dancer: it is worth recollecting that certain of Pavlova's colleagues and admirers, notably Troy Kinney, the writer, and Ivan Clustine, the ballet master, considered Genée academically the finer dancer. The section of photographs does not adequately illustrate the first two periods, or Parts I and II, which were among the finest and most productive of Van Vechten's career.

VAN ZILE (JUDY). DANCE IN INDIA. An Annotated Guide to Source Materials Providence, Asian Music Publications 1973.

Med. 8vo (9 × 6 ins.). xi + 129 pp. incl. a map. Orig. dec. wrapps.

Contents: I. Works of Reference; II. History and Theory; III. Dance Forms; IV. Films; V. Recordings; VI. Labanotation; VII. Resource Organizations; Index of Periodicals; Index of Authors. Under Dance Forms the Folk and Tribal Dance Forms may be placed in their proper *locale* by consulting the map on p. ix.

VASILIEVA-ROJDESTVENSKAYA (M.). ISTORIKO-BITOVOI TANETS. Moskva, Izdatelstvo Iskusstvo 1963.

Demy 8vo (8·4 × 6·4 ins.). 389 + (ii) pp. illus. with drwgs., engravings, diags. and a large section of music. Orig. dec. tan cloth.

A technical and historical survey of the dance (Historical and Social) beginning with the *Branle* and *Rigodon* through the 19th century *Waltz*. A work in the category of Melusine Wood's three volumes on Historical Dances, and Maria Drabeca's *Tance Historyczne*.

VATSYAYAN (KAPILA). INDIAN CLASSICAL DANCE.. [New Delhi], Publications Division [Ministry of Information and Broadcasting Government of India Patiala House 1974].

Med. 8vo (9·3 × 6·6 ins.). viii + 61 pp. + plates + index (pp. 63–66). Orig. black cloth.

Contents: I. History of Dance (p. 1); 2. Theory and Technique (p. 5); 3. Bharatanatyam (p. 15); 4. Kathakali (p. 25); 5. Orissi (p. 34); 6. Manipuri (p. 48); 7. Kathak (p. 48); 8. Modern Dance (p. 57); Index (p. 63). As the nomenclature of the Indian Classical Dance is extensive and complex, it might be well to remember three main categories, *natya* (drama), *nritya* (gesticulation when it is performed to the words sung in a musical melody) and *nritta* (pure dancing where the movements of the body do not express any mood). *Nritya* is also termed *abhinaya* and examples of *nritta* and *abhinaya* will be found in the section of photographs. See also Judy Van Zile's *Dance in India* for listing of these two works and several others.

VATSYAYAN (KAPILA). TRADITIONS OF INDIAN FOLK DANCE. New Delhi, Indian Book Co. 1976.

Demy 8vo (8·1 × 5·1 ins.). 280 pp. illus. Orig. dec. cloth.

Dividing the book to cover eight regions of India, the author provides for the dances, the settings, costumes, accessories, moods and group patterns which include drawings and diagrams. Descriptions of steps are simple but do convey both the mood and the action. In the *Jhora* (danced in the villages of Kumaon pp. 60–61), for instance: '. . . the left leg of the dancers sways in front or sideways, while the right foot holds the weight of the body.' The torsos are all slightly bent forward. This is followed by a small hop on the right foot and bringing back the left leg to its original position; this time the torso is thrown a little backward – The forward backward swaying of the legs and the torsos, creates a beautiful undulating pattern of waves. The torso is used more in Kumaon dances than in those of Himachal Pradesh.'

VAUGHAN (DAVID). FREDERICK ASHTON AND HIS BALLETS. London, Adam & Charles Black [1977].

Cr. 4to (9·6 × 7·1 ins.). xx + 522 pp. incl. appendices. Illus. Orig. tan cloth.

A fine book about Ashton written with care and respect. The Appendices are most important, the Bibliography particularly so as it includes many articles by and about Ashton that make further research most pleasant. See also *Bibliography*, Part III, Dominic, Zoe and Barnes, Clive.

VAUGHAN (DAVID). LYNN SEYMOUR. Brooklyn, New York, Dance Horizons 1976.

Med. 8vo (9 × 7 ins.). 22 + (ii) pp. incl. both wrapps. Illus.

A monograph with photographs by Anthony Crickmay. One of *Dance Horizons Spotlight Series*. See also Gruen, John, *The Private World of Ballet* (pp. 131–135).

VAUGHAN (DAVID). THE ROYAL BALLET AT COVENT GARDEN. London, Dance Books Ltd. [1975].

Demy 4to (11·2 × 8 ins.). (vii) + 145 numbered plates. Orig. dec. wrapps.

A book of photographs by Leslie E. Spatt, Jennie Walton, Edward Griffiths, Mike Humphrey and Rosemary Winckley. See also *Bibliography*, Part III, Vaughan, David.

VERDAK (GEORGE). ERAS OF THE DANCE. The George Verdak Collection. Montgomery, Montgomery Museum of Fine Arts 1977.

Sq. (9·2 × 9·2 ins.). 90 pp. incl. index. Illus. Orig. dec. wrapps.

A very attractive catalogue of important dance material. It lists 131 items, not too large to have had better proof reading than is evident: for instance, *Marco Spada* was first performed in 1857 not 1837 (p. 52); Lacauchie (Alexandre) is spelled Lacouchie (pp. 47, 48), and there is a reference to *Bacchus* by Jules Massenet, choreography by Jules Massenet. I believe this must be Hartmann's *Bacchus*, choreography by Hansen, music by Henri Busser, Paris Opera 1902 (p. 56 items a and b).

VERDE GAIO. BALLET PORTUGAIS. Portugal, Organization du Secretariat National de L'Information 1949.

Demy 4to (11·1 × 8·6 ins.). pp. n.n. illus. with photogs. and des. in colour. Orig. black dec. wrapps.

A collection of 24 ballets and divertissements presented mainly in Lisbon with choreography by Francis Gracia and Ivo Cramer, and decor and costumes by Paulo Ferreira, José Barbossa and others. See also Sasportes, José, *História Da Dança em Portugal* and *Bibliography*, Part III, Sasportes, José, *Dance in Portugal*.

VERNOY DE SAINT GEORGES (J. H.). GISELLA ELLER WILIERNA. Romantisk Ballet I Two Akter. Uppsatt för Kongl. Theaterns scen af Herr Balletmastären Alexandre, och uppförd för första gängen den 3 Dec. 1845. Stockholm, Tryct Hos. 1 Marcus 1845.

F'cap 8vo (6·7 × 4·1 ins.). 21 pp. Boards with fabric spine.

A photographic facsimile of the Swedish synopsis of *Giselle*. Leading dancers: Hr. Alexandre (*Hertig Albrecht af Schlesien*); Melle Paulus (*Gisella*); *Myrtha* (Melle. Nordberg).

VERNOY DE SAINT GEORGES (J. H.). GISELLE. Ballet in two acts. Designer B. Volkov. London Coliseum June 12–July 20 1974.

Med. 8vo (9 × 5·2 ins.). 24 pp. illus. Orig. black wrapps.

An illustrated house programme with synopsis of *Giselle* as performed by the Bolshoi Ballet. The choreography is by Petipa-Coralli-Perrot, revised by Leonid Lavrovsky. The role of *Giselle* was alternated by Bessmertnova, Maximova and Timofeyeva, that of *Albrecht* by Vasiliev, Lavrovsky and Liepa. See also *Bolshoi Teatr SSSR* Part 2 *Balet, Jizel*.

VERNOY DE SAINT GEORGES (J. H.). KORSAR. Balet v 3 Aktakh 5 Kartinakh. Moskva, Nemirovich-Dantchenko [1964].

Demy 8vo (8·5 × 5·6 ins.). 5 pp. n.n. Orig. printed white wrapps.

A cast and artist list with synopsis for the ballet *Le Corsajre* as performed by the Nemirovich-Dantchenko Theatre with Violetta Bovt and Sofia Vinogradova as *Medora*, and Yuri Grigoriev as *Conrad*. See *Bibliography*, Part II, Vernoy de Saint Georges, for original libretto.

VESTOFF-SEROVA STUDIO. THE DANCE IN THE MAKING. Technical Combinations of the Dance by Veronine Vestoff. New York, Vestoff-Serova Studio.

Cr. 4to (10·4 × 6·7 ins.). 2 vols. 15 pp. (1). 19 pp. of music (2). Orig. dec. wrapps. (Betsy Rees).

See also *Bibliography*, Part II, Serova, Sonia.

VESTOFF-SEROVA STUDIO. INTERPRETATIVE EXERCISES AND STUDIES SUMMER 1922. New York, Vestoff-Serova Studio.
 Cr. 4to (10·4 × 6·7 ins.). 12 pp. Orig. printed white wrapps.

VESTOFF-SEROVA STUDIO. INTERPRETATIVE STUDIES AND EXERCISES 1921. By Sonia Serova. New York, Vestoff-Serova Studio.
 Cr. 4to (10·4 × 6·7 ins.). 2 vols. 11 pp. (1). 17 pp. of music (2). Orig. printed wrapps.

VESTOFF-SEROVA STUDIO. INTERPRETATIVE STUDIES AND EXERCISES & STUDIES 1924. New York, Vestoff-Serova Studio.
 Cr. 4to (10·4 × 6·7 ins.). 2 vols. 11 pp. (1); 15 pp. (2). Orig. printed white wrapps.
 Vol. 1 contains the instructions and Vol. 2 the music.

VESTOFF-SEROVA STUDIO. PASTELS. Seven Interpretative Exercises 1927. Arranged by Sonia Serova. New York, Vestoff-Serova Studio 1927.
 Cr. 4to (10·4 × 6·7 ins.). 2 vols. 21 pp. (1); 19 pp. (2). Orig. printed white wrapps.
 Vol. 1 contains the instructions and Vol. 2 the music.

VESTOFF-SEROVA STUDIO. PLASTIQUE & TECHNIQUE. Dance Arranged by Veronine Vestoff. New York, Vestoff-Serova Studio 1924.
 Cr. 4to (10·4 × 6·7 ins.). 2 Vols. 8pp. (1); 11 pp. (2). Orig. printed white wrapps.
 Vol. 1 contains the instructions and Vol. 2 the music.

VESTOFF-SEROVA STUDIO. POETRY OF MOTION. A Short Collection of Interpretative Studies. By Sonia Serova. New York, Studio.
 Cr. 4to (10·4 × 6·7 ins.). 20 pp. Orig. white printed wrapps.
 The instructions only for 10 studies ranging from *Andante* to *Crescendo Religioso*.

VESTOFF-SEROVA STUDIO. TECHNIQUE-PLASTIQUE SUMMER 1921. New York, Vestoff-Serova Studio.
Cr. 4to (10·4 × 6·7 ins.). 2 Vols. 13 pp. (1); 17 pp. (2). Orig. wrapps.

A dance arranged by Veronine Vestoff with Vol. 1 containing the instructions and Vol. 2 the music.

VESTOFF-SEROVA STUDIO. TRAINING ON THE TOES. Vestoff-Serova Studio 1921.
Cr. 4to (10.4 × 6·7 ins.). 11 pp. Orig. printed white wrapps.

Instructions for dancing on pointe, with exercises at the barre and centre floor. See also Bibliography, Part II, Serova, Sonia and Vestoff, Veronine. See also Belknap, *Guide to Dance Periodicals* until 1941, and *Dance Index* Vol. III Nos. 4, 5, 6, *European Dance Teachers in The United States*. A son, Veronine Vestoff also, became famous as a stage and film dancer and actor under the name of Buster West: a thrilling dancer.

VESTRIS (MR.). ILDAMOR AND ZULÉMA. A Grand Ballet in Three Acts. Performed for his Benefit at the King's Theatre on Thursday, 30th May 1811. London, Printed by T. Harper 1811.
Cr. 8vo (8·1 × 5·2 ins.). 29 pp. with an engraved frontis. Unbound.

A synopsis of the ballet with Mr. Vestris (*Ildamor*), Mad. Angiolini (*Zuléma*) and Mr. Deshayes (*Orezimba*). According to Ivor Guest in *The Romantic Ballet in England* (p. 122), Armand Vestris and Fortunata Angiolini made their London debut at the King's Theatre in 1809. This was either the first or second ballet choreographed by Armand Vestris for the King's Theatre.

VICTOR (THOMAS). THE MAKING OF A DANCE. Mikhail Baryshnikov and Carla Fracci in Medea. Choreography by John Butler. London, Dance Books Ltd. 1976.
Oblong (8·4 × 10·7 ins.). pp. n.n. illus. Orig. green cloth.

An album of photographs of John Butler's *Medea*, photographed and edited by Thomas Victor. See also Baryshnikov for further studies of this unique dancer-mime and Austin, *Birth of a Ballet* for other books dealing with composition.

VICTORICIA (VICTORIA GARCIA). EL ORIGINAL BALLET RUSSE EN AMERICA LATINA. Prologo de Fernando Emery. Argentina, Ediciones Arturo Jacinto Alvarez 1948.
Demy 4to (11·3 × 9·6 ins.). 263 + (i) pp. illus. with some plates in colour. Orig. stamped white buckram.
A splendidly illustrated album of photographs about The Original Ballet Russe of Colonel de Basil in Latin American between 1942–1946. Edition limited to 3,000 copies. Cyril Beaumont's own copy, including a typewritten letter from the author Victoricia.

VLAD (ROMAN). STRAVINSKY. Translated from the Italian by Frederick and Ann Fuller. London, Oxford University Press [1960].
Demy 8vo (8·3 × 5·7 ins.). (vi) + 232 pp. incl. index. Illus. with a frontis. and num. mus. ex. Orig. cloth.
There is a short Bibliography on pp. 225–26 in which the author remarks to readers that the most complete list of Stravinsky's works and those about him are to be found in Paul Magriel's Bibliography published in Minna Lederman's, *Stravinsky in the Theatre*. See Lederman, Minna for further details.

VOLININE (ALEXANDRE). MY DANCE OF LIFE. Part III. New York, Dance Magazine, Mar. 1930.
Roy. 4to (12·5 × 8·6 ins.). pp. 34, 35, 55 illus. Orig. dec. wrapps. (Dorothy Stone).
Part III of a IV part article in the March issue of *Dance Magazine*. See also *Bibliography*, Part II, Leslie, Serge, *Seven Leagues of a Dancer*, the Index.

VOLKOV (NICOLAI). GOLUBOI DUNAI. Balet v 3k deistviyakh, 7 kartinakh. Malyi Opernyi Teatr. Leningrad 1957.
Cr. 8vo (7·4 × 5·4 ins.). 4 pp. n.n. Orig. dec. wrapps.
A house programme for *Goluboi Dunai* (The Blue Danube), with music by Johann Strauss and choreography by Tatyana Bruni. Cast and artists with short synopsis given. First performed at this theatre Dec. 13, 1956. Listed in Slonimsky's *Vse o Balete*. See article, Some Soviet Choreographers in *The Dancing Times* Feb. 1945 (p. 199).

VOLKOV (NICOLAI). SPARTACUS. The Bolshoi appears at the London Coliseum June 12th to July 20th 1974. London, Bentley Bros. Printers.

Med. 8vo (9 × 5·2 ins.). 24 pp. n.n. illus. Orig. black wrapps.

A synopsis of *Spartacus* with choreography by Yuri Grigorovich, which includes some useful historical notes. There were performances of *Spartacus* by Vasiliev, Vladimirov, and Lavrovsky; *Crassus* by Akimov and Liepa; *Phrygia* by Bessmertnova, Maximova and Sorokina; *Aegina* by Adirkhayeva and Timofeyeva and a *Gladiator* by Yagudin. See also *Teatr Wielki, Spartakus* for a Polish version.

VOLKOV (NICOLAI). SPARTAK. Balet v 4 deistviyakh. Muzika A. I. Kachaturyan. Leningrad 1957.

Cr. 8vo (7·7 × 5·6 ins.). 48 pp. illus. Orig. dec. wrapps.

A synopsis of *Spartacus* in Russian in its first version with choreography by L. V. Yakobson (Jacobson), produced for the Kirov Dec. 27, 1956. Booklet contains an (8 pp.) insert programme for May 7, 1957 performance with Makarov (*Spartak*), Subkovskaya (*Frigiya*), and Shelest (*Zgina*). The latest and perhaps most successful version was by Grigorovich for the Bolshoi with Vasiliev, Maximova and Timofeyeva. See *Bolshoi Teatr SSSR* book 2 *Balet, Spartak*.

VOLKOV (NICOLAI). SPARTAK. Balet v trekh deistviyakh deveti kartinakh. Moskva 1958.

Med. 8vo (9 × 6 ins.). 32 pp. with a frontis. of Khachaturyan. Orig. dec. wrapps.

A synopsis of the ballet *Spartacus* in Russian as presented by the Bolshoi. The synopsis is autographed to Cyril Beaumont by Yuri Bakhrushin.

VOLKOV (NICOLAI). ZOLUSHKA. Bolshoi Teatr 1946.

Cr. 8vo (8 × 5 ins.). 8pp. with a portrait of Prokofiev. Orig. white wrapps.

A synopsis of the ballet *Cinderella* in Russian, artists not listed. See *Bibliography*, Part III, *Soviet Ballet, The, Zolushka* for an illustrated libretto. See also *Bolshoi Teatr SSSR* book 2 *Balet, Zolushka*.

VOLLMER (JURGEN). NUREYEV IN PARIS. Le Jeune Homme et la Mort. Photographed by Jurgen Vollmer. New York Modernismo Publications 1975.

Demy 4to (11 × 8·4 ins.). pp. n.n. illus. Orig. dec. wrapps. boxed.

An Album of Photographs with text by John de Vere. A television performance of the ballet *Le Jeune Homme et la Mort* danced by Nureyev and Jeanmaire, originally created by Roland Petit for Jean Babilée. See also Crisp and Brinson, *The International Book of Ballet* (pp. 277, 78, 79) for short synopsis of the ballet.

VUILLIER (GASTON). A HISTORY OF DANCING. From the Earliest Ages to our Own Times. With a sketch of Dancing in England by Joseph Grego. London, Wm. Heinemann 1898.

Roy. 4to (12·2 × 8·4 ins.). xvi + 446 pp. with 20 full page plates and 409 illus. Orig. full vellum gilt edges.

One of the early illustrated histories of dancing which many later historians and critics have branded as 'popular' or mediocre while they have at the same time feasted mightily on its rich and varied illustrations. See *Bibliography*, Part II, Vuillier, Gaston for other editions.

WALLMANN (MARGHERITA). THE PLACE OF BALLET IN OPERA. Opera Annual No. 5. London, John Calder 1958.

Med. 8vo (9·2 × 7 ins.). pp. 91–93. Orig. black cloth.

An article in *Opera Annual* No. 5. A short but good essay on a part of Opera only slightly touched upon by writers of today. See also Turner, Harold, *Ballet in Opera* in *The Dancing Times* April 1958 and Hussey, Dyneley, *Opera and the Ballet* in *The Dancing Times* July through November 1945.

WARRACK (JOHN). TCHAIKOVSKY. London, Hamish Hamilton [1973].

Med. 8vo (9·6 × 7·1 ins.). 287 pp. incl. index. Many illus. incl. 28 in colour. Orig. blue cloth.

An attractive work on Tchaikovsky containing information on his ballets. See also *Muzikalnoe Nasldene Chaikovskogo*.

WARREN (LARRY). LESTER HORTON. Modern Dance Pioneer. New York, Marcel Dekker Inc. [1977].

Med. 8vo (9 × 6 ins.). xvi + 265 + (iii) pp. illus. Orig. dec. black paper boards.

See also *Dance Perspectives* No. 31, The Dance Theatre of Lester

Horton and Belknap, *Guide to Dance Periodicals* Vol. 3 on, for articles and information about Lester Horton.

WEBSTER (T. B. L.). THE GREEK CHORUS. London, Methuen & Co. [1970].

Demy 8vo (8·3 × 5·3 ins.). xiv + 223 pp. with eleven num. illus. Orig. brown cloth.

This book is primarily concerned with relating the history of the dance, an aspect of the chorus, and with presenting emphasis on the development of the metre, which was fundamental in providing the rhythm for words, music, and dance.

WECHSBERG (JOSEPH). THE WALTZ EMPERORS. The Life and Times and Music of the Strauss Family. London, Weidenfeld and Nicholson [1973].

Cr. 8vo (9·5 × 7·2 ins.). 272 pp. incl. index. Illus. with many in colour. Orig. rose cloth.

See also Klingenbeck, Fritz, *Unsterblicher Walzer* and Carner, Mosco, *The Waltz, Bibliography* Part III. Also Wilson, Thomas, *The Correct Method of German and French Waltzing*, Part II.

WENTINK (ANDREW MARK). PATRICIA MCBRIDE. Photographs by Martha Swope. Dance Horizons Spotlight Series.

Med. 8vo (9 × 7 ins.). 24 pp. illus. Orig. dec. wrapps.

A monograph. See also Gruen, John, *The Private World of Ballet*, Patricia Mcbride (pp. 287–294), and *Dance Magazine Portfolio* for August 1977, Tobias, Toni, Patricia Mcbride.

WHALON (MARION K.). PERFORMING ARTS RESEARCH. A Guide to Information Sources. Detroit, Gale Research Co. [1976].

Demy 8vo (8·3 × 5·2 ins.). xi + 280 pp. incl. index. Orig. dec. cloth.

A guide listing a tremendous amount of material on the Performing Arts. For the dance: the bibliographies of Beaumont, Forrester, Leslie, Magriel, New York Public Library, and Petermann are listed. Missing are pamphlets by Fletcher, Guest and Haskell as well as a major 6 volume work by Irena Ostrowska, *Bibliografia Zagadnien Sztuki Tanecznej* 1950–1966.

WILLIAMS (HARCOURT, Editor). VIC-WELLS. The Work of Lilian Baylis. London, Cobden-Sanderson 1938.
Med. 8vo (9·5 × 7·2 ins.). vii + 106 pp. illus. Orig. buckram.
See The Vic-Wells Ballet by Ninette de Valois (p. 95), and Dance it Trippingly by Robert Helpmann (p. 100).

WILLIAMS (PETER). BETWEEN HEAVEN AND CHARING CROSS. London, Dance & Dancers July 1951.
Demy 4to (11 × 8·4 ins.). (p. 8) with one illus. Orig. dec. wrapps.
An article in the July 1951 issue of *Dance and Dancers* concerning Cyril Beaumont, Alice Beha (his wife) and the establishment of the book shop that embellished 75 Charing Cross Road for so many years.

WILLIS (JOHN). DANCE WORLD 1969, 1968–1969 Season Volume 4. New York, Crown Publishers 1970.
Med. 8vo (9 × 6·1 ins.). 209 pp. + index. Illus. Orig. cloth.
See *Bibliography*, Part III, Willis, John, for listing of the first 3 volumes.

WILLIS (JOHN). DANCE WORLD 1970, 1969–1970 Season Volume 5. New York, Crown Publishers 1970.
Med. 8vo (9·1 × 6·1 ins.). 224 pp. incl. index. Illus. Orig. cloth.

WILLIS (JOHN). DANCE WORLD 1971, 1970–1971 Season Volume 6. New York, Crown Publishers 1971.
Med. 8vo (9 × 6·1 ins.). 229 pp. incl. index. Illus. Orig. cloth.

WILLIS (JOHN). DANCE WORLD 1972, 1971–1972 Season Volume 7. New York, Crown Publishers 1973.
Med. 8vo (9 × 6·1 ins.). 226 pp. incl. index. Illus. Orig. cloth.

WILLIS (JOHN). DANCE WORLD 1973, 1972–1973 Season Volume 8. New York, Crown Publishers 1974.
Med. 8vo (9 × 6·1 ins.). 222 pp. incl. index. Illus. Orig. cloth.

WILLIS (JOHN). DANCE WORLD 1974, 1973–1974 Season Volume 9. New York, Crown Publishers 1975.
   Med. 8vo (9 × 6·1 ins.). 220 pp. incl. index. Illus. Orig. cloth.

WILLIS (JOHN). DANCE WORLD 1975, 1974–1975 Season Volume 10. New York, Crown Publishers 1976.
   Med. 8vo (9 × 6·1 ins.). 222 pp. incl. index. Illus. Orig. cloth.

WILLIS (JOHN). DANCE WORLD 1976, 1975–1976 Season Volume 11. New York, Crown Publishers 1977.
   Med. 8vo (9 × 6·1 ins.). 220 pp. incl. index. Illus. Orig. cloth.

WILLIS (JOHN). DANCE WORLD 1977, 1976–1977 Season Volume 12. New York, Crown Publishers 1978.
   Med. 8vo (9 × 6·1 ins.). 224 pp. incl. index. Illus. Orig. cloth.

WILSON (G. B. L.). A DICTIONARY OF BALLET. London, Adam & Charles Black [1974].
   Demy 8vo (8·4 × 5·2 ins.). xi + 539 pp. with 8 pp. of photogs. and 20 line drwgs. Orig. red cloth.
   The third edition, revised, enlarged and reset.

W[ILSON] (P[AULINE]). DANCERS OF TODAY. Volume I. London, Pendulum Publications Ltd. 1947.
   Cr. 4to (10·1 × 7·4 ins.). iv + xxiv plates. Orig. dec. wrapps.
   The text includes a statement of policy for this venture, short biographies of the dancers chosen, and the plates themselves.

WINTER (MARIAN HANNAH). LE CIRQUE ET LE BALLET. Paris, Le Vieux Papier, Avril 1973.
   Cr. 4to (11 × 7·4 ins.). pp. 33–38 with illus. Orig. wrapps.
   Fascicule No. 248 of the Bulletin de la Société Archéologique, Historique et Artistique, *Le Vieux Papier*. See also *Bibliography*, Part II, Winter, Hannah.

WINTER (MARIAN HANNAH). THAT MAGNIFI-CENT MUTE. Paris, Opera Ballet Music-Hall in the World III 1952–53.
Roy. 4to (12 × 9·3 ins.). pp. 8–17 illus. Orig. dec. wrapps.
An article appearing in issue No. 3 of *Opera Ballet Music-Hall*, about the *mime* Charles Deburau, with illustrations from the collection of the author. The issue also contains other articles on *mime* by Marcel Marceau, Jean-Louis Barrault, Serge Lifar, Svend Ericksen and Clifford Williams.

WINTER (MARIAN HANNAH). THE PRE-ROMANTIC BALLET. [London], Pitman Publishing [1974].
Demy 4to (10·6 × 8·3 ins.). xxii + 306 pp. with 18 illus. in colour and many in monochrome. Orig. red cloth.
In 1966 Peter Brinson published a book, *Background to European Ballet*, which was a Note-Book to the Archives of European dance. He mentions eight countries and states (rightly) that in the study of the life of a choreographer or a dancer, or of a movement in ballet, these countries' traditions must all be consulted. Hannah Winter's independent researches have carried her over much of the same ground (and into the archives) that Brinson mentions. The result is that for the first time we see the Pre-Romantic Ballet as a coherent movement: the distance between Noverre and Hilverding and Angiolini is narrowed, while Austria and Germany are shown to be among the three or four countries from which the Pre-Romantic Ballet principally evolved.

WINTER (MARIAN HANNAH). THE PRICES. An Anglo-Continental Theatrical Dynasty. London, Theatre Notebook 1974.
Demy 8vo (8·4 × 5·5 ins.). pp. 117–123 illus. Orig. dec. wrapps.
An article in *Theatre Notebook* Vol. XXVIII No. 3. See also *Bibliography*, Part II, Veale, Tom, *The Dancing Prices of Denmark*.

WINTER (MARIAN HANNAH). THE THEATRE OF MARVELS. Preface by Marcel Marceau. New York, Benjamin Blom [1962].
Demy 4to (11·3 × 8·3 ins.). 208 pp. incl. notes, bibliography and index. With 188 black and white illus. and 11 in colour. Orig. white buckram.
'*The Theatre of Marvels* is the theatre peopled by shadows and

lights in which wicked genies, fairies, heroes and gods mingle; where angels and demons link hands and, with beating wings and tossing Manes, pass through dream clouds in a shower of stardust'. Marcel Marceau (Preface). English translation by Charles Meldon.

WOOD (PETER). THE PERFORMING ARTS. Catalogue three. Summer 1974. Cambridge, Peter Wood.

Demy 8vo (8·1 × 5·5 ins.). 89 pp. Orig. dec. wrapps.

Ballet and Dance begins on p. 75 and occupies numbers 1960 to 2118. Other sections are Theatre, Music, Broadcasting, Television and Cinema.

WOOD (PETER). THEATRE. Catalogue six. Cambridge, Peter Wood.

Demy 8vo (8·1 × 5·5 ins.). 61 pp. Orig. dec. wrapps.

Ballet and Dance begin on p. 51 and consist of items numbered 1222 to 1405. There is also a section on Souvenir Programmes and one on Periodicals. With the exception of Vuillier and a few important reprints the material is 20th century.

WOOD (PETER). THEATRE. Catalogue 13. Cambridge, Peter Wood 1976.

Cr. 8vo (7·6 × 5·5 ins.). 89 pp. Orig. dec. wrapps.

Ballet and Dance begin with No. 1079 and continue to 1350 c. Mostly modern books, item 1210 Fuller, Loie (an 8 pp. appreciation in French with 8 illus.) seems of particular interest.

WOOD (ROGER). STUDIES OF CLASSICAL CHOREOGRAPHY BEING PHOTOGRAPHS OF THE SLEEPING BEAUTY. London, Ballet Feb. 1952.

Demy 8vo (8·4 × 5·3 ins.). pp. 4–11 illus. Orig. dec. wrapps.

A series of 21 numbered photographs listed in the Key to the Studies (p. 11). Beryl Grey and Violetta Elvin represent *Aurora* in these studies.

WOODARD (ROBIN). IN A REHEARSAL ROOM. A Portrait of two dancers Cynthia Gregory and Ivan Nagy. New York, Modernismo Publications 1976.

Demy 4to (8·4 × 10·7 ins.). pp. n.n. illus. Orig. grey cloth.

A book about a film by David Hahn with choreography by William Carter. See Péres, *Dance Horizons Spotlight Series* for a monograph on each artist. See also *Dance Magazine* April 1975, Conversations with Cynthia Gregory and *Dance Magazine Portfolio* July 1975, ABT's Ivan Nagy.

WOOLLIAMS (ANNE). BALLETT SAAL. Photeas Andreas Heumann. Vorvort John Cranko. [Stuttgart], Belser Verlag [1973].

Demy 4to (11·5 × 8·1 ins.). 140 pp. + (ii) illus. in half-tone. Orig. dec. boards.

Inhalt: Vorwort von John Cranko (p. 9); Vorbemerkung der Autorin (p. 11); Ballett als Berauf (p. 14); Ballettunterricht (p. 26); Kleidung (p. 40); A la Barre (p. 50); Port de Bras (p. 61); Adage (p. 72); Pirouette (p. 78); Sur les Pointes (p. 86); Batterie (p. 94); Elevation (p. 100); Pas de Deux (p. 108); Mimik (p. 122); Rhythmus und Musikalitat (p. 130); Gesundheit (p. 136). Anne Woolliams, connected with the Stuttgart Ballet since 1963, was appointed director of the Australian Ballet from September 1976. The book bears a signature and a letter to Doris Niles and Serge Leslie.

WOOLLIAMS (ANNE) & TETLEY (GLEN). BALLETT EXERCISES DAS STUTTGARTER BALLETT. Augsburg, Verlag Die Brigg [1976].

(11·2 × 10·5 ins.). pp. n.n. illus. Orig. dec. wrapps.

An album of photographs by René Gebbhardt with text by Anne Woolliams and Glen Tetley.

WOSIEN (MARIA-GABRIELE). SACRED DANCE. Encounters with the Gods. London, Thames and Hudson [1974].

Demy 4to (11 × 8 ins.). 128 pp. illus. in colour and black and white. Orig. dec. wrapps.

An excellent picture book accompanied by a dignified text. See also Oesterley, *The Sacred Dance*; Frazer, *The Golden Bough*; Hambly, *Tribal Dancing and Social Development*, and Shawn, *Gods Who Dance*.

WYNNE (DAVID W.). THREE YEARS WITH CHARLES WEIDMAN. New York, Dance Perspectives, Winter 1974.

Cr. 4to (9 × 7·3 ins.). 49 pp. illus. Orig. dec. wrapps.

No. 60 of *Dance Perspectives*. See also McDonagh, Don, *The Complete Guide to Modern Dance* (pp. 110–120).

ZAKHAROV (R[OSTISLAV VLADIMIROV]). ZAPISKI BALETMEISTERA. Moskva, 'Iskusstvo' 1976.

Demy 8vo (7·7 × 4·7 ins.). 349 + (iii) pp. illus. Orig. dec. wrapps.

Zapiski Baletmeistera (Notes or Memoirs of a Ballet Master), contains also information on other ballet masters and pedagogues such as E. Valukin, K. Y. Goleizovskii, V. I. Vainonen, V. M. Chabukiani, Y. Grigorovich and R. V. Zakharov as well as earlier 19th century figures. Cleanly printed with the exception of the photographs which sometimes have blurred captions. See also *Bibliography*, Part II, Zakharov, *Besedi O Tantse*.

ZHDANOV (LEONID). MAĬYA PLISETSKAYA. Fotoalbum. Moskva, Izdatelstvo Iskusstvo 1965.

Cr. 4to (10·3 × 8·1 ins.). About 22 pp. n.n. illus. Orig. dec. boards.

A (5 pp.) Preface by Victor Komissarchevsky in Russian, English and French followed by the album of photographs of Plisetskaya in her principal roles. See also *Bibliography*, Part II, Roslavleva, N., *Maya Plisetskaya* and Part III, Avdeyenko. A. A., *Maya Plisetskaya*.

ZHDANOV (LEONID). SHKOLA BOLSHOGO BALETA. Moskva, Izdatelstvo 'Planeta' 1974.

Cr. 4to (10·1 × 7·4 ins.). 192 pp. n.n. profusely illus. Orig. white boards.

A short history of the Bolshoi Ballet followed by eight grades of classwork with emphasis on the barre work, closing with scenes of performance. A picture book, not a manual. See Asaf Messerer and Agrippina Vaganova for detailed class work. *Bibliography*, Part III.

ZHITOMIRSKY (S.). BALETI CHAIKOVSKOGO. Moskva, Gosudarstvennoe Muzikalnoe Izdatelstvo 1947.

Demy 8vo (8·6 × 7·2 ins.). 119 pp. + 40 pp of plates. Orig. dec. wrapps.

Studies of Tchaikovsky's three main ballets: *Swan Lake, Sleeping Beauty* and *Nutcracker*. See also Shaverdyana, *Chaikovskii I Teatr*; Slonimsky, P. I. *Tchaikovskii I Baletnyi Teatr*; also *Muzikalnoe Nasledne Chaikovskogo*, and Warrack, John, *Tchaikovsky*.

ZHORNITSKAYA (M. I.). NARODNIE TANTSI YAKUTII. Izdatelstvo 'Nauka', Moskva 1966.

Cr. 8vo (7·6 × 4·6 ins.). 166 pp. + (ii) illus. With photogs. drwgs. and diags. Orig. dec. wrapps.

National dances of the Yakutii (Esquimaux of Eastern Siberia). The work closes with a very good list of literature about the Yakutii.

ZINKHEISEN (DORIS). DESIGNING FOR THE STAGE. London, The Studio [1948].
    Cr. 8vo (9·6 × 7·2 ins.). 79 pp. with 46 num. illus. with 2 in colour. Orig. grey cloth.
    First published in 1938; this is a reprint of 1948. See also *Bibliography*, all IV Parts, under Design: Costumes and Settings.

ZORN (FRIEDRICH ALBERT). GRAMMAR OF THE ART OF DANCING THEORETICAL AND PRACTICAL. Edited by Alfonso Joseph Sheafe. [Brooklyn], A Dance Horizons Republication.
    Cr. 8vo (8 × 5 ins.). xviii + 302 pp. with frontis. of author, drwgs. symbols, choreographic notation and mus. Orig. wrapps.
    An unabridged republication of the 1905 edition. See *Bibliography*, Part II, Zorn, Friedrich Albert, for the original edition in English and also in German.

ZORN (FRIEDRICH ALBERT). MUSICAL SCORE OF THE GRAMMAR OF THE ART OF DANCING. Edited by Alfonso Joseph Sheafe. [Brooklyn], Dance Horizons.
    Cr. 8vo (5·3 × 8 ins.). 37 pp. of music. Orig. wrapps.
    An unabridged republication of the first edition published in 1905 comprising 124 numbered airs. Dances that still command interest and study are the *Vestris Gavotte* and the *Fanny Elssler Cachuca*.

INDEX

Acrobatics and Gymnastics

Ausgewählte Probleme des Trainings im Turnier-tanz, H. Raede, 193, 194
Danses Gymnastiques, G. Demeny & A. Sandoz, 106
Khudojestvennoe Vospitanie Sovetskogo Shkolinka, The Soviet Ballet, 223
Osnova Obucheniya Dishaniya v Khoreografii, E. Y. Popova, 192

Ancient and Classical Dance

The Antique Greek Dance, M. Emmanuel, 112, 113
The Court Ballet in France 1615–1641, M. F. Christout, 91
Les Feés des Forêts de S. Germain, Ballet de Cour, J. H. Baron, 28
The Greek Chorus, T. B. L. Webster, 255
Indian Classical Dance, K. Vatsyayan, 247
The Mathers on Dancing, J. Marks III, 154
Musica, Ballo e Drammatica alla Corte Medicea dal 1600 al 1637, A. Solerti, 220
The Parson on Dancing, R. J. B. Gross, 126
The Pre-Romantic Ballet, M. H. Winter, 258
Sacred Dance, M. G. Wosien, 260
Splendour at Court, R. Strong, 230

Autobiography, Biography, Memoirs

Aleksi Ermolaev, C. M. Abramovna, redaktor, 17
Alexandra Danilova, A. E. Twysden, 244
Alicia Alonse, At Home and Abroad, T. De Gamez, 105
Alicia Markova, H. Fisher, 115
Amalia Molina, A. G. Carraffa, 89
André Eglevsky, H. Sheridan, 210
Anna Pavlova, An Album of Original Photographs, 178, 179
Anna Pavlova, An Album of Press Cuttings, 179
Anna Pavlova, Ivy House Reception Album, 179, 180
Anna Pavlova Miscellany, 179
Anna Pavlova, O. Kerensky, 139, 140
Anna Pavlova, V. Svetlov, 230
Anthony Dowell, L. F. Rosen, 197
Antoinette Sibley, D. Harris, 131
The Art of Alexandra Danilova, B. H. Haggin & E. Denby, 102
The Art of Margot Fonteyn, K. Money, 170
Avdotyia Istomina, N. Elyash, 112
Balanchine, B. Taper, 234
Balanchine: The Early Years, Y. Slonimsky, 217
Baletnoe Iskusstvo i S. V. Fedorova 2-ya, S. Grigorov, 126
La Belle Otero, A. H. Lewis, 155
Bookseller at the Ballet, C. W. Beaumont, 35, 36
Castles in the Air, I. Castle, 90
Choura, Alexandra Danilova, A. Danilova Fan Club, 102
Cynthia Gregory, L. Péres, 181, 182
Dancing Around the World, A. L. Haskell, 132

La Dansarina Roseta Mauri, 1850–1923, F. Canyameres i J. Inglésias, 88
David Garrick and his French Friends, F. A. Hedgcock, 133
David Wall, A. Todd, 242
The Divine Comedy of Pavel Tchelitchew, P. Tyler, 244
The Divine Virginia, I. Guest, 128
Doris Humphrey: An Artist First, S. J. Cohen, 136
Fanny Cerrito. The Life of a Ballerina, I. Guest, 128
Fifteen Years of a Dancer's Life, L. Fuller, 119
Fonteyn, K. Money, 170
Frederick Ashton, D. Vaughan, 247, 248
Galina Ulanova, F. Fühmenn, 119
Galina Ulanova, V. Golubov, 123
Gene Kelly, C. Hirschorn, 134
The Gypsy in my Soul, J. Greco, 125
Heinz Bosl, M. Niehaus, 174, 175
Helgi Tomasson, A. Kisselgoff, 143
Igor Stravinsky, F. Herzfelt, 133
Impresario, A Memoir by S. Hurok & R. Goode, 136, 137
Isamu Noguchi, J. Gordon, 124
Isamu Noguchi, T. Tobias, 241
Ivan Nagy, L. Péres, 182
Jacques D'Amboise, L. F. Rosen, 197
John Cranko, W. E. Schafer, 204
Lester Horton. Modern Dance Pioneer, L. Warren, 254, 255
A Loftier Flight, M. G. Swift, 232
Lola Montez, A. Darling, 102
Ludmila Semenyaka, W. Terry, 240
Lynn Seymour, D. Vaughan, 248
Maiya Plisetskaya, L. Zhdanov, 261
Marcia Haydée, H. Kilian, 141
Margot Fonteyn, G. Anthony, 21
Margot Fonteyn, M. Clarke, 93
Margot Fonteyn, H. Fisher, 115
Margot Fonteyn, M. Fonteyn, 117
Margot Fonteyn in Australia, M. Frostick & C. Swinson, 118
Marie Taglioni (1804–1884), translated by C. W. Beaumont, A. Levinson, 58
Maris Liepa, P. Barnes, 28
M. I. Petipa (1847–1907), A. Plescheev, 190
Marius Petipa 1822 CXXV 1947, *Spyasha Krasavits* (Sleeping Beauty), 186
Markova. Her Life and Art, A. Dolin, 108
Le Marquis de Cuevas, P. Daguerre, 99
Martha Graham, D. Mcdonagh, 167
The Master of the Russian Ballet, O. Racster, 193
Maya Plisetskaya, Moscow Progress Publishers, 191
Melissa Hayden off Stage and on, M. Hayden, 132, 133
Memoirs of Joseph Grimaldi, C. Dickens, 107
Merle Park, P. W. Manchester, 162
Michel Fokine and His Ballets, C. W. Beaumont, 59
Michio Ito, H. Caldwell, 88
Mikhail Baryshnikov, L. Péres, 182
Mikhail Gabovich, M. Gabovich, 119
Moira Shearer. Portrait of a Dancer, P. Crowle, 98
My Life in Art, C. Stanislavski, 226
Natalia Bessmertnova, H. V. Atlas, 23
Natalia Makarova, D. Makarova, 162
Nicolas Legat. Heritage of a Ballet Master, A. Eglevsky & J. Gregory, 111
Nijinskii, V. Krasovskaya, 147
Nijinsky, R. Buckle, 86
Nijinsky, R. Nijinsky, 175
Nureyev, R. Nureyev, 175

SUBJECT INDEX 265

Nureyev, J. Percival, 181
Olga Spessivtzeva. The Sleeping Ballerina, A. Dolin, 108
Patricia Mcbride, A. M. Wentink, 255
Perche' Carla Fracci, L. Arruga, 22
Peter Martins, A. Todd, 242
Richard Collins, Behind the Bolshoi Curtain, R. Collins, 95
Roland Petit, P. Craig-Raymond, 97
Rudolf Nureyev, L. Péres, 182
Sacheverell Sitwell, D. Parker, editor, 178
Serge Diaghilev, His Life, His Work, His Legend, S. Lifar, 157
Sophie Fedorovitch, a Biographical Sketch, S. Fleet, 115, 116
Speak to Me, Dance with Me, A. de Mille, 106
Split Seconds, T. Geva, 121
Step by Step, N. de Valois, 106
Suzanne Farrell, A. M. Kriegsman, 148
Taken care of, E. Sitwell, 213
Teatralinaya Ulitsa, T. P. Karsavina, 139
Thi Kendes for Ret-? Erindringer, H. Lander, 149
Two or Three Muses, M. Sert, 207
Vida de Nijinsky, R. Nijinsky, 175
Violette Verdy, B. H. Haggin, 129
Vladimir Vasiliev, A. Kisselgoff, 143
Vospominaniya Baletmeistera, A. P. Gluszkovskii, 122
Ya Balerina, I. Shovire (Chauviré), 211
Your Isadora, F. Steegmuller, 227
Yuri Faier o Sebe o Muzike o Balete, Y. Faier, 114

Collective Biography

Baletniya Znamenitosti i Natshionalvnie Tantsi, K. Blazisa, 81
Bolshoi's Young Dancers, N. Avaliani & L. Zhdanov, compilers, 24
Dancers of the Ballet, M. F. Atkinson & M. Hillman, 23
Essays on Dancing and Dancers, eleven Vol., C. W. Beaumont, 42–46
Le Monde Dramatique, Tome Ier., 169
Nijinsky, Pavlova, Duncan. Three Lives in Dance, P. Magriel, editor, 162
The Private World of Ballet, J. Gruen, 126
Sibley and Dowell, N. Dromgoole, 110
Sju Danskonst-Närer, B. Häger, 129
Some Professional Dancers of or from Queensland, M. Hollinshed, 135

Ballet Synopses, Divertissements, Operas and Plays

Amleto, L. Henry, 133
Anastasia, K. Macmillan, 161
The Christmas Tree, C. W. Beaumont, 40
The Circus, C. W. Beaumont, 40
La Commedia Umana, G. Boccaccio, 82
Deburau, A play, S. Guitry, 128
Dvenadchat Mesyatsev, B. L. Bitov, 80
La Fille Mal Gardée, J. Dauberval, 103
Facade, E. Sitwell (booklet accompanying Columbia record No. ML 5341), 212
Gavrosh, B. L. Bitov, 81
Gisella eller Wilierna, J. H. Vernoy de Saint-Georges, 249
Giselle, J. H. Vernoy de Saint Georges (London Coliseum), 249
La Gitana, P. Taglioni, 233, 234
Goluboi Dunai, N. Volkov, 252
Gorda, V. Tsignadze & V. Chabukiani, 243
Gusmano D'Almeida, A. Monticini, 171

Ildamor and Zuléma, Mr. Vestris, 251
Ines de Castro, S. Taglioni, 234
Jezorio Labedzie, Teatr Wielki, 236
Kamennii Shvetok, P. P. Bajov, 24
Korsar, J. H. Vernoy de Saint-Georges, 249
Le Lac des Cygnes, K. Bednar, 77
Laurencia, E. M. Mandelberg, 163
Lebedinoe Ozero, V. P. Begichev & V. F. Geltser, 77
Leili I Medjnun, A. S. Shenin, 210
A Midsummer Night's Dream, M. Swope, 233
Miracle in the Gorbals, N. Bartholomew, 28
Napoli, A. Bournonville, 84
The Nutcracker, M. Petipa (Bolshoi), 186
The Nutcracker, M. Petipa (Canada), 186
L'Oiseau de Feu, C. W. Beaumont (typescript), 63
Otello, V. Chabukiani, 90
Les Plaisirs de l'Hiver, ou Les Patineurs, P. Taglioni, 233
Picasso Theatre, P. Picasso (*L'Avant Scène*), 188, 189
Pietruszka, Teatr Wielki, 236
Pozadanie, Teatr Wielki, 236
La Princesa Durmiente, C. Perrault, 182
Programme of Danse-Divertissements, C. W. Beaumont, 65
Programme of a Grand Matinee Presented by the Cremorne Company, C. W. Beaumont, 65
Raimonda, L. Pashkov & M. Petipa, 178
Raymonda, M. Petipa (*Ballet Review*), 187
The Red Detachment of Women, The Peoples Republic of China, 181
The Red Shoes, C. W. Beaumont (typescript), 66
Rodnye Polya, N. Chervinskii, 91
Romeo i Djulietta, L. M. Lavrovsky (Bolshoi), 151
Romeo i Djulietta, L. M. Lavrovsky, 151
Romeo e Giuletta, W. Shakespeare (San Giorgio), 208
Romeo e Giuletta, W. Shakespeare (La Scala), 208
Sampo, I. Smirnov, 219
Satanella, P. Taglioni, 233
Schaste, G. A. Ovanesyana, 177
Schlagobers, R. Strauss, 228
Sem Krasavits, I. Idayatzade, Y. Slonimskogo, S. Rakhamana, 137
Serdtse Gor, G. D. Leonidze & N. D. Volkov, 153
Shelkunchik, M. Petipa (Bolshoi), 187
Shurale, A. Faizie, 114
Skaz o Kamennon Shvetke, P. P. Bajov, 24, 25
The Sleeping Beauty, C. Perrault, 182, 183
The Sleeping Beauty, M. Petipa (Covent Garden), 188
The Sleeping Beauty, M. Petipa (San Francisco), 187, 188
Solovei, Y. Slonimsky & A. N. Ermolaev, 219
Spartacus, N. Volkov (London Coliseum), 253
Spartacus, Teatr Wielki, 236
Spartak, N. Volkov (Leningrad), 253
Spartak, N. Volkov (Moskva), 253
Swan Lake, V. P. Begichev & V. F. Geltser, 77
The Tale of Igor, H. de Vere Beauclerk, 106, 107
The Taming of the Shrew, W. Shakespeare (Covent Garden), 208
Taras Bulba, V. Solovyov-Sedoi, 220
Tatyana, V. E. Meskheteli, 167
The Three Cornered Hat, P. A. de Alarcon, 17
Vesennyaya Skaza, Y. I. Slonimsky, 218
Yunost, Y. Slonimsky, 219
Zolotopryaki, L. Algvere & P. Abolimov, 19
Zolushka, N. Volkov, 253

SUBJECT INDEX 267

Ballets, collections of

Balanchine's Complete Stories of the Great Ballets, G. Balanchine & F. Mason, 26
Ballet Guide, W. Terry, 240
Beauties of the Opera and Ballet, C. Heath, 133
Coppélia a Storiau Eraill o'r Falé, E. Davies, 103
Dramaturgiya Baletnogo Teatre XIX Veka, Y. Slonimsky, 217
The Fire-Bird and Petrushka, E. Evans, 114
The International Book of Ballets, P. Brinson & C. Crisp, 85
Kobbé's Complete Opera Book, Earl of Harewood editor, 144
More Ballet Stories for Young People, G. Davidson, 103
101 Stories of the Great Ballets, G. Balanchine & F. Mason, 26
Opernführer, Operette und Ballett, J. Schöltze, 206
Przewodnik Baletowy, I. Turska, 243
Reclams Ballettfuhrer, O. F. Regner, 195
Sem Baletnikh Istorii, Y. Slonimsky, 217
Wieczor Baletowy, Teatre Wielki, 237

Beaumont, C. W., Letters to and programmes

The Ballet Guild present a performance in Honour of Mr. Cyril W. Beaumont (programme), 33
Hoebridge School for Boys, C. W. Beaumont, a report on, 52
A Letter to Cyril Beaumont, Ambassade de France, 19
A Letter to Cyril Beaumont, A. Benois, 78
A Letter to Cyril Beaumont, A. Benois, 78
A Letter to Cyril Beaumont, J. Cornell, 96
A Letter to Cyril Beaumont, A. Benois, 78
A Letter to Cyril Beaumont, L. Knight, 144
A Letter to Cyril Beaumont, A. Levinson, 154
A Letter to Cyril Beaumont, R. Page, 177
A Letter to Cyril Beaumont, A. Stokes, 227
A Letter to Cyril Beaumont, V. Svetlov, 231
A Letter to Cyril Beaumont, J. Target, 235
A Letter to Cyril Beaumont, A. Todd, 242
Letters to Cyril Beaumont, W. Payne, 180
Letters to Cyril Beaumont, M. Shearer, 209, 210
Menu-Dinner to Celebrate the Coming of Age of Cyril Beaumont, 59
Mr. Serge Diaghilev Requests the Honour of the Company of Mr. Beaumont to Assist at the Final Rehearsal of Stravinsky's Reynard, Royal Opera House, 60

Beaumont, C. W. Manuscripts & Typescripts

The Origin of the Taglioni Cake Ceremony, C. W. Beaumont (typescript), 63
The Complete Book of Ballets, C. W. Beaumont (typescript), 75

Bibliography, Catalogues etc.

Aesthetics for Dancers: A Selected Annotated Bibliography, M. H. Kaprelian, 138
Background to a Great Society, The Imperial Society (brochure), 137
Bakst, L. Bakst. Catalogue of an Exhibition at the Fine Art Society 1973–1974, 25
Bakst, C. Spencer. An Exhibition at the Fine Art Society, 225
Ballet, a Reader's Guide, A. L. Haskell, 131
Ballet and Theatre Material, Sotheby's, Day of Sale Thurs. June 5th 1975, 220
Ballet and Theatre Material, Sotheby's, Day of Sale Wed. May 25, 1977, 220, 221
Ballet and Theatre Material, Sotheby Parke-Bernet Wed. May 17, 1978, 221
Ballet et Danse, Hachette (catalogue), 129
Le Ballet et la Danse à L'Epoque Romantique 1800–1850, S. Lifar, 186
Ballets Russes de Diaghilev 1909–1929, S. Lifar, 156

Ballets Russes de Serge Diaghilev, Strasbourg, 1969, 27
Bibliografia Zagadnień Sztuki Tanecznej, Centralnia Poradnia Amatorskie Ruchu Artystycznego, 5 Vol's, 79, 80
Bibliographical Descriptions of Forty Rare Dance Books, I. K. Fletcher, 116
A Bibliography of Dancing, P. D. Magriel (First Supplement), 162
A Bibliography of the Dance Collection of Doris Niles & Serge Leslie, 153, 154
Bibliothèque Musicale du Théâtre de L'Opéra, T. de Lajarte, 105
Books Relating to the Diaghilev Ballet, I. K. Fletcher (Diaghilev Exhibition Catalogue), 116
Catalogue of Ballet & Theatre Material, June 5th 1975, Sotheby & Co., 220
Catalogue of the Highly Important Toulouse–Philidor Collection, June 26th, 1978, Sotheby Parke Bernet & Co., 221
A Catalogue of Most Desirable Books, C. W. Beaumont, 38
Catalogues, The Dance Mart, 100
Catalogues of Dance Books Ltd. New Books & Additions to Stock April 1977, J. O'Brien and D. Leonard, 100
The Constitution and Activities of the Cecchetti Branch of the Imperial Society of Teachers of Dancing, 90
Dance, I. K. Fletcher (catalogue), 116
Dance in India, J. Van Zile, 246
Dance, Theatre, Opera, Dec. 15, 1977, Sotheby Parke Bernet Inc., 221, 222
Decor and Costume Designs, Portraits, Manuscripts and Posters Principally for Ballet, Thurs. 21st June 1973, Sotheby & Co., 221
The Diaghilev Ballet, The Dance Mart, 100, 101
The Diaghilev–Lifar Library, Sotheby Parke-Bernet, Monaco, 222
Dramatic Bibliography, B. Baker, 25
Eras of the Dance, The George Verdak Collection, 248
An Exhibition of Costume and Set Designs Chiefly from the Diaghilev Ballets, J. C. Doughty, 109
Exhibition of Drawings, Masks, and Models, R. Mason editor, 165
An exhibition of Paintings and Decors, C. Bérard, 78
La Famille Benois (Arthur Tooth & Sons), 78
Films on Ballet and Modern Dance, J. Mueller, 172
Guide to Dance Periodicals Vol. VIII 1957–1958, S. Y. Belknap, 77
Harlequinade, Second Hand & Antiquarian Books, C. Morris, 130
Homage to Designers of Diaghilev 1909–1929, R. Buckle, 86
Impressionist and Modern Paintings, Drawings and Ballet and Theatre Material, 20th Oct. 1976, Sotheby's, 222
The Jack Cole Dance and Theatre Collection, J. Cole, 95
Le Lac des Cygnes, The London Archives of the Dance, 158, 159
Maggs Musical Miscellany, Maggs, 161
Michel Larionov, W. George (catalogue), 120, 121
Mr. Beaumont's Books, H. Sims, 60
Nathalie Gontcharova, W. George (catalogue), 121
The Performing Arts, Catalogue Three, P. Wood, 259
Performing Arts Research, M. K. Whalon, 255
Printed & Manuscript Music, Autograph Letters of Musicians & the Theatre and Dance, 8th & 9th Nov. 1976, Sotheby's, 222
Retrospective Larionov, Galerie de Paris (catalogue), 150
Ritratti di Musicisti ed Artisti di Teatro, P. Arrigoni & A. Bertarelli, 21, 22
The Russian Ballet, Paintings and Drawings, L. Knight (catalogue), 144
Russian Painters and the Stage 1884–1965, coll. of Mr. & Mrs. D. Lobanov–Rostovsky, 158
Sale of Material Relating to the Theatre, Opera Ballet etc. Dec. 20th 1976, Sotheby's, 222, 223
Tanzbibliographie, K. Petermann (28 Lieferung) parts issued to date, 183–85
Ten Years of Films on Ballet and Classical Dance 1956–1965, Unesco, 244
Theatre, Catalogues 6 and 13, P. Wood, 259

Criticism, Essays and Belles Lettres

El Acierto de la Danza Española, V. M. Suarez, 230
L'Amour au Theatre Italien, S. Sitwell (Nijinska's finger variation), 214
At the Vanishing Point, M. B. Siegel, 211, 212

SUBJECT INDEX 269

Badinerie, S. Sitwell (poems), 214
Baletni Stroki Pushkina, Y. Slonimsky, 217
The Ballerina, R. Austin, 23
Ballet. A Complete Guide to Appreciation, A. L. Haskell, 131
Ballet in the U.S.S.R., J. Lawson, 151
Balletomania then and now, A. L. Haskell, 132
Ballets Soviétiques, G. Oulanova, 176, 177
The Beautiful Danger, E. Aschengreen, 22
Bookseller at the Ballet, C. W. Beaumont, 35, 36
The Bridge of the Brocade Sash, S. Sitwell, 214, 215
C. W. Beaumont, O. Sitwell (*Laughter in the Next Room*), 213
A Call to Order, J. Cocteau, 94
The Crystal Salt Cellar, M. Sandoz, 203
Dance as Life, F. Stevens, 227
Dance Data No. 1, A. J. Pischl & B. N. Cohen editors, 189, 190
Dance Data No. 2, A. J. Pischl & B. N. Cohen editors, 190
The Dance has Many Faces, W. Sorell, 220
The Dance in Art, S. Longstreet, 159
The Dance Writings of Carl Van Vechten, C. Van Vechten, 246
Diaghilev's Oversight: and the Aftermath, J. Gregory, 125, 126
Duncan, Isadora, The Art of the Dance, S. Cheney editor, 110
Echoes of American Ballet, L. Moore, 171
Edith Sitwell, Selected Letters 1919–1964, J. Lehmann & D. Parker, 153
Encounters with Stravinsky, P. Horgan, 136
Enrico Cecchetti, A. Clarke (typescript), 92
Entries from an Early Diary for John Martin, L. Kirstein, 142
For Want of the Golden City, S. Sitwell, 215
The Function of Dance in Human Society, F. Boas, 82
Gothic Europe, S. Sitwell, 215
Great Morning, O. Sitwell (notes on Diaghilev), 213
The History of the Pheasantry Chelsea 1766–1977, N. Macdonald, 160
The Hunters and the Hunted, S. Sitwell, 215
Images of the Dance, R. Austin, 24
Impugnacion Literaria a la Crotalogia Erudita, o Cience de las Castañuelas, J. L. Polinario, 191, 192
An Indian Summer, S. Sitwell (poems about dancing), 215
Laughter in the Next Room, O. Sitwell (notes on Bakst etc.), 213
Left Hand Right Hand, O. Sitwell (notes on Henriette d'Or, Taglioni), 214
Let's Meet the Ballet, D. Samachson, 202
Light on a System of Classical Dance, J. Gregory, 126
Little Italy in London, S. Sitwell, 216
Mastera Baleta, A. Levinson, 155
The Muscovite Peacock, R. Lister, 158
The Nature of Ballet, A. Monahan, 169
Noble Essences, O. Sitwell (notes on Tchelitchew), 214
The Omnibus Box, M. E. Perugini, 183
Prelude to Ballet, A. L. Haskell, 132
Pushkin i Baletnii Teatr, N. Elyash, 112
A la Recherche d'un Langage, R. Goldron, 122, 123
The Russian Ballet Gift Book, E. Sitwell, 212, 213
The Scarlet Tree, O. Sitwell (notes on the Ballet), 214
The 7 Lively Arts, G. Seldes, 207
Silken Dalliance, J. H. Bruce, 86
Southern Baroque Revisted, S. Sitwell (notes on Scarlatti), 216
Stati o Balete, V. Krasovskaya, 148
Strana Volchebnaya Balet, Z. Bocharnikova, 82
Stravinsky and the Dance, New York Public Library, 173
Stravinsky: The Chronicle of a Friendship, R. Craft, 97
A Tayle of Ye Danse, Jo. Count G. Satelli, 138
Temple of Segesta, S. Sitwell (poem containing theatre information), 216
Three Essays in Dance Aesthetics, G. Beiswanger, W. Hoffmann, D. M. Levin, 77

Three Years with Charles Weidman, D. W. Wynne, 260
To the Ballet, I. Deakin, 104, 105
A Tribute to John Cranko, Peter Rosenwald (programme), 198, 199
Truffle Hunt, S. Sitwell (poems, many about the ballet), 216
Ulanova, Moiseyev, Zakharov on Soviet Ballet, P. Brinson, editor, 244
The World of Ballet, O. Kerensky, 140
Writings on Dance 1938–68, A. V. Coton, 97
Your Book of Ballet, P. Moldon, 169
Zapiski Baletmeistera, R. Zakharov, 261
Zritelu o Balete, N. Elyash, 112

Dance in Education

History of the Dance in Art and Education, R. Kraus, 148
Making a Ballet, M. Clarke & C. Crisp, 94
Making a Ballet, C. Crisp & M. Clarke, 98
The School of American Ballet Inc., L. Kirstein (brochure), 143

Dance Notation

Choreographie ou L'Art de décrire la Danse, R. A. Feuillet, 115
Dance Studies Vol. I, R. Lange, 149
Dances from Cuiavia, Kinetograms & Music, R. Lange, 149
Grammar of the Art of Dancing, F. A. Zorn, 262
The Language of Movement, R. Laban, 148
Massine on Choreography, L. Massine, 165, 166
Metodo de Castañuelas, R. Escudero, 113, 114
Reading Dance. The Birth of Choreology, R. & J. Benesh, 78
A Third Reader, A. Hutchinson, 137

Dance Periodicals

About the House. The Friends of Covent Garden Vol. 4 No. 3 to Vol. 5 No. 5, 199–202
The American Dancer, R. E. Howard, managing director, 19
Ballett 1973, H. Koegler, editor, 145
Ballett 1974, H. Koegler, editor, 145
Ballett 1975, H. Koegler, editor, 145
Ballett 1976, H. Koegler, editor, 145
Ballett 1977, H. Koegler, editor, 145
Ballet Review No. 1, Albyn Press, 26
The Bulletin of the London Ballet Circle, Petit Tour Vol. 2 No. 3 Dance and Dancers, P. Williams, editor, 188
Dance and Dancers, P. Williams, editor, 99
Dance Magazine 1949–1979, W. Como, editor, 100
Dance Magazine Portfolio 1968–1979, W. Como, editor, 100
Dance Perspectives 1972–1976, S. J. Cohen, editor, 101
Dance World, J. Willis, editor (Vol's 4–12), 256, 257
Dancers of Today, Vol. I, P. Wilson, 257
Dancing Times, The, 1951–62; 1963–78, 101, 102
La Danza, Revista Espanola del Mondo del Ballet, M. Menkes, editor, 102
The Director, M. B. Gilbert, 121, 122

Dance Technique: Academic Dance & Classical Ballet

Ballett Exercises das Stuttgarter Ballett, A. Woolliams & G. Tetley, 260
Ballet School, J. Gabriel, 119, 120

SUBJECT INDEX 271

Las Bases de la Danza Clásica, A. Vaganova, 245
Basic Ballet, J. Mackie, 161
Birth of a Ballet, R. Austin, 23, 24
Bournonville & Ballet Technique, E. Bruhn & L. Moore, 86
The Cecchetti Method of Teaching Classical Ballet, C. W. Beaumont, 38
Classes in Classical Ballet, A. Messerer, 167, 168
Clendenen's Treatise on Elementary and Classical Dancing, F. L. Clendenen, 94
The Code of Terpsichore, C. Blasis, 81
Dance. Therapy for Dancers, B. Dunn, 111
The Dance in the Making, Vestoff–Serova Studio, 249
Do's and Dont's of Basic Ballet Barre, T. Mara, 163
Khoreograficheskie Otktrovennosti, F. Lopukhov, 159
Klassicheskii Tanets, N. Bazarova, 29
Klassicheskii Tanets, N. Tarasov, 234, 235
Klassischer Tanz, N. I. Tarassow, 235
Leningradskoe Gosudarstvennoe Khoreograficheskie Uchiliste, L. Pantukova, 178
Making a Ballet, C. Crisp and M. Clarke, 98
The Making of a Dance, Mikhail Baryshnikov & Carla Fracci in *Medea*, T. Victor, 251
Manual of Dancing Steps, E. Pohl, 191
A Manual of the Theory and Practice of Classical, Theatrical Dancing, C. W. Beaumont & S. Idzikovski, 57
Pas de Deux, N. Serebrennikov, trans. E. Kraft, 207
Pas de Deux im Klassischen Tanz, N. Serebrennikow, 207
Podderjka v Duztnom Tantse, N. N. Serebrennikov, 207
Programmi Spetsialnikh Distsiplin Khoreografischesikh Uchilishche, The Soviet Ballet, 223
The Russian Ballet School, L. Harris, 131
Le Secret de la Ligne par la Danse, I. Lidova, 156
Shkola Klassicheskogo Tantsa, V. Kostrovitskaya & A. Pisarev, 147
Tam Gde Rojdaetsya Tanets, Y. Aleksandrov, editor, 18
The Teaching of Classical Ballet, J. Lawson, 152
Teaching Young Dancers, J. Lawson, 152
Training on the Toes, Vestoff-Serova Studio, 251
A Treatise on the Principles and Evolution of the Port de Bras, E. Faust (typescript), 114, 115

Dance Technique: Ballroom and Modern Social Dance

The Tango and How to Dance it, G. B. Crozier, 99
Tantsevat Mogut Vse, R. L. Cherekhovskaya, 91

Dance Technique: Historical Dance and Historical Social Dancing

Arte ou Methodo Facil de Apprender a Dancar as Contradancas Francezas, Anonymous, 20
Curious Character Dances, A. Heyworth and K. M. Powell-Tuck, 134
Dancing Made Easy, C. J. Coll and G. Rosière, 95
Historical Dances for the Theatre, J. Guthrie, 129
Istoriko-Bitovoi Tanets, M. Vasilieva-Rojdestvenskaya, 246, 247
John Playford's The English Dancing Master, J. Playford, 190
Pre-Classic Dance Forms, L. Horst, 136
Taenze mit Muzik, Herrn Lauchery, 151
El Triunfo de las Castañuelas, D. A. Moya, 172

Design: Costumes and Settings

Bakst: The Story of the Artist's Life, A. Levinson, 154
Ballettstudien, F. Marshall, 165
The Christmas Tree, W. Payne (20 original designs), 180
Circus, W. Payne (14 paper cutouts), 180
The Decorative Art of Léon Bakst, A. Alexandre, 18

SUBJECT INDEX

Designing for the Stage, D. Zinkheisen, 262
Léon Bakst, C. Spencer, 225, 226
Marc Chagall, J. Lassaigne, 150
Painters in the Theatre, D. Hays, 133
Stage Designs, W. Jeudwine, 138
The Theatre of Eugene Berman, G. Amberg, 19

Dictionaries and Encyclopaedias

ABC'S of Dance Terminology, M. O'Moore, 176
Ballet van A tot Z, L. Kersley & J. Sinclair, 140
The Book of Ballet, G. Guillot & G. Prudommeau, 128
Concise Encyclopedia of Ballet, F. Reyna, 196
The Concise Oxford Dictionary of Ballet, H. Koegler, 146
The Dance Encyclopedia, A. Chujoy and P. W. Manchester, 92
A Dictionary of Ballet, G. B. L. Wilson, 257
A Dictionary of Ballet Terms, L. Kersley & J. Sinclair, 140
Dictionary of the Dance, W. G. Raffé, 194
Mastera Tantsa, Materali k Istorii Leningradskogo Baleta 1917–1973, A. Degen and I. Stupnikov, 105

Extracts from Periodicals

Adolph Bolm, C. W. Beaumont (*Ballet Annual*), 29
Agnes de Mille and Warren Leonard, C. W. Beaumont (Dance Journal), 29
Alicia Markova, C. W. Beaumont (*Ballet Annual*), 29
American Ballet Theatre's Roller Coaster Repertoire, R. J. Pierce (Dance Magazine Portfolio), 100
Anna Pavlova, C. W. Beaumont (Dance Journal), 30
Anna Pavlova—A Votive Offering, T. Kinney (Dance Magazine), 141
Annals of the Sleeping Beauty, F. Lopukhov and B. Asafiev (Ballet Review), 159
Anthony Tudor: Choreographer, C. W. Beaumont in *British Ballet* ed. Peter Noble, 30
Antická Choreografie a Isadora Duncanová, V. Svetlov (Taneční Listy), 230, 231
Approach to Ballet, C. W. Beaumont (Critic's Circular), 30
Les Archives Internationales de la Danse, C. W. Beaumont (Dance Journal), 30
The Art and Profession of the Academic Dancer II, C. W. Beaumont (Opera and Ballet), 30
The Art of Enrico Cecchetti, C. W. Beaumont (Dancing World), 30
The Art of Maud Allan, C. W. Beaumont (Dancing World), 31
The Art of Ninette de Valois, C. W. Beaumont (Dancing Life), 31
The Art of Ruth St. Denis, C. W. Beaumont (Dancing World), 31
The Art of Troy Kinney, A. Macmahon (Dance Magazine), 161
As an Oriental Looks at Art (Michio Itow), K. Porter (Dance Magazine), 192
Ashton's Cinderella, C. W. Beaumont (Ballet), 31
Ashton's Don Juan, C. W. Beaumont (Ballet), 31
Assoluta: Alicia Alonso and her Ballet Nacional de Cuba, W. Terry (Opera News), 240
Audrey Ashby. Some Remarks on Training, C. W. Beaumont (Dancing World), 31
Auguste Vestris, C. W. Beaumont (Ballet), 32
The Autobiography of a Prima Ballerina, C. W. Beaumont (Dance Journal), 32
The Autobiography of a Premier Danseur, C. W. Beaumont (Dance Journal), 32
Balanchine: Demigod of the Dance (Newsweek), 25, 26
Balanchine's Ballet Imperial, C. W. Beaumont (Ballet), 32
Balet Sadlers Wells v Praze, C. W. Beaumont (Britzky Magazin Zari), 32
Ballet—American Version, M. Turbyfill (Dance Magazine), 243
The Ballet Club, C. W. Beaumont (Dance Journal), 32
The Ballet Club—The Camargo Society, C. W. Beaumont (Dance Journal), 32
Ballet Dancing, A. L. Haskell (Theatre and Stage), 132
A Ballet Followed by Some Divertissements, C. W. Beaumont (Dancing World), 33
The Ballet Girl—Then and Now Part I, C. W. Beaumont (Dancing Times), 33

SUBJECT INDEX 273

The Ballet Girl—Then and Now Part II, C. W. Beaumont (Dancing Times), 33
The Ballet: Good Thing for Painters, N. Lansdale (Art News), 150
The Ballet of the Lilac Fairy, C. W. Beaumont (Dancing World), 33, 34
Ballet Rambert, C. W. Beaumont (Ballet), 34
The Ballet Theatre, C. W. Beaumont (Ballet), 34
Ballet's Debt to Fairy Tale, C. W. Beaumont (Ballet), 34
Les Ballets des Champs-Elysées, C. W. Beaumont (Ballet), 34 & 35
Les Ballets des Champs-Elysées, C. W. Beaumont (Dans Kroniek), 34
Ballets des Champs-Elysées (Realités), 26
Les Ballets des Champs-Elysées, C. W. Beaumont (The Studio), 35
Il Balletto Italiano, O. R. Signorelli (Venezia Festivale Internazionale di Musica Contemporaneo, 212
The Beaumont Press 1917–1932, B. T. Jackson (The Private Library), 138
Behind the Scenes at the Opera in Taglioni's Day, C. W. Beaumont (Dancing Times), 35
Berain and the French Costume Tradition, A. Levinson (Theatre Arts Monthly), 154
Between Heaven and Charing Cross, P. Williams (Dance and Dancers), 256
Bonne Bouche, C. W. Beaumont (Ballet), 35
The British Dancer, C. W. Beaumont (Dance Journal), 36
The British Dancer, C. W. Beaumont (Opera), 36
A Burmese Puwè at Wembley, C. W. Beaumont (Operator and the Ballet), 36
La Camargo, C. W. Beaumont (Dance Journal), 36
The Camargo Society, C. W. Beaumont (Dance Journal), 37
The Camargo Society—The Vacani Matinee, C. W. Beaumont (Dance Journal), 37
Canada Land of Promise, (Dancing Times), 101
The Career and Tragedy of Vaslav Nijinsky, C. W. Beaumont (Dance Journal), 38
Carlotta Grisi and Giselle, C. W. Beaumont (Dance Journal), 38
Carlotta Zambelli, I, II Guest (Dance Magazine), 127, 128
Cartophily—Applied to Dancers, C. W. Beaumont (Dancing Times), 38
Cecchetti Choreographic Competition, C. W. Beaumont (Dancing Times), 38
Cecchetti's Legacy to the Dance, C. W. Beaumont (*Ballet Annual*), 39
The Centenary of Enrico Cecchetti, C. W. Beaumont (Dancing Times), 39
Century Old Dancers, C. W. Beaumont (Opera and the Ballet), 39
The Characters in Swan Lake, C. W. Beaumont (Ballet), 39
Checkmate and Mam'zelle Angot, C. W. Beaumont (Ballet), 39
The Choregraphe Michael Fokine, C. W. Beaumont (Dancing World), 40
The Classical Ballet, B. W. Findon, editor, (The Play Pictorial), 190
The Christensen Brothers, O. Maynard (Dance Magazine Portfolio), 166
Commedia dell'Arte and Opera, N. Pirotta (The Musical Quarterly), 189
The Complete Book of Ballets, C. W. Beaumont (Ballet), 41
Christian Berard 1902–1949, C. W. Beaumont (The Studio), 40
A Christmas Dream for Balletomanes, C. W. Beaumont (Dancing World), 40
Le Cirque et le Ballet, M. H. Winter (Le Vieux Papier), 257
Coppelia 1946, C. W. Beaumont (Ballet), 41
Costume for Ballet, C. W. Beaumont (Robes of Thespis, ed. Sheringham), 41
The Costume of the Male Ballet Dancer, C. W. Beaumont (Dance Journal), 41
Cranko's Pineapple Poll, C. W. Beaumont (Ballet), 41
Le Creature di Prometeo, G. Frangini (XIX Maggio Musicale Fiorentino), 118
Critical Notes on Some Recent Dancing, C. W. Beaumont (Dancing World), 42
The Criticism of Ballet, I. Deakin (At the Ballet), 104
C. W. Beaumont Gives up Historic London Bookshop, M. Clarke (Dance News), 93
Cyril Beaumont, N. Bowden (Dancing Times), 84, 85
Cyril Beaumont, S. Leslie (Seven Leagues of a Dancer), 154
Cyril Beaumont, S. Leslie (Theatre Notebook), 154
Cyril Beaumont on Ballet Books (Sunday Times), 42
Dance Criticisms Appearing in The Sunday Times 1950–1959, C. W. Beaumont, 42
The Dance in Art and History, (Hobbies), 135
Dance Magazine Portfolios 1968–1978, W. Como, R. Philp & H. Migdoll, 100
The Dance of Spain, T. Kinney (Dance Magazine), 141
The Dance of the Sprouting Corn, D. H. Lawrence (Theatre Arts Monthly), 151
The Dance Journal XI Vols, C. W. Beaumont, editor, 42–46

Dancer on the Horizon, C. W. Beaumont (Dance Journal), 46
Dancers in Unexpected Places, C. W. Beaumont (Dancing Times), 46
The Dancer's Library, C. W. Beaumont (Dancing Times), 46
Dancing From Burma, V. Pilcher (Theatre Arts Monthly), 189
The Dancing Master, P. Rameau (Dance Journal), 46, 47
Dancing Schools or Robot Factories, C. W. Beaumont (Dancing World), 47
Danse, J. Silvant (Intermède), 212
The Danseuses Viennoises, C. W. Beaumont (Dance Journal), 47
Darja Collin en Edmee Monod, C. Conyn (De Fakhel), 95
Le Decalogue de Vicente Escudero, (Revue Chorégraphique de Paris), 195
Derra de Moroda: Marion Morgan Dancers, C. W. Beaumont (Dancing World), 47
Designs for Ballet, C. W. Beaumont (An Exhibition for Theatre and Ballet), 47
Deux Lettres de Jacques Anselme à Antoine Bournonville, J. Anselme, 20, 21
De Valois' Don Quixote, C. W. Beaumont (Ballet), 47
A Devotee of the Orient (Vera Mirova), T. Kinney (Dance Magazine), 141
The Diaghileff Company, C. W. Beaumont (Opera), 47, 48
Diaghilev—The Trail Blazer, V. Svetlov 3 Parts (Dance Magazine), 231
Diamond Jubilee Dinner Speech for The Imperial Society of Teachers of Dancing, C. W. Beaumont (Dance Journal), 48
A Disappointment and a Surprise, C. W. Beaumont (Dancing World), 48
Emma Livry, C. W. Beaumont (Dance Journal), 48
The Emperor and the Nightingale, C. W. Beaumont (The Studio), 48
Enchanted Realm, (News from Home), 173
An English Ballet in Spain, W. Goodman (The Theatre), 124
Enrico Cecchetti. The Jubilee of a Great Artist, C. W. Beaumont (The Observer), 48
E. P. Eduardova, V. Fride (Jar Ptitsa), 118
Les Etoiles de la Danse, C. W. Beaumont (Ballet), 48
A Familiar Subject Viewed at a New Angle, C. W. Beaumont (Dancing World), 49
Fanny Elssler, C. W. Beaumont (Dance Journal), 49
Fifty Years a Follower of Ballet, C. W. Beaumont (Balley Today), 49
Fifty Years of Male Dancing, C. W. Beaumont (Dancing Times), 49
Fokine's Ballets, C. W. Beaumont (Dancing Times), 49
Forty Years Writing on the Ballet, C. W. Beaumont (*Ballet Annual*), 49
Four Giselles, C. W. Beaumont (Ballet), 50
Four Opinions on Ashton's Sylvia: An Account, C. W. Beaumont (Ballet), 50
Frederick Ashton—English Choreographer, C. W. Beaumont (*Souvenirs du Ballet*), 50
A Friend for all Seasons, C. W. Beaumont (Sacheverell Sitwell, A Symposium), 50
From Pavlova to ABT, W. Terry (Opera News), 240
The Funeral of Nijinsky, C. W. Beaumont (*Ballet Annual*), 50
Gaetano and Auguste Vestris in English Caricature, C. W. Beaumont (Ballet), 50
Gaetano Vestris Gives a Lesson in Deportment to the Prince of Lanmarck, C. W. Beaumont (Dance Journal), 51
Garland for Nijinsky—Artist and Dancer, C. W. Beaumont (*Ballet Annual*), 51
Giselle ou les Wilis, trans. by C. W. Beaumont (Dance Journal), 51
Grand Ballet de Monte Carlo, C. W. Beaumont (Ballet), 51
Le Grand Ballet de Monte Carlo, C. W. Beaumont (Ballet), 51
The Growth of Style in English Ballet, C. W. Beaumont (C.O.I. for the British Council), 51
The Haunted Ballroom, C. W. Beaumont (Dance Journal), 52
Haunting Disclaimed, C. W. Beaumont (Ballet), 52
Het Wezen van den Spaanschen Dans, C. Conyn (Elsevier's), 96
A History of Ballet in Russia, from 1613–1880, C. W. Beaumont (Dance Journal), 52
A History of Ballet in Russia, C. W. Beaumont (Dance World), 52
Homage à Balanchine, (Revue Chorégraphique de Paris), 195, 196
Homage to Diaghilev (1872–1929), C. W. Beaumont (Columbia Gramophone), 53
Hommage à Jeanmaire, C. W. Beaumont (*Ballet Annual*), 53
Hopi Kachina Artist James Makya, A. J. Makya (Arizona Highways), 162
Horse Ballets, C. W. Beaumont (Ballet), 53
Hugh Stevenson, C. W. Beaumont (The Studio), 53
Il Mio Maesstro Cecchetti, L. Albertieri and S. Palmer (Dance Magazine), 17, 18
In Memoriam—Giuseppina Cecchetti, C. W. Beaumont (Dance Journal), 53

SUBJECT INDEX

The International Ballet, C. W. Beaumont (Ballet), 53, 54
International Ballet's Swan Lake, C. W. Beaumont (Ballet), 53
An Interview with Stanislas Idzikovsky, C. W. Beaumont (Dancing World), 54
Isadora Reexamined, N. Macdonald, (Dance Magazine), 161
Is Modernism Modern? M. Fokine (Dance Magazine), 116, 117
Jean-Etienne Despréaux, C. Fleury (Revue de la France Moderne), 116
Jean Target, C. W. Beaumont (The Studio), 54
Le Jugement de Paris, C. W. Beaumont (Dance Journal), 54
Jules Perrot, C. W. Beaumont (Dance Journal), 54
Kirstein, Balanchine, and Others, C. W. Beaumont (Tempo), 54
The Kurt Jooss Ballet, C. W. Beaumont (Dance Journal), 55
Le Lac des Cygnes at Covent Garden, C. W. Beaumont (Ballet), 55
The Last Years of Isadora Duncan, C. W. Beaumont (Dance Journal), 55
The Legacy of Hurok, G. Dorris (Ballet Review), 108
Leontine Beaugrand, C. W. Beaumont (Dance Journal), 55
A Letter from Editions Hypérion, C. W. Beaumont (Editions Hypérion), 55
Lifar—His Book and Theories, M. Fokine (Dancing Times), 117
The Life of a Ballet Girl in the 'Sixties', C. W. Beaumont (Dancing Times), 56
Lights that Dance, V. Svetlov (Dance Magazine), 232
The Literature of the Ballet, C. W. Beaumont (British Book News), 56
The London Archives of the Dance and Some of its Treasures, C. W. Beaumont (*Ballet Annual*), 56
London's Overdue Festival of Ballet, C. W. Beaumont (Opera and The Ballet), 56
Madeleine Guimard, C. W. Beaumont (Dance Journal), 56
Margot Fonteyn, C. W. Beaumont (*Ballet Annual*), 57
Maria Mercandotti, C. W. Beaumont (Ballet), 58
Marie Sallé, C. W. Beaumont (Dance Journal), 58
Marie Taglioni, C. W. Beaumont, translated by (Dance Journal), 58
Marie Taglioni, and La Sylphide, C. W. Beaumont (Dancing World), 58
Mario e il Magio, V. Castiglioni (Teatro alla Scala), 89
Marius Petipa, C. W. Beaumont (Dance Journal), 58
Markova and Dolin in Giselle, C. W. Beaumont (Ballet), 59
Martha Graham: Three New Dances, G. Beiswanger (Theatre Arts), 77
Mary Wigman, C. W. Beaumont (Dance Journal), 59
The Massine Ballet, C. W. Beaumont (Dancing World), 59
Michel Fokine, C. W. Beaumont (Dance Journal), 59, 60
Michel Fokine Dance Studios (brochure), 117
Milady of Milan (Rosina Galli), R. Harper (Dance Magazine), 130
A Mirror for Witches, C. W. Beaumont (Ballet), 60
The Monte Carlo Ballet Russe, C. Beaton (Vanity Fair), 29
The Monument of Diaghilev, L. Kirstein (Dance News), 142
More Light on Giselle, C. W. Beaumont (Dancing Times), 60
More Taglioni Treasures, C. W. Beaumont (Dancing Times), 61
Musings from Near the Museum, C. W. Beaumont (Dancing Times), 61
My Dance of Life, A. Volinine (Dance Magazine), 252
The National Ballet of Lithuania, C. W. Beaumont (Dance Journal), 61
New York City Ballet: Two of Robbins, C. W. Beautmont (Ballet), 61
Nicholas Grigorievich Sergeyev, C. W. Beaumont (*Ballet Annual*), 62
The Nijinsky Galas, C. W. Beaumont (Ballet), 62
Nimura—Dancer of the Samurai, T. E. Harré (Dance Magazine), 130, 131
Not Although but Because: A Dialogue with Michel Fokine, C. W. Beaumont translator (Dance Journal), 62
A Note on Léon Bakst, C. W. Beaumont (Opera and The Ballet), 62
A Note on the Swedish Ballet, B. H. Clark (The Drama), 92
Notes on the Changes in Dance in Fifty Years, C. W. Beaumont (Dancing Times), 62
Notre Dame de Paris, P. Bourcier (L'Opéra), 84
Le Nouveau Ballet de Monte Carlo, C. W. Beaumont (Ballet), 62
Od Krakowiaka Do Polki, A. Michalek, 168
On Examinations in the Cecchetti Syllabus, C. W. Beaumont (Dance Journal), 63
On Teaching of Dance History, C. W. Beaumont (Dance Journal), 63
On Theatrical Dancing, C. W. Beaumont (Theatre Arts), 63

Our First National School of Dancing, C. W. Beaumont (Dancing Times), 63, 64
The Passing of a Great Artist Enrico Cecchetti, C. W. Beaumont (The Mask), 64
Pauline Duvernay, C. W. Beaumont (Dance Journal), 64
Pavlova, C. W. Beaumont (Opera and The Ballet), 64
Pavlova, Lopokova and "Hassan", C. W. Beaumont (Dancing World), 64
Petit's Ballabile, C. W. Beaumont (Ballet), 64
Petrouchka, E. Schwarz (Dans Kroniek), 206
Petrushka in London, C. W. Beaumont (*Petrushka* edited by Charles Hamm), 64
The Place of Ballet in Opera, M. Wallmann (*Opera Annual*), 254
A Polish Dancer New to London, C. W. Beaumont (Dancing World), 65
The Practice of Ballet Criticism, C. W. Beaumont (*Dancers and Critics* edited by C. Swinson), 65
The Prices an Anglo-Continental Theatrical Dynasty, M. H. Winter (Theatre Notebook), 258
Printed Editions of André Campra's Europe Galante, J. R. Anthony (Musical Quarterly), 21
The Promise of Svetlana Beriosova, C. W. Beaumont (Ballet Today), 66
Pushkin, and His Influence on Russian Ballet, C. W. Beaumont (Ballet Part I), 66
Pushkin, and His Influence on Russian Ballet, C. W. Beaumont (Ballet Part 2), 66
The Return of Ballet Theatre, C. W. Beaumont (Ballet), 66
The Return of Lopokova, C. W. Beaumont (Dancing Life), 66
The Return of Markova and Dolin, C. W. Beaumont (*Ballet Annual*), 67
A Revitalized Ballet, J. Percival (Danish Foreign Office Journal), 181
Les Robes de Bakst, G. Mourey (Gazette de Bon Ton), 172
Roland Petit's Ballets de Paris, C. W. Beaumont (Ballet), 67
The Romantic Ballet, C. W. Beaumont (Time and Tide), 67
Ross's Caprichos, C. W. Beaumont (Ballet), 67
The Royal Danish Ballet, C. W. Beaumont (Ballet), 67
The Russian Ballet 1921-1929, C. W. Beaumont (Art Work No. 28), 67
The Sakharoffs: The Blue Bird Theatre, C. W. Beaumont (Dancing World), 68
Sally Gilmour, C. W. Beaumont (Dancing World), 68
Schools and Methods of Dance Training, C. W. Beaumont (World Ballet News), 68
See How They Dance, C. W. Beaumont (Programme Royal Albert Hall), 68
Serge Diaghilev, C. W. Beaumont (Dancing Times), 68
Serge Grigoriev, C. W. Beaumont (Dancing Times), 68
Simon Slingsby, C. W. Beaumont (Ballet), 69
The Sitwells at the Ballet, E. Ricco (Ballet Review), 196
The Sleeping Princess, C. W. Beaumont (Dancing Life), 69
Some Classic Dances of Japan, C. W. Beaumont (Dance Journal), 69
Some Dancers of the Diaghilev Ballet, C. W. Beaumont (Ballet), 69
Some Dancers of the Sadler's Wells Theatre Ballet, C. W. Beaumont (Foyer), 69
Some Memorable Occasions, C. W. Beaumont (Tempo), 70
Some New Paintings of the Russian Ballet, C. W. Beaumont (Dancing World), 70
Some Notes on the Ballet Shoes worn by Anna Pavlova, C. W. Beaumont (Dance Journal), 70
Some Observations on the Production of Swan Lake, C. W. Beaumont (Dancing Times), 70
Some Postcards of the Imperial Russian Ballet, C. W. Beaumont (Ballet), 70
Some Prints of the Romantic Ballet, C. W. Beaumont (Print Collectors Quarterly), 71
Some Recent Revivals by the Original Ballet Russe, C. W. Beaumont (Ballet), 71
Some Stages in the Development of the Academic Ballet, C. W. Beaumont (Dancing World), 71
Speech for the Critic's Circle, C. W. Beaumont (typescript), 71
Stage Decorations and the Dance, C. W. Beaumont (Dancing World), 71
Stage Movement and Mime, M. G. Pickersgill (Theatre and Stage), 189
Studies of Classical Choreography, R. Wood (Sleeping Beauty) (Ballet), 259
Sur Le Plateau, S. Lifar (Formes et Couleurs), 157
Sur les Pointes, C. W. Beaumont (Dance Journal), 72
Swan Lake at Covent Garden, C. W. Beaumont (Ballet), 72
Swan Lake at Stockholm, C. W. Beaumont (Ballet Today), 72
The Swedish Ballet, C. W. Beaumont (Ballet), 72
La Sylphide 1832-1947, C. W. Beaumont (Ballet), 72
Les Sylphides Televised, C. W. Beaumont (Ballet Today), 72
Taglioni, C. W. Beaumont (Dance and Dancers), 72
Taglioni Treasures, C. W. Beaumont (Dancing Times), 72
Tamara Toumanova: A Unique Career, V. H. Swisher, 232

SUBJECT INDEX 277

A Terpsichore of the Eighteenth Century, Madeleine Guimard 1743–1816, C. W. Beaumont (Dancing World), 73
That Magnificent Mute, M. H. Winter (Opera Ballet et Music-Hall in the World), 258
They're Turning to Ballet, L. Massine (Theatre Arts), 166
Three Dance Performances, C. W. Beaumont (Dance Journal), 72
Three Polish Dancers, C. W. Beaumont (*Ballet to Poland*, A. L. Haskell, editor), 73
Three Studies in Character, C. W. Beaumont (Ballet), 73, 74
A Tribute to Cecchetti, C. W. Beaumont (*Ballet Annual*), 74
Tribute to Fokine, C. W. Beaumont (Editions du Trident), 74
A Tribute to John Cranko, Royal Ballet, The, 198
A Tribute to Nijinsky, C. W. Beaumont (Ballet), 74
A Tribute to Wanda Evina, C. W. Beaumont (Dancing Times), 74
True Cecchetti, C. W. Beaumont (Dancing Times), 74
The Truth About Nijinsky, J. G. Dunton (Dance Magazine 2 parts), 111
The Truth About the Diaghileff Company, C. W. Beaumont (Dancing World), 75
1200 Books on Dancing, S. Palmer (Dance Magazine), 177
Two Massine Ballets, C. W. Beaumont, (Ballet), 75
Two Shows, C. W. Beaumont (Dance Journal), 75
Uday Shan Kar, B. K. Roy (Dance Culture), 198
U.S. Ballet Soars (Gelsey Kirkland), F. Gray (Time Magazine), 125
A Valuable Contribution, C. W. Beaumont (Dancing Times), 75
Verleden Heden en Toekomst van het Sadler's Wells Ballet, C. W. Beaumont (Dans Kroniek), 75, 76
Virginia Zucchi, V. Svetlov (Dancing Times), 232
Visiting Fracci, T. Tobias (Dance Magazine), 100
Watching Bournonville, K. Cunningham (Ballet Review), 99
The Way of a Ballerina, Y. Geltser (Soviet Travel), 120
The Wedding of Nijinsky, C. W. Beaumont (Dancing Times), 76
Will We Ever Have An American Ballet?, D. Barney (Dance Lovers Magazine), 28
A Wreath for Montie, C. W. Beaumont (Dancing Times), 76
The Year in Ballet, C. W. Beaumont (Year's Work in the Theatre), 76
The Year in Ballet, P. Hope-Wallace (The Year's Work in the Theatre), 135, 136
Yvette Chauviré as Princess Aurora, C. W. Beaumont (Ballet Today), 76

Fiction

Fanni Ballerina della Scala, G. Adami, 17
Recital in Paris, S. Stokes, 227

Folk, National and Ethnological Dance

All That Strange and Mysterious Folk, (Dance Perspectives), 101
The Art of Flamenco, D. E. Pohren, 191
The Art of the Sleeve in Chinese Dance, G. B. Strauss, 228
Belorusskie Tantsi, I. M. Khvorost, 140
Canciones y Danzas de Espana 9 a. edición, Seccion Feminina de F.E.T.Y. las J.O.N.S., 88
China on Stage, L. W. Snow, 219, 220
Classical and Folk Dances of India, Marg Publications, 163
Dance, M. L. E. Moreau de Saint Méry, 171, 172
Dance Dialects of India, R. Devi, 107
Dance in Ghana, O. Blum, 82
The Dance of Shiva, A. K. Coomaraswamy, 96
Dance-Rituals of Manipur, India, An Introduction to "Meitei Jagoi," L. Lightfoot, 157
Dancing Catalans, J. Langdon-Davies, 149
Les Danses Grecques, lien Vivant avec le Grece de L'Antiquité, D. Stratou, 228
Danzas Populares de Espana, M. G. Matos, 166
English Folk Song and Dance, F. Kidson and M. Neal, 140, 141
Ferganskii Tanets, R. Karimova, 139
Folk Dance Company of the U.S.S.R., M. Chudnovsky, 92

Folk Dances from Old Homelands, E. Burchenal, 87
Folk Dances and Games, C. Crawford, 97
Folk Dances and Singing Games, E. Burchenal, 87
Folk Dances of the Greeks, T. and E. Petrides, 188
Folk Dancing in High School and College, G. Fox and K. G. Merril, 117
Gagaku, R. Garfias, 120
Grundlagen der Struktur und Formanalyse des Volkstanzes, R. Ehm-Schulz and Dr. Kurt Petermann, 112
Gruzinskie Narodnie Tantsi, D. D. Djavrishvili, 107
The Kabuki Handbook, A. Halford and G. M. Halford, 129, 130
The Kabuki Theatre, E. Ernst, 113
Khoreografischeskoe, Iskusstvo Moldavii, E. Koroleva, 146
Knights of the Steppes, Mongolian Peoples Republic, 170, 171
The Lancashire Morris Dance, M. Karpeles, 139
Latin and American Dances for Students and Teachers, Pierre, 189
Libretto for the Concert of Mongolian Art, The Mongolian Peoples Republic, 170
Mallorcan Folk Dances, A. Galmes, 120
Mongolian National Wrestling, The Mongolian Peoples Republic, 170
The Mongolian Peoples Republic, (a film), 170, 171
Music and Dance in the New England States, including Maine, New Hampshire, Vermont, Massachusetts, Rhode Island and Connecticut, Bureau of Musical Research, 87
Music and Dance in Pennsylvania, New Jersey and Delaware, Bureau of Musical Research, 88
Narodnie Tantsi Yakutii, M. I. Zhornitskaya, 261, 262
The Nature of Dance, R. Lange, 149, 150
Shorashim: The Roots of Israel, J. B. Ingber, 138
Soviet Art Festivals 1967, Ministry of Culture of the USSR, 223
Sujetnie Tantsi, The Soviet Dance, 224
Tantsi Narodov SSSR, The Soviet Dance (3 Vols.), 224
The Traditional Dance, V. Alford and R. Gallop, 19
Traditions of Indian Folk Dance, K. Vatsyayan, 247
Tri Sujetnikh Tantsa, The Soviet Dance, 224, 225
Turkish Dancing, M. And, 20
Vokabular Deutscher Volkstanzschritte, A. Goldschmidt, 123
Zhizn v Tantse, E. Lutskaya, 160

History of Ballet and Ballet Companies

American Ballet Theatre, L. Péres, 181
Association Philanthropique des Artistes de L'Opéra, 22
The Australian Ballet 1962–1965, I. F. Brown, editor, 85, 86
Australian Notes on the Ballet, J. Garling, 120
Balet Bolshogo Teatr SSSR, The Soviet Ballet, 223
Baletnoe Iskusstvo Kazakhstana, L. P. Sarinova, 203
Ballet, M. Clarke and C. Crisp, 93
Le Ballet de l'Opéra de Paris, I. Guest, 127
Ballet in Australia, H. P. Hall, 130
Ballet in Britain Since the War, C. Barnes, 27
The Ballet of the Second Empire, L. Guest, 127
Ballet Portugais, Verde Gaio, 248, 249
Ballet Gestern und Heute, E. Rebling, 194
Ballett vom Sonnenkönig bis Balanchine, H. Schmidt-Gare, 205
Balletten 1945–52, S. Kragh-Jacobsen, 147
Il Ballo alla Scala 1778–1970, L. Rossi, 198
Belo Ruskii Balet, Y. Churko, 92
Bulletin des Lois No. 1261 (France), 87
Ceskoslovensky Balet, L. Schmidova, 205
Christian Johansson och Hans Brev till August Bournonville, A. Lilliestam, 157
Conseil d'Etat, Extrait du Registre des Délibérations (Sr. Pilatte) France, 169
Das Lettische Ballett der Rigar Oper, G. Stals, 226

SUBJECT INDEX 279

Diaghilev et les Ballets Russes, B. Kochno, 144, 145
Diaghilev Observed, N. Macdonald, 160
Een eeuw Danskunst in Nederland, Dr. E. Rebling, 194, 195
English Ballet, J. Leeper, 152
50 Years of Ballet Rambert, C. Crisp, A. Sainsbury and P. Williams, 98
Het Ballet, N. Loeser, 158
Istoriya Russkogo Baleta, Y. A. Bakhrushin, 25
Istoriya Russkago Baleta, S. Lifar, 157
Marius Petipa Meister des Klassischen Balletts, Selbstzeugnisse Dokumente, M. Petipa herausgegeben von E Rebling, 185, 186
Mastera Bolshogo Baleta, B. Lvov-Anokhin, 160
O Balete, P. Karp, 139
El Original Ballet Russe en America Latina, V. G. Victoricia, 252
Pravda Baleta, E. I. Shumilova, 211
Rigas Balets, J. Tihonovs, 241
The Royal Danish Ballet, S. Kragh-Jacobsen, 147
Royal Festivals and Romantic Ballerinas 1600–1850, E. Binney 3rd, 80
The Sadler's Wells Theatre Ballet, M. Clarke, 93
Segodnya na Stsene Bolshogo Teatr 1776–1976, Bolshoi Teatr, 83
Sovetskii Balet. Materiali k Istorii Sovetskogo Baletnogo Teatr, Y. Slonimsky, 218
Sovetskii Baletni Teatr 1917–1967, V. Krasovskaya, editor, 147, 148
The Soviet Ballet, Y. Slonimsky, 218
Spektakl Baletmeister Tantsovshtsnik, E. Koroleva, 147
The Story of the Royal Ballet, H. Fisher, 115
The Story of Sadler's Wells, D. Arundell, 22
The Stravinsky Festival of the New York City Ballet, N. Goldner, 122
Svensk Balett, B. Idestam-Almquist, 137
Den Svenska Baletten, K. Rootzen, 197
Teatr Operi I Baleta, M. Alexandrovich, 18, 19
Teatr Operi I Baleta, S. M. Kirova, 142
The World of Diaghilev, J. Percival, 181
The World of Serge Diaghilev, C. Spencer, P. Dyer and M. Battersby, 226

History of Dance

Alle Leven Danst, J. A. M. Merloo, 167
America Learns to Dance, J. E. Marks III, 164
A Chronicle of Dance in Baltimore, C. T. Bond, 84
Dance, J. Anderson, 20
The Dance. A Historical Survey of Dancing in Europe, C. J. Sharp and A. P. Oppé, 209
Historia da Dança em Portugal, J. Sasportes, 203, 204
A History of Dancing, G. Vuillier, 254
In the Shadow of the Swastika, H. Koegler, 146
A Pictorial History of the Dance, J. Marks, 164, 165
Un Siglo de Baile en Barcelona, A. Capmany, 89
Stravinsky and the Dance, The New York Public Library, 173
Tańce Historyczne, M. Drabeca, 109, 110
Der Tanz, O. Bie, 80
Der Tanz als Bewegungsphänonen, D. Günther, 129
Theatre in the East, F. Bowers, 85
Vom Hoppelrei Zum Beat, N. Molkenbur, K. Petermann and J. Schultz, 169
World History of the Dance, C. Sachs, 202

Mime and Pantomime

Angna Enters (Press Material), 113
Ben Jonson: Selected Masques, S. Orgel, editor, 176
Creative Miming, G. Sayre, 204

The History of the Harlequinade, M. Sand, 203
Masks, Mimes and Miracles, A. Nicoll, 174
The Mime, J. Dorcy, 108, 109
The Mime Theatre of Etienne Decroux, A. Epstein, 113
Mime Training and Exercises, I. Barlangy, 27
Pantomime, R. Mander and J. Mitchenson, 163
Pantomime, Elements and Exercises, D. Alberts, 18
Piccola Storia delle Maschere Italiane, A. M. Gianella, 121
Practical Illustrations of Rhetorical Gesture and Action, H. Siddons, 211
Stuart Masks and the Renaissance Stage, A. Nicoll, 174
Tanets Pantomima Balet, G. Dobrovolskaya, 107, 108
The World of Harlequin, A. Nicoll, 174

Modern Dance, Central European and American

The Complete Guide to Modern Dance, D. Mcdonagh, 166, 167
The Dancer Prepares, J. Penrod and J. G. Plastino, 180, 181
Interpretative Exercises and Studies Summer 1922, Vestoff-Serova Studio, 250
Interpretative Studies, Vestoff-Serova Studio, 250
Interpretative Studies and Exercises and Studies 1924, Vestoff-Serova Studio, 250
Modern Dance, E. E. Pease, 180
The Notebooks of Martha Graham, M. Graham, 124, 125
Pastels, Vestoff-Serova Studio, 250
Plastique and Technique, Vestoff-Serova Studio, 250
Poetry of Motion, Vestoff-Serova Studio, 250
Prechistenka: The Isadora Duncan School in Moscow, N. Roslavleva, 197, 198
The Professional Appearances of Ruth St. Denis and Ted Shawn, C. Schlundt, 205
The Professional Appearances of Ted Shawn and His Men Dancers, C. Schlundt, 205
Tamiris. Chronicle of her Dance Career 1927–1955, C. Schlundt, 205
Technique-Plastique Summer 1921, Vestoff-Serova Studio, 251
The Use of Stanislavsky within Modern Dance, V. Litvinoff, 158

Music

And Music at the Close, L. Libman, 155
Aram Khachaturyn, G. Schneerson, 206
Baleti Arama Khachaturyana, G. Tigranov, 241
Baleti Chaikovskogo, S. Zhitomirsky, 261
Baleti Asafiev, M. Ribnikova, 196
Ballet and its Music, J. Knight, 144
Ballet Music, H. Searle, 206
Constant Lambert, R. Shead, 209
Conversations with Igor Stravinsky, I. Stravinsky and R. Craft, 228
Dialogues and a Diary, I. Stravinsky and R. Craft, 229
Erinnerungen, I. Strawinsky, 230
Expositions and Developments, I. Stravinsky and R. Craft, 229
A History of Russian Music, R. A. Leonard, 153
The Interpretation of the Music of the XVII and XVIII Centuries, A. Dolmetsch, 108
Listen Here, V. Duke, 110
Magyar Táncmüvesvészek Szövetsége, Táncmüvészeti Ertésitö (3 vols), 234
Manuel de Falla and Spanish Music, J. B. Trend, 242
The Margin of Music, E. Evans, 114
Memories and Commentaries, I. Stravinsky and R. Craft, 229
Music for the Ballet, R. Gilbert, 122
Musical Score of the Grammar of the Art of Dancing, F. A. Zorn, 262
Muzika i Khoreografiya Sovremennogo Baleta, I. V. Golubov, redaktor, 123, 124
Muzika i Khoreografiya Sovremennogo Baleta, Vipusk 2, I. V. Golubov, redaktor, 124

SUBJECT INDEX

Muzikalnaya Foneteka v Shkola (I–III klass), S. A. Kartseva, 139
Muzikalinaya Kultura Belorusskoi SSR, T. A. Sherbakov, compiler, 210
Muzikalnoe Nasledie Chaikovskogo, Akademii Nauk SSSR, 172
A New History of Music, H. Prunières, 192
Prokofiev, C. Samuel, 202, 203
Retrospectives and Conclusions, I. Stravinsky and R. Craft, 229
Russian Symphony, D. Shostakovich and others, 211
Simfonicheskie Printsipi Baletov Chaikovskogo, Y. Rozanova, 202
Soviet Music, L. Polyakova, 192
Stravinsky, R. Siohan, 212
Stravinsky, R. Vlad, 252
Stravinskys Russische Ballette, H. Kirchmeyer, 141, 142
Tchaikovsky, J. Warrack, 254
Themes and Episodes, I. Stravinsky and R. Craft, 229, 230
The Waltz Emperors, J. Wechsberg, 255
A Working Friendship. The Correspondence between R. Strauss and H. V. Hofmannsthal, 228

Photographic Records and Illustrated Books

El Arte del Baile Flamenco, A. C. Puig, 193
Background to a Ballet, J. F. Speed, 225
Ballerina. Portraits and Impressions of Nadia Nerina, C. Crisp, 97, 98
Ballet, A. Brodovitch and E. Denby, 85
Ballet Guyed, P. Revitt, 195
Ballet Portraits, M. Seymour, 208
Les Ballets de Bolchoi, Ballets du Grand Theatre de Moscou, 27
Ballets et Danseurs dans le Monde, S. Lido, 155
Ballett, S. Enkelmann, 113
Ballett Saal, A. Woolliams, 260
Ballett von Heute, S. Lido, 155, 156
Ballettens Bog. V. Cavling, 90
Balletzeichnungen, P. Picasso, 188
Baryshnikov at Work, M. Baryshnikov and M. Swope, 28, 29
Bolshoi Ballet, Dance Books Ltd, 82
Bolshoi Teatr SSSR—Balet, Pod. Redaktsiei, V. A. Boni, 83
Bolshoi Teatr SSSR—Opera, Pod. Redaktsiei, V. A. Boni, 83
A Camera at the Ballet, G. Anthony, 21
Cante Hondo, A. Martin and J. Bergamin, 165
Dance Drawings of Martha Graham, C. Trowbridge, 242
Dancers Through the Ages, P. Hooreman, 135
La Danse, G. Truc, 243
The Duel, R. Baldick, 26
Dynamisches Ballett, R. Betz, 79
Les Etoiles de la Danse dans le Monde, S. Lido, 156
Fanny Elssler in America, A. Delarue, 106
The Fred Astaire and Ginger Rogers Book, A. Croce, 98
100 Years of Dance Posters, W. Terry and J. Rennert, 241
In a Rehearsal Room, R. Woodward, 259, 260
Inside American Ballet Theatre, C. Barnes, 27, 28
The New York City Ballet, L. Kirstein, 142
Nijinsky Dancing, L. Kirstein, 142, 143
Nureyev, D. Leonard and P. Moldon, 176
The Nureyev Image, A. Bland, 81
Nureyev in Paris, J. Vollmer, 253, 254
Paris Cancan, P. Mariel and J. Trocher, 164
Picasso Theatre, D. Cooper, 96
Princess Ballet Book No. 4, M. Davis, 103
Princess Ballet Book No. 5, M. Davis, 103
Princess Tina Book No. 6, M. Davis, 103

Princess Tina Ballet Book No. 7, M. Davis, 103
Princess Tina Ballet Book No. 8, J. Davis, 103
Princess Tina Ballet Book No. 9, J. Davis, 103
The Royal Ballet at Covent Garden, D. Vaughan, 248
The Sadler's Wells Ballet, G. Anthony, 21
Serge Lifar à L'Opéra, P. Valery, J. Cocteau, S. Lifar and L. Pageot-Rousseaux, 245
Sevilla y la Semana Santa, E. Gomez, 124
Shkola Bolshogo Baleta, L. Zhdanov, 261
Soviet Dancers in Britain, British Soviet Friendship Society, 85
Stravinsky at Rehearsal, M. Cosman, 96
Taniec w Polsce (1945–1959), I. Turska, 243, 244
Teatralnii Kalendar 1963–1977, 237–240
Teatralnyi Portret, E. A. Pankratkova, 177
Twenty-One Drawings of the Russian Ballet, L. Knight, 144

Personal Letters

Letters to Doris Niles and Serge Leslie, C. W. Beaumont, 55, 56

Stage Effects

Iskusstvo Grima, S. P. Shkolnikov, 210
Le Merveilleux et le Théâtre du Silence, M.-F. Christout, 91, 92
Russkaya Sovetskaya Zstrada 1917–1929, E. D. Uvarova, 245
Stage Dancing, P. J. S. Richardson, 196
Stage Lighting, T. Fuchs, 118
Stsenicheskie Belorusskie Tantsi, S. M. Grebenshikov, 125
Stsenicheskie Belorusskie Tantsi, The Soviet Dance, 224
Stravinsky and the Stage, B. Goldovsky and B. Hastings, 122
The Theatre of Marvels, M. H. Winter, 258, 259

Tap Dancing

American Tap Dancing, Z. Raye, 194
A Glossary of Technical Terms with Abbreviated Definitions Tap Technique, Z. Raye, 194
Jazz Dance, M. & J. Stearns, 227

Theatres and Theatrical Companies

Bolshoi Teatr, Y. A. Bakhrushin and Others, 83
Bolshoi Teatr SSSR, Balet, Y. Grigorovich, 83, 84
Bolshoi Teatr SSSR, Opera, B. Pokrovskii, 83
Crowded Nights-and Days, A. Croxton, 99
Dance as a Theatre Art, S. J. Cohen, 94
The Development of the Theatre, A. Nicoll, 173
Drury Lane, B. Dobbs, 107
Etiudy Baletowe, Teatr Wielki (2 vols), 235
40 Years of Opera in Chicago 1889–1928, E. Moore, 171
The Golden Horseshoe, Metropolitan Opera House, 168
A History of Theatre, G. Freedly and J. A. Reeves, 118
The King's Arcadia: Inigo Jones and the Stuart Court, J. Harris, S. Orgel and R. Strong, 131
The King's Theatre 1704–1867, D. Nalbach, 172
Kronika Sezonu 1970–1971, Teatr Wielki, 236
The Metropolitan Opera 1883–1935, I. Kolodin, 146
The New Spirit in Drama and Art, H. Carter, 89

SUBJECT INDEX

L'Opéra de Versailles, Rose-Marie Langlois, 150
The Other Theatre, N. Marshall, 165
Reforma Kitaiskoi Klassecheskoi Drami, L. N. Menchikov, 167
The Russian Theatre, R. Fülöp-Miller and J. Gregor, 119
The Russian Theatre, P. M. Sayler, 204
Russian Theatre from the Empire to the Soviets, M. Slonim, 216, 217
Das Russische Theater, J. Gregor and R. Fülöp-Miller, 125
Russkii Narodnii Teatr, N. I. Savuchkina, 204
Segodnya na Stsene Bolshogo Teatr 1776-1796, Bolshoi Teatr, 83
Shakespeare and His Players, M. Holmes, 135
Soviet Stars, Lenin Prize Winners, Progress Publishers, 153
Stage by Stage, P. Daubeny, 103
The Story of the Metropolitan Opera 1883-1950, I. Kolodin, 146
The Story of World Opera, K. V. Burian, 88
Stravinsky and the Theatre, New York Public Library, 173
Stravinsky in the Theatre, M. Lederman (Peter Owen), 152
Stravinsky in the Theatre, M. Lederman (da Capo), 152
Tadzhikskii Teatr, N. Nurdjanov, 175
Teatr Operi i Baleta, S. M. Kirova, 142
Theater und Ballett in Schweden, G. Hilleström, 134
The Theatre. Three Thousand Years of Drama Acting and Stagecraft, S. Cheney, 91
Theatre and Ballet in Sweden, G. Hilleström, 134
Theatre Arts Anthology, R. Gilder, editor, 241
Tonight and Every Night, V. Van Damm, 246
Troupers of the Gold Coast, or the Rise of Lotta Crabtree, G. Rourke, 198
25 Lat Opery Warszawskiej w Polsce Ludowej 1945-1970, Teatr Wielki, 237
Vic-Wells, The Work of Lilian Baylis, H. Williams, editor, 256

Ref Z 7514 D2 L4 pt.4

JAN 1 0 1986